Tobias Schoenberger

Building blocks for a modern privacy law

Global and Comparative Data Law

Edited by
Moritz Hennemann
Lea Katharina Kumkar
Linda Kuschel
Björn Steinrötter

Volume 6

Tobias Schoenberger

Building blocks for a modern privacy law

A comparative study of the U.S. Consumer Online Privacy Rights Act

DE GRUYTER

ISBN 978-3-11-914511-4
e-ISBN (PDF) 978-3-11-221571-5
e-ISBN (EPUB) 978-3-11-221590-6
ISSN 2751-0174

Library of Congress Control Number: 2025941646

Bibliographic information published by the Deutsche Nationalbibliothek
The Deutsche Nationalbibliothek lists this publication in the Deutsche Nationalbibliografie; detailed bibliographic data are available on the Internet at http://dnb.dnb.de.

Cover image: peshkov / iStock / Getty Images
Typesetting: jürgen ullrich typosatz, Nördlingen
Printing and binding: CPI books GmbH, Leck

www.degruyterbrill.com
Questions about General Product Safety Regulation:
productsafety@degruyterbrill.com

MIX
Papier | Fördert gute Waldnutzung
FSC® C083411

Acknowledgement

In the winter semester of 2024/25, the Faculty of Law at the University of Freiburg accepted this study as a dissertation in law. The manuscript was last updated in February 2025.

I extend my deepest gratitude to my esteemed supervisor, Prof. Dr. Moritz Hennemann, M. Jur. (Oxon.), whose guidance and support have been invaluable throughout my dissertation work. His many inputs and suggestions have significantly strengthened this study and I have learned a great deal from him on the topics of data privacy, data regulation, and beyond.

Thank you also to Prof. Dr. Hanno Merkt, LL.M. (Univ. of Chicago), who kindly agreed to review and grade my work.

This book was printed with the kind support of the Verein zur Förderung des Deutschen, Europäischen und Vergleichenden Wirtschaftsrechts e.V.

Lausanne, February 2025 Tobias Schoenberger, LL.M. (Berkeley)

https://doi.org/10.1515/9783112215715-202

Contents

List of abbreviations

BDSG	Bundesdatenschutzgesetz (“German Federal Data Protection Law”)
BVerfG	Bundesverfassungsgericht (“German Federal Constitutional Court”)
BVerfGE	Bundesverfassungsgerichtsentscheidung (“Decisions of the German Federal Constitutional Court”)
BT-Drs.	Bundestagsdrucksachen (“Official Journal of the German Parliament”)
Cf	Confer (“Compare”)
CFR	Code of Federal Regulations
CJEU	Court of Justice of the European Union
COPRA	Consumer Online Privacy Rights Act
CR	Computer und Recht (“Journal of Computer & Law”)
EDPB	European Data Protection Board
EDPL	European Data Protection Law Review
ECFR	European Charter of Fundamental Rights
E.g.	Exempli gratia (“For example“)
EO	Executive Order no. 14086 on Enhancing Safeguards For U.S. Signals Intelligence Activities
ETSI	European Telecommunications Standards Institute
EU	European Union
EU CFR	Charter of Fundamental Rights of the European Union
EuZW	Europäische Zeitschrift für Wirtschaftsrecht (“European Journal of Business Law”)
FTC	Federal Trade Commission
GDPR	General Data Protection Regulation
GG	Grundgesetz (“German basic law/ German Constitution”)
GRUR	Gewerblicher Rechtschutz und Urheberrecht (“Journal of Intellectual Property and Copyright Law”)
GWU	The George Washington University
IAPP	International Association of Privacy Professionals
Ibid	Ibidem (“in the same place”)
ICLQ	International and Comparative Law Quarterly
IEEE	Institute of Electrical and Electronics Engineers
InTeR	Zeitschrift zum Innovations- und Technikrecht (“Journal of Innovation & Technology Law”)
ISJLP	Information Society Journal of Law and Policy
JZ	Juristenzeitung (“Journal of Law”)
LR	Legal Revolutionary Journal of Digital Economy

https://doi.org/10.1515/9783112215715-203

MMR	Multimedia & Recht Zeitschrift für IT-Recht und Recht der Digitalisierung ("Journal of IT and Digitization Law")
No	Number
NJW	Neue Juristische Wochenschrift ("New Weekly Journal of Law")
NVwZ	Neue Zeitschrift für Verwaltungsrecht ("New Journal of Administrative Law")
NZKart	Neue Zeitschrift für Kartellrecht ("New Journal of Competition Law")
OECD	Organization for Economic Co-operation and Development
OJ	Official Journal of the European Union
PNAS	Proceedings of the National Academy of Sciences of the U.S. of America
RabelsZ	Rabels Zeitschrift für ausländisches und internationales Privatrecht ("Rabels Journal of International Law")
Sec.	Section
TFEU	Treaty on the Functioning of the European Union
UCLA	University of California Los Angeles
U.S.	United States of America
U. S. C.	U.S. Code
WIPO	World Intellectual Property Organization
ZD	Zeitschrift für Datenschutz ("Journal for Data Protection")
ZEuP	Zeitschrift für Europäisches Privatrecht ("Journal for European Civil Law")
ZfDR	Zeitschrift für Digitalisierung und Recht ("Journal of Digitization & Law")
ZUM	Zeitschrift für Urheber- und Medienrecht ("Journal of Copyright and Media Law")

Introduction

When *Tim Berners-Lee* proposed an information management system in 1989 thereby laying the foundation of the internet as we know it, his supervisor commented on his idea *"vague but exciting"*.[1] More than 30 years later, the comment still holds true: We have witnessed the rapid development of the world wide web, today more than 50 % of the global population are using the internet.[2] Still, only recently have we started to grasp the power of *Berners-Lee's* idea to organize and manage data and information. In an ever more connected world, modern data-focused technology is used for the mass creation, accumulation and processing of data, likely with a comparable impact on today's economy and society than mass production and industrialization in the 1900's.[3] For example, large language models as a form of artificial intelligence technology leverage the great quantity of available data to generate new text and images.[4] Looking into the future, data-focused technologies such as big data and algorithmic decision-making may replace money-based market interaction and lower transaction costs to a minimum.[5] More data, better quality of data, and superior forms of organizing data may soon help public authorities and policymakers to make better informed decisions, new forms of digital participation may facilitate more meaningful interaction between politicians and their constituents.[6]

---

1 Tim Bernes-Lee, 'Proposal of an information management system' (1989) <http://info.cern.ch/Proposal.html> accessed 10 August 2023; on the invention of the internet generally see Tim Bernes-Lee and Mark Fischetti, *Weaving the web: The original design and ultimate destiny of the world wide web by its inventor* (Harper Collins 1999).

2 Cf. World Bank, 'Individuals using the Internet' (2020) <https://data.worldbank.org/indicator/it.net.user.zs> accessed 11 August 2020.

3 Christopher Freeman and Francisco Louçã, *As time goes by: From the industrial revolutions to the information revolution* (Oxford University Press 2002) 257–300; Wolfgang Hoffmann-Riem, *Recht im Sog der digitalen Transformation* (Mohr Siebeck 2022) 287–288.

4 Cf. Andreas Hepp, 'Die Herausforderungen der Regulation und Governance von kommunikativer KI: Drei Thesen aus kommunikations- und medienwissenschaftlicher Sicht' 2023 ZUM 553, 554; IBM, 'What are large-language-models?' (2023) <https://www.ibm.com/topics/large-language-models> accessed 12 January 2024.

5 Viktor Mayer-Schönberger and Thomas Ramge, *Reinventing capitalism in the age of big data* (John Murray 2018) 81.

6 Advocating for the generation and use of open government data cf. German Data Ethics Commission, 'Opinion' (2019) 16 <https://datenethikkommission.de/wp-content/uploads/191023_DEK_Kurzfassung_en_bf.pdf> accessed 26 October 2020; Jamie Susskind, *Future politics: Living together in a world transformed by tech* (Oxford University Press 2018) 227–257.

https://doi.org/10.1515/9783112215715-001

Despite the opportunities of modern data-focused technology, in Germany the public debate has often been dominated by concerns and fears about its risks and challenges. Since the time *Berners-Lee* began working on the creation of the world wide web, Germans have been discussing the peril of becoming *"transparent citizens"* whose personal sphere of life is intruded by public and private actors (*gläserner Bürger*).[7] The German view has been one of vague skepticism and fear that data-focused technology in the hand of the malevolent can be used to the detriment of the individual and society.[8] Such skepticism has recently been spurred by scandals of industrial malpractice, for example the instrumentalization of 50 million *Meta*, formerly *Facebook*, user profiles to influence political campaigns by *Cambridge Analytica*,[9] and *TikTok's* undisclosed harvesting of millions of unique identifiers from their users' mobile phones.[10]

Arguably, this skepticism towards modern data-focused technology and personal data use can be discerned as a common pattern in Europe even beyond German borders.[11] This is because Germany's view on data-focused technology as expressed in its early data protection laws in the 1970s has deeply influenced a string of subsequent data protection laws in the EU culminating in the passing of the 2016 *General Data Protection Regulation* ("GDPR").[12] Many of the GDPR's bedrock principles originate in German public law and legal theory; for instance, its processing ban as set out in Art. 6 para. 1 and Art. 9 para. 1 GDPR draws on the German concept of *Verbotsprinzip mit Erlaubnisvorbehalt* according to which any government action requires

7 Cf. Friedrich Westphalen, 'Auf dem Weg zum gläsernen Bürger?' 1983 Die neue Ordnung 136; Hoffmann-Riem (n 3) 145–147.

8 Wilhelm Steinmüller and others, 'Grundfragen des Datenschutzes, Anlage 1' 1972 Drucksache VI/3826, 38; Lothar Determann, 'California Privacy Law Vectors for Data Disclosures' in Moritz Hennemann and others (eds), *Data Disclosure: Global developments and perspectives* (De Gruyter 2023) 135–136.

9 Emma Graham-Harrison and Carole Cadwalladr, 'Revealed: 50 million Facebook profiles harvested for Cambridge Analytica in major data breach' (2018) <https://www.theguardian.com/news/2018/mar/17/cambridge-analytica-facebook-influence-us-election> accessed 8 December 2020; Federal Trade Commission, 'FTC Imposes $5 Billion Penalty and Sweeping New Privacy Restrictions on Facebook' (2020) <https://www.ftc.gov/news-events/press-releases/2019/07/ftc-imposes-5-billion-penalty-sweeping-new-privacy-restrictions> accessed 14 October 2020.

10 Kevin Poulsen and Robert Mcmillan, 'TikTok Tracked User Data Using Tactic Banned by Google' (2020) <https://www.wsj.com/articles/tiktok-tracked-user-data-using-tactic-banned-by-google-11597176738?mod=djemalertNEWS> accessed 12 August 2023.

11 Urs Gasser, 'Futuring Digital Privacy' in Mira Burri (ed), *Big data and global trade law* (Cambridge University Press 2021) 197.

12 Data protection law of the German State of Hesse 1970; cf. Thomas Streinz, 'The Evolution of European Data Law' in Paul P Craig and Gráinne de Búrca (eds), *The evolution of EU law* (Oxford University Press 2021) 7; sub Chapter 1 B. Concept and status of EU data protection law.

a legal justification.[13] In its original sphere of existence, *i.e.* the government's authority to intervene in a citizen's constitutional right (*Eingriffsrecht*), the concept ensures the citizen's protection against arbitrary surveillance – accordingly, the police may only search an apartment when equipped with a lawfully obtained search-warrant or in a situation of imminent danger. In its transplanted sphere of data protection law, the GDPR's absolute processing ban equally applies between private actors where it fundamentally shapes their interaction and communication by imposing strict limitations on the disclosure and processing of personal data.[14] In the pointed critique of *Veil*, data protection law in the EU thereby risks morphing into a *"fundamental super-right"* which tilts the playing field to the detriment of those that process personal data, *inter alia* by abridging their constitutional right to free speech and to freely exercise their profession (*Meinungs- und Berufsfreiheit*).[15]

While the objective of the GDPR to protect individual sovereignty in the digital world is laudable, several of its concepts and means arguably appear outdated, and some of its effects on the individual citizen, on society, and on the economy undesirable.[16] For instance, critics have long argued that the GDPR is overly focused on individual privacy concerns and largely ignores the effects and interdependencies of personal data processing and innovation, *e.g.* in the field of medicine which could greatly benefit from a more sophisticated use of personal data.[17] As a case in point, Art. 6 para. 1, Art. 9 para. 1 and 2, and Art. 5 para. 1 lit. c GDPR aim at minimizing the disclosure of personal data and how processing entities use it.[18] In the eyes of the critics, the EU data protection regulation does little to foster the development and positive use of modern data-focused technology and personal data.[19]

---

13 Steffen Detterbeck, *Allgemeines Verwaltungsrecht* (C.H. Beck 2020) para. 504; Yoan Hermstrüwer, *Informationelle Selbstgefährdung* (Mohr Siebeck 2015) 72–73; Johannes Masing, 'Herausforderungen des Datenschutzes' 2012 NJW 2305, 2306.

14 Cf. Hermstrüwer (n 13) 72–73.

15 Masing (n 13), 2307; Winfried Veil, 'Die Datenschutz-Grundverordnung: des Kaisers neue Kleider' 2018(10) NVwZ 686–696, 689.

16 Yafit Lev-Aretz and Katherine J Strandburg, 'Privacy Regulation and Innovation Policy' 2020(22) Yale Journal for Law and Technology 256, 269–270, 308–309; Lothar Determann, 'Healthy Data Protection' 2020(26) Michigan Telecommunications and Technology Law Review 229, 262–265, 277.

17 Cf. Determann, 'Healthy Data Protection' (n 16) 262–265, 277; Kai von Lewinski, 'Einführung' in Martin Eßer, Philipp Kramer and Kai von Lewinski (eds), *DSGVO/BDSG* (Carl Heymanns Verlag 2023) para. 72–73; Lev-Aretz and Strandburg (n 16), 269–270, 308–309; Streinz (n 12) 46–47.

18 Determann (n 8) 141; Alexander Roßnagel, 'Art. 5' in Spiros Simitis, Gerrit Hornung and Indra Spiecker Döhmann (eds), *Datenschutzrecht* (Nomos 2019) para. 118–121.

19 Paul Schwartz and Karl-Nikolaus Pfeifer, 'Transatlantic Data Privacy Law' 2017(106) Georgetown Law Journal 115, 131; von Lewinski, 'Einführung' (n 17) para. 34–36; Moritz Hennemann, 'Wettbewerb der Datenschutzrechtsordnungen' 2020(4) RabelsZ 864, 893; Michal S Gal and Oshrit Aviv, 'The Competitive Effects of the GDPR' 2020(3) Journal of Competition Law & Economics 349, 353–355.

Irrespective of how much the GDPR is to blame, it is a fact that, today, cutting-edge technology is increasingly developed outside of Europe, namely in the U.S., in China and in the Republic of Korea.[20]

EU policymakers, on the other hand, have repeatedly expressed high hopes about the GDPR's positive secondary effects on digital innovation in the EU.[21] However, empiric evidence suggests the contrary: According to a survey by the *Institut der deutschen Wirtschaft*, only 5 % of the participants believe the EU data protection regulation has positively influenced their business; mostly, businesses criticized high implementation cost and the chilling effect on their activities due to legal uncertainty.[22] Similarly, *Gal* and *Aviv* contend that the GDPR has hampered competition in the digital sphere by rendering market-entry more difficult for newcomers. In their analysis, the regulatory approach to collecting personal data as set out in Art. 6 para. 1 and Art. 9 para. 1 and 2 GDPR favors large data platforms and their accumulation and use of personal data across their multiple services.[23]

The EU has since shifted its efforts to pursue a European data strategy to outside of data protection law.[24] A set of new data regulation aims at unlocking the potential of the digital economy *inter alia* by nudging organizations into sharing more

---

20 WIPO, 'The Geography of Innovation: Local Hotspots, Global Networks' (2019) 9, 35 <https://www.wipo.int/edocs/pubdocs/en/wipo_pub_944_2019.pdf> accessed 15 December 2022.

21 European Commission, 'Data protection as a pillar of citizens' empowerment and the EU's approach to the digital transition: Two years of application of the General Data Protection Regulation' COM(2020)264 final, 1–2; European Data Protection Supervisor, 'Opinion on the European Commission's White Paper on Artificial Intelligence' (2020) 8 <https://edps.europa.eu/data-protection/our-work/publications/opinions/edps-opinion-european-commissions-white-paper_en> accessed 26 October 2020; see also Recital 7 of the GDPR which states that the regulation will help grow *"the trust that will allow the digital economy to develop across the internal market."*

22 Cf. Institut der deutschen Wirtschaft, 'Wettbewerbseffekte der Europäischen Datenschutz-grundverordnung' (2020) 12 <https://www.iwkoeln.de/fileadmin/user_upload/Studien/Report/PDF/2020/IW-Report_2020_DSGVO_und_Wettbewerb.pdf> accessed 15 December 2021.

23 Gal and Aviv (n 19), 353–355.

24 European Commission, 'A European strategy for data: Communication from the Commission to the European Parliament, the Council, A European strategy for data: Communication from the Commission to the European Parliament, the Council, the European Economic and Social Committee and the Committee of the Regions' [2020] COM(2020)66 final; see also Deutsche Bundesregierung, 'Datenstrategie der Bundesregierung' (2021) 25, 26 <https://www.bundesregierung.de/breg-de/service/publikationen/datenstrategie-der-bundesregierung-1845632> accessed 13 September 2023; Moritz Hennemann and Björn Steinrötter, 'Data Act: Fundament des neuen EU-Datenwirtschaftsrechts?' 2022(21) NJW 1481, 1481–1482; also Moritz Hennemann and Björn Steinrötter, 'Der Data Act: Neue Instrumente, alte Friktionen, strukturelle Weichenstellungen' 2024 NJW 1.

data, see Recital 5 and 32 *Data Governance Act*,[25] and by introducing broad access and usage rights to data, see Art. 4 et seq. *Data Act*.[26]

Regarding the effectiveness of the GDPR's data protection provisions, several of its core concepts have been criticized to provide only insufficient protection in real life by allowing data controllers to shift risk on to the data subject.[27] As a case in point, informed consent as required by Art. 6 para. 1 lit. a and Art. 9 para. 2 lit. a GDPR frequently appears to be but a legal fiction.[28] According to a survey requested by the *European Commission*, only 13 % stated they *"fully read privacy statements online"* and only 22 % of the respondents felt *"always informed"* about the collection and use of their personal data.[29] Instead, many users of data-focused technology and the internet face a decision of take-it-or-leave-it – with the consequence that consent is regularly granted as a necessary evil to access the content of a website or to use a particular technology or service.[30]

Therefore, it is important to acknowledge that we are rather at the beginning than the end of a vague but exciting journey to a modern privacy law which embraces today's data-focused technology and can cope with its shortcomings.[31] In the EU, we must continuously review whether our regulatory approach offers

---

25 European Parliament and Council, 'Regulation 2022/868 of the European Parliament and the Council of 30 May 2022 on European data governance and amending Regulation 2018/1724' OJL152/1; Moritz Hennemann and Lukas von Ditfurth, 'Datenintermediäre und Data Governance Act' 2022(27) NJW 1905; see also Moritz Hennemann and Louisa Specht-Riemenschneider, Data Governance Act (Nomos 2023) Einleitung para. 20, 22.

26 European Parliament and Council, 'Regulation 2023/2854 on harmonised rules on fair access to and use of data and amending Regulation 2017/2394 and Directive 2020/1828 (Data Act)' OJ L series; Hennemann and Steinrötter (n 24), 1484.

27 Cf. Veil (n 15), 686, 688–689; Hermstrüwer (n 13) 86.

28 Veil (n 15), 688–689; Gordian Ebner, *Weniger ist Mehr?* (Nomos 2022) 103–107; Gordian Ebner, 'Information Overload 2.0?: Datenwirtschaftsrecht IV: Die Informations-pflichten gem. Art. 3 Abs. 2 Data Act-Entwurf' 2022(7) ZD 364, 365–366; Determann, 'Healthy Data Protection' (n 16) 252–255; Marlene Voigt, *Die datenschutzrechtliche Einwilligung: Zum Spannungsfeld von informationeller Selbstbestimmung und ökonomischer Verwertung personenbezogener Daten* (Nomos 2020) 100–101.

29 European Commission, 'Special Eurobarometer 487a: The General Data Protection Regulation' (2019) 2 <https://cnpd.public.lu/dam-assets/fr/actualites/international/2019/ebs487a-GDPR-sum-en.pdf> accessed 15 December 2021; Gordian Ebner, *Weniger ist Mehr?* (Nomos 2022) 45–48.

30 Frederik Zuiderveen Borgesius and others, 'Tracking Walls, Take-It-or-Leave-It Choices, the GDPR, and the ePrivacy Regulation' 2017(3) EDPL 353, 354, 360 et seq.; Fred H Cate, 'The Failure of Fair Information Practice Principles' in Jane Winn (ed), *Consumer Protection in the Age of the 'Information Economy'* (Ashgate 2007) 364–365; Maximilian Becker, 'Ein Recht auf datenerhebungsfreie Produkte' 2017 JZ 170, 174.

31 Cf. Oskar J Gstrein and Andrej J Zwitter, 'Extraterritorial application of the GDPR: promoting European values or power?' (2021) 10(3) Internet Policy Review 2, 23; Lev-Aretz and Strandburg (n 16), 308–309; Streinz (n 12) 4–5.

effective risk mitigation against modern privacy challenges and whether it strikes the right balance between protecting individuals and society and fostering technological progress. This is all the more true – and arguably even becomes an ethical imperative – because of the GDPR's global reach and the EU's endeavor to export its data protection rules to third countries.[32] By imposing our expectations on third countries and their citizens to adopt elements of EU data protection law, we may negatively impact the local people and economy.[33] For instance, a GDPR transplant may cause friction when the perception and appreciation of privacy and personal data sharing in a third country starkly differs from German and EU expectations.[34] Already, there is evidence about the adverse effect of an export of the EU data protection law and system on some of Africa's digital technology industry if countries and companies are left with the choice between implementing the EU data protection standard or losing projects and work for which the receipt of EU personal data is essential.[35]

A. Scope, thesis, and structure of the study

On the journey to a modern privacy law, this study strives to further pave the way towards a common understanding about personal data processing and how it should be regulated. In particular, we focus on U.S. privacy law in comparison to EU data protection law because U.S. privacy law offers a historically distinct regulatory approach which may prompt us to question established EU data protection concepts and regulatory means.[36] More generally, the U.S. law and system are of inter-

32 Cf. Hennemann, 'Wettbewerb der Datenschutzrechtsordnungen' (n 19) 870–873, 895; Streinz (n 12) 40; Hoffmann-Riem (n 3) 216–217; Katharina Reiling, 'Transnationale Ordnung der Digitalwirtschaft durch die Datenschutzgrundverordnung' in Christoph Krönke (ed), Regulierung in Zeiten der Digitalwirtschaft (Mohr Siebeck 2019) 51–53.

33 Cf. Gstrein and Zwitter (n 31), 3; Flora Wang, 'Cooperative Data Privacy: The Japanese Model of Data Privacy And The EU-Japan GDPR Adequacy Agreement' 2020(33) Harvard Journal of Law & Technology 661, 687.

34 Cf. Daniela Wawra, 'Parameters of Personal Data Disclosure Decisions in Cross-Cultural Comparison' in Moritz Hennemann and others (eds), *Data disclosure: Global developments and perspectives* (De Gruyter 2023) 54–55.

35 Cara Mannion, 'Data Imperialism: The GDPR's Disastrous Impact on Africa's E-Commerce Markets' 2020 Vanderbilt Journal of Transnational Law 685, 701–702; Moritz Hennemann, Patricia Boshe and Ricarda von Meding, 'Datenschutzrechtsordnungen in Afrika: Grundlagen, Rechtsentwicklung und Fortentwicklungspotenziale' 2021(3) ZfDR 193, 231–232.

36 Sub Chapter 1 A. Concept and status of U.S. privacy law; cf. Gregory Voss, 'Obstacles to transatlantic harmonization of data privacy law in context' 2019 University of Illinois Journal of Law, Technology & Policy 405, 411; Schwartz and Pfeifer (n 19), 117–118.

est because the economic and technological interdependencies between the U.S. and the EU continue to proof very strong. In 2023, more than 50 % of Europe's and about 50 % of the U.S. data flow has been transatlantic, surpassing data exchange with any other partner.[37] Besides, the U.S. remains at the forefront of technological innovation exporting many of the goods and services EU citizens use on a daily basis.[38] In 2022, U.S. imports of high-technology products into the EU totaled a volume of about 90 billion EUR ranking second behind imports from China with about 180 billion EUR and ahead of Switzerland with slightly above 20 billion EUR.[39]

In the first part of this study which is divided into two chapters, Chapter 1 will briefly trace the historical development of personal data regulation in the U.S. and in the EU. The chapter explores how, although the U.S. and EU law and system have influenced each other multiple times over the years, they have ended up with distinctly different because historically grown regulatory approaches, concepts and means. As will be examined throughout this study, many elements of traditional U.S. privacy and EU data protection regulation lag behind technological progress and have arguably become ignorant or ineffective vis-à-vis modern privacy risks. Chapter 1 therefore sets the background for this study's discussion about the shortcomings of existing regulation.[40] Besides, in Chapter 1 we will see that in the U.S. a new trend of broader privacy regulation has emerged on a state level while on a federal level similarly broad regulation has not yet been passed into law.[41] The analysis of a proposal for such a broad federal privacy law is the topic of the second part of this study.

Against this backdrop, Chapter 2 will propose building blocks for a modern privacy law, in particular it attempts a categorization of modern privacy risks. The suggested risk categories shall be free from any local, regional, and national particularities so that they can be discussed and used globally. The idea to collect and organize in an abstract manner what shapes personal data processing today is taken from the 1973 *Fair Information Practices Principles* and similar endeavors

---

37 Daniel Hamilton and Joseph Quinlan, 'The Transatlantic Economy 2023' (2023) <https://transatlanticrelations.org/publications/transatlantic-economy-2023/> accessed 20 June 2024.

38 WIPO, 'The Geography of Innovation: Local Hotspots, Global Networks' (2019) 33 <https://www.wipo.int/edocs/pubdocs/en/wipo_pub_944_2019.pdf> accessed 15 December 2022, since the 1970, the U.S.'s share of the world's issued patents and publications has continuously been at least 20 %; Voss, 'Obstacles to transatlantic harmonization of data privacy law in context' (n 36) 411.

39 Eurostat, 'Imports of high-tech products in 2022' (2022) <https://ec.europa.eu/eurostat/statistics-explained/index.php?title=International_trade_and_production_of_high-tech_products#Main_conclusions> accessed 20 May 2024.

40 Sub Chapter 2 A. Categorization of modern privacy risks – a call for capacity-apt regulation.

41 Sub Chapter 1 A. Concept and status of U.S. privacy law.

thereafter.[42] In light of the existing research and scholarship which mostly discusses selected privacy risks, this study argues that a new attempt should be made to broadly categorize privacy risks given the very recent advancements in technology and their impact on human behavior.[43]

Similar to the effect of the *Fair Information Practices Principles*, these categories of modern privacy risks could help law- and policymakers across jurisdictions to agree on common challenges in personal data processing which modern privacy regulation should address.[44] The categories may serve as building blocks when updates to existing privacy rules or altogether new privacy regulation are conceived, or when international transfers of personal data and a country's level of data protection are discussed. Such a value-based approach in the form of established building blocks is characterized by the agreement to common values rather than giving in to economic, political, or institutional power.[45] Conceivably, a value-based approach to privacy and data protection regulation in different countries and international data transfers would go beyond the EU's current transfer-mechanism as set out in Art. 44 sentence 1 and 2 GDPR which has been described by *Bradford* and others as power-based in its influence on global privacy regulation.[46]

In all, the first thesis of this study is that we can and should (re-)focus our attention on several selected core challenges of today's personal data processing which any modern privacy law should address; and that these focus points encompass, at a minimum, the categories of modern privacy risks suggested in this study.

In the second part of this study, we take a close look at the *Consumer Online Privacy Rights Act* ("COPRA"), a recent proposal for a broad U.S. federal privacy law.[47] COPRA is among the most comprehensive privacy bills currently discussed

---

42 Cf. U.S. Department of Health, Education and Welfare, 'Records, Computers and the Rights of Citizens' (1973) <https://aspe.hhs.gov/reports/records-computers-rights-citizens> accessed 24 February 2023; a more detailed presentation of the *Fair Information Practices Principles* and similar categorizations follows sub Chapter 2 A. Categorization of modern privacy risks – a call for capacity-apt regulation.

43 Sub Chapter 2 A. Categorization of modern privacy risks – a call for capacity-apt regulation

44 Similarly, the idea that countries can converge on "*first principles*" in privacy and data protection regulation is discussed in Anupam Chander and Paul Schwartz, 'Privacy and/or Trade' 2022 University Chicago Law Review forthcoming, 48 <https://papers.ssrn.com/sol3/papers.cfm?abstract_id=4038531> accessed 8 September 2023.

45 Gstrein and Zwitter (n 31), 5.

46 Anu Bradford, *The Brussels Effect: How the European Union rules the world* (Oxford University Press 2021) 25–26; Gstrein and Zwitter (n 31), 4–5.

47 Senate Bill 2968, 116th Congress (2019–2020); Senate Bill 3195, 117th Congress (2021–2022); full version at the end of this study, Annex U.S. Consumer Online Privacy Rights Act.

in the U.S. which qualifies it as an excellent object of study to better understand in which direction U.S. federal privacy law may be heading, and from which to draw inspiration for EU data protection law. To this end, Chapter 3 will use the building blocks and modern privacy risk categories developed in Chapter 2 as the benchmark against which to assess the COPRA bill and the effectiveness of its provisions. Until today, no in-depth analysis of COPRA has been published.

Finally, in Chapter 4 we assume COPRA is successfully passed into law and examine whether the level of data protection established in the U.S. by COPRA would meet the standard of adequacy as set out in Art. 45 para. 1 sentence 1 and para. 2 GDPR. Here, the benchmark will not be the modern risk categories from Chapter 2 but the adequacy standard which is applied in the European Union by the *Court of Justice of the European Union* ("CJEU") and the *European Commission.*[48] The analysis in Chapter 4 should be of interest in particular to practitioners because the European Commission's decision according to Art. 45 para. 3 sentence 1 GDPR about an adequate protection level in the U.S. *post* COPRA would allow companies to transfer personal data from the EU to the U.S. without additional requirements according to Art. 45 para. 1 sentence 2 GDPR and Recital 103 sentence 2 GDPR.[49]

To conclude, the thesis of the second part of the study is that, first, COPRA can be considered a strong update to existing U.S. privacy law because the bill's privacy concepts and means – when viewed in the aggregate – are capable of effectively mitigating against modern privacy risks; secondly, that as a consequence, the European Commission should designate to the U.S. *post* COPRA adequacy-status to facilitate the transatlantic transfer of personal data from the EU to the U.S.

B. Method and terminology

To identify modern privacy risks which hold true beyond a particular jurisdiction, we will examine in Chapter 2 common processing phenomena of modern data-focused technology and how humans interact with it. The latter suggests that we look to research in behavioral economics to consider the observed actual

48 Sub Chapter 4 A. The adequacy threshold.

49 European Commission, 'Commission Implementing Decision on the adequate level of protection of personal data under the EU-US Data Privacy Framework' (n 39) para. 2 sentence 2, para. 8 sentence 1; Moritz Hennemann, 'Wettbewerb der Datenschutzrechtsordnungen' 2020(4) RabelsZ 864, 883–884; Daniel Pauly, 'Art. 45' in Boris Paal and Daniel Pauly (eds), *DSGVO, BDSG* (C.H. Beck 2021) para. 1; Jörg Hladjk, 'Art. 45' in Martin Eßer, Philipp Kramer and Kai von Lewinski (eds), *DSGVO/BDSG* (Carl Heymanns Verlag 2023) para. 3.

behavior of humans rather than a mostly fictitious belief that humans are solely motivated by reason.[50] While this study does not directly apply behavioral economics' method of observational studies, it is informed by the latest research and methodology in this field and to the extent relevant for privacy and data protection law.[51]

Furthermore, we introduce a categorization of modern privacy risks so that it may help to conceive *effective* privacy regulation. In this study, *effectiveness* as a consequentialist measure is similar to how adequacy can be interpreted in Art. 45 para. 1, 2, and 3 GDPR, *i.e.* whether a foreign data protection system *"delivers the required protection"*.[52] When we examine what effective protection means in the various risk categories of Chapter 2, we look at which values are to be protected and how to best protect them. In doing so, we are again influenced by behavioral economic research and method. For instance, the desired outcome of regulating privacy risks may be technical, economic, or behavioral, *e.g.* how should we address structural privacy risks associated with the use of specific processing technology such as algorithmic decision-making technology, how can we foster the non-harmful disclosure and use of personal data to boost innovation, or how can we avoid personal data-based discrimination?[53] In line with our objective to describe privacy risks which are valid across jurisdictions, we focus on common values which transcend local, regional, and national particularities. For instance, we will disregard for the purpose of this study a specific country's constitutional rights or political agenda which may constitute values the country's privacy regulation would want to protect.

When we analyze the COPRA bill and U.S. privacy law in Chapter 3, we will apply methods of comparative law. To understand the functioning of COPRA provisions, the bill will not be interpreted in isolation; instead, we will examine its provi-

---

50 Saul Levmore, 'The Evolutionary Force of Behavioral Economics in Law' 2021 17(2) Review of Law & Economics 465; Daniel Kahneman, *Thinking, fast and slow* (Penguin Books 2012) 419–432.

51 In particular sub Chapter 2 A. II. 1. Intellectual (in)capacity.

52 European Commission, 'Commission Implementing Decision on the adequate level of protection of personal data under the EU-US Data Privacy Framework' (n 39) para. 3 sentence 2, para. 4 sentence 1–4; cf. Judgement of 16 July 2020, *Data Protection Commissioner v Facebook Ireland, Maximilian Schrems*, C-311/18, ECLI:EU:C:2020:559 – *Schrems II* para. 188 (CJEU); a detailed discussion of the adequacy threshold in Art. 45 para. 1, 2, and 3 GDPR follows sub Chapter 4 A. The adequacy threshold.

53 Cf. Gasser (n 11) 207–208; Hennemann, 'Wettbewerb der Datenschutzrechtsordnungen' (n 19) 868; Determann, 'Healthy Data Protection' (n 16) 262–265, 277; Sonia Katyal, 'Private Accountability in the Age of Artificial Intelligence' 2019(66) UCLA Law Review 54, 56, 71–73.

sions in the context of existing U.S. privacy regulation.[54] In the absence of COPRA case law, we will look at the text, the systematic structure, and the regulatory objective of its provisions as expressed by the COPRA's authors in their preparatory report.[55] Where the study refers to EU data protection law and the GDPR, we will rely on methods suitable for European law. In light of Art. 4 para. 3 *Treaty on the European Union* we strive for an interpretation in conformity with European law (*europarechtskonforme Auslegung*), an autonomous and uniform interpretation of terms in EU law, and one which gives effect to the objective of European law and the GDPR provisions (*effet utile*).[56] In the cross-cultural comparison between U.S. privacy law and EU data protection law, we are aware of and strive to avoid the risk that our analysis is tinged by methodological shortcomings, for instance a restricted focus on positive law in the ocean of wealth that is U.S. privacy case law, or an erroneous assumption of U.S. legal and cultural homogeneity, *e.g.* privacy expectations and legal standards likely differ between the States of California and Texas.[57]

At times, this study wishes to examine and support legal theory by referring to existing empirical and statistical research; yet it does not itself produce new statistical or empirical data. The main purpose of such reference to data shall be to better assess whether and to which extent legal privacy concepts and theory are operational in real life.

Finally, given the different terminology the law, academia, and public discourse in the U.S. and in Europe use in the field of privacy and data protection, this study applies the term most closely linked to the subject matter in discussion.[58] For example, when we reference the GDPR we speak of data protection, personal data,

---

54 For the functional approach in comparative law cf. Konrad Zweigert and Hein Kötz, *Einführung in die Rechtsvergleichung auf dem Gebiete des Privatrechts* (Mohr Siebeck 1996) 33–34; Ralf Michaels, 'The Functional Method of Comparative Law' in Mathias Reimann and Reinhard Zimmermann (eds), *The Oxford handbook of comparative law* (Oxford University Press 2019) 345–348; Harald Koch, Ulrich Magnus and Peter Winkler von Mohrenfels, *IPR und Rechtsvergleichung* (C.H. Beck 2010) § 13 para. 11–14; confirming the functional approach in comparative studies while highlighting its limitations Uwe Kischel, *Rechtsvergleichung* (C.H. Beck 2019) § 3 para. 179–197.

55 Maria Cantwell, 'The State of Online Privacy and Data Security' (2019) <https://www.cantwell.senate.gov/imo/media/doc/The%20State%20of%20Online%20Privacy%20and%20Data%20Security.pdf> accessed 6 August 2020.

56 Sibylle Seyr, *Der effet utile in der Rechtsprechung des Europäischen Gerichtshofs* (Duncker & Humblot 2010) 275–280.

57 Cf. Ralf Michaels and Lena Salaymeh, 'Decolonial Comparative Law: A Conceptual Beginning' 2022(1) RabelsZ 166, 170–172.

58 Cf. Voss, 'Obstacles to transatlantic harmonization of data privacy law in context' (n 36) 408–409.

and data subjects; for U.S. privacy law, we use the terminology applied in the respective privacy law such as personal identifiable information, personal information, or covered data. When we discuss U.S. privacy law generally, we choose the term personal data.[59]

59 Cf. Schwartz and Pfeifer (n 19), 121–122.

Chapter 1
The privacy landscape in the U.S. and in the EU

In both the U.S. and in Europe, data privacy and data protection as a political topic and legal category started to emerge from the 1970s. With the advent of computers and digital databases, the question arose about whether and how to regulate the processing of personal data.[60] Despite the common starting point and understanding that some form of regulation was needed, the U.S. and Europe subsequently parted into different directions: Whereas in the U.S. the new data and digital economy thrived and influenced the legislature to solely regulated where necessary,[61] the public debate in several European countries and in the EU from early on centered around the risks and potential misuse of personal data with the consequence that legislators were generally favorable to broad data protection regulation.[62]

To put it simply, the U.S. has traditionally followed a risk-based approach whereby it regulates the processing of personal data in specific industry sectors or to protect selected consumer groups (sub Chapter 1 A. Concept and status of U.S. privacy law).[63] By contrast, the EU has passed comprehensive data protection laws to broadly regulate the processing of personal data irrespective of a particular industry, sector, or group of individuals (sub Chapter 1 B. Concept and status of EU data protection law).[64] As a consequence, privacy law in the U.S. and data protection law in the EU today look and function quite differently.[65] Yet they share the commonality that many of their elements are ignorant of or ineffective against modern privacy risks.[66] The summary below thus provides the background for the

---

60 Cf. Daniel Solove and Paul Schwartz, *Information Privacy Law* (Wolters Kluwer Law & Business 2018) 77–79; Cate (n 30) 343–344; Streinz (n 12) 6–7; Lee Bygrave, *Data privacy law: An international perspective* (Oxford University Press 2014) 9–11.

61 Cf. Schwartz, 'Global Data Privacy: The EU Way' 2019 New York University Law Review 771, 798, 815–816.

62 Cf. Westphalen (n 7); Hoffmann-Riem (n 3) 145–147; supra Introduction.

63 Solove and Schwartz (n 60) 1032–1033.

64 Stefan Ernst, 'Art. 2' in Boris Paal and Daniel Pauly (eds), *DSGVO, BDSG* (C.H. Beck 2021) para. 2–10; Kai von Lewinski, 'Art. 2' in Martin Eßer, Philipp Kramer and Kai von Lewinski (eds), *DSGVO/BDSG* (Carl Heymanns Verlag 2023) para. 5.

65 Voss, 'Obstacles to transatlantic harmonization of data privacy law in context' (n 36) 418–422; as we will see, this is true despite the recent trend in the U.S. that some states have passed new privacy laws which in several elements converge closer to EU data protection law cf. IAPP, 'U.S. State Privacy Legislation Tracker' (2024) <https://iapp.org/media/pdf/resource_center/State_Comp_Privacy_Law_Chart.pdf> accessed 23 May 2024; sub Chapter 1 A. Concept and status of U.S. privacy law.

66 Sub Chapter 2 A. Categorization of modern privacy risks – a call for capacity-apt regulation.

https://doi.org/10.1515/9783112215715-002

discussion in Chapter 2 about building blocks for a modern privacy law. Furthermore, it provides the context for the COPRA updates and how the bill would fit with existing U.S. privacy law.[67] Finally, the summary of the legal foundation of EU data protection law is relevant for our analysis in Chapter 4 when we define the adequacy threshold as set out in Art. 45 para. 1, 2, and 3 GDPR, the standard for transfers of EU personal data to the U.S. *post* COPRA according to Art. 45 para. 1 sentence 1 GDPR.[68]

A. Concept and status of U.S. privacy law

For the U.S., the start of the public debate about opportunities and risks of the early computer technology and data use is well documented in the 1973 report on *Records, Computers and Rights of Citizens* by the U.S. Department of Health, Education and Welfare.[69] Notably, the report discusses in its appendices parallel developments in Europe of the passing of data protection regulation in the German State of Hesse in 1970 and in Sweden in 1973.[70] The report culminates in suggesting five so-called *Fair Information Practices Principles, i.e.* fundamental guidelines on how to handle *"records of identifiable personal data"*.[71] The principles were later voted into the *Privacy Act of 1974*, amended in 5 U. S.C. § 552a, where they govern until today how U.S. federal agencies may keep records on individuals.[72]

The U.S. has subsequently followed a risk-based approach largely focused on the regulation of different industry sectors, in particular on sectors in which businesses typically held large amounts of sensitive information.[73] For instance, in 1996 the U.S. regulated health care providers and insurers in the *Health Insurance Portability and Accountability Act*, Public Law No. 104–191,[74] and in 1999 the financial industry in the *Gramm Leach-Bliley Act*, Public Law No. 106–102, 15 U. S.C.

67 Sub Chapter 3 Assessing the COPRA bill.
68 Sub Chapter 4 A. The adequacy threshold.
69 U.S. Department of Health, Education and Welfare, 'Records, Computers and the Rights of Citizens' (1973) <https://aspe.hhs.gov/reports/records-computers-rights-citizens> accessed 24 February 2023.
70 Ibid Appendices 'Computers and Privacy': The Reaction in Other Countries.
71 Ibid IX. Action Agenda for the Secretary of Health, Education and Welfare; cf. Cate (n 30) 343–344; Data protection law of the German State of Hesse (n 12); Voss, 'Obstacles to transatlantic harmonization of data privacy law in context' (n 36) 405, 463.
72 Cf. Streinz (n 12) 909.
73 Solove and Schwartz (n 60) 1032–1033.
74 Ibid 683–684.

§§ 6801 to 6809.[75] An additional element of U. S. federal privacy regulation has been targeted privacy laws to protect particular consumer groups, *e.g.* the *Children's Online Privacy Protection Act*, 15 U. S. C. §§ 6501–6506, regulates how personal identifiable information from children under the age of 13 years can be collected.[76]

Beyond the sectoral regulation, U. S. law has not regulated the processing of personal identifiable information. Instead, the U. S. has largely trusted in industry self-regulation.[77] Processing entities have been free to set their own processing rules in contracts and privacy policies.[78] Consumers are considered sovereign actors in the marketplace who, following their notice about and their consent to a company's privacy policy, are in a position to choose whether or not they disclose their personal identifiable information to the processing entity.[79] If and when companies deviate from their self-set processing standards, they can be held accountable for their breaking of (privacy policy) promises to the consumer.[80] In particular the *Federal Trade Commission* ("FTC"), a U. S. federal agency and the leading U. S. authority for privacy enforcement, has enforced breaches of a company's privacy policy pursuant to § 45 (a) (1) FTC Act 15 U. S. C. 41 et seq. as an *"unfair or deceptive"* practice.[81] In this pattern of sector- and group-specific laws, a patchwork of privacy regulation spanning across different U. S. states and the federal level has formed over time.[82] Reportedly, the U. S. legislator has been reluctant to consider broad privacy regulation out of fear that comprehensive privacy regulation would stifle innovation and the growth of the U. S. technology sector.[83]

As a consequence, in the Unites States, the processing of personal identifiable information has remained generally permitted unless it is specifically restricted by existing privacy laws.[84] Importantly, the U. S. regulatory approach to personal data

---

75 Ibid 1015–1019.

76 Ibid 1157–1159.

77 Chris Hoofnagle, 'Privacy Self-Regulation: A Decade of Disappointment' in Jane Winn (ed), *Consumer Protection in the Age of the 'Information Economy'* (Ashgate 2007) 382.

78 Schwartz and Pfeifer (n 19), 137–138; Schwartz, 'Global Data Privacy: The EU Way' (n 61) 797–798; Solove and Schwartz (n 60) 1033–1034; 1089.

79 Cf. Daniel Solove, 'Privacy Self-Management and the Consent Dilemma' 2013(126) Harvard Law Review 1880, 1883–1884; Schwartz and Pfeifer (n 19), 132, 155–156.

80 Chris Hoofnagle, *Federal trade commission privacy law and policy* (Cambridge University Press 2016) 156–158.

81 Cf. Solove and Schwartz (n 60) 1034; Solove, 'Privacy Self-Management and the Consent Dilemma' (n 78) 1884.

82 Cf. ibid 1033; cf. Art. 29 Data Protection Working Party, 'Working Party on the Protection of Individuals with regard to the Processing of Personal Data' (1999) Working Paper 15, 2.

83 Schwartz, 'Global Data Privacy: The EU Way' (n 61) 797–798.

84 Schwartz and Pfeifer (n 19), 120.

processing has been and still is consistent with the broader U.S. legal framework and with U.S. constitutional law. According to *Schwartz* and *Pfeifer*, "[t]*he most significant constitutional safeguards for information in the U.S. concern the free flow of data, not personal privacy*".[85] In particular, the U.S. Constitution's First Amendment provides strong protection for free speech and the free flow of information.[86] By contrast, the Fourth Amendment which protects the individual in the integrity of her house and home is limited to the legitimacy of government searches without effect on personal data processing by private actors.[87] Besides, over time case law has considerably weakened the protection granted by the amendment even in its narrow scope of application.[88]

The year 2013 marked a turning point in the public debate, perception, and regulation of personal data use in the U.S. In particular two events triggered a change of course: First, *Edward Snowden* helped surface U.S. surveillance practices which broadly accessed personal identifiable information from U.S. citizens and foreigners.[89] The second event was the meddling of *Cambridge Analytica* in the 2016 U.S. presidential elections; the company had perverted profiling and targeted political messaging to influence voters.[90] Public outrage transformed into the quest to reform the U.S. *laissez-faire* approach to personal data processing and to establish new privacy regulation. In 2018, a ballot initiative in the State of California which proposed comprehensive state privacy regulation rapidly gained traction with voters. It was eventually picked up by the Californian legislator and voted into law as the *California Consumer Privacy Act*, California Civil Code § 1798.100–178.199.[91] Other U.S. states have since followed the Californian example and have proposed or passed their own non-identical comprehensive state privacy laws. By May 2024, privacy laws existed or have been signed into law in 30 of the 50 U.S. States.[92]

The emergence of numerous U.S. state privacy laws raises the question whether a turning point for U.S. privacy law may soon catalyze also on the federal level? Until today, no comprehensive U.S. federal privacy law exists. There are,

---

85 Ibid 134–135.

86 Ibid 134.

87 Ibid 133.

88 Cf. Thomas Wischmeyer, *Überwachung ohne Grenzen: Zu den rechtlichen Grundlagen nachrichtendienstlicher Tätigkeiten in den USA* (Nomos 2017) 43–45.

89 For a summary of the events and content of the Snowden revelations Susan Landau, 'Making Sense from Snowden: What's Significant in the NSA Surveillance Revelations' 2013 11(4) IEEE Security & Privacy 54; Wischmeyer (n 87) 26–27; Maria H Murphy, 'Assessing the implications of Schrems II for EU US data flow' 2022 71 ICLQ 245, 247, 249; Schwartz and Pfeifer (n 19), 118.

90 Cf. Federal Trade Commission (n 9); Graham-Harrison and Cadwalladr (n 9).

91 Felix Glocker, Der California Consumer Privacy Act (Mohr Siebeck 2022) 1–2.

92 IAPP (n 65).

however, numerous proposals and bills on how to comprehensively regulate privacy on a federal level. This study will analyze COPRA which stands alongside similar proposals such as the *American Data Privacy and Protection Act*, H.R. 8152, and the *American Privacy Rights Act of 2024*.[93] Authored and sponsored by the same *Senator Cantwell*, the American Privacy Rights Act closely resembles COPRA in concept, structure, and content. At the end of the COPRA analysis below, we will briefly summarize and compare the American Privacy Rights Act to COPRA.[94] Until a comprehensive federal privacy law is passed, business leaders and privacy stakeholders alike will keep calling on the legislator to take action.[95] The historic fragmentation of U.S. privacy law has made it difficult and costly for businesses to steer their operations in full compliance with the law(s), which is why they are urging the legislator to overcome the fragmentation by harmonizing privacy rights for consumers across state borders.[96]

B. Concept and status of EU data protection law

In Europe, the passing of the data protection law in the German State of Hesse in the year 1970 marks the starting point of data protection regulation. A federal data protection law followed for all of (West) Germany in 1977.[97] Inspired by Hesse's pioneering state regulation, several other European countries, although far from the majority, introduced national data protection laws shortly after, *e.g.* Sweden in 1973, France and Denmark in 1978.[98] Above country-level in the EU, however, reluctance to adopt broad data protection regulation prevailed at first. Similar to the

---

93 U.S. Congress, 'American Data Privacy and Protection Act' 117th Congress, House of Representatives 8152; Committee on Energy and Commerce, 'Committee Chairs Rodgers, Cantwell Unveil Historic Draft Comprehensive Data Privacy Legislation' (2024) <https://energycommerce.house.gov/posts/committee-chairs-rodgers-cantwell-unveil-historic-draft-comprehensive-data-privacy-legislation> accessed 23 May 2024.

94 Sub Chapter 3 F. Interim summary.

95 Cf. Business Roundtable, 'CEO letter to members of the U.S. Senate and House of Representatives' (2019) <https://s3.amazonaws.com/brt.org/BRT-CEOLetteronPrivacy-2.pdf> accessed 6 June 2020; cf. Cantwell (n 54) 3; cf. Daniel Solove and Paul Schwartz, 'ALI Data Privacy: Overview and Black Letter Text' 2022 UCLA Law Review 1252; Voss, 'Obstacles to transatlantic harmonization of data privacy law in context' (n 36) 410.

96 Business Roundtable (n 9532(2)32) 2; Schwartz, 'Global Data Privacy: The EU Way' (n 61) 814; Cate (n 30) 369–370.

97 Cf. von Lewinski, 'Einführung' (n 17) para. 4–5; Streinz (n 12) 6–7; Hoffmann-Riem (n 3) 145–147; Determann, 'Healthy Data Protection' (n 16) 276–277.

98 Cf. Streinz (n 12) 7; von Lewinski, 'Einführung' (n 17) para. 7.

concerns and preferences discussed in the U.S., the European Commission initially feared broad regulation would hamper the free flow of information and stifle innovation and economic growth.[99]

Without a European initiative to pursue harmonization, other international organizations picked up the topic to work out data protection concepts and ideas that could be used internationally. In 1980, the *Organization for Economic Co-operation and Development* ("OECD") issued guidelines on how to prevent and remove barriers that blocked international data exchange. Despite their lack of legally binding effect, the guidelines have substantially shaped EU data protection law until today, for instance by introducing the terminology of the *data controller* and the principles of a collection and use limitation in Art. 7 and 10 of the guidelines.[100]

Of similar influence has been the 1981 *Convention No. 108 for the Protection of Individuals with regard to Automatic Processing of Personal Data*, a binding treaty of international public law prepared under the helm of the *Council of Europe*.[101] Its signatories have committed to fundamental processing principles including to fair data processing in Art. 5 lit. a, and to data rights of the individual such as a right to access and correct collected personal data according to Art. 8 lit. b and c of the Convention.[102] In 2018, an approved update to the Convention added further obligations for data controllers, *e.g.* an obligation to notify a data protection supervisory authority according to Art. 7 para. 2 in case of a relevant data breach, and the right for individuals pursuant to Art. 9 para. 1 lit. a to *"have his or her views taken into consideration"* when personal data is used in automated decision-making.[103]

In light of the patchwork of different national data protection laws, the EU Commission eventually took an interest to harmonize the law on an EU level. In 1995, the passing of the *Data Protection Directive* streamlined the Member State's data protection laws regarding the transfer of EU residents' personal data to third countries, the directive introduced in its Art. 25 para. 1 and 2 the prerequisite that the receiving third country must provide for *"an adequate level of* [data] *protec-*

---

99 Cf. Streinz (n 12) 7–8.

100 OECD, 'Guidelines on the Protection of Privacy and Transborder Flows of Personal Data' [1980] <http://www.oecd.org/internet/ieconomy/oecdguidelinesontheprotectionofprivacyandtransborderflowsofpersonaldata.htm> accessed 5 August 2020; cf. Streinz (n 12) 8.

101 Cf. Lee Bygrave, 'The 'Strasbourg Effect' on data protection in light of the 'Brussels Effect': Logic, mechanics and prospects' 2021 40(105460) Computer Law & Security Review 1, 13.

102 Council of Europe, 'Convention for the Protection of Individuals with regard to Automatic Processing of Personal Data' (1981) <https://rm.coe.int/1680078b37> accessed 24 February 2023; cf. Streinz (n 12) 8.

103 Council of Europe, 'Update to Convention for the Protection of Individuals with regard to Automatic Processing of Personal Data' (2018) <https://search.coe.int/cm/Pages/result_details.aspx?ObjectId=09000016807c65bf> accessed 24 February 2023.

tion".[104] The Data Protection Directive set a minimum harmonization obligation for EU Member States which left them free to surpass the harmonized protection level with more onerous legislation. The result was differing levels of data protection and varying enforcement from country to country.[105] Consequently, the EU legislator pushed to further harmonize EU data protection law and, in 2016, passed the GDPR which directly took effect in EU Member States from 2018 onwards.[106]

From the 1970 Hesse data protection law via the 1995 Data Protection Directive to the 2016 GDPR, EU data protection law has been characterized by a comprehensive or omnibus approach, a regulative effort to broadly govern the processing of personal data irrespective of industry sector or consumer group regulation alike in the U.S.[107] As a consequence, the processing of personal data of EU residents today generally requires a legal basis pursuant to Art. 6 para. 1 and Art. 9 para. 1 GDPR, with only a few exceptions provided by law and limited in scope and application, *e.g.* a processing privilege for journalistic, academic, artistic or literary expression in Art. 85 para. 2 GDPR.[108]

Finally, EU data protection law has been conceptually anchored in constitutional law with data protection as a fundamental human right.[109] It is the human rights foundation of EU data protection law which has been at the heart of the EU-U.S. debate about personal data processing and its adequate regulation.[110] Again originating in Germany, the *German Federal Constitutional Court* in its 1983 decision about the legitimacy of a national census first held that citizens had a fundamental right to decide about their own affairs and information in the digital realm (*Recht auf informationelle Selbstbestimmung*).[111] With the *Charter of Fundamental Rights of the European Union* becoming EU primary law in 2009, the Charter's explicit mentioning of privacy and data protection in Art. 7 and Art. 8 para. 1

---

104 For a detailed discussion of today's EU adequacy standard sub Chapter 4 A. The adequacy threshold.

105 Cf. Streinz (n 12) 11.

106 Cf. Jan P Albrecht, 'Das neue EU-Datenschutzrecht – von der Richtlinie zur Verordnung' 2016 (32(2)) CR 88, 98.

107 Ernst, 'Art. 2' (n 63) para. 2–10; von Lewinski, 'Art. 2' (n 63) para. 5.

108 Philipp Kramer, 'Art. 6' in Martin Eßer, Philipp Kramer and Kai von Lewinski (eds), *DSGVO/BDSG* (Carl Heymanns Verlag 2023) para. 1; Eike Frenzel, 'Art. 6' in Boris Paal and Daniel Pauly (eds), *DSGVO, BDSG* (C.H. Beck 2021) para. 7–8; for the exceptions sub Chapter 4 B. I. 4. Limitations to derogations.

109 Schwartz and Pfeifer (n 19), 122–127.

110 Ibid 117–119; Judgement of 6 October 2015, *Maximilian Schrems v Data Protection Commissioner, Digital Rights Ireland Ltd*, C-362/14, ECLI:EU:C:2015:650 – *Schrems I* (CJEU); *C-311/18 – Schrems II* (n 52).

111 *Volkszählungsurteil* [1983] BVerfGE 1 (BVerfG).

and 2 further strengthened the anchoring of EU data protection in constitutional law.[112]

112 Schwartz and Pfeifer (n 19), 122–127; Streinz (n 12) 15–16; *C-362/14 – Schrems I* (n 110); *C-311/18 – Schrems II* (n 52).

Chapter 2
Building blocks for a modern privacy law

Looking back at the evolution of European data protection and U.S. privacy law, we can distinguish how regulatory concepts and ideas from the early computer years in the 1970s shape the law until today.[113] In the EU, the GDPR focuses on hypothetical privacy risks (*vertyptes Risiko*) at the beginning of the processing chain.[114] As *von Lewinski* has illustratively explained, such upstream regulation (*Vorfeldschutz*) builds on the idea that computer-enabled data processing may negatively affect the individual who should thus decide about the processing.[115] As a consequence of the upstream regulation with the decision-making point at the time of the initial data disclosure and before any data processing has occurred, the GDPR is largely ignorant of any *actual* processing risk or data protection infringement which may materialize after the initial data disclosure and later on in the processing chain.[116] Besides, with the regulatory control point set prior to any processing and without regard to the processing results, the GDPR's purpose of protection (*Schutzzweck*) is blurred – is its purpose to shield the data subject from harmful data processing or, as Art. 1 para. 2 GDPR seems to suggest, much more broadly to enable the data subject to realize her "*fundamental rights and freedoms*" in the digital realm?[117] Due to its failure to identify specific processing risks and its uncertainty about which aspects of human life to protect, *von Lewinski* has pointedly criticized the GDPR as "*largely vague*" and "*sometimes even dysfunctional*" in today's world of modern data-focused technology.[118]

In the U.S. and on a federal level, modern data-focused technology has largely remained unregulated amidst the patchwork of limited federal privacy laws.[119] In particular because of surging compliance cost and heightened market-entry barriers for newcomers, a public debate has been triggered about how to harmonize U.S. privacy law, *e.g.* by passing a comprehensive federal privacy law.[120]

---

113 Determann, 'Healthy Data Protection' (n 16) 276–277; Gstrein and Zwitter (n 31), 2.

114 Cf. von Lewinski, 'Einführung' (n 17) para. 13, 18–19; Hennemann, 'Wettbewerb der Datenschutzrechtsordnungen' (n 19) 871.

115 Kai von Lewinski, *Die Matrix des Datenschutzes* (Mohr Siebeck 2014) 78–83; von Lewinski, 'Einführung' (n 17) para. 26; Steinmüller and others (n 8), 86; supra Introduction and Chapter 1 B. Concept and status of EU data protection law.

116 Von Lewinski, 'Einführung' (n 17) para. 13, 18–19.

117 Veil (n 15), 694, 695; von Lewinski, 'Einführung' (n 17) para. 16–17; Streinz (n 12) 5.

118 Von Lewinski, 'Einführung' (n 17) para. 13, 18–19.

119 Supra Chapter 1 A. Concept and status of U.S. privacy law.

120 Cf. Business Roundtable (n 95) 2; Determann (n 8) 128; Solove and Schwartz, 'ALI Data Privacy: Overview and Black Letter Text' (n 95) 1254, 1284.

https://doi.org/10.1515/9783112215715-003

Against this background, this chapter reflects on what a modern privacy law should look like. We suggest an abstract categorization of modern privacy risks which can be used as common building blocks in the discussion about how personal data should be regulated (sub Chapter 2 A. Categorization of modern privacy risks – a call for capacity-apt regulation). We will then examine the concept and effect of output- and downstream-based privacy regulation in comparison to input- and upstream-based regulation alike in the GDPR (sub Chapter 2 B. Output and downstream regulation). Finally, we will summarize elements of an existing standard which has previously been used to assess whether privacy regulation has been effectively implemented (sub Chapter 2 C. Effective implementation of privacy regulation).

In all, Chapter 2 tests the first hypothesis of this study that law- and policymakers should (re)focus their attention on core challenges in personal data processing when they evaluate existing or conceive modern privacy regulation, in particular that they should concentrate on the categories of modern privacy risks suggested in the below.[121] Later on in this study, we will use these building blocks and risk categories as the benchmark against which we assess the COPRA bill in Chapter 3.

A. Categorization of modern privacy risks – a call for capacity-apt regulation

In November 2019, the authors of the COPRA bill published a preparatory report titled *The State of Online Privacy and Data Security* in which they discussed typical risks U.S. consumers and society face in today's online world and regarding the processing of their personal data.[122] For instance, the report describes how many consumers feel they lack sufficient understanding and control about how their personal data is used by companies.[123] Also, the report talks about the risk of data breaches and cyber-attacks due to insufficient data security and by which large amounts of sensitive personal data can be compromised.[124] Evidently, the report's enumeration of examples is not comprehensive. Any attempt to exhaustively list privacy risks is doomed to remain a fragment of the full picture because technologies, devices, and applications evolve rapidly, and so does human behavior which

121 Supra A. Scope, thesis, and structure of the study.

122 Cantwell (n 54).

123 Ibid 3, 8.

124 Ibid 4.

is influenced by the interaction with such technology.[125] Instead, an abstract description and categorization of these risks promises to be a more suitable approach to sketch out the focal points of any modern privacy regulation which strives to offer effective privacy protection.

The idea to conceptualize and organize into general categories of privacy risks the innumerous privacy challenges and infringements we experience every day is not new. In 1973, the U.S. *Department of Health, Education and Welfare's* report on *Records, Computers and Rights of Citizens* first grouped and discussed general concerns about the emerging computer technology to then articulate its *Fair Information Practices Principles* which have become the building blocks of U.S. and international privacy laws.[126] The 1980 guidelines by the *Organisation for Economic Co-operation and Development* contain an *Explanatory Memorandum* which summarizes technical problems and privacy challenges.[127] In 2014, *Bygrave* gave an account of technical and organizational developments and how humans have reacted to them in an effort to trace and predict the evolution of privacy law; in particular, *Bygrave* highlighted the phenomenon of personal data being (re-)used in and across organizations and by automated means.[128] In 2019, the *American Law Institute*, a U.S. legal research and advocacy group best known for its influential restatements of existing U.S. law, issued so-called *Data Privacy Principles*. However, the principles are neither a restatement of law nor do they conceptualize modern privacy risks; instead, they suggest to U.S. law- and policymakers a set of spelled-out privacy rules which can be directly implemented as black-letter law.[129] Similarly, the 2020 *NIST Privacy Framework* by the *U.S. National Institute of Standards and Technology* sets forth proposed elements of a privacy program by which companies can mitigate against common privacy risks.[130] There are many others who have discussed selected privacy risks that root in technology or human behavior.[131] Still, it is

---

125 Cf. Hoffmann-Riem (n 3) 68–70, 276–277.

126 Solove and Schwartz (n 60) 78–79; Cate (n 30) 343–344; supra Chapter 1 A. Concept and status of U.S. privacy law.

127 OECD, 'Guidelines on the Protection of Privacy and Transborder Flows of Personal Data' [1980] <http://www.oecd.org/internet/ieconomy/oecdguidelinesontheprotectionofprivacyandtransborderflowsofpersonaldata.htm> accessed 5 August 2020; Solove and Schwartz (n 60) 82, 1427.

128 Bygrave (n 60) 9–11.

129 Solove and Schwartz, 'ALI Data Privacy: Overview and Black Letter Text' (n 95) 1261–1262.

130 National Institute of Standards and Technology, 'Privacy Framework' (2020) <https://www.nist.gov/privacy-framework> accessed 20 May 2024.

131 For example, Urs Gasser, 'Futuring Digital Privacy' in Mira Burri (ed), *Big data and global trade law* (Cambridge University Press 2021); Moritz Hennemann and others (eds), *Data Disclosure: Global developments and perspectives* (De Gruyter 2023); Daniel Solove, 'Privacy Self-Management and the Consent Dilemma' 2013(126) Harvard Law Review 1880.

the very recent advancements in new data processing technology such as in artificial intelligence and big data technology that, according to this study, justify another fresh attempt to broadly categorize technical risks and how humans react to them, thereby building on *Bygrave's* work from 2014.

Admittingly, an abstract description and categorization of privacy risks must radically simplify and reduce the complexity of today's privacy challenges. In turn, this simplification may help conceptualize new approaches in privacy law. Consider, for instance, how privacy and technological advancements have often been perceived as incompatible – the introduction to this study gives a short recount of how German skepticism towards personal data processing and technology has shaped EU data protection regulation.[132] By contrast, the categories laid out below demonstrate that technology can and must be part of the solution.[133] For instance, we should look for scalable privacy tools and solutions which technically control processing preferences, we should have experts from IT and other disciplines spell out what constitutes acceptable privacy risks and nudge processing entities into strong privacy commitment by granting them regulatory safe haven when they comply with predefined privacy standards.[134]

This chapter contends that, to identify today's privacy risks irrespective of a particular country or system, we need to first look at the capacity and capabilities of modern data-focused technology, *i.e.* the technical phenomena of how personal data can be processed, and at actual human behavior in relation to this technology. This is why we suggest to first organize modern privacy risks into two main categories depending on their respective main driver of risk: Privacy challenges which are essentially caused by *technical capacities* (sub Chapter 2 A. I. Technical capacities) and privacy challenges at the root of which lay – many times interlocked with technical capacities – *human (in)capacities* (sub Chapter 2 A. II. Human (in)capacities). Effective regulation of personal data processing must identify, acknowledge, and embrace these technical and human (in)capacities, and in that sense a modern privacy law must be *capacity-apt*.[135]

---

132 Supra Introduction and Chapter 1 B. Concept and status of EU data protection law; cf. Determann (n 8) 135–136.

133 Similarly, Gasser (n 11) 207–208; Hoffmann-Riem (n 3) 143–144, 196–198.

134 Cf. Gasser (n 11) 207–208; Hoffmann-Riem (n 3) 143–144; Determann, 'Healthy Data Protection' (n 16) 270–271, 273; James Dempsey and others, 'Breaking the Privacy Gridlock: A Broader Look at Remedies' (2021) SSRN Journal, 19 <https://dx.doi.org/10.2139/ssrn.3839711> accessed 30 October 2023.

135 The theoretical foundation of which we find in behavioral economics as explained supra B. Method and terminology.

Within these two main categories of technical capacities and human (in)capacities, any modern privacy risk then falls into one or several subcategories each associated with either a technical or a human driver. The subcategories will be presented and discussed in the below. When we attempt to propose effective privacy regulation and mitigation measures together with the identified modern privacy risks, we want to conceive elements which are adaptive and responsive to the identified technical and human (in)capacities.[136] It follows that, to assess the quality of a modern privacy law, the benchmark will be as to how many of the below building blocks the law manages to address, and how effectively it mitigates against the identified risks. As will be discussed throughout this study, traditional privacy and data protection regulation in the U.S. and the EU share the commonality that many of its core concepts and means lack behind technological progress and have become ignorant of or even dysfunctional vis-à-vis modern privacy risks.[137] The summary of important developments leading up to today's privacy landscape in the U.S. and in the EU therefore sets the background for this study's discussion about building blocks for a modern privacy law.[138] It furthermore provides the context for COPRA and how the proposal for a comprehensive federal privacy regulation would fit with existing U.S. law.[139] Finally, the summary of important developments and the legal foundation of EU data protection law is important for our analysis in Chapter 4 when we define the adequacy threshold as set out in Art. 45 para. 1, 2, and 3 GDPR, the standard for transfers of personal data of EU data subjects to the U.S. *post* COPRA according to Art. 45 para. 1 sentence 1 GDPR.[140]

I. Technical capacities

The COPRA report about *The State of Online Privacy and Data Security* illustrates how a great part of modern privacy challenges originate in recent technological developments. For instance, the success of internet-connected consumer devices capable of producing and processing personal data which is or can be made available almost instantaneously and almost anywhere. The technological progress and the falling prices associated with development of these devices have led to a new scale and level of integration of the technology into consumers' everyday

136 Similarly regarding the role of technology Gasser (n 10) 207–208; discussing the role of humans and technology also Hoffmann-Riem (n 3) 143–144.
137 Sub Chapter 2 A. Categorization of modern privacy risks – a call for capacity-apt regulation.
138 Sub Chapter 2 Building blocks for a modern privacy law.
139 Sub Chapter 3 Assessing the COPRA bill.
140 Sub Chapter 4 A. The adequacy threshold.

life.[141] More generally, we see the trend that technology is getting ever more capable and that consumers, on average, happily embrace the newly available and affordable technology, also consider the recent fascination with and success of large language models such as *Open AI's* ChatGPT.[142]

The success story of these recent technical developments in hard- and software and the proliferation of the technology could not have been known in the 1970s when the first privacy laws were initially drafted.[143] Back then and compared to today's reality of modern data-focused technology, the quantity and quality of processed personal data was negligible, capable technology was not omnipresent and lacked the global connectivity of data and systems we experience today.[144] The notion instead was to protect the consumer against the one or the few computers with limited computing power which the government owned and started using to better understand its constituents.[145] Still, the outdated idea from the 1970s of a cybernetic and monocausal system of data processing by a few government computers remains at the heart of European data protection law.[146] Furthermore and as will be described in detail below, the GDPR generally does not distinguish between the quantity and quality of personal data that is being processed, the different processing technology in use, and their capacity and associated risks.[147]

Today, we can arguably conceive more effective ways of addressing risks related to new *technical capacities* of devices and technology which process personal data. Ideally, it is some of the same technical capacities that are posing privacy challenges which can be made operable to alleviate and offer solutions.[148] In figure 1 below, we suggest the following non-exhaustive taxonomy of privacy risks associated with technical capacities.

141 Cantwell (n 54) 9.

142 IBM (n 4); Cantwell (n 54) 9; cf. Gasser (n 11) 207–208.

143 Supra Chapter 1 B. Concept and status of EU data protection law.

144 Sub Chapter 2 A. I. 1. Data quantity; Chapter 2 A. I. 2. Data quality; generally Hoffmann-Riem (n 3) 68–70, 276–277.

145 Steinmüller and others (n 8); Westphalen (n 7); generally supra Chapter 1 B. Concept and status of EU privacy law.

146 Von Lewinski, 'Einführung' (n 17) para. 26.

147 Cf. ibid para. 13, 18–19; Veil (n 15), 694, 695; Hoffmann-Riem (n 3) 68–70, 276–277; German Data Ethics Commission (n 6) 5 (5th bullet point), 17–26.

148 Gasser (n 11) 207–208; Hoffmann-Riem (n 3) 143–144, 196–198; Philipp Hacker, *Datenprivatrecht* (Mohr Siebeck 2020) 555–561; Determann, 'Healthy Data Protection' (n 16) 270–271, 273; Luciano Floridi, *The ethics of information* (Oxford University Press 2013) 235–236, 243.

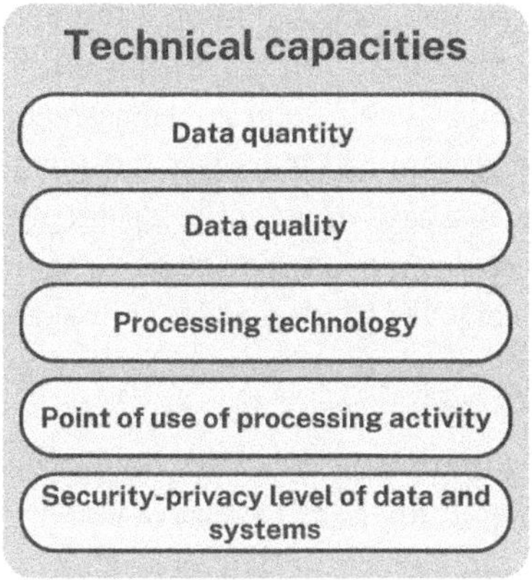

Figure 1: Technical capacities

1. Data quantity

Should we apply the same set of privacy rules to persons and companies that collect and process little personal information about individuals than to those that hold or process a lot? In the abstract, it may be difficult to argue a causal link between the quantity of personal data a person or company collects and processes about an individual and the privacy risk this person or company potentially poses: Even a data-holder with little information about an individual can do considerable harm, for instance when sensible information is breached. Accordingly, the EU Commission has held that the size of the operator in itself is not a valid indication of privacy risk.[149]

Empirically though, there is evidence that the accumulation of large quantities of individual pieces of personal information over time and by multiple organizations frequently lies at the root of privacy risks and violations.[150] The preparatory COPRA report, for instance, points to the common practice of data commercialization by which large quantities of personal data are accumulated and traded.[151] In fact, data commercialization has been the path of growth for many if not for all of today's large data companies: By acquiring and integrating existing data pools (or

149 European Commission, 'European Commission, Data protection as a pillar of citizens' empowerment and the EU's approach to the digital transition' (n 21) 9.

150 Cf. Solove, 'Privacy Self-Management and the Consent Dilemma' (n 78) 1881, 1889–1890; Bygrave (n 59) 9–11; Hoofnagle (n 80) 147; German Data Ethics Commission (n 6) 8; interestingly, the new EU Digital Services Act now recognizes a structural risk associated with data quantity European Parliament and Council, 'Regulation (EU) 2022/2065 on a Single Market for Digital Services and amending Directive 2000/31/EC' OJ L 277/1, Recital 76.

151 Cantwell (n 54) 5.

entire companies that possess large data sets), data companies reinforce the network-effect of their products thereby expanding their data and market power.[152] *Meta* is a known example of how large data companies thrive upon the amassment of personal data, and *Meta's* acquisition and integration of *WhatsApp* and *Instagram* totaling in 2.6 billion users across platforms is a case in point.[153] Repeatedly, *Meta* has been criticized for its carelessness or even open opposition to privacy. In 2019, the FTC's investigation against *Meta* for privacy violations and following the *Cambridge Analytica* scandal culminated in a USD 5 billion settlement and a reorganization of *Meta's* corporate structure.[154]

Building on this argument, this study suggests that modern privacy regulation should acknowledge and adequately address data quantity as a category of modern privacy risk. Considering that some processing entities process relatively little personal while others process a lot, adequate regulation of data quantity must go both ways.

At one end of the spectrum, there should be a required minimum threshold of processed data or of processing activities to subject companies to privacy regulation.[155] Below this threshold, any processing of personal data should be considered a socially and legally accepted risk. This minimum threshold could be set, for instance, at the quantity of data which typically constitutes interpersonal communication.[156] In the same line of reasoning, the *American Law Institute's Data Privacy Principles* do not regulate person-to-person processing of personal data because "[t]*ort law and sometimes even criminal law are better at dealing with these situations.*"[157] To give an example, there are many good reasons why a kindergarten, a schoolteacher, or a small handyman shop do not need to be held to the same regulatory standards as a large data-holder. Similarly, certain minimally-invasive processing activities do not have to be regulated by privacy law. There already exist adequate remedies at law which address libel and similar offenses. Consider,

152 Hoofnagle (n 80) 147; cf. Lev-Aretz and Strandburg (n 16), 273–274.
153 Mike Isaac, 'Zuckerberg Plans to Integrate WhatsApp, Instagram and Facebook Messenger' *New York Times* (2019) <https://www.nytimes.com/2019/01/25/technology/facebook-instagram-whatsapp-messenger.html> accessed 10 October 2020.
154 Federal Trade Commission (n 9).
155 Veil (n 15), 686, 695; contrary to European Commission, 'European Commission, Data protection as a pillar of citizens' empowerment and the EU's approach to the digital transition' (n 21) 9; Jan P Albrecht and Florian Jotzo, *Das neue Datenschutzrecht der EU* (Nomos 2017) 64.
156 A more precise quantification, at best a range of how much and which personal data is commonly exchanged in an interpersonal conversation, would have to be researched in a quantitative examination which lies out of scope of this study.
157 Solove and Schwartz, 'ALI Data Privacy: Overview and Black Letter Text' (n 95) 1265.

for instance, the law of torts generally, §§ 185–187 German Criminal Code, §§ 823–853, § 1004 para. 1 sentence 2 together with § 249 para. 1 German Civil Code which includes a right to rectify false facts (*medienrechtlicher Berichtigungsanspruch*), § 3 German *Netzwerkdurchsetzungsgesetz* and Art. 16 in connection with Art. 6 para. 1 European *Digital Services Act* which establish accountability for platform host and providers of hosting services to monitor and moderate information within their sphere of influence.[158] Generally, companies that possess little information about an individual and will be less often and less likely in a position to exploit this data to the detriment of the individual than a company which holds a lot of personal information. By introducing a minimal threshold of required data processing activities to be subjected to privacy regulation, low-risk persons and companies would be spared the often time-intensive and costly burden of keeping up with privacy compliance obligations.[159]

At the other end of the spectrum, one may argue for stricter and more targeted privacy regulation to mitigate against privacy risks which are commonly associated with large data holders.[160] The same tone strikes the German Data Ethics Commission's call at legislators to consider "*possible future cumulative effects, network effects and effects of scale*" when defining future standards for data governance.[161] Generally speaking, the idea is to link data-quantity-apt measures which are likely more costly to implement and more time-consuming to administer (and thus appear particularly burdensome to small industry players) to risk-scenarios which are commonly present among large data holders and large-sized data pools.

Such regulation could monitor from a privacy point of view how large data companies exercise their market and data power utilizing collected personal data, similar to competition law control which regulates large data companies' *market*

---

158 Oliver Spiecker, '§ 39 Äußerungs- und Medienrecht' in Christoph Hamm (ed), *Beck'sches Rechtsanwalts-Handbuch* (C.H. Beck 2022) para. 32–33; Gerhard Wagner, 'Haftung von Plattformen für Rechtsverletzungen (Teil 2)' 2020 GRUR 447, 448; Marc Liesching, 'Fünf Jahre Netzwerkdurchsetzungsgesetz' 2023 MMR 56, 56.

159 Cf. Institut der deutschen Wirtschaft (n 22) 12, according to which 96 % of the participating businesses complained about high expenses incurred to implement the GDPR; European Commission, 'European Commission, Data protection as a pillar of citizens' empowerment and the EU's approach to the digital transition' (n 21) 9, acknowledging the fact that SMEs are complaining about the challenges of implementing the GDPR.

160 Cf. Daniel Solove, 'The Myth of the Privacy Paradox' 2021(89) The George Washington Law Review 1, 50; Lauren Scholz, 'Private rights of action in privacy law' 2022 William & Mary Law Review 1639, 1678–1683.

161 German Data Ethics Commission (n 6) 8.

dominance and *prohibited conduct*.[162] For instance, there could be additional rules for large data companies to strengthen their privacy compliance system by designating data privacy and data security officers or to conduct regular privacy and security impact assessments.[163] Besides, there could be targeted technical provisions which help reduce the privacy risks frequently associated with large data companies or large data sets, for example, by limiting databases in size, organizing databases by statistical properties only, or storing smaller databases separately without integrating them so that they remain "*comparatively small and unspecific*" and individuals cannot be identified.[164]

Compared to EU data protection law, data quantity regulation starkly contrasts with the GDPR's one-size-fits-all approach which governs companies of all sizes and irrespective of the amount of personal data they process. Once more, the one-size-fits-all approach demonstrates how German and EU skepticism towards all of data processing has shaped the law: If any single processing act of personal data and irrespective of the data quantity at stake carries the potential risk of a privacy violation, there is no room to privilege data controllers or processors which process only small amounts of personal data.[165] The European Commission has explicitly refuted the idea of exempting small(er)-sized companies from the application of the GDPR in the future, and does not recognize the size of a data controller or processor or the quantity of personal data they process as a general indication of privacy risk.[166]

The Commission's disregard for data quantity as an important building block for data protection regulation has been met with critique by European stakeholders and policymakers. For example, in 2019, the *German Data Ethics Commission*, an advisory committee to the German government on the topic of protecting individuals and society in the information age, explicitly acknowledged data quantity as a building block and category of data regulation. It recommends integrating

---

162 Cf. § 18 et seq. German Act against Restraints of Competition (*Gesetz gegen Wettbewerbsbeschränkungen*); on the applicability of competition law to large data companies and an access to data sets see Sebastian Louven, 'Datenmacht und Zugang zu Daten' 2018 NZKart 217; Heike Schweitzer, 'Datenzugang in der Datenökonomie: Eckpfeiler einer neuen Informationsordnung' 2019 GRUR 569, 579–580; Streinz (n 12) 30.

163 Cf. Katyal (n 52), 56, 112; cf. Dempsey and others (n 129), 2, 8.

164 Dirk Helbing, *Thinking Ahead – Essays on Big Data, Digital Revolution, and Participatory Market Society* (Springer International Publishing 2015) 140.

165 Von Lewinski, 'Einführung' (n 17) para. 13, 18–19; Determann (n 8) 135–136; on German and EU skepticism towards technology supra Introduction and Chapter 1 B. Concept and status of EU data protection law.

166 European Commission, 'European Commission, Data protection as a pillar of citizens' empowerment and the EU's approach to the digital transition' (n 21) 9.

into future regulation *"foresighted responsibility [which is mindful of] possible future cumulative effects, network effects and effects of scale* [...]".[167] Interestingly, new EU data regulation beyond EU data protection law now integrates data quantity as a building block, albeit sparsely. The new *Data Governance Act* aims at strengthening trust in data sharing via data intermediaries and at increasing data availability and reuse of data; yet, the act applies a one-size-fits-all approach treating entities with little data just the same as platform hegemons which already today possess and control a large part of the most valuable data that has been collected.[168] The new European *Data Act* which proposes regulation to facilitate data access and data use across various data holders does not distinguish in its scope of application in Art. 1 para. 2 lit. a and b Data Act between manufacturers of products, suppliers of related services and data holders and how much data they hold. On the other hand, in Art. 7 para. 1 Data Act exempts *microenterprises, small enterprises,* and *medium-sized enterprises* the data sharing obligations in Chapter 2 of the Data Act.[169] Finally, without regard to the quantity of data but at least acknowledging the average quantity of monthly recipients of their services, the new EU *Data Services Act* now sets additional accountability obligations for *very large online platforms* and *very large online search engines* as defined in Art. 33 para. 1 Digital Services Act and compared to regular providers of intermediary services.[170]

Conceptually speaking, data quantity as a building block and category of modern data protection regulation would be compatible with EU data protection law. Given the focus of this chapter to propose abstract categories of modern privacy risks, the following reference to GDPR articles does not mean to propose precise new measures for EU data protection regulation; rather, it wants to demonstrate the feasibility of quantity-based regulation in EU data protection law generally. In the GDPR, at least three provisions exist which build on data quantity or the quantity of processing activities by a data controller or processor. First, Art. 30 para. 5 GDPR exempts enterprises with less than 250 employees from keeping records on their processing activities. The idea is to reduce the impact of compliance cost on small organizations given their important role as employers.[171]

167 German Data Ethics Commission (n 6) 8.

168 European Parliament and Council 'Regulation (EU) 2022/868 of the European Parliament and the Council of 30 May 2022 on European data governance and amending Regulation (EU) 2018/1724' OJ L152, 1; cf. Hennemann and Ditfurth (n 25), 1907; Hennemann and Specht-Riemenschneider (n 25) Einleitung para. 20, 22.

169 European Parliament and Council (n 26); cf. Hennemann and Steinrötter (n 24), 1482.

170 European Parliament and Council, 'Regulation (EU) 2022/2065 on a Single Market for Digital Services and amending Directive 2000/31/EC' (n 145) Recital 76.

171 Mario Martini, 'Art. 30' in Boris Paal and Daniel Pauly (eds), *DSGVO, BDSG* (C.H. Beck 2021) para. 26, 28.

Secondly, the threshold of *large scale* – the term is not defined in the GDPR – triggers the obligation to designate a data protection officer according to Art. 37 para. 1 lit. b and c GDPR. Importantly, the threshold of large scale monitoring or processing is not restricted to data quantity and can also be met because a large quantity of people is concerned by the data processing, because the data processing is geographically extensive, or because the duration and retention of the data processing is large.[172] Last but not least, Art. 35 para. 3 lit. b and c GDPR stipulates impact assessments in cases of *large scale* processing of special categories of personal data or in cases of systematic monitoring of publicly accessible areas on a *large scale*. The GDPR does not define the quantity of data necessary to meet the threshold of large scale processing of special categories of data; instead, data controllers and processors have to assess according to Art. 35 para. 1 sentence 1 GDPR whether the special categories of personal data processed amount to a high risk for the rights and freedoms of natural persons.[173] Finally, public surveillance requires a data processing impact assessment because of the structural risk that data subjects feel intimidated when an extended and systemic monitoring of public places takes place.[174]

To summarize, data quantity regulation is cognizant of the amount of personal data which is being collected and processed. By introducing thresholds into the scope of application of the regulation or for specific regulatory measures, we can establish privacy regulation on a sliding scale. Thereby, stricter regulation of high-risk companies or high-risk data pools will go hand in hand with a relief from financially and administratively burdensome regulation for low-risk processors of personal data.

2. Data quality

The type and substance of personal data collected and processed, and the composition of data pools containing accumulated personal data greatly influence the results of modern data-focused technology and data processing activities.[175] In this study, the category of data quality refers to the substance of personal data both in

---

172 Boris Paal, 'Art. 37' in Boris Paal and Daniel Pauly (eds), *DSGVO, BDSG* (C.H. Beck 2021) para. 8–9.

173 Mario Martini, 'Art. 35' in Boris Paal and Daniel Pauly (eds), *DSGVO, BDSG* (C.H. Beck 2021) para. 14.

174 Ibid para. 30–31.

175 Cf. Scholz, 'Private rights of action in privacy law' (n 160) 1679; German Data Ethics Commission (n 6) 8 (4th bullet point).

individual pieces of data and when accumulated in data sets or pools.[176] By substance we mean the content or message an information or data conveys to its recipient. In the absence of a standardized and widely accepted definition of the term data quality in law or the IT-industry, data quality in this study is to be understood broadly and includes quality-defining criteria such as accuracy, completeness, relevance, and usability of personal data.[177]

The extent to which the output of modern data-focused technology depends on the quality of individual pieces of data and of data sets can be exemplified by algorithmic decision-making. Sec. 2 para. 2 COPRA defines algorithmic decision-making as a *"computational process, including one derived from machine learning, statistics, or other data processing or artificial intelligence techniques that makes a decision or facilitates human decision-making with respect to covered data"*. In simple terms, algorithmic decision-making technology can be described as a set of machine-implemented rules which perform a string of calculations to solve a given problem.[178] The technology builds on data as input-material to train the algorithms.[179]

When algorithms are trained on low-quality data or data pools which contain incorrect, biased, or incomplete data, the technology risks unwanted or even unlawful outputs.[180] The challenge with data quality is that low-quality data often has deep roots in the data creation or collection which are not easily rectifiable.[181] Frequently, low-quality data is linked to systemic shortcomings in the real world which are mirrored in data; for example, the misrepresentation of minorities in society many times penetrates into data. If a certain group of people does not own property or owns considerably less property than another group of people, there will be no or considerably less data on property ownership of this group.[182] Data mirrors real life participation and (mis)representation of people in society in many other aspects:

---

176 Already on data quality as a category of privacy regulation cf. the 1980 OECD (n 97), Part Two: Basic Principles Of National Application, para. 8, and Detailed Comments, para. 53; supra Chapter 1 B. Concept and status of EU data protection law.

177 Cf. Thomas Hoeren, 'Thesen zum Verhältnis von Big Data und Datenqualität Erstes Raster zum Erstellen juristischer Standards' 2016(1) MMR 8, 10–11; Moritz Hennemann, 'Datenrichtigkeit' [2020] LR 77, 78–80; Frank Sarre and Michael Pruß, '§ 2 Daten, Datenbanken und Datensicherheit' in Astrid Auer-Reinsdorff and Isabell Conrad (eds), *Handbuch IT- und Datenschutzrecht* (C.H. Beck 2019) § 2 Daten, Datenbanken und Datensicherheit para. 71–110.

178 Hoffmann-Riem (n 3) 35–36.

179 Cf. Katyal (n 52), 56, 67–77; European Data Protection Supervisor (n 21) 10.

180 Cf. Federal Trade Commission, 'Warning about using Artificial Intelligence to Combat Online Problems' (2022) <https://www.ftc.gov/news-events/news/press-releases/2022/06/ftc-report-warns-about-using-artificial-intelligence-combat-online-problems> accessed 4 August 2023.

181 Cf. Katyal (n 52), 56, 71–73.

182 Ibid.

When a group of individuals on average is less participative in or has less access to goods and services, the data representation of such group will be inferior in quality and quantity to the default group. The lack of such data in a data pool impacts the quality of the input-data on which an algorithm is trained which, in turn, may trigger the algorithm to arrive at conclusions that are false or discriminatory.[183]

Moreover, false and discriminatory processing results may also be caused by an intentional (mis)use of data quality.[184] The COPRA report illustrates a number of examples of targeted advertisement in which a consumer's data quality was used as a basis for deliberate discrimination, *e.g. Meta* has been found to exclude users of a certain race, age, and gender from housing, work, and credit advertisement, *Alphabet*, formerly *Google*, has been found to show to women only lower-paying jobs and related advertisement compared to male profiles.[185]

The traditional answer how to mitigate against this privacy challenge has been to classify and regulate more strictly sensitive data such as gender or race which is thought to be particular prone to misuse and discrimination. Art. 9 para. 1 GDPR is the manifestation of this approach.[186] In today's data reality, however, this thick-brush approach misses the complexity of data quality. Most of all, data quality is a moving target which cannot be appropriately addressed in an exhaustive and fixed list of sensitive personal data: What does not constitute discriminatory-prone data today may be used to produce the same discriminatory results tomorrow.[187] The COPRA report highlights how digital discrimination not only occurs when specific sensitive personal information such as race is directly processed but also when seemingly secondary information can be linked to the person or group of people who is being discriminated against, *e.g.* geolocation data or the postal code of an area known to be under economic distress has been shown to oftentimes work as a proxy for race.[188]

---

183 Katyal (n 52), 56, 71–73; similarly, Eike Frenzel, 'Art. 5' in Boris Paal and Daniel Pauly (eds), *DSGVO, BDSG* (C.H. Beck 2021) para. 39 on the functionality of data as a representation of reality; *European Data Protection Supervisor (n 21) 21–22.*

184 Cf. Scholz, 'Private rights of action in privacy law' (n 160) 1681; Katyal (n 52), 56, 71–73.

185 Cantwell (n 54) 8; Katyal (n 52), 56; Amit Datta, Michael C Tschantz and Anupam Datta, 'Automated Experiments on Ad Privacy Settings' 2015 Proceedings on Privacy Enhancing Technologies 92, 105.

186 Eike Frenzel, 'Art. 9' in Boris Paal and Daniel Pauly (eds), *DSGVO, BDSG* (C.H. Beck 2021) para. 6–9.

187 Cf. Paul Ohm, 'Changing the Rules: General Principles for Data Use and Analysis' in Julia Lane and others (eds), *Privacy, big data, and the public good* (Cambridge University Press 2014) 104–105.

188 Cantwell (n 54) 8; similarly, on the phenomenon of "*sensor fusion*" to combine data which helps identify an individual Scott Peppet, 'Regulating the Internet of Things: First Steps Toward Managing Discrimination, Privacy, Security & Consent' 2014(93) Texas Law Review 85, 117–124.

It follows from the above examples of involuntary and of deliberate (mis)use of data quality and its effect on processing outputs that any modern privacy regulation must ensure (the use of) a high standard of data quality.[189] Although there likely is no medicine to cure privacy risks based on data quality such as discrimination altogether, there are targeted privacy measures which can substantially increase the quality of individual pieces of personal data and of aggregated data in data pools. The discussion inevitably starts with a standardization of the criteria we apply to measure the quality of data in the first place.[190] To this end, a technical precondition for transparency and comparability are standard data formats, standardized data ontology, and a data infrastructure which allows us to easily exchange and transfer data.[191] The approach for law- and policymakers could be to work with standard-setting bodies to propose internationally attractive default data formats, ontology, and infrastructure similar to what the *European Telecommunications Standard Institute*, a not-for-profit organization, has done for standard-setting in the mobile phone industry.[192] Companies could be nudged into using these standards by way of incentives such as access to lucrative public procurement projects.[193] Finally, there could be new legally binding standards for companies to adhere to, consider for instance the EU's recent decision to regulate mobile phone chargers with a required use of only USB-C ports from the end of 2024 in all of Europe.[194]

Moreover, we should require more transparency from companies which collect and commercialize data, and from developers and entities that create data-focused technology to disclose the source, content, and composition of their data or data pools.[195] We should create reference data pools with existing statistical data

189 German Data Ethics Commission (n 6) 8 (4th bullet point).

190 As early as in 1980, the criteria of "*accuracy, completeness, and up-to-dateness* [...] *related to the purpose of data*" were presented to assess data quality by the OECD (n 97), Part Two: Basic Principles Of National Application, para. 8, and Detailed Comments, para. 53; Sarre and Pruß (n 172) § 2 Daten, Datenbanken und Datensicherheit para. 71–110.

191 Cf. Olga Batura and Roel Peeters, 'EU Commission DG Internal Policies, Policy Department for Economic, Scientific, and Quality of Life Policies: European Union data challenge' (2021) 5 <https://www.europarl.europa.eu/RegData/etudes/BRIE/2021/662939/IPOL_BRI(2021)662939_EN.pdf> accessed 3 October 2023.

192 ETSI, '4th Generation (LTE)' (2023) <https://www.etsi.org/technologies/mobile/4g?jjj=1698915313158> accessed 2 November 2023.

193 Generally on the idea of nudging Richard Thaler and Cass Sunstein, *Nudge* (Yale University Press 2009).

194 European Parliament, 'USB-type C to become EU's common charger by end of 2024' (2022) <https://www.europarl.europa.eu/news/en/headlines/society/20220413STO27211/usb-type-c-to-become-eu-s-common-charger-by-end-of-2024> accessed 15 January 2024.

195 Cf. Hoffmann-Riem (n 3) 61–63.

which can be used to train data-focused technology or against which we measure the quality of existing data pools.[196] Moreover, obligatory testing can help increase data quality, for instance, when impact assessments share light on the functioning of technology and the results they are likely to produce.[197] Such testing can be done as mandatory self-assessment linked to mandatory reporting and on the level of the owner of the data-focused technology, or by way of external audits, possibly strengthened by standardized review and certification.[198]

With regard to data quality and the prevention of unwanted or unlawful processing output such as discriminatory results, the shortcomings of current EU data protection law become apparent. Simply put, the GDPR has been focused more on preventing the disclosure and use of personal data than on ensuring the quality of selected input data, of data pools, or on impartial, unbiased, or fair processing and processing result.[199] This is true despite the regulation's containing at least three provisions which directly or indirectly relate to data quality – Art. 5 para. 1 lit. d, Art. 9 para. 1 lit. d, and Art. 35 para. 3 lit. b GDPR – because, generally speaking, the EU regulation and the provisions cited before miss the full picture of data quality risks and its structural roots illustrated above. In the below, we outline how they provide for limited control of data quality in *individual* pieces of personal data but largely ignore the broad idea of data quality such as in in data sets and pools.[200]

Art. 5 para. 1 lit. d GDPR demands the accuracy of individual pieces of personal data but is largely ineffective vis-à-vis the results derived from data sets.[201] To build an example similar to the structural problem of data representation described above: Consider cases in which the individual pieces of information in a large set of personal data are accurate but in which the lack of certain personal data on an aggregated level nevertheless causes the data set to be biased or inaccurate.[202] Art. 16 sentence 1 and 2 GDPR together with Art. 5 para. 1 lit. d GDPR further strengthens this argument: The individual data subject is entitled to claim the rectification or completion of her or his inaccurate personal data, however, there is no right to question the data quality in a data pool and the accuracy of aggregated data of a group of individuals.[203]

---

196 Cf. European Data Protection Supervisor (n 21) 21–22, calling for an obligation to use *"representative"* data sets to train artificial intelligence technology.

197 Cf. Katyal (n 52), 56, 112; Dempsey and others (n 129), 12.

198 Cf. Determann, 'Healthy Data Protection' (n 16) 274.

199 Cf. Hoeren (n 172), 10; Determann (n 8) 123; von Lewinski, 'Einführung' (n 17) para. 72–73.

200 Cf. Hoeren (n 172), 10.

201 Cf. Frenzel, 'Art. 5' (n 178) para. 39–42.

202 Cf. Katyal (n 52), 56, 71–73.

203 Cf. Susanne Stollhoff, 'Art. 16' in Martin Eßer, Philipp Kramer and Kai von Lewinski (eds), *DSGVO/BDSG* (Carl Heymanns Verlag 2023) para. 20–21.

Art. 9 para. 1 GDPR regulates data quality by generally banning the disclosure and processing of *special categories of personal data*. The reason to subject special categories of personal data to more rigorous treatment in comparison to other personal data is the attempt to mitigate the risk of discrimination because of the data quality or substance of the personal data. Consequently, the article has sometimes been called the *"anti-discrimination measure in the digital world"* (*informationelles Diskriminierungsverbot*).[204] Yet the processing ban largely fails to comprehend the effect of data aggregation and the composition and functionality of data sets. First, data sets can be incorrect, incomplete, or biased in other ways despite or even due to the lack of special categories of personal data.[205] In the above, we explained how conclusions can be derived on an individual or a group of individuals precisely because there only exists a lack of data, incorrect or biased data related to the person or group of persons – data largely mirrors life in the real world and a lack of participation of a person or a group of persons in real life situations can easily result in their misrepresentation in data, *e.g.* the issuance of bank credit to an individual or a group of individuals.[206] Secondly, a considerable risk of discrimination remains because the list of special categories of personal data in Art. 9 para. 1 GDPR is incomplete: There is more personal data essential to the safeguarding of an individual's fundamental rights and freedoms than listed, for example, the list of special categories of personal data does not include information about the economic situation of individuals or about their place of residence.[207] A person may consequently have to pay higher interest on a bank credit because information about her economic situation indicates that she will take longer to repay their credit than the average consumer, a person's place of residence may be directly or indirectly instrumentalized to advertise or withhold the advertisement of jobs, goods, or services, *e.g.* because their place of residence is associated with a lower-income population.[208] Thirdly, such fixed-list approach alike Art. 9 para. 1 GDPR is anachronistic: What constitutes non-sensitive personal data today likely is intelligible enough for technology tomorrow to arrive at the same conclusions as from sensitive personal data directly.[209] In short, the idea of banning sensitive personal data as a counter-measure to discrimination is unable to keep up with today's data rea-

204 Holger Greve, 'Art. 9' in Martin Eßer, Philipp Kramer and Kai von Lewinski (eds), *DSGVO/BDSG* (Carl Heymanns Verlag 2023) para. 2.

205 Cf. Katyal (n 52), 56, 71–73.

206 Cf. Ibid.

207 Cf. Frenzel, 'Frenzel, Art. 9' (n 181) para. 7.

208 Cf. Cantwell (n 54) 8; Katyal (n 52), 56.

209 Cantwell (n 54) 8; Solove, 'Privacy Self-Management and the Consent Dilemma' (n 78) 1889–1890; Ohm (n 182) 104–105.

lity with data quality as a moving target. Fourthly, protection against discriminatory results can be circumvented because Art. 9 para. 2 lit. a GDPR allows the data controller to shift the risk and legal liability of discrimination back on to the data subject by asking for explicit consent. In a typical take-it-or-leave-it situation in which the processing of special categories of personal data is the precondition to obtain insurance coverage, the issuance of credit, or to be considered for a medical treatment, how good of a protection against discrimination is explicit consent?[210] While coercion and institutional power imbalances, *e.g.* between a public authority and an individual or between an employer and an employee, may be filtered out by the requirement in Art. 4 para. 11 GDPR and Recital 43 GDPR of *"freely given"* consent by the data subject, Art. 9 para. 2 lit. a GDPR arguably fails to consider the structural risk of the situational constraints and distress an individual will often find herself in when confronted with a take-it-or-leave-it situation.[211]

Finally, Art. 35 para. 1 and 3 GDPR requires privacy impact assessments for high-risk processing activities which, in principle, can be helpful tools to detect shortcomings also in data quality.[212] Unfortunately, the GDPR provisions are limited because data quality analysis arguably remains a nice-to-have exercise rather than a core-obligation in impact assessments. First, Art. 35 para. 7 GDPR does not explicitly include data quality as an obligatory component of an impact assessment. Even if one reads the requirement of a *"systematic description of the envisaged data processing operations"* in Art. 35 para. 7 lit. a GDPR to also cover the analysis of processed data and data formats, it remains unclear whether and to which extent data quality in data pools and the accuracy of aggregated data must be discussed.[213] To the same point, important guiding material by the French data protection authority on how to conduct data protection impact assessments is silent on whether a detailed assessment of the software and algorithm development process and the data quality used for the training is expected.[214]

Secondly, Art. 35 para. 3 lit. b 1st alternative GDPR does not apply generally but only in the exceptional situation of large scale-processing of special categories of

---

210 Cf. Zuiderveen Borgesius and others (n 30), 354, 360 et seq.; *Cate*, in: Winn (ed.), Consumer Protection in the Age of the 'Information Economy', 2007, p. 341, 364–365; *Maisch*, Informationelle Selbstbestimmung in Netzwerken, 2015, p. 298; Becker (n 30), 172.

211 The constraints of consent as a basis for personal data processing are discussed in more detail sub Chapter 2 A. II. 1. Intellectual (in)capacity.

212 Dempsey and others (n 129), 12; Katyal (n 52), 56, 112.

213 Cf. Bertram Raum, 'Art. 35' in Martin Eßer, Philipp Kramer and Kai von Lewinski (eds), *DSGVO/ BDSG* (Carl Heymanns Verlag 2020) para. 51; Hoffmann-Riem (n 3) 64–65.

214 Commission Nationale de l'Informatique et des Libertés, 'Private Impact Assessment: Methodology' (2022) <https://www.cnil.fr/en/privacy-impact-assessment-pia> accessed 31 October 2023.

personal data.[215] Consequently, a large number of processing activities is out of scope, in particular during early-stage data accumulation, product design, model programming and training, and other development work because these activities are likely not judged high-risk processing activities and of which the related risk level can be properly understood only in hindsight.[216] Art. 35 para. 3 lit. b 1st alternative GDPR hence fails to grasp the seminal role data quality plays in the building, functionality, and the results of modern data-focused technology.

In sum, data quality should be regarded an essential category of modern data processing because it provides the basis for technological developments and has a direct impact on the results of data processing activities and of technology.

3. Processing technology

Some modern data-focused technology breeds inherent privacy risks which escape traditional regulatory concepts. In these cases, tailored privacy regulation focusing on specific processing technology may offer more effective solutions than generally technology-agnostic one-size-fits-all approaches alike in the GDPR.[217] Today, much attention in research and development, as well as in the public debate and policy is given to the potential opportunity and risk of artificial intelligence and big data technology. Artificial intelligence technology uses a set of computing techniques such as machine learning and statistical approaches to solve a given problem by imitating human intelligence, *e.g.* the algorithm further refines outputs and develops new models without human intervention.[218] Already today, the technology is ubiquitous in software where algorithms assist or substitute human decision-making.[219] Big data technology makes use of the abundance of available data and the increasing computing power in data processing.[220] The idea is to leverage large

---

215 With a similar critique of the GDPR's privacy impact assessment obligation and its limited scope Dariuz Kloza, 'A Behavioural Alternative To The Protection Of Privacy' in Dan J B Svantesson and Dariuz Kloza (eds), *Trans-Atlantic Data Privacy Relations As A Challenge For Democracy* (Intersentia 2017) 488.

216 Cf. Hoffmann-Riem (n 3) 62–63.

217 Cf. German Data Ethics Commission (n 6) 5 (5th bullet point), 17–26.

218 Cf. the definition of artificial intelligence technology in Annex 1 European Parliament and Council 'Proposal for a Regulation of the European Parliament and of the Council Laying Down Harmonised Rules On Artificial Intelligence', COM(2021) 206 final; Hoffmann-Riem (n 3) 39–40.

219 Cf. Katyal (n 52), 56; Hoffmann-Riem (n 3) 35–36; Cantwell (n 54) 9.

220 Cf. the description of big data technology in Art. 2 bullet point 2 European Parliament and Council 'Proposal for a Regulation of the European Parliament and of the Council on European data governance' COM(2020) 767 final.

data quantity to identify and make useful in an inductive manner patterns, structures, and models to generate new insights.[221]

But how do these technologies challenge traditional privacy concepts? To start with, the mounting complexity in modern data-focused technology renders the traditional privacy approach of information rights and obligations as the basis for an informed decision by the individual largely ineffective.[222] Big data technology is a case in point: The technology is able to infer from a large set of data conclusions that are often surprising or even inexplainable for the human observer including for skilled big data experts because of how the technology combines and processes information, *e.g.* by creating data patterns and models in a way that is unintelligible for the human mind.[223] However, according to existing regulatory concepts like notice-and-consent in U.S. privacy law and informed consent in EU privacy law,[224] companies using big data technology are required to explain the functioning and logic of big data technology to the consumer in their privacy policies and data processing information.[225] This puts companies in the following dilemma: If you cannot explain how and why big data produces a certain result in the first place, it is difficult to inform about it in a privacy policy.[226]

The use of automated decision-making and artificial intelligence technology faces similar challenges. The GDPR's information rights and obligations such as the ones spelled out in Art. 13 para. 2 lit. f and Art. 14 para. 2 lit. g GDPR require if not an explanation of the specific decision produced by automated decision-making technology so at least an *ex ante* explanation of the decision process and the general functionality of the technology.[227] Yet the technical capacity of artificial intelligence, its

---

221 Salon Barocas and Helen Nissenbaum, 'Big Data's End Run around Anonymity and Consent' in Julia Lane and others (eds), *Privacy, big data, and the public good* (Cambridge University Press 2014) 46.

222 Cf. Ebner, *Weniger ist Mehr?* (n 29) 45–48; cf. Solove, 'The Myth of the Privacy Paradox' (n 155) 5.

223 Hoffmann-Riem (n 3) 41; Barocas and Nissenbaum (n 216) 56–63; Ohm (n 182) 105–106.

224 Solove, 'Privacy Self-Management and the Consent Dilemma' (n 78) 1883–1884; Kramer, 'Art. 6' (n 104) para. 21; Boris Paal and Moritz Hennemann, 'Art. 13' in Boris Paal and Daniel Pauly (eds), *DSGVO, BDSG* (C.H. Beck 2021); supra Chapter 1 A. Concept and status of U.S. privacy law and Chapter 1 B. Concept and status of EU data protection law.

225 Boris Paal and Moritz Hennemann, 'Big Data im Recht: Wettbewerbs- und daten(schutz)rechtliche Herausforderungen' 2017 NJW 1697, 1701; Ohm (n 182) 105–106.

226 Cf. Ohm (n 182) 100–101; Barocas and Nissenbaum (n 216) 56–63; Hoffmann-Riem (n 3) 41; Voigt (n 28) 88–89.

227 Sandra Wachter, Brent Mittelstadt and Luciano Floridi, 'Why a Right to Explanation of Automated Decision-Making Does Not Exist in the General Data Protection Regulation' 2017 7(2) International Data Privacy Law 76, 82–83; see also Paal and Hennemann, 'Art. 13' (n 219) Art. 13 para. 31 and Art. 14 para. 32.

ability to self-enhance or auto-teach its algorithms to solve problems is what makes it increasingly difficult even for programmers and technical experts to explain in a easily understandable manner the logic and functionality of the technology.[228]

Even regarding less complex technology, finding the right balance between using processing technology and adequately informing about it is a difficult exercise for many processing entities, and one which comes with legal uncertainty and liability risks.[229] Likely, we will have to agree on accepted standards of simplified information, in particular regarding the logic of big data technology and artificial intelligence technology, and value the assessment and certification by technical experts more than we have so that companies understand how to meet their privacy compliance obligations.[230]

The friction between information obligations and modern processing technology further triggers the question whether in light of the mounting technical complexity of processing technology we can truthfully uphold the fundamental privacy concept of the sovereign (data) citizen (*mündiger Bürger*): Can the individual adequately understand the risks and benefits of modern data-focused technology, are individuals able to form an informed opinion and decision about the processing of their personal data by complex processing technology such as big data technology or artificial intelligence technology, and should the law continue to strongly rely on individual privacy rights as a tool to counterbalance risky or undesired processing activities?[231] The *European Data Protection Supervisor* and regarding artificial intelligence technology has answered this question in the negative: In April 2020, the supervisor urged regulators to temporarily ban artificial intelligence in high-risk situations where the impact of the use of such technology on the individual or on society is *"not yet fully understood"*.[232] We examine the question of intellectual capacity in more detail sub Chapter 2 A. II. 1. Intellectual (in)capacity.

The availability of large quantities of data together with new capabilities in technology such as in big data technology could even shake at the very foundation of privacy law as we know it because of the technology's capacity to identify and infer conclusions about individuals from seemingly secondary and non-personal

228 Hoffmann-Riem (n 3) 41.

229 Cf. Institut der deutschen Wirtschaft (n 22) 12.

230 Cf. Gasser (n 11) 206; cf. Ebner, *Weniger ist Mehr?* (n 29) 78; sub Chapter 2 B. II. Intellectual (in) capacity.

231 Cf. Veil (n 15), 687; Solove, 'Privacy Self-Management and the Consent Dilemma' (n 78) 1881, 1886–1888; Alessandro Acquisti and Jens Grossklags, 'What Can Behavioral Economics Teach Us about Privacy?' in Alessandro Acquisti (ed), *Digital privacy: Theory, technologies, and practices* (Auerbach Publications 2008) 368, 371; Daniel Solove, 'The Limitations of Privacy Rights' 2022(30) GWU Law School Public Law Research Paper 1, 10–17.

232 European Data Protection Supervisor (n 21) 10, 14.

information.[233] Consequently, when non-personal data suffices to identify an individual, the rationale to regulate only personal information, to advocate for the anonymization of personal data, and to restrict the processing of sensitive data such as gender or race becomes ineffective.[234] For instance, already today we know of cases in which heightened scrutiny for sensitive covered data or special categories of personal information as spelled out in Sec. 2 (20) COPRA and Art. 9 para. 1 GDPR is circumvented by using proxies to derive at conclusions that could have previously been derived only from sensitive personal information directly, *e.g.* the usage of area codes of people's home address to derive at their race or religion.[235] Similarly, *Montjoye* and others have shown how we are *"unique in the crowd"* meaning that about 95 % of all individuals can be identified when we have as little as four spatio-temporal data points on them.[236] For the near future, *Peppet* predicts technology capable of organizing non-personal data in a way that produces the same results as the processing of personal and sensitive personal data. *"Everything reveals everything"* when non-personal data generated from the sensors of internet-connected consumer devices such as smart watches, cars, and refrigerators is combined and processed, *e.g.* by big data technology, to reveal our whereabouts, personal preferences, or current health status.[237]

The GDPR claims that it already provides an adequate framework which fosters the potential while mitigating against the risk of automated decision-making technology, an important building block in big data and artificial intelligence technology.[238] A closer look reveals that, although generally technology-agnostic, the EU data protection regulation contains a set of technology-targeted provisions in Recital 71 (automated decision-making, profiling); Art. 4 para. 4 (profiling), Art. 13 para. 2 lit. f and Art. 14 para. 2 lit. g (information about automated decision-making and profiling), Art. 15 para. 1 lit. h, Art. 21 para. 1 sentence 1 (right to object to pro-

---

233 Barocas and Nissenbaum (n 216) 55–56; Solove, 'Privacy Self-Management and the Consent Dilemma' (n 78) 1889–1890; Peppet (n 183), 118–124.

234 Gasser (n 11) 200; Ohm (n 182) 100–102; Andreas Solti, Sushant Agarwal and Sarah Spiekermann-Hoff, 'Privacy in Location-Sensing Technologies' in Claudio B Aris Gkoulalas-Divanis (ed), *Handbook of mobile data privacy* (Springer 2018) 58.

235 Cf. Cantwell (n 54) 8.

236 Yves-Alexandre de Montjoye and others, 'Unique in the Crowd: The privacy bounds of human mobility' 2013 Nature 1376; Igor Bilogrevic, 'Privacy in Geospatial Applications and Location-Based Social Networks' in Claudio B Aris Gkoulalas-Divanis (ed), *Handbook of mobile data privacy* (Springer 2018) 216–220.

237 Peppet (n 183), 118–124.

238 Cf. Recital 157 GDPR highlights the potential for scientific researchers to use big data technology *e.g.* "by *coupling information from registries*"; cf. Recital 71 GDPR on the risk of profiling "*based solely on automated processing and which produces legal effects.*"

filing), Art. 22 (right not to be subjected to automated decision-making and profiling), Art. 35 para. 3 lit. a (data impact assessments for automated decision-making and profiling), Art. 47 para. 2 lit. e GDPR (binding corporate rules must address data subject's right not to be subject to automated decision-making and profiling).

However, the listed GDPR provisions only insufficiently address the modern privacy risks described above because they preserve traditional privacy concepts and means which are largely dysfunctional vis-à-vis new technology, consider, for instance, the above-discussed examples of the concept of the sovereign (data) citizen who is perfectly capable of making an informed decision about automated decision-making technology, the feasibility and effectiveness of information rights and obligations, and the regulation of personal data or specific sets of sensitive personal data as a means of privacy protection despite modern technology's technical capacity to rely on non-personal data.[239] Moreover, the GDPR applies to modern data-focused technology its general processing-ban as set out in Art. 6 para. 1 sentence 1 GDPR, and its general processing principles including the principles of purpose limitation, of data minimization, and of a limited storage period as set out in Art. 5 para. 1 lit. b and lit. c and lit. e GDPR.[240] This approach likely causes friction with modern data-focused technology, for instance, because big data technology builds on the availability of a lot of (ideally high-quality) data which is to be collected over an extended period of time and often without a pre-identified and clearly defined processing purpose.[241] *Determann* pointedly argues that the GDPR's approach is out of synchronization with today's data reality: "*The genie of extensive data collection is long out of the bottle and cannot be put inside again.*"[242]

In sum, the problem with the GDPR and how it regulates modern processing technology is that the EU data protection regulation's technology-targeted provisions come short of what is technically needed while its general provisions make it difficult for technology to prosper. Instead of trying to keep the disclosure and processing of individual pieces of personal data to a minimum, we should instead focus on alternative ways of reducing privacy risks, for example by increasing the chances that processing technology can be used without producing harmful results.[243] To this end, we may decide to enforce stricter accountability and trans-

---

239 Cf. Veil (n 15), 686, 688–689; Ebner, *Weniger ist Mehr?* (n 29) 45–48; Gasser (n 11) 200.

240 Paal and Hennemann, 'Big Data im Recht' (n 220) 1700.

241 Cf. Ohm (n 182) 100–102; Streinz (n 12) 945–946; Hoffmann-Riem (n 3) 175.

242 Determann, 'Healthy Data Protection' (n 16) 262–265, 277; Hoeren (n 172), 10; Solove, 'The Myth of the Privacy Paradox' (n 155) 30.

243 Cf. Determann, 'Healthy Data Protection' (n 16) 270–271, 273; Gasser (n 11) 207–208; Hoffmann-Riem (n 3) 198–199; Michael M Maisch, *Informationelle Selbstbestimmung in Netzwerken* (Duncker & Humblot 2015) 107–118, 340; Becker (n 30), 172.

parency standards regarding big data and algorithmic decision-making technology, *e.g.* by recording access to personal data, log files, and data queries, and by subjecting them to independent review and certification.[244] Furthermore, we should consider an obligation that artificial intelligence and big data outputs must be reproducible, and, looking into the future, that the technology can detect and autocorrect undesired outputs, a design structure IT-experts refer to as *"self-regulating systems"*.[245]

Admittingly, retiring ineffective concepts and means in EU data protection and in U.S. privacy law may often be difficult given the path dependency of the respective laws and systems.[246] Still, where possible already a cumulative approach (while keeping the established concepts and means) could improve the *status quo*, for example by deploying resources and energy into a law and system that better fosters high-quality data, and the use of processing technology so that they produce non-harmful results.

To close the circle, it is worth noting that, outside of privacy and data protection law, both the U.S. and the EU are currently preparing regulation which specifically targets modern data-focused processing technology and related risks. In the U.S., President Biden signed the Executive Order on the *Safe, Secure, and Trustworthy Development and Use of Artificial Intelligence* in October 2023 which lays out eight principles and priorities of how artificial intelligence technology should be developed and used.[247] In particular, the Executive Order spells out the need to develop safe and secure technology which requires standardized testing and risk mitigation, the responsible use and development of the technology which respects U.S. values and interests, and the wish to work with international allies towards a global artificial intelligence technology framework.[248]

In the EU, the European Parliament formally adopted in March 2024 the final text of the new EU AI Act, the first of its kind legally binding framework governing the development and use of artificial intelligence technology and products.[249]

---

244 Cf. Determann, 'Healthy Data Protection' (n 16) 274; Dempsey and others (n 129), 3.

245 Helbing (n 159) 15–16; Gasser (n 11) 207–208; Ohm (n 182) 102–104.

246 Supra Chapter 1 The privacy landscape in the U.S. and in the EU.

247 President of the United States, 'Executive Order on the Safe, Secure, and Trustworthy Development and Use of Artificial Intelligence' (2023) <https://www.whitehouse.gov/briefing-room/presidential-actions/2023/10/30/executive-order-on-the-safe-secure-and-trustworthy-development-and-use-of-artificial-intelligence/> accessed 1 November 2023.

248 Ibid Sec. 2 lit. a, c, e, and h.

249 European Parliament, 'Legislative resolution on the proposal for a regulation of the European Parliament and of the Council on laying down harmonised rules on Artificial Intelligence (Artificial Intelligence Act) and amending certain Union Legislative Acts (COM(2021)0206 – C9-0146/2021 – 2021/0106(COD)' [2024] P9_TA(2024)0138.

Although the analysis of the AI Act is out of scope of this study, it is worth noting that, in many aspects, the act seems to address the technical capacities discussed in this chapter and often with a similar approach. For instance, the AI Act proposes measures of *how* the technology should be used which are aimed at fostering the use of high-quality data, good data governance, and transparency, for instance as set out in Art. 10 para. 1–4, Art. 12 para. 1 and 2, Art. 13 para. 1–3, and Art. 15 para. 1 AI Act. Finally, in Chapter II Art. 5 para. 1 and 2 AI Act proposes a list of use cases in which the technology is banned, for instance according to Art. 5 para. 1 lit. a AI Act when it deploys *"purposefully manipulative or deceptive techniques"*. The motivation and regulatory means in Art. 5 para. 1 and 2 AI Act resemble the ideas proposed in this chapter under the risk categories of processing technology (real-time remote biometric identification systems in Art. 5 para. 2 AI Act), point of use of the processing activity (social monitoring Art. 5 para. 1 lit. c AI Act), and individual and collective privacy (an output-based control which is triggered when the outcome or effect of use is harmful Art. 5 para. 1 lit. a AI Act).

In addition to the AI Act, the EU has introduced broad data regulation in an effort to boost and safeguard Europe's data economy. For example, the Data Act strives to facilitate access to and usage of data generated by products and services according to Art. 1 para. 1 Data Act.[250] The Data Governance Act regulates gatekeepers or data intermediaries such as data platforms according to Recital 27 and Art. 10 lit. a Data Governance Act.[251] Importantly, in the relationship between these new laws and EU data protection law, the minimum level of protection provided by the GDPR provisions remains unchanged.[252]

The above demonstrates how modern processing technology challenges traditional concepts and means in privacy and data protection law. Processing technology and its technical capacity should thus be integrated into modern privacy regulation or addressed as an ancillary measure to privacy and data protection law.

4. Point of use of the processing activity

The processing and processing result of one and the same piece of personal information may have very different consequences for an individual depending on the

---

250 European Parliament and Council 'Regulation (EU) 2022/868 of the European Parliament and the Council of 30 May 2022 on European data governance and amending Regulation (EU) 2018/1724' OJ L152, 1; cf. Hennemann and Ditfurth (n 25), 1910; Hennemann and Steinrötter (n 26).

251 European Parliament and Council (n 26); cf. Hennemann and Steinrötter (n 24), 1482; Hennemann and Specht-Riemenschneider (n 25) Einleitung para. 38–39.

252 Louisa Specht-Riemenschneider, 'Datennutz und Datenschutz: Zum Verhältnis zwischen Datenwirtschaftsrecht und DSGVO' 2023 ZEuP 638, 642–644.

context and situation in which her data is being processed. This link between personal data and the quality of a processing situation or context which lies outside of the information is referred to in this study as the point of use of the processing activity. This chapter argues that a modern privacy regulation should be cognizant of the point of use of the processing activity and shield individuals from privacy risks in situations which have been identified as particularly prone to privacy violations or as situations of outstanding importance to an individual's private life.

For instance, the COPRA report lists processing related to credit, housing, employment, and education as situations in which consumers are especially vulnerable to discrimination.[253] These processing situations are similar in quality because the consumer likely faces severe negative consequences if the processing of her collected covered data produces an unfavorable processing result. This is due to the fact that these situations or outside-qualities linked to the processing of personal information are regularly perceived by the average consumer as high-stake situations or inflection points which stick out from everyday life. For example, housing typically is a very expensive commitment and decisions linked to housing are singular and high-stake for most consumers; a recent survey by the U.S. *Bureau of Labor Statistics* revealed that in 2021 the biggest expenditure in consumers' budgets of 33.8 % was spent on housing.[254] Moreover, these situations are often marked by a power and information imbalance which disadvantage the consumer in making effective privacy choices.[255]

The effect of point of use situations on the individual's capacity to make privacy-informed decisions has widely been discussed in literature and practice alike. Particularly poignant is the critique of *Veil* who raises general doubts about individuals being able to consent *voluntarily* in situations of a strongly desired outcome, *e.g.* the seeking of medical treatment.[256] *Veil* points to processing situations in which the disclosure of personal data is regularly set as a prerequisite to gain access or receive a desired good or service – which, he argues, leaves the consumer without meaningful privacy choice.[257] In the same direction, the European Data Protection Supervisor acknowledged in an opinion about the regulation of artificial

253 Cantwell (n 54) 8; for a detailed discussion of the high-risk situations regulated in Sec. 108 (a) and (b) COPRA see sub Chapter 3 D. I. 2. a. Point of use regulation.

254 U.S. Bureau of Labor Statistics, 'Consumer Expenditures 2021' (2021) <https://www.bls.gov/news.release/cesan.nr0.htm> accessed 5 March 2023.

255 Cf. Ebner, *Weniger ist Mehr?* (n 29) 190–191.

256 Veil (n 14), 687; similarly, Zuiderveen Borgesius and others (n 25), 354, 360 et seq.

257 Veil (n 15), 687; Hoffmann-Riem (n 3) 167Cate (n 30) 364–365; Becker (n 30), 174; Solove, 'The Limitations of Privacy Rights' (n 226) 10–17; Hermstrüwer (n 13) 84–85.

intelligence technology the existence and the need to identify certain processing situations or outside-qualities of processing activities as particularly prone to privacy violations.[258]

In all of the above described processing examples, individual privacy protection can appear weak or ineffective because of the situation the individual finds herself in, in which a particular processing technology is deployed, or in which a processing activity occurs.[259] In these situations, point of use privacy regulation which factors into the level of privacy protection the link between the information and the outside-quality or processing situation will likely increase privacy protection for individuals.

There are several ways of how point of use regulation can acknowledge high-risk situations in privacy law. Whereas the point of use examples described above gravitate around a limited number of identified risk situations (punctual approach), *e.g.* COPRA focuses on processing situations related to housing, credit, education, and employment, the idea of a point of use regulation may go even further: Point of use regulation may also be combined with the traditional concept of staggered personal spheres (spheric approach, *Sphärentheorie*), and as proposed, for instance, by the *German Constitutional Court*: In many of its decisions, the Court has applied incrementally increased levels of protection to different levels of intimacy distinguishing between the most fragile and guarded sphere of intimacy (*Intimssphäre*), a common private sphere (*Privatssphäre*), and a less protected social or public sphere (*Sozialsphäre*).[260] In this direction, *Veil* has suggested a staggered approach to privacy protection as a combination of existing privacy law with the spheric approach established in German case law and depending on which personal sphere is being targeted.[261] Similarly, *Hoffmann-Riem* and *Becker* have suggested to reduce global connectivity and introduce decentralized closed-systems for software and data use in point of use situations which are particularly sensitive or to offer consumers the choice between technology which uses personal data and such which does not.[262]

A parallel discourse about the point of use of a processing technology or activity can be traced also in the U.S.: First and foremost, in her work on privacy and democracy, *Cohen* argues that as a precondition for individual self-development

258 European Data Protection Supervisor (n 21) 14.

259 Cf. Veil (n 15), 686, 687–689.

260 *Tonbandaufnahme* BVerfGE 34, 238, 245; 35, 39; Udo Di Fabio, 'Art. 2 (1)' in Theodor Maunz and Günter Dürig (eds), *Grundgesetz* (C.H. Beck 2020) para. 157–162.

261 Veil (n 15), 695.

262 Hoffmann-Riem (n 3) 197; more generally advocating for a legal right to choose between digital products which do not process personal data and those which do Becker (n 30), 175–176.

and social integrity in any democratic system there should be a processing-free "*zone of personal space that permits (degrees of) unconstrained, unobserved physical and intellectual movement*".[263] From this, the common idea of point of use privacy regulation emerges which demands stronger privacy protection in high-risk or high-stake situations, or in a processing situation linked to an outside-quality.[264] To consider an example from the COPRA report: If put into practice, strict privacy regulation in our personal home and most private spaces may be able to effectively tackle the privacy risks associated with the new scale and level of integration of data-focused technology into our personal life and as highlighted in the COPRA report, for instance regarding home surveillance devices.[265]

Yet even where we have successfully identified point of use situations or spheres, the discussion will be about the form and degree of point of use regulation – which processing limitation in a selected situation or sphere is adequate to effectively address today's privacy risks? The theoretical spectrum spans from establishing rules on *how* to process certain categories of personal data or *how* to use a particular data-focused technology to a complete *processing ban* on certain categories of personal data or data-focused technology in a defined point of use situation.[266] And where should we start? A processing ban seems *ultima ratio* and would require further research into which data, categories of data, or processing technology causes an undue risk and whether such appreciation of risk could be generalised to arrive at the (paternalistic) decision of a ban for a group of individuals or for society. The first approach should thus likely be a reinforced debate about *how* personal data can be used.

Besides, we will have to further develop and improve technology to effectively implement such fine-tuned privacy regulation. Here, it is important to point out that point of use privacy regulation has started to become technically feasible: In his article about *context-adaptive privacy*, *Schaub* sketches out how technology is able to adapt to pre-defined situations and how this can be leveraged to enhance privacy.[267] In essence, *privacy-smart* devices such as wearables are increasingly capable of identifying where the device is located, who or which entities are present in its proximity, and even why the user is initiating certain actions or requests, a technical capacity whereby systems and devices can be set to adhere to different

---

263 Julie Cohen, *Configuring the Networked Self* (Yale University Press 2012) 143; Ohm (n 182) 105; Ohm (n 182) 105.

264 Ohm (n 182) 105; cf. Solove, 'The Myth of the Privacy Paradox' (n 155) 49–50.

265 Cantwell (n 54) 9.

266 Cf. Hoffmann-Riem (n 3) 197; Becker (n 30), 175–176.

267 Florian Schaub, 'Context-Adaptive Privacy Mechanisms' in Claudio B Aris Gkoulalas-Divanis (ed), *Handbook of mobile data privacy* (Springer 2018) 345–362.

levels of privacy protection in point of use situations where they (dis)allow particular processing activities.[268]

Would such point of use privacy regulation be compatible with existing EU data protection law? A closer look at the GDPR reveals the regulation does not explicitly apply the concept of point of use regulation. Mostly, it is ignorant of situations and contexts in which a processing technology is deployed or in which a processing activity occurs.[269] Art. 9 para. 1 GDPR, for example, regulates the processing of special categories of personal data irrespective of the place, time, or audience in which the processing activity takes place, causing *Frenzel* to observe:

> *"One and the same information can have very different, positive, or negative consequences at a different place, at a different time, or facing a different audience. Art. 9 para. 1 in connection with para. 2 is only partially able to capture this problem because it does not distinguish between different contexts, processing situations and audiences."*[270] [translation by the author]

Neither does point of use regulation apply as part of the purpose limitation in Art. 5 para. 1 lit. b GDPR. Purpose limitation protects the consumer in that she is aware of and concedes to her personal data being used for a disclosed purpose; the objective of purpose limitation is to bind the data controller and processor to use the collected personal data solely within the limits of the disclosed purpose.[271] However, purpose limitation in EU data protection law does not factor context and point of use situations into the level of data protection granted to the data subject. In the high-stake processing situation to determine whether somebody is creditworthy, purpose limitation does not require heightened scrutiny or stricter protection, all it does is to limit the use of personal data to the specific purpose.

On the other hand, Art. 35 para. 3 lit. c GDPR may serve as an example that point of use regulation as a general concept already exists in and therefore is compatible with EU data protection law: According to the provision, an impact assessment is required in the case of a systematic monitoring of a *publicly accessible area* which occurs on a large scale.[272] Here, a location where the processing technology is used triggers privacy control, *i.e.* the obligation to run an impact assessment. The reason why the use of processing technology is regulated in this situation lies in its specific point of use, *i.e.* surveillance of a publicly accessible area which, as Reci-

---

268 Ibid 339–340.

269 Arguing that the GDPR does in fact take into account specific point of use situations, albeit without conclusive evidence Albrecht and Jotzo (n 151) 77–82.

270 Frenzel, 'Frenzel, Art. 9' (n 181) para. 6.

271 Philipp Kramer, 'Art. 5' in Martin Eßer, Philipp Kramer and Kai von Lewinski (eds), *DSGVO/BDSG* (Carl Heymanns Verlag 2023) para. 23.

272 Martini, 'Martini, Art. 35' (n 168) para. 30–31.

tal 91 sentence 3 GDPR highlights, is thought to cause the structural privacy risk that individuals feel intimidated by cameras in the public sphere and refrain from exercising their civil rights and freedoms including their participation in a demonstration or free speech.[273]

The above illustrates why the point of use of processing technology or activities should be a building block of modern privacy or data protection regulation when such point of use has been observed to cause a structural privacy risk, *e.g.* because individuals are particularly prone to privacy violations.

5. Security-privacy level of data and systems

The COPRA report describes how insufficient IT- and data security many times lies at the root of privacy violations. For example, data-thieves and cyber-attacks frequently attack poorly secured personal data online which they misappropriate for identity-theft or to levy illegitimate charges on consumers and companies.[274] According a study from 2019, 97 % of all cyber-attacks in this year were aimed at retrieving personal data such as birth dates and social security numbers.[275] In a recent consumer survey, 61 % of U.S. consumers confirmed they had seen their personal data compromised by a data breach or a similar incident, and 74 % declared that they were concerned about the risks and possible ramifications caused by insufficient IT- and data-security.[276]

Numerous large data holders and large data pools have fallen prey to data breaches and cyber-attacks resulting in the disclosure and dissemination of very large quantities of personal data. As a case in point, *Meta* had to report the breach of customer data on multiple occasions, in one incident in 2019 reportedly more than 540 million *Facebook* user records were openly shared on an *Amazon* cloud computing service.[277]

Looking back at how privacy law and data protection has evolved, the risk related to inferior IT- and data-security is no new phenomenon: Already in the

273 Ibid para. 31.

274 Cantwell (n 54) 4, 9; Peppet (n 183), 133–140.

275 ForgeRock, 'U. S. Consumer Data Breach Report' (2019) 3 <https://www.forgerock.com/resources/view/92170441/industry-brief/us-7> accessed 30 September 2020.

276 Lena Kessel, 'Vectors of data disclosure – A comparative study of the use of personal data from a legal, cultural, and information systems perspective: Cultural Influences on Personal Data Disclosure Decisions – US-American Perspectives' (2022) 23–24 <https://www.jura.uni-passau.de/irdg/publikationen/research-paper-series/> accessed 15 February 2023.

277 Jason Silverstein, 'Facebook data breach: Hundreds of millions of records exposed on Amazon server, according to UpGuard cybersecurity research firm' (2019) <https://www.cbsnews.com/news/millions-facebook-user-records-exposed-amazon-cloud-server/> accessed 27 January 2021.

1973 *Fair Information Practices Principles*, one of the five pillars of fair data processing addressed IT- and data-security *"to prevent the misuse of data"*.[278] What is new is that there is more loosely secured personal data online, generated, for instance, by the widespread use of consumer wearables such as watches and phones which remain connected to the internet allowing for a constant flow of (personal) data from and to the devices. These devices regularly lack sufficient computing and battery power to leverage resource-intensive security technology such as encryption and data pseudonymization which makes them particularly vulnerable to security failures.[279] As a general trend we see that the affordability and omnipresence of these devices has lowered the technical entry-barrier for malevolent surveillance and cyber-attacks.[280] This is why modern privacy regulation should stimulate the use of more sophisticated IT- and data-security then what we have seen in the past. Preferably, a modern approach IT- and data-security will identify and effectuate different levels of security protection of personal data and systems depending on the respective privacy risk.[281]

Including as a critique of the GDPR's conceptual approach to mitigate privacy risks by trying to minimize the disclosure and collection of personal data and of processing activities, this study contends that our answer to cloudy skepticism vis-à-vis modern data-focused technology and in cases where the processing of personal data is essential, *e.g.* in the field of medicine and to advance scientific and technological progress, should routinely be better technology and better data security.[282]

To this end, we suggest that a processing activity and its associated IT- and data security risk should be defined in context of any of the technical capacity subcategories listed in this study, *i.e.* data quantity, data quality, processing technology, and point of use situations or spheres. Similar to the above-discussed idea of staggered privacy levels according to the point of use situation, *e.g.* which or how much *personal data* can be processed,[283] we propose the idea of a gradual data security according to a particular privacy risk, *e.g.* which measures or quality of *data security* is required. We term this idea *security-privacy levels of data and systems*.[284] It is

278 Cate (n 30) 344.

279 Peppet (n 183), 133–140; cf. Cantwell (n 54) 4.

280 Cantwell (n 54) 9.

281 Similarly, German Data Ethics Commission (n 6) 8 (5th bullet point).

282 Determann, 'Healthy Data Protection' (n 16) 270–271, 273; Floridi (n 143) 235–236, 243; Maisch (n 238) 107–118, 340; Hacker (n 143) 559–561.

283 See supra Chapter 2 A. I. 4. Point of use of the processing activity.

284 Similar to the established term of security safeguards in OECD (n 97), Part Two: Basic Principles Of National Application, para. 11, Detailed Comments, para. 56.

worth noting that already today security technology can be technically organized in staggered security-privacy levels so that technology automatically adapts to context, for instance, by linking security features to point of use situations: So-called *privacy-smart* devices increasingly understand the proximity of and interactions between users and processing technology and can precisely leverage security technology such as encryption to adjust the level of protection to the point of use situation.[285]

Given the scale, integration, and complexity of personal data processing today as illustrated in the chapters about the COPRA report and technical capacities above, adequate security-privacy levels of data and systems today are of supra-individual and societal concern.[286] Consequently, new standards and improvements require more than company-driven corrections. Privacy law and policy should set incentives and obligations to drive structural security-privacy reinforcement. First and foremost, we should develop technical solutions which are effective, scalable, and accountable and which address privacy problems such as data storage, access control, analysis, and release as well as trustworthy data sharing.[287] Technical solutions can be advanced data encryption, the idea of personal data stores by which the individual can determine via access rights when and how personal data can be processed, and secure multiparty computation which allows parties to work without the disclosure of data sets by way of a coordinated computing effort.[288]

When developing software and solution, security-privacy levels of data and systems should be strengthened as a decision-making category in organizations.[289] Organizations should dedicate sufficient staff and resources to data security; conversely, privacy regulation should set incentives or obligations for companies to designate a data security officer akin to the function and authority of the GDPR data protection officer as set out in Art. 37–39 GDPR.

On a policy level, discussions about security-privacy in the EU have rightfully focused on necessary investment, research and development, and a more important role for public actors: For instance, in 2021 the German government announced plans to rival *Amazon* and *Microsoft* with a European cloud service

285 Cf. Schaub (n 265) 358–359.

286 Cf. Solove, 'Privacy Self-Management and the Consent Dilemma' (n 78) 1881, 1886–1888; cf. Hoffmann-Riem (n 3) 73–74.

287 Gasser (n 11) 207–208.

288 Gasser (n 11) 207–208; Hoffmann-Riem (n 3) 196.

289 Cf. Hoffmann-Riem (n 3) 62–63; Maisch (n 238) 107–118, 340; the idea of privacy on the ground and the importance of elevating topics of importance to the decision-making bodies within organizations is explained at Kenneth A Bamberger and Deirdre K Mulligan, *Privacy on the Ground: Driving Corporate Behavior in the United States and Europe* (MIT Press 2015) 242–243.

provider by the name of *GAIA-X*; the idea is to set up data storage on servers located in the European Union and according to new EU security-privacy standards built on European values.[290] Today, technical standards including in IT- and data security are mostly prepared and rolled out by important industry players with other companies adapting and arguably sometimes bowing to the market power of the norm-creator.[291] Here, public review, certification of the data- and IT-standards, or other forms of stronger public engagement to foster security-privacy is advisable to ensure the adequate balancing of interests.[292]

An intellectual cousin of security-privacy levels of data and systems as suggested in this chapter – albeit less nuanced – can already be found in the GDPR where it is frequently referred to as a manifestation of the regulation's risk-based approach.[293] Art. 5 para. 1 lit. f and Art. 32 para. 1 and 2 GDPR require the implementation of *appropriate* security-privacy and depending on the respective privacy risk at stake. According to Art. 24 para. 1, Art. 28 para. 1 GDPR and Recitals 75 to 77 and Recital 83 GDPR, it is both the data controller's and the processor's responsibility to establish technical and organizational measures to this regard.[294] Importantly, the GDPR, does not provide any explicit reference to and guidance on which specific security technology or security measure to implement because such restricted selection would risk being outdated by the rapid evolution of data- and IT-security.[295] It follows that, instead, technical experts and case law should spell out the details of which security standards and measures are appropriate in a given processing situation.

To conclude, the recommendation for a modern privacy law on how to address security-privacy levels of data and systems is to generally follow a technology-agnostic security-privacy approach akin to the GDPR with additional guidance on how to structure and stagger security-privacy levels and more incentives for organizations to adequately staff and allocate resources.[296]

290 Deutsche Bundesregierung (n 24) 25, 26.

291 Cf. ETSI (n 187).

292 Cf. Hoffmann-Riem (n 3) 198–199; Ulrich Alt, 'Datensicherheit, Datenschutz und Technik – ein risikoorientierter Ansatz' 2020 Der Sachverständige 169, 171–172.

293 Mario Martini, 'Art. 32' in Boris Paal and Daniel Pauly (eds), *DSGVO, BDSG* (C.H. Beck 2021) para. 46; cf. w.

294 Mario Martini, 'Art. 24' in Boris Paal and Daniel Pauly (eds), *DSGVO, BDSG* (C.H. Beck 2021) para. 21–23.

295 Philipp Kramer and Martin Meints, 'Art. 32' in Martin Eßer, Philipp Kramer and Kai von Lewinski (eds), *DSGVO/BDSG* (Carl Heymanns Verlag 2023) para. 18.

296 Without an obligation to use a specific security technology also OECD (n 97), Part Two: Basic Principles Of National Application, para. 11, Detailed Comments, para. 56.

II. Human (in)capacities

The second category of modern privacy risks summarizes privacy challenges which are – rather than by modern data-focused technology itself – predominantly caused by a human decision or behavior of the owner of technical capacities, of the technology user, or of the person affected by the technology.[297] By owner of technical capacities, we mean the human actors who have developed or who are responsible for a particular data-processing technology, a data processing entity, or a point of use situation in which a processing activity occurs. The category of technology users comprises persons of all age including children and young people who actively use data processing technology. Finally, the third category describes persons who are affected by modern data-focused technology without their decision to actively engage with the technology but rather as a reflex of a technology owner's or user's usage of data-focused technology. In other words, the technology owner's or technology user's decision or behavior has the consequence that the affected person's personal data or other information is being processed by the technology in a way that identifies the affected person.[298]

Overall, this chapter deals with *human (in)capacities* when humans interact with and are exposed to the technical capacities of modern data-focused technology. The category of human (in)capacities opens the door to a wide range of questions about human decision-making and behavior some of which can only be briefly touched upon in this study, *inter alia* how individuals operate technology, to what extent they understand how modern data-focused technology works, whether they read and understand privacy policies, and how they value privacy and the processing of their personal data, how personal data processing and the usage of data-focused technology affects the collective beyond the individual? To aggregate and conceptualize these questions, this study suggests that privacy risks caused by human (in)capacities can be further organized into the three subcategories set out in figure 2. Each of the subcategories will be examined in more detail in the below.

297 Cf. Hoffmann-Riem (n 3) 61–63.
298 Ibid 73–74; Kai von Lewinski, *Die Matrix des Datenschutzes* (Mohr Siebeck 2014) 55–56.

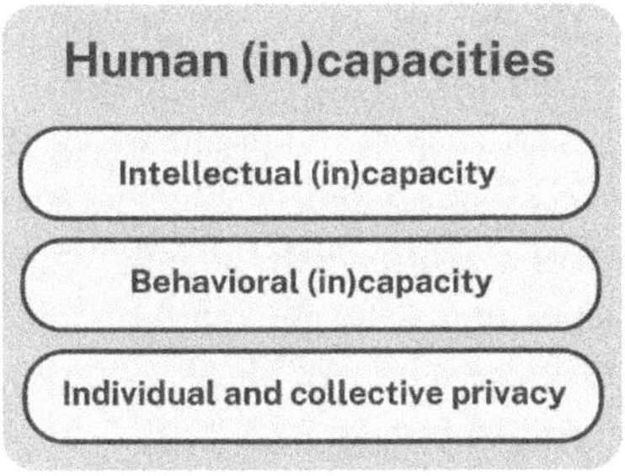

Figure 2: Human (in)capacities

1. Intellectual (in)capacity

At the heart of German and EU data protection law and of U.S. consumer privacy law lies the belief that the individual is intellectually capable of mastering the technological challenges she routinely faces. Despite systemic differences in their regulatory approach to privacy, the axiom of their bedrock concepts is the individual's ability to take control and to make rational decisions about privacy, *i.e.* the German right to decide about one's own affairs and information in the digital realm (*informationelle Selbstbestimmung*), the EU right to privacy, and the U.S. concept of notice-and-consent.[299]

Building on the research of *Acquisti*, *Grossklags* and many others, this study argues that the assumption of human intellectual capacity vis-à-vis personal data processing and technology is increasingly called into question by the ubiquity and mounting complexity of modern data-focused technology, and by recent scientific findings about human decision-making generally.[300] As research has shown, human intellectual capacity regarding personal data disclosure and privacy is substantially influenced by innate human cognitive limitations: We tend to oversimplify technical complexity, we tend to overrate the short-term gain of access to a par-

299 Johanna Heberlein, *Datenschutz im Social Web* (Nomos 2017) 297–298; Jan H Klement, 'Art. 7' in Spiros Simitis, Gerrit Hornung and Indra Spiecker Döhmann (eds), *Datenschutzrecht* (Nomos 2019) para. 19; Solove, 'Privacy Self-Management and the Consent Dilemma' (n 78) 1881; Paal and Hennemann, 'Art. 13' (n 219); Cate (n 30) 358; Hermstrüwer (n 13) 71; supra Chapter 1 A. Concept and status of U.S. privacy law and Chapter 1 B. Concept and status of EU data protection law.

300 Cf. Acquisti and Grossklags (n 226) 364, 371, 374; Ebner, *Weniger ist Mehr?* (n 29) 45–48; Louisa Specht, *Diktat der Technik* (Nomos 2019) 167–168; Barbara Sandfuchs, *Privatheit wider Willen* (Mohr Siebeck 2015) pp. 218–221; Cate (n 30) 360–361; Solove, 'Privacy Self-Management and the Consent Dilemma' (n 78) 1880, 1881–1882, 1886; Solove, 'The Myth of the Privacy Paradox' (n 155) 43–44; Voigt (n 28) 90–91; Veil (n 15), 687–689; Thaler and Sunstein (n 188) 31–60; Lev-Aretz and Strandburg (n 16), 287.

ticular good or service over the aggregated and sometimes long-term risk of repeatedly disclosing bits and pieces of personal data, and we tend to disregard more abstract external effects of privacy decisions and behavior such as the implications of aggregated privacy behavior by individuals for society as a whole.[301] Given these limitations, we must wonder whether, in the moment of truth when the individual is asked to decide about whether or not to disclose personal data, she is able to adequately assess the effect and risk associated with the aggregation of pieces of personal data over time and from different sources?[302] Limited human intellectual capacity may be even more pronounced in certain groups of individuals who thus appear particularly vulnerable when they use or are exposed to modern data-focused technology, *e.g.* children and depending on their age and state of personal development.[303]

How can we address this challenge of intellectual (in)capacity? Many individuals seem unaware of how data-focused technology works and how their personal data is being processed. According to a recent survey by the European Commission *"only one in five participants said they are always informed about the conditions attached to the collection and use of their personal data online"*.[304] Yet more information hardly is the solution. As the COPRA report correctly highlights, privacy policies are, on average, already too long to read and difficult to understand.[305] On the internet and on internet-connected devices, a flood of *"do you consent?"* pop-ups and privacy notices today many times causes an *"information overload"* to individuals, *i.e.* the recipient receives more information than she can intellectually process or is asked to take an action so frequently that it becomes a nuisance.[306] According to research, such information overload likely triggers some of the above-mentioned human intellectual biases and heuristics and may thus even lead to adverse effects on privacy by clouding transparency efforts and by

301 Cf. Solove, 'Privacy Self-Management and the Consent Dilemma' (n 78) 1881–1882, 1886; Acquisti and Grossklags (n 231) 368; Solove, 'Privacy Self-Management and the Consent Dilemma' (n 78) 1881, 1886–1888; Solove, 'The Myth of the Privacy Paradox' (n 155) 43–44; see generally on cognitive limitations in human decision-making Kahneman (n 49).

302 Solove, 'Privacy Self-Management and the Consent Dilemma' (n 78) 1888–1891; Voigt (n 28) 88–89.

303 Art. 29 Data Protection Working Party, 'Stellungnahme zum Schutz der personenbezogenen Daten von Kindern' (2009) Working Paper 160, 3; Albrecht and Jotzo (n 151) 80; German Data Ethics Commission (n 6) 12; Maisch (n 238) 296–298; Sandfuchs (n 298) pp. 135–138.

304 European Commission (n 29) 2.

305 Cantwell (n 54) 5; affirming Solove, 'Privacy Self-Management and the Consent Dilemma' (n 78) 1885; Hermstrüwer (n 13) 86.

306 Ebner, *Weniger ist Mehr?* (n 29) 103–107; Ebner, 'Information Overload 2.0?' (n 28) 365.

causing individuals to make inferior decisions.[307] A common phenomenon is that people do not fully read or altogether ignore privacy notices, according to a survey by the European Commission *"only a minority (13 %)* [of the survey participants] *fully read privacy statements online"*.[308]

Likely, the response how to best address intellectual (in)capacity is a balancing exercise between fostering individual autonomy and sound decision-making, and strengthening privacy-friendly personal data processing as such and so that it does not depend on the individual's decision and active participation.[309] Given the limitations of human intellectual incapacity and the trends of modern data-focused technology illustrated above in the chapter on technical capacities, the focus of a modern privacy law should be less on individual decision-making as a privacy control mechanism and more on the improvement of personal data processing systems and technology and privacy compliance as such.[310]

If, in the short run, we continue entertaining the idea of information rights and obligations as a cornerstone of privacy control, we should replace long privacy policies with more digestible notices which are less strenuous and time-consuming to read.[311] For instance, privacy notices which are predominantly visual such as privacy labels or pictograms are quicker to absorb and may be able to offer, if not the same, a reasonable amount of information to technology users but without less pitfalls of common human heuristics.[312] Ideally, privacy notices should offer true choice for individuals how their personal data is processed, otherwise it makes little sense for individuals to give much attention to privacy notices in the first place.[313] We should furthermore strengthen intellectual capacity by better educating individuals – in particular children and young people – about how to make privacy-friendly decisions; an important aspect is to teach how data-focused technology and associated business models work and how tech-

307 Acquisti and Grossklags (n 231) 364, 374; Sandfuchs (n 298) pp. 218–221; Voigt (n 28) 87–89; Ebner, 'Information Overload 2.0?' (n 28) 365–366; Boris Paal and Moritz Hennemann, 'Art. 12' in Boris Paal and Daniel Pauly (eds), *DSGVO, BDSG* (C.H. Beck 2021) para. 4 and 5; Specht (n 298) 167–168; Ebner, 'Information Overload 2.0?' (n 28) 365.

308 European Commission (n 29) 2.

309 Cf. Max Schrems, *Kämpf um deine Daten* (Edition a 2014) 204–206; Solove, 'The Limitations of Privacy Rights' (n 226) 10–17.

310 Similarly Solove, 'The Limitations of Privacy Rights' (n 226) 10–17.

311 Supportive also Hermstrüwer (n 13) 86.

312 Ebner, *Weniger ist Mehr?* (n 29) 116–120; Paal and Hennemann, 'Art. 12' (n 295) para. 75–76.

313 Cf. Christina Kühnl, *Persönlichkeitsschutz 2.0* (De Gruyter 2016) 342–348; Paal and Hennemann, 'Art. 12' (n 305) para. 75–76.

nology users should use and live with the technology.[314] Also, we should nudge technology users into making more privacy-friendly decisions by exploring more than we have the concepts and ideas of privacy-by-design and privacy-by-default and as already suggested by the GDPR in Art. 25 para. 1 and 2 and Recital 78 sentences 2–5 GDPR.[315] Additionally, we should strengthen data processing entities' internal compliance system. As *Bamberger/Mulligan* have impressively demonstrated, such privacy on the ground in the form of privacy compliance within organizations often is the best catalyst for better privacy protection.[316] They argue in favor of a strong network and collaboration between privacy stakeholders in- and outside of organizations. We can strengthen such alliance *inter alia* by allocating more money to (technical) privacy research and development.[317]

In the medium- to long-term, we should consider more radical changes to how we regulate personal data processing: Less weight should be given to individual consent and whether individuals leverage their privacy rights, instead, the focus should be on strengthening the protective effect of privacy regulation without individual's taking action.[318] This could be achieved by moving from input-based privacy regulation alike in Art. 6 para. 1 lit. a, Art. 9 para. 2 lit. a GDPR and the U.S. notice-and-consent approach with the individual's consent that justifies a processing activity to a more output-oriented privacy control whereby processing results which are actually harmful are regulated and sanctioned.[319] The concept of input- and output regulation will be discussed in more detail below.[320]

Given our innate human intellectual incapacity to factor into our privacy decisions long-term and external effects, we should furthermore consider shifting from an upstream-based privacy regulation which is primarily concerned with the initial data disclosure and to a lesser degree with processing activities down the value chain to a more downstream-based regulation which hones in on the above-listed technical capacities which are commonly associated with privacy risks such as ris-

---

314 Sandfuchs (n 298) 108; German Data Ethics Commission (n 6) 5; Schrems (n 307) pp. 204–206; Hoffmann-Riem (n 3) 292–293.

315 Sandfuchs (n 298) 109–115; Barbara Sandfuchs and Andreas Kapsner, 'Coercing Online Privacy' 2016(12) ISJLP 185, 222–230; cf. Albrecht and Jotzo (n 151) 92; Thaler and Sunstein (n 188); Kloza (n 210) 466–467; Maisch (n 238) 296–298.

316 Bamberger and Mulligan (n 287) 241–242.

317 Cf. Hoffmann-Riem (n 3) 207–208; Gasser (n 11) 206.

318 Cf. Solove, 'The Limitations of Privacy Rights' (n 226) 10–17; cf. Determann, 'Healthy Data Protection' (n 16) 270–271, 273; Hacker (n 143) 559–561.

319 Cf. Hoffmann-Riem (n 3) 73–75; Hoeren (n 172), 11; Determann, 'Healthy Data Protection' (n 16) 252–255; Boris Paal and Daniel Pauly, 'Introduction' in Boris Paal and Daniel Pauly (eds), *DSGVO, BDSG* (C.H. Beck 2021) para. 16.

320 Sub Chapter 2 B. Output and downstream regulation.

ky processing situations or processing technology.[321] The concept of upstream- and downstream-regulation will be discussed in more detail below.[322]

Finally, we can derive from the above that, in light of our intellectual (in)capacity to appropriately deal with modern data-focused technology, privacy and data protection law should focus more on strengthening the protective effect of regulation, *e.g.* by implementing measures in line with the examples above, and less on privacy and data protection concepts and means which are dependent on the individual's taking action.[323]

2. Behavioral (in)capacity

Human behavior is adapting to modern data-focused technology and privacy regulation must keep up. This category describes both behavioral adaptation to technology because of our conscious decision to engage with it (here, the category is heavily interdependent with the category of intellectual (in)capacity), and behavioral adaptation because technology *"happens"* to us, *i.e.* because we are affected by existing technology without an active decision to engage with it, and often as a reflex of other people using the technology.[324] For instance, the uploading of a group picture on social media without the consent of every single person depicted on the photo affects the persons who have not consented, often they do not even know about the upload of the photo. The challenge with existing data protection and data privacy regulation is that protection against unwanted personal data use today gravitates around and mostly depends on the action of the individual, it only insufficiently protects against the reflex and effect of technology use by other technology users.[325]

How human interaction with and reaction to modern data-focused technology is evolving is repeatedly illustrated also by the COPRA report: Online-shopping surpasses offline-shopping, internet-connected devices have become omnipresent, people commonly and often unknowingly share personal and sensitive personal information with third parties, and vulnerable individuals such as children increasingly use or are exposed to modern data-focused technology. We are facing a new scale and degree of integration of modern data-focused technology into our

---

321 Solove, 'Privacy Self-Management and the Consent Dilemma' (n 78) 1902–1903.

322 Sub Chapter 2 B. Output and downstream regulation.

323 Leading to the idea of more collective privacy as examined sub Chapter 2 A. II. 3. Individual and collective privacy.

324 Cf. Veil (n 15), 687; Hoffmann-Riem (n 3) 73–74; Lev-Aretz and Strandburg (n 16), 280–281.

325 Von Lewinski, *Die Matrix des Datenschutzes* (n 296) 55–56; Hoffmann-Riem (n 3) 73–74; cf. Ohm (n 182) 105.

lives, and, as a consequence, human interactions with and reactions to data-focused technology changes as well.[326]

In an effort to protect their privacy, some consumers may decide to renounce modern data-focused technology, for instance by turning off location-tracking on their mobile phones or sticking a physical cover on their laptop cameras. Yet given the ubiquity of modern data-focused technology, even increased efforts to attempt a life of former times without technology and to shield one's personal life from personal data use will likely be in vain.[327] Or, as *Solove* has pointedly put it: *"If people really wanted to keep all their information concealed, they would have to live in a shack in the woods".*[328] Similarly, we have to acknowledge that calls to legally require owners of technical capacities to offer consumer products or solutions which do not process personal data beyond what is technically necessary for their functionality are neither today's reality nor, perceivably, a realistic scenario in the near future.[329] More importantly, evidence shows that the majority of consumers happily embrace new technology and that the growth-trend to integrate modern-data technology into our lives continues.[330]

How consumers interact with and react to data-focused technology shapes privacy both on an individual and on a societal level. As a common behavior, *Specht-Riemenschneider* and others have observed that consumers often show passivity and inaction towards personal data processing by modern data-focused technology, for instance people frequently do not read privacy notices.[331] And passivity arguably seems to be an accurate description at large for human behavior regarding privacy and modern data-focused technology.[332] Partially, the reason for such behavioral (in)capacity has been explained above – but there is more to it than intellectual incapacity.[333] First and foremost, privacy-mindful behavior in today's data reality, vis-à-vis modern data-focused technology, and within the cur-

326 Cantwell (n 54) 9; *Solove*, The George Washington Law Review 2021, 1, 37; Hoffmann-Riem (n 3) 68–70, 276–277.

327 Cf. Kloza (n 210) 491–504; Veil (n 15), 687.

328 Solove, 'The Myth of the Privacy Paradox' (n 155) 30.

329 Becker (n 30), 175–176.

330 The overall market size for internet connected devices including consumer devices has doubled between 2017 and 2021 according to Ann Bosche and others, 'Unlocking Opportunities in the Internet of Things' (2018) 1–2 <https://www.bain.com/contentassets/5aa3a678438846289af59f62e62a3456/bain_brief_unlocking_opportunities_in_the_internet_of_things.pdf> accessed 20 December 2020.

331 Specht (n 298) 422; European Commission (n 29) 2; Voigt (n 28) 93; Ebner, 'Information Overload 2.0?' (n 28) 365–366.

332 Cf. Hermstrüwer (n 13) 340–341; Solove and Schwartz (n 60) 1113.

333 Supra Chapter 2 A. II. 1. Intellectual (in)capacity.

rent regulatory framework is difficult and strenuous.[334] *Solove* is correct when he points to the structural challenges consumers routinely face and which regularly impede the effectiveness of any privacy-mindful behavior, consider, for example, the myriad of data collecting and processing entities the individual must engage with to control her privacy, and the privacy-averse effect of data aggregation across platforms and entities.[335] To always consider privacy notifications, to continuously assess the privacy risk of modern data-focused technology which surrounds us, and to adapt one's individual behavior accordingly requires an elevated level of technical, legal, and social knowledge and a lot of perseverance, concentration, and continuous diligent work. Likely, many people today would say it is an impossible task to do.[336]

Moreover, technical privacy protection to control and minimize personal data processing largely remains a privilege of the tech-savvy and experienced consumer and has only insufficiently been used by the general public.[337] This is because technical privacy protection, on average, requires technical interest, knowledge, and effort. To give an example, about two thirds of all smartphone applications leave proprietary and irreversible *unique strings* as personal identifiers on phones which allow profiling and tracking even if and when technology users manage to manually configure the default *Android advertisement-ID* or the *iOS Ad-ID*. Also, do-not-track add-ons come pre-installed only on a handful of internet browsers such as *Firefox*, *Tor*, or *Brave* which are used but by a minority of consumers who browse the internet.[338]

Against this background, modern data privacy regulation should acknowledge human behavioral (in)capacity in adapting to modern data-focused technology and strive for effective privacy protection nevertheless.[339] Privacy regulation should, first, facilitate privacy-mindful behavior and, secondly, more effectively shield people from harm caused by their behavioral (in)capacity including as a reflex of data-focused technology and personal data processing "*happening*" to them. To the first point, we argue that privacy regulation should broadly foster a privacy-friendly industrial and societal environment. Risking some overlap with the examples listed

334 Solove, 'Privacy Self-Management and the Consent Dilemma' (n 78) 1881, 1886–1888; Solove, 'The Myth of the Privacy Paradox' (n 155) 5; Lev-Aretz and Strandburg (n 16), 295.

335 Solove, 'Privacy Self-Management and the Consent Dilemma' (n 78) 1881, 1886–1888; Solove, 'The Myth of the Privacy Paradox' (n 155) 5; Lev-Aretz and Strandburg (n 16), 295.

336 Solove, 'The Myth of the Privacy Paradox' (n 155) 5.

337 Kloza (n 210) 489–491.

338 Hacker (n 143) 559–561; Kloza (n 210) 489–491.

339 Cf. Sandfuchs (n 298) 135–138; pointing out the recent evolution in human-technological interaction also Hoffmann-Riem (n 3) 276–277.

above in the category of intellectual (in)capacity, we believe a sound privacy culture in schools, companies, business relationships, and society will favor the design, development, and consumption of privacy-friendly technology;[340] as a knock-on effect, the privacy-friendly culture and technology will empower and protect the individual, groups of individuals, and society to both intellectually[341] and factually engage in better privacy behavior.

To the second point of providing better privacy protection in the face of human behavioral (in)capacity, we contend that technology can frequently be used to mitigate some of the negative consequences. This is true also with regard to technology-use and personal data processing *"happening"* to consumers. For instance, the above-described categories of processing technology and point of use of a processing activity could be leveraged to create surveillance-free spaces or privacy-spheres of different degrees that allow the individual to retreat to a low- or a no-processing zone whenever she wishes to do so.[342] To this end, context-intelligent technology could be programed to prevent the involuntary disclosure of personal data, to disallow certain processing activities whenever others are affected, and to make privacy self-management more user friendly and effective.[343]

Finally, context-intelligent technology could further be used to adjust the respective privacy protection level to the needs of consumer groups whose interaction with or reaction to technology and personal data processing is particularly prone to privacy infringements or digital discrimination.[344] The group of individuals with such behavioral (in)capacity should generally be interpreted broadly to include children, elderly people, persons with disabilities, and ethnic or other minorities.[345] While conceptually ready today, the solution of context-intelligent technology will likely be market-standard only in the medium- to long-term.

In the short term, the most promising technical solution how technology can be configured to respect the technology user's and third party's personal privacy preferences seems to be so-called *personal information management systems*.[346] Their purpose is to facilitate the management of online-identities and how perso-

---

340 Cf. Sandfuchs (n 298) 108; *Solove*, The Myth of the Privacy Paradox, The George Washington Law Review 2021, 1, 49–50.

341 Cf. Sandfuchs (n 298) 108; see also generally on better education to hedge against limited human rationality supra Chapter 2 A. II. 1. Intellectual (in)capacity.

342 Cohen (n 261) 143; Veil (n 15), 695; Ohm (n 182) 105.

343 Cf. Sandfuchs (n 298) 227–228, 260; Schaub (n 265) 345–362.

344 Specifically on the privacy risk caused by artificial intelligence technology, cf. European Data Protection Supervisor (n 21) 21; the also supra Chapter 2 A. I. 2. Data quality.

345 Cf. German Data Ethics Commission (n 6) 12; on artificial technology specifically European Data Protection Supervisor (n 21) 21; Sandfuchs (n 298) 135–138.

346 Cf. Hoffmann-Riem (n 3) 196–198; cf. Gasser (n 11) 207–208.

nal data can be processed and shared across products and services by offering a one-stop-solution to centrally register individual privacy preferences.[347] Instead of interacting which each data processing entity individually, the consumer can record her privacy preferences in a central register which data processing entities are required to consult prior to engaging in any processing activity of the consumer's personal data. Accordingly, modern data-focused technology could be configured to verify with the privacy information management system whether and to which extent the consumer has agreed to the processing of her personal data.[348] Theoretically, privacy preferences can be registered in privacy information management systems with as much detail as useful and necessary, *e.g.* whether the consumer has consented to the processing of a particular data quality, by a particular processing entity or technology and for particular point of use situations.[349]

An early example of a privacy information management system can be found in the German *Telecommunication and Telemedia Data Privacy Act* (*Telekommunikation-Telemedien-Datenschutz-Gesetz*), replaced in 2024 by the *Telecommunication and Digital Services Data Privacy Act* (*Telekommunikation-Digitale-Dienste-Datenschutz-Gesetz*). Art. 26 para. 1 of the Act defines privacy information management systems as "*user-friendly and competition-compliant*" technology whereby data subject can manage their consent.[350] The provision stipulates for privacy information management systems to be independent and without a proprietary economic interest in the data subject's consent or her personal data, the data subject's consent must be registered only for the purpose of managing her consent. Additionally, the system must be able to demonstrate an appropriate IT-security program.[351] Considering how the privacy information management systems pool highly valuable personal data which could make them sought targets for hackers, the heightened scrutiny required by the German *Telecommunication and Telemedia Data Privacy Act* is convincing.[352] Until privacy information management systems become part of privacy regulation, we will likely first see vendor-driven privacy control tools. They may come with similar functionality, however, they will not be true one-stop-solutions

347 Cf. with a particular emphasis on identity- and data-management for children German Data Ethics Commission (n 6) 12; Maisch (n 238) 296–298; Hoffmann-Riem (n 3) 143–144.

348 A similar idea for a opt-in personal data management regime also in Hermstrüwer (n 13) 340–341.

349 Supra Chapter 2 A. I. Technical capacities.

350 Cf. Glocker (n 91) 97–98.

351 Cf. Diana Ettig, 'Art. 26' in Jürgen Taeger and Detlev Gabel (eds), *DSGVO – BDSG – TTDSG: Kommentar* (Deutscher Fachverlag GmbH 2022) para. 6.

352 Ibid; cf. Cantwell (n 54) 4.

but rather vendor-specific or platform-limited technical solutions.[353] A case in point is the existing feature of *Family Privacy Disclosure for Children* on *Apple* devices which allows parents to control how their children can use the technology and to which extent personal data can be shared across *Apple* devices.[354]

Beyond privacy, a broad implementation of privacy information management systems for handling personal data would be a highly impactful building block also within the wider EU data strategy and new European data regulation. For instance, data intermediaries that are bound according to Art. 1 para. 3 and 4 together with Recitals 35, 37, 60 Data Governance Act to fully comply with EU data privacy regulation could leverage privacy information management system technology to systemically, efficiently, and cost-effectively identify, monitor, and document data subjects' consent and the limitations of their approved data processing to ensure privacy compliance.[355] Economically speaking, the increase in transparency and efficiency for businesses interested in using shared data via data intermediaries and data sharing platforms and which chose to broadly rely on privacy information management systems would likely lead to a decrease of their transaction cost, in particular because their compliance risk that personal data has been shared within the limits of the GDPR should be significantly lower than without using privacy information management systems.[356]

An important building block of modern privacy and data protection regulation should be concepts and means which embrace behavioral (in)capacity of individuals vis-à-vis data processing. Even when individuals declare that they care about how their personal data is being processed, on average, individuals have been observed to remain passive, and to not act on their privacy rights or leverage the technical solutions which offer better protection.

3. Individual and collective privacy

The above chapters have focused on the capacity of the individual to intellectually and behaviorally comprehend and interact with modern data-focused technology. Similarly, U.S. consumer privacy law and, to a lesser degree but still importantly,

---

353 Cf. Aline Blankertz and Louisa Specht-Riemenschneider, 'What regulation for data trusts should look like' (2021) 29 <https://www.stiftung-nv.de/sites/default/files/regulation_for_data_trusts_0.pdf> accessed 8 September 2023.

354 Apple, 'Family Privacy Disclosure for Children' (2022) <https://www.apple.com/legal/privacy/en-ww/parent-disclosure/> accessed 2 July 2022.

355 Cf. Hennemann and Ditfurth (n 25), 1910; on the conflict between GDPR and DGA cf. Hennemann and Specht-Riemenschneider (n 25) Einleitung 87–92; Gal and Aviv (n 19), 353, 370–373.

356 Cf. Gal and Aviv (n 19), 353–355.

EU data protection law have predominantly gravitated around the individual's privacy expectations and actions; by contrast, they have given less weight to collective aspects of personal data use such as innovation or communication in groups and communities.[357] The examples we discussed above are the German notion of the individual's deciding about her own affairs and information in the digital realm (*informationelle Selbstbestimmung*) which is visible also in EU data protection law, and the concept of notice-and-consent in U.S. privacy self-management, both of which build on the individual's capacity to effectively control personal data and technology use.[358]

While the regulatory focus on the individual can be explained as a relic of data protection and privacy law's origin, it has become clear in the above chapters that the technical reality today has little to do with the time and world when the regulatory focus and concepts were first conceived.[359] As a consequence, the regulatory focus on the individual and the belief, or at least the assertion in law, that the individual is sufficiently capable of broadly addressing privacy challenges by herself has largely become misplaced and illusional.[360] This study has demonstrated how in today's modern data world many of the privacy risks are beyond the individual's control because they are structural and systemic.[361] We discussed how individuals, on average, lack the experience, knowledge, and resources to meaningfully address privacy challenges and infringements, how individual action cannot amount to the scale of corrective action needed to address systemic privacy shortcomings *inter alia* in data quality or processing technology, and how individual control frequently fails when owners of technical capacities or other technology-users decide to process another individual's personal data (processing "*happening*" to the individual).[362]

To state it bluntly, the restraint focus of current U.S. privacy and EU data protection regulation on individual privacy actions and expectations puts an unproportionate burden on the individual and effectively means holding on to a regula-

357 Schwartz and Pfeifer (n 19), 132, 155–156; cf. Hennemann, 'Wettbewerb der Datenschutzrechtsordnungen' (n 19) 893.

358 Jan H Klement, 'Art. 7' in Spiros Simitis, Gerrit Hornung and Indra Spiecker Döhmann (eds), *Datenschutzrecht* (Nomos 2019) para. 19; Hoffmann-Riem (n 3) 166; Solove and Schwartz (n 60) 1436; Solove, 'Privacy Self-Management and the Consent Dilemma' (n 78) 1881; supra Chapter 2 A. II. 1. Intellectual (in)capacity and supra Chapter 1 A. Concept and status of U.S. privacy law.

359 Supra Chapter 1 The privacy landscape in the U.S. and in the EU.

360 Cf. Veil (n 15), 686, 687–689; Hoffmann-Riem (n 3) 167; Solove, 'The Limitations of Privacy Rights' (n 226) 10–17.

361 Supra Chapter 2 A. I. Technical capacities.

362 Cf. Acquisti and Grossklags (n 226) 368, 371; Solove, 'The Limitations of Privacy Rights' (n 226) 17.

tory approach which has largely become ineffective.[363] Meanwhile, the new technical capacities, in particular the scale, sophistication, and impact of modern data-focused technology and personal data use, have transformed privacy from an originally predominantly individual concern, *i.e.* preventing government authorities from processing one's personal data, to a collective concern where personal data use and privacy shape all of society.[364]

This dimension of privacy as a value beyond the individual and for democracy and society as a whole has since been discussed in great depth. For example, *Cohen* and others have stressed the importance of privacy as a necessary precondition for the functioning of any modern democratic society in which privacy works as a boundary management tool against increasing data collection and surveillance.[365] Another strand of research has focused on the operability of privacy within groups and communities (*Gruppen- /Kollektivdatenschutz*).[366] In a community, the use of personal data and the delineation of privacy structure and form intra-group communication and organization. Frequently, the common denominator for privacy boundaries in a group and community is not determined by the person who has the strictest privacy expectations, instead members of the community may find their individual privacy expectations and actions interlinked with or predetermined by the privacy expectations and actions of the community.[367] In particular in cultural settings of strong community membership, privacy regulation without meaningful integration of group-privacy elements risks abridging the interdependencies between community members and their community, thereby largely ignoring the importance communities play in these settings.[368] Current EU data protection regulation does not recognize a privacy right of the collective as such (*Gruppen-/Kollektivdatenschutz*), for instance the GDPR does not provide for a delegation of privacy rights to a community representative or for community-based enforcement rights.[369]

---

363 Cf. Solove, 'The Limitations of Privacy Rights' (n 226) 10–17; Solove, 'Privacy Self-Management and the Consent Dilemma' (n 78) 1881.

364 Supra Chapter 1 The privacy landscape in the U.S. and in the EU.

365 Cohen (n 261) 148f.; Gasser (n 11) 198; Solove, 'The Myth of the Privacy Paradox' (n 155) 34; supra Chapter 2 A. I. 4. Point of use of the processing activity.

366 Gasser (n 11) 198; Hennemann, Boshe and Meding (n 35), 225–226; cf. Hoffmann-Riem (n 3) 73–74.

367 With a focus on group-privacy in African communities Hennemann, Boshe and Meding (n 35), 225–226; similarly, Gasser (n 11) 198.

368 Cf. Hennemann, Boshe and Meding (n 35), 227–228; Mannion (n 35), 702–704; the EU's endeavor to export EU data protection values and law has been discussed supra Introduction.

369 Von Lewinski, 'Art. 2' (n 63) para. 12.

With privacy as a super-individual and societal concern, modern privacy regulation must consider more than it has the collective angle of personal data processing and privacy.[370] By collective privacy we mean a regulatory approach which does not depend on individual privacy preferences and on the individual's taking action, but which establishes generally applicable guardrails to personal data processing as a framework for processing entities about what constitutes legitimate processing of personal data.[371] Furthermore, collective privacy in modern privacy law must integrate, at least, two elements: First, the protection of groups of individuals and of society against harmful effects of personal data processing and, secondly, the enablement of personal data processing by modern data-focused technology at large for societal advancement and the common good.[372]

Conceptually speaking, the reinforcement of privacy law with collective guardrails does not have to substitute but can accompany individual privacy. The GDPR may serve as an (imperfect) example of such integration of elements of individual with collective data protection regulation.[373] Whereas Chapter 3 (Art. 12–23) GDPR *Rights of the data subject* centers around the data subject who is entitled to exercise individual data control rights to access her personal data according to Art. 15 para. 1 GDPR, or to demand the deletion of her personal data according to Art. 16 para. 1 GDPR, the EU data protection regulation establishes in Art. 5 GDPR generally applicable *Principles relating to the processing of personal data*, in particular the principle of purpose limitation in Art. 5 para. 1 lit. b GDPR, data minimization in Art. 5 para. 1 lit. c GDPR, and storage limitation in Art. 5 para. 1 lit. e GDPR.[374] As Recital 39 GDPR explains, the EU *Principles relating to the processing of personal data* apply for data processing entities generally and irrespective of the legal processing basis such as the data subject's consent according to Art. 6 para. 1 lit. a GDPR.[375]

However, the GDPR has been criticized for providing insufficient incentives to achieve a better use of personal data at large for societal advancement and the

370 Cf. Determann, 'Healthy Data Protection' (n 16) 262–265, 277; von Lewinski, 'Einführung' (n 17) para. 72–73; Lev-Aretz and Strandburg (n 16), 269–270, 308–309; Streinz (n 12) 46–47; Gasser (n 11) 198.

371 Cf. Cohen (n 261) 148f.; von Lewinski, 'Einführung' (n 17) para. 34–36; Solove, 'Privacy Self-Management and the Consent Dilemma' (n 78) 1902–1903.

372 Cf. Hennemann, 'Wettbewerb der Datenschutzrechtsordnungen' (n 19) 893; von Lewinski, 'Einführung' (n 17) para. 34–36.

373 Schwartz and Pfeifer (n 19), 120; Hoffmann-Riem (n 3) 111–112; supra Chapter 1 B. Concept and status of EU data protection law.

374 Cf. Schwartz and Pfeifer (n 19), 122–127.

375 Cf. Frenzel, 'Art. 5' (n 178) para. 11; Kramer, 'Art. 5' (n 269) para. 23.

common good.[376] Arguably, this has recently been acknowledged even by EU policy- and lawmakers, albeit outside of data protection law: As part of the EU's data initiative, the new EU *Data Act* aims at improving access to and usage of personal and non-personal data generated by the use of products and related services according to Art. 1 para. 1 Data Act, and the *Data Governance Act* encourages broad data exchange via data intermediaries according to Recital 27 and Art. 10 lit. a Data Governance Act.[377] EU data protection law, by contrast, remains largely dominated by German and EU technology-skepticism and arguably misses a strong catalyzer for positive data use; a case in point is the GDPR's approach of addressing abstract privacy risks upstream by limiting data disclosure generally according to Art. 6 para. 1 and Art. 9 para. 1 GDPR, and to subject modern data-focused technology like big data technology to data processing principles, see in particular the principles of purpose limitation in Art. 5 para. 1 lit. b, data minimization in Art. 5 para. 1 lit. c and storage limitation in Art. 5 para. 1 lit. e GDPR.[378]

To better protect groups of individuals and society, this study argues that modern privacy regulation should move away from an upstream and input-based control at the beginning of the processing chain alike in the GDPR and give more weight to the output and actual processing results in the downstream of processing activities.[379] Thereby modern privacy regulation will arguably be in a better position to balance at scale the benefits of processing activities against its risks. Conceivably, such balancing test would broadly capture processing activities, *e.g.* by way of a catch-all provision (*Generalklausel*) which generally demands good data use while sanctioning unfair processing activities.[380] Leaving the technical explanation of output regulation to the following subchapter,[381] the general idea of such an out-

376 Cf. Gal and Aviv (n 19), 353–355; Hennemann, 'Wettbewerb der Datenschutzrechtsordnungen' (n 19) 868; Determann, 'Healthy Data Protection' (n 16) 276–277.

377 European Parliament and Council (n 26); cf. Hennemann and Steinrötter (n 24), 1484; European Parliament and Council 'Regulation (EU) 2022/868 of the European Parliament and the Council of 30 May 2022 on European data governance and amending Regulation (EU) 2018/1724' OJ L152, 1; cf. Hennemann and Ditfurth (n 25), 1907; Hennemann and Specht-Riemenschneider (n 25) Einleitung para. 38–39.

378 Cf. Paal and Hennemann, 'Big Data im Recht' (n 220) 1700; supra Chapter 2 B. I. 3. Processing technology.

379 The concepts of input- and output- and of upstream- and downstream-based regulation will be explained in detail sub Chapter 2 B. Output and downstream regulation; cf. von Lewinski, 'Einführung' (n 17) para. 13, 18–19; Solove, 'Privacy Self-Management and the Consent Dilemma' (n 78) 1902–1903.

380 Cf. von Lewinski, 'Einführung' (n 17) para. 13; seemingly supportive of this idea also Veil (n 15), 695.

381 Sub Chapter 2 B. Output and downstream regulation.

put-based fair processing standard is that it would able to address more effectively than current privacy regulation many if not all of the privacy challenges illustrated in the chapters above: By endorsing fair processing activities and processing results while sanctioning unfair processing practices, we remain focused on the actual output, result, or effect of data processing;[382] in the balancing exercise about what constitutes fair data processing, we can better account for the societal weight of personal data processing and privacy and allow more room for processing which advances the common good;[383] finally, a reasonably open and malleable fair processing standard in the form of a catch-all provision is likely better able to keep up with technological progress.[384] Consider, for instance, how a fair processing standard could open the door for courts and practitioners to privilege personal data processing in the field of medicine where a less restrictive personal data collection and use compared to the GDPR standard would likely advance medication to the benefit of the individual and all of society.[385]

A broader look at U.S. and EU law reveals that the idea of a comprehensive fair practice standard as an output control is not new and has had a track-record of success. In the U.S., the FTC has enforced privacy violations on the basis of its general prohibition of *"unfair or deceptive acts or practices in or affecting commerce"* in § 45(a) FTC Act.[386] Remarkably, the FTC has leveraged this catch-all fair practice standard broadly to enforce not only unfulfilled privacy promises in companies' privacy policies but also insufficient data security programs and concealed practices of personal data collection.[387] A fair processing provision in modern privacy law could further be informed by the fair use standard in U.S. copyright law which has been successfully used in practice to delineate legitimate copyright use from otherwise unauthorized exploitation of a protected work. The standard builds on, first, a non-exhaustive list of examples of permitted use in 17 U.S.C. § 107, *e.g.* the reuse of copyright protected works is allowed for news reporting or teaching, and, secondly, on four criteria to help identify cases of fair use – whether the use is commercially motivated or for non-profit, the nature of the copyrighted work, how

---

382 Cf. Hoffmann-Riem (n 3) 73–75; cf. Solove, 'The Myth of the Privacy Paradox' (n 155) 25, 43; Gasser (n 11) 198.

383 Cf. von Lewinski, 'Einführung' (n 17) para. 13; Hennemann, 'Wettbewerb der Datenschutzrechtsordnungen' (n 19) 893.

384 Cf. Gasser (n 11) 207–208; cf. Ohm (n 182) 105.

385 Cf. Determann, 'Healthy Data Protection' (n 16) 234–236.

386 Solove and Schwartz (n 60) 1105–1107; 1270–1272; see generally supra Chapter 1 A. Concept and status of U.S. privacy law.

387 Hoofnagle (n 80) 163; Daniel Solove and Woodrow Hartzog, 'The FTC and the New Common Law of Privacy' 2014(114) Columbia Law Review 583, 628–638; Solove and Schwartz (n 60) 1270.

much of the copyrighted work was reused, and the effect of the reuse on the market value of the copyrighted work.[388]

In the EU, we find a fair use output-based provision, for instance, in the German *Act against Unfair Competition* (*Gesetz gegen den unlauteren Wettbewerb*). Therein, Art. 3 para. 1 and 2 rules that any *"unfair commercial practices shall be illegal"*, an implementation into national law of the fair practice standard in Art. 5 para. 2 of the EU *Unfair Commercial Practices Directive*.[389] EU data protection law has known a fair processing principle since many years; however, the provisions primarily serve as input- and upstream-control, not as output control. The 1995 *Data Protection Directive* broadly stipulated in Art. 6 para. 1 lit. a that *"personal data must be processed fairly and lawfully"*, Art. 5 para. 1 lit. a GDPR today demands that *"personal data shall be processed lawfully, fair and in a transparent manner in relation to the data subject"*.[390] Similarly, Art. 6 para. 1 lit. f GDPR aims at a fair balancing of the interests of the controller or a third party with the interests of the data subject at the time of the disclosure of personal data and at any processing stage.[391]

In sum, given today's importance of personal data processing beyond the individual and for all of society, a modern data privacy or data protection law should give considerable weight to the actual processing outputs and effects of processing activities on the collective, *e.g.* how the processing fosters innovation or whether the processing has negative effects on the community or society. Privacy regulation should shift to a more output- and downstream-based approach, arguably a comprehensive fair processing standard in the form of a catch-all provision can be an effective tool to balance risks and opportunities of personal data processing vis-à-vis individual and collective privacy.

---

388 Achim Förster, *Fair Use: Ein Systemvergleich der Schrankengeneralklausel des US-amerikanischen Copyright Act mit dem Schrankenkatalog des deutschen Urheberrechtsgesetzes* (Mohr Siebeck 2008) 18–20.

389 Helmut Köhler, '§ 3' in Helmut Köhler, Joachim Bornkamm and Jörn Feddersen (eds), *Gesetz gegen den unlauteren Wettbewerb* (C.H. Beck 2020) para. 3.1; European Parliament and Council 'Directive 2005/29/EC concerning unfair business-to-consumer commercial practices in the internal market' OJ L 149/22.

390 Cf. Frenzel, 'Art. 5' (n 178) para. 14–18.

391 Cf. Kramer, 'Art. 6' (n 104) para. 64–89.

B. Output and downstream regulation

In the following, we examine the concepts of input, output, upstream, and downstream control in privacy and data protection regulation and discuss how a modern privacy law should leverage them effectively.

Analogous to the functionality of a computer where information as the raw material goes *into* the machine and in order to produce an *output*, input and output regulation describes a single moment in time when privacy control is applied or, in the case of output-based control, privacy regulation which acknowledges the effect or result of a processing activity.[392] Upstream and downstream regulation, by contrast, focuses on the continuum *when* processing rules shall take effect (*at the beginning of or later on in the processing chain*?).[393] Although the elements in each pair of input and output and of upstream and downstream regulation may at first appear as alternatives, the approaches often work cumulatively or continuously. Consider, for example, the GDPR's processing ban in Art. 6 para. 1 and Art. 9 para. 1 GDPR which governs if and which data can be disclosed and processed and before any actual processing takes place – the approach is a combination of input and upstream regulation.[394] At other times, the approach is continuous, *e.g.* the processing principle of purpose limitation in Sec. 106 COPRA and in Art. 5 para. 1 lit. b GDPR applies upstream and downstream where it restricts how personal data can be collected and used at the time of the first disclosure and later on in the processing chain.[395]

Looking at input, output, upstream, and downstream regulation and its effect, the question is whether and which form of privacy regulation appears more apt to mitigate against the modern privacy risks described above? For instance, is input or output regulation better suited to promote the collective dimension of personal data use to the benefit of innovation, economy, and society?[396]

Starting with input and output regulation, we see that input regulation controls whether data can initially be processed, for instance, at the point in time the

392 Steinmüller and others (n 8), 75; Hoffmann-Riem (n 3) 73–75; Hoeren (n 169), 11.

393 Cf. Solove, 'Privacy Self-Management and the Consent Dilemma' (n 78) 1881; Solove, 'The Myth of the Privacy Paradox' (n 155) 50; Hoffmann-Riem (n 3) 73–75; Hoeren (n 172), 11.

394 Cf. von Lewinski, 'Einführung' (n 17) para. 13, 18–19; Kramer, 'Art. 6' (n 104) para. 1; Frenzel, 'Frenzel, Art. 9' (n 181) para. 6–9.

395 Sub Chapter 3 D. I. 5. Purpose limitation, data minimization, limitations on waivers of privacy rights.

396 Cf. the call that modern data privacy regulations must strike the balance between privacy-risk management and fostering innovation for instance Hennemann, 'Wettbewerb der Datenschutzrechtsordnungen' (n 19) 868; von Lewinski, 'Einführung' (n 17) para. 72–73; cf. Hoffmann-Riem (n 3) 73–75.

individual first discloses her personal data to the processing entity, whereas output control is triggered if and when the result of a processing activity meets a predefined quality or threshold, *e.g.* in case the processing result proves discriminatory. From this processing result, output regulation then traces the causal link back to the processing activity which caused the result and in order to subject this processing activity to privacy control. Conceptually speaking, output regulation thus takes an *ex post* or backward looking perspective to privacy control whereas input regulation builds on an *ex ante* risk assessment.

As a consequence of its *ex ante* assessment, input regulation is often forced to speculate about the risk of processing activities before the actual processing activity occurs. Consider, for instance, how the EU data protection regulation conceptualizes in Art. 6 para. 1 and Art. 9 para. 1 GDPR at the beginning of the processing chain and before any processing has taken place typical privacy risks irrespective of whether any actual privacy risk or infringement has actually materialized (*vertyptes Risiko*).[397] In the logic of the GDPR's input-based control, already at the point in time of the initial disclosure of personal data from the data subject to the data controller, the disclosure is deemed to contain the risk of harmful or undesired processing or producing a harmful or undesired processing result.[398] This is the motivation why the GDPR regulates the processing *input* and whether personal data can be processed at all.[399] Only exceptionally and as an additional element to consider in the balancing test within the framework of input-based regulation does the GDPR take into account the results of processing activities, for instance, when the processing of personal data is necessary to protect vital interests of the data subject or of another natural person pursuant to Art. 6 para. 1 lit. d and Art. 9 para. 1 lit. c GDPR, or to enable preventive or occupational medicine according to Art. 9 para. 2 lit. h GDPR.[400]

In light of the modern privacy risks illustrated above such as data quantity, data quality, and the capabilities of modern data-focused technology, the input-based control regime in EU data protection law and in the GDPR today often seems anachronistic and ineffective.[401] At the time of its conception in the 1970s, personal

397 Cf. von Lewinski, 'Einführung' (n 17) para. 13, 18–19; Hennemann, 'Wettbewerb der Datenschutzrechtsordnungen' (n 19) 871; Kramer, 'Art. 6' (n 104) para. 1; Frenzel, 'Frenzel, Art. 9' (n 181) para. 6–9.

398 Determann, 'Healthy Data Protection' (n 16) 276–277.

399 Kramer, 'Art. 6' (n 104) para. 1; Frenzel, 'Art. 6' (n 104) para. 7–8; cf. Hennemann, 'Wettbewerb der Datenschutzrechtsordnungen' (n 16) 871.

400 Hoffmann-Riem (n 3) 75; Greve, 'Art. 9' (n 199) para. 23 and 31.

401 Cf. Determann, 'Healthy Data Protection' (n 16) 276–277; Lewinski, von 'Einführung' (n 17) para. 13, 18–19; Hoeren (n 172), 10.

data collection and use was scarce, occurred primarily in the relationship between the government and the individual, and was mostly insignificant for private processing entities.[402] Back then, the idea of protecting privacy by overall limiting data disclosure seemed feasible because it was an effective way to prevent the government from accumulating and processing more personal data.[403] In today's data reality in which data processing technology and personal data processing is ubiquitous and without geographic limitations, data quantity can no longer effectively be kept small by a national or regional processing limitation.[404] Today, instead of trying to limit personal data generation, we should strive to generate and make fruitful more high quality data.[405]

To this point, recent economic research has shown how the EU's input- and consent-based approach favors big technology companies in their internal data collection and does little to improve market-entry, data generation and collection by smaller processing entities and overall market competition about personal data.[406] This means the EU's input-based regulation could even intensify data quality problems such as the mis- and underrepresentation in data pools of marginalized groups and individuals.[407] To generate more high quality data, output regulation seems the better regulatory approach, ideally when combined with incentivizes for high data-quality such as increased transparency and comparability of data through standardized data formats, ontology, and infrastructure.[408]

Moreover, output regulation's *ex post* view allows privacy regulation to be more responsive and adaptive to the technical capacities of modern data-focused technology than input regulation.[409] This is because the hindsight risk assessment allows to better identify and factor into the mitigation action than input control's *ex ante* perspective which category of modern data risks has led to a particular privacy violation, for instance, whether the violation roots in the functionality of a particular processing technology. *Ex post*, more information and context related to the processing chain and the processing of personal data is available than at the beginning of the processing chain which facilitates better informed decisions and, over time, more bespoke privacy regulation by privacy authorities and stake-

---

402 Supra Chapter 1 B. Concept and status of EU privacy law.

403 Cf. Determann, 'Healthy Data Protection' (n 16) 276–277.

404 Cf. Cantwell (n 54) 9; Determann, 'Healthy Data Protection' (n 16) 276–277.

405 Supra Chapter 2 A. I. 2. Data quality.

406 Gal and Aviv (n 19), 363–364.

407 Cf. Katyal (n 52), 56, 71–73; supra Chapter 2 B. I. 2. Data quality.

408 Batura and Peeters (n 186) 5; cf. European Data Protection Supervisor (n 18) 21–22; Katyal (n 136), 56, 112; Dempsey and others (n 129), 12.

409 Supra Chapter 2 A. Categorization of modern privacy risks – a call for capacity-apt regulation.

holders.[410] As a case in point, consider big data technology for which large quantities of data are amassed and later on leveraged for a particular purpose, *e.g.* to find new cures for diseases in the field of medicine.[411] At the time of the data collection, it is often unclear which information can be made fruitful in the future and for which purpose; frequently, it is only long after the data has been collected that the decision is taken about how to use the available data. Hence, it is ultimately these subsequently formed motivations and decisions which determine whether the processing activity and its output is beneficial or harmful to the individual and society.[412]

Considering human incapacities when individuals deal with modern data-focused technology, the *ex post* risk assessment in output regulation arguably embraces better than input regulation does human intellectual and behavioral (in)capacities.[413] Even where privacy or data protection regulation empowers individuals to make decisions about how their personal data should be processed, consumers frequently remain passive and do not take privacy-friendly action.[414] This could be because, from the perspective of the consumer, considering and forming an opinion *ex ante* about the implications of their personal data being processed and before any actual processing activity has occurred may often seem vague and difficult. Moreover, the above-described structural privacy challenges linked to the scale and complexity of modern data processing discourage or even make it impossible for consumers to take action, for instance, the consumer would have to make sense of the often complex processing activities and pick and choose whom to confront from the myriad of processing entities that process their personal data.[415] Moving the decision-making point closer to the processing action for individuals in the form of output regulation likely increases their ability and motivation to form

---

410 Cf. Gasser (n 11) 198; von Lewinski, 'Einführung' (n 17) para. 13, 18–19; Schaub (n 265) 358–359; Hoffmann-Riem (n 3) 73–75; Hoeren (n 172), 11; Solove, 'Privacy Self-Management and the Consent Dilemma' (n 78) 1902–1903.

411 Cf. Determann, 'Healthy Data Protection' (n 16) 262–265, 277; Hoffmann-Riem (n 3) 37.

412 Cf. Ohm (n 182) 100–102; Gasser (n 11) 200; Boris Paal and Moritz Hennemann, 'Big Data im Recht: Wettbewerbs- und daten(schutz)rechtliche Herausforderungen' 2017 NJW 1697, 1700 on how purpose limitation and data minimization under the GDPR equally apply to big data technology.

413 Cf. Hoffmann-Riem (n 3) 73–75; cf. Hoeren (n 172), 11; cf. Determann, 'Healthy Data Protection' (n 16) 252–255.

414 Specht (n 298) 422; Acquisti and Grossklags (n 226) 371; Sandfuchs (n 298) 135–138; generally supra Chapter 2 A. II. 2. Behavioral (in)capacity.

415 Solove, 'Privacy Self-Management and the Consent Dilemma' (n 78) 1881, 1886–1888; Lev-Aretz and Strandburg (n 16), 295; Acquisti and Grossklags (n 226) 371; Ebner, *Weniger ist Mehr?* (n 29) 45–48.

better-informed decisions because they can be aware of the actual consequences of their decision in a particular processing situation.[416]

Secondly, output regulation appears favorable to input control in terms of human (in)capacities when it puts the onus of securing non-harmful data processing and results on the processing entities.[417] For example, the rule for processing entities could be that they are only allowed to process personal data to the extent that it does not do harm to the individual or to society.[418] Such output-based control dispels the myth and disbelief that solely by empowering the individual to make privacy decisions we will be able to correct common privacy shortcomings.[419] The above-illustrated modern privacy risks have become structural risks and, given our innate human intellectual and behavioral (in)capacities, are thus mostly beyond the individuals' capacity to solve.[420] As a consequence, the action must first and foremost be on the owner of technical capacities and on processing entities rather than on the individual consumer to ensure that personal data is processed without harming or disadvantaging the consumer or the collective.[421]

Looking at upstream and downstream regulation which governs how personal data can be processed after the initial data disclosure and later on in the value chain, many of the observations and arguments about input and output control hold true. Today, data processing typically is not a singular one-off processing activity in the relationship between the individual and the government or one specific processing entity; instead, personal data is commonly aggregated, combined, and processed over time, from a variety of different sources, and by multiple processing entities.[422] Upstream regulation alike in Art. 6 para. 1 and Art. 9 para. 1 GDPR must often anticipate and conceptualize typical processing risks that may occur in the future, downstream regulation, by contrast, can move the point of scrutiny or regulatory intervention closer to the processing activity. This can make downstream control more context-specific with more and better quality informa-

416 Cf. Solove, 'Privacy Self-Management and the Consent Dilemma' (n 78) 1902–1903; von Lewinski, 'Einführung' (n 17) para. 13; Sandfuchs (n 298) 109–115.

417 Cf. Solove, 'The Limitations of Privacy Rights' (n 226) 10–17.

418 Von Lewinski, 'Einführung' (n 17) para. 13; Veil (n 15), 695.

419 Solove, 'Privacy Self-Management and the Consent Dilemma' (n 78) 1881; Veil (n 15), 686, 687–689; cf. Acquisti and Grossklags (n 226) 368; Specht (n 298) 422; Ebner, *Weniger ist Mehr?* (n 29) 45–48.

420 Veil (n 15), 686, 687–689; Solove, 'Privacy Self-Management and the Consent Dilemma' (n 78) 1881, 1886–1888; Ebner, *Weniger ist Mehr?* (n 29) 45–48; supra Chapter 2 A. II. Human (in)capacities.

421 Solove, 'The Limitations of Privacy Rights' (n 226) 10–17.

422 Cf. Solove, 'Privacy Self-Management and the Consent Dilemma' (n 78) 1881, 1886–1888; Cantwell (n 54) 5.

tion about the processing activity at stake.[423] For example, downstream regulation can hone in on particular qualities of data processing in a way that upstream regulation cannot – imagine processing decisions which directly answer to technical capacities downstream such as the use of a particular processing technology, data quality, or in a specific point of use processing situation.[424]

This context-specificity and a more detailed understanding of the processing situation and effect in downstream regulation could prove particularly helpful when balancing risks and benefits of personal data processing.[425] For instance, whether personal data retrieved from clinical studies in a hospital should later on be (re-)used by a research entity could be assessed downstream with a closer focus on the actual processing situation at the research entity, and with less importance given to the initial data collection.[426] In the same direction albeit outside of EU data protection law, EU public policymakers are currently discussing how to regulate more situationally the re-use of personal data from clinical studies to free it from some of the tarnish which regulatory upstream control has caused it.[427]

Similar to output-based regulation, downstream regulation often appears more apt to embrace intellectual and behavioral (in)capacities than upstream control.[428] This is because, in downstream regulation, individuals can focus on the decisive processing step and context, *e.g.* when they receive pertinent information about a particular processing activity and are asked whether they are aware and in agreement.[429] As *Schwartz* puts it, consumers should always have a *"right to exit from bad bargains"*.[430] And considering common human passivity and inaction about data processing, individuals should be more motivated to take ownership and voice their privacy choice when their right to exit is put downstream where they face a specific processing activity and the consequences of their action or inac-

423 Supra Chapter 2 A. I. Technical capacities; cf. Solove, 'The Myth of the Privacy Paradox' (n 155) 50; Solove, 'Privacy Self-Management and the Consent Dilemma' (n 78) 1902–1903; Ohm (n 165) 105; von Lewinski, 'Einführung' (n 16) para. 13; Hoffmann-Riem (n 4) 73–75; Hoeren (n 134), 11.

424 Cf. Solove, 'Privacy Self-Management and the Consent Dilemma' (n 78) 1901–1902.

425 Cf. Hennemann, 'Wettbewerb der Datenschutzrechtsordnungen' (n 19) 893; von Lewinski, 'Einführung' (n 17) para. 72–73.

426 Cf. Determann, 'Healthy Data Protection' (n 16) 234–236.

427 European Commission, 'Proposal for a regulation – The European Health Data Space' (2022) <https://health.ec.europa.eu/publications/proposal-regulation-european-health-data-space_en> accessed 12 November 2023.

428 Supra Chapter 2 A. II. Human (in)capacities.

429 Cf. Solove, 'The Myth of the Privacy Paradox' (n 155) 43–44; von Lewinski, 'Einführung' (n 17) para. 13.

430 Paul Schwartz, 'Privacy inalienability and the regulation of spyware' 2005 Berkeley Technology Law Journal 1269, 1274.

tion.[431] Still, in light of the structural privacy risks described above, the individual's capacity to assess and adequately respond to data processing downstream should not be overestimated.[432] This is why downstream regulation should preferably focus on substantive processing rules which address technical capacities instead of human (in)capacities; the processing rules, in turn, should not be linked to an individual consumer's action or privacy preference but apply generally in the character of a collective privacy provision.[433]

To summarize the above, output- and downstream- based control in privacy and data protection regulation seems superior compared to input- and upstream-based control because, overall, such regulation can be more capacity-apt. The later point of scrutiny and the close link between the regulatory intervention and the root cause of a privacy violation may lead to improved decision-making when regulating technical capacities. Also, it may motivate and educate individuals to be better informed and more active in exercising their privacy control rights.

C. Effective implementation of privacy regulation

In addition to the above-described modern privacy risk categories which are presented for the first time in this study, we want to summarize in the below an already existing standard first introduced by *Bamberger/Mulligan* in their renown work *Privacy on the ground* which can be used to assess how effectively countries and systems have implemented privacy regulation.[434] The benchmark to assess the effectiveness of the COPRA bill and the U.S. privacy law and system *post* COPRA shall be the building blocks for a modern privacy law in Chapter 2 including the elements taken from *Bamberger/Mulligan's* work.

The remarkable finding of *Bamberger/Mulligan* is that they were able to show how effective privacy protection significantly depends on the broader privacy system, *i.e.* how processing entities, oversight and enforcement authorities implement and practice processing rules. Effective privacy protection for *Bamberger/Mulligan* meant that organizations in a given country showed a *"broad, substantive understanding of privacy values that must be protected* [...]", for example, by *"incorporat*

431 Specht (n 298) 422; Cate (n 30) 360–361; cf. Solove, 'The Myth of the Privacy Paradox' (n 152) 43, 50; Ebner, *Weniger ist Mehr?* (n 29) 103–107.

432 Solove, 'Privacy Self-Management and the Consent Dilemma' (n 78) 1902–1903; Solove, 'The Myth of the Privacy Paradox' (n 155) 5; Solove, 'The Limitations of Privacy Rights' (n 226) 10–17.

433 Solove, 'Privacy Self-Management and the Consent Dilemma' (n 78) 1902–1903; von Lewinski, 'Einführung' (n 17) para. 13.

434 Bamberger and Mulligan (n 287).

[ing] privacy *'by design' into corporate structures"*.[435] In order to identify characteristic elements, they conducted comparative studies on organizations in different countries. In particular for organizations in EU countries which are subject to the same EU data protection rules, the authors observed the impact the different implementation and practice of data protection rules by processing entities and oversight and enforcement authorities had on a country's privacy system and overall privacy protection.[436]

Bamberger/Mulligan identified the following elements as building blocks for effective privacy protection: First, whether privacy was set as a corporate priority ("*making the board's agenda*"); secondly, whether processing entities tasked high-status privacy representatives to liaise between internal and external privacy needs ("*a boundary-spanning privacy professional*"); and, thirdly, whether privacy was a decision-making category in the organization which informed and formed the design of technology and processes ("*the 'managerialization' of privacy*").[437] Extrapolating from these findings, *Bamberger/Mulligan* furthermore found that a given system could foster a strong privacy culture in organizations by nudging processing entities into broadly mandating privacy representatives to define and put into practice what privacy regulation sets out in broad strokes, by reinforcing transparency and information disclosure within organizations about privacy failures and data breaches, and by meaningfully enforcing privacy law so that processing entities are encouraged to further invest into their privacy compliance programs.[438]

D. Interim summary

In Chapter 2, we discussed how traditional concepts and means in EU data protection and U.S. privacy law are increasingly called into question by new technical capacities of modern data-focused technology. The scale, sophistication, and integration of technical capacities today have far surpassed the ones present when many of these ideas and means were conceived which poses new regulatory challenges.[439] Additionally, human (in)capacities in dealing with modern data-focused

---

435 Ibid 174.

436 Ibid 173–174.

437 Ibid 241–242; overlapping in the description of some of the elements also with Hoffmann-Riem (n 3) 62–63; Solove, 'The Myth of the Privacy Paradox' (n 180) 49–50; Dempsey and others (n 129), 2, 8.

438 Bamberger and Mulligan (n 287) 242–243; Dempsey and others (n 129), 2, 11; Schwartz and Pfeifer (n 19), 177.

439 Supra Chapter 2 A. I. Technical capacities.

technology further aggravate privacy risks: Essentially, humans use, adapt, and react to technology in an imperfect way because they are, on average, unable to adequately comprehend or respond to today's technical capacities.[440] In the face of these technical and human (in)capacities, it has become even more apparent that personal data use and privacy are of a collective and societal concern.[441]

Answering the first hypothesis of this study, this is why any modern privacy law should attempt new answers to mitigate against today's privacy risks. In the search for new answers, effective privacy regulation should be *capacity-apt* and embrace *technical* and *human (in)capacities* instead of clinging on to traditional regulatory concepts and means which were designed for a different data processing reality. Although EU data protection and U.S. privacy regulation likely suffer from considerable path dependency due to the law and system's very different genesis,[442] there is opportunity for change and convergence as the U.S. still awaits comprehensive privacy regulation on a federal level (and several of its recent state privacy laws indicate a new openness to concepts and means familiar to EU data protection law), and because many of the proposed new regulatory ideas and means seem conceptually feasible for integration into the GDPR.

As a minimum, modern privacy regulation should integrate the following building blocks which are summarized at figure 3 below: The quantity and quality of personal data and data sets, the use of particular processing technology, the processing of personal data in particular use-situations, and the technical safeguarding of personal data and data sets against third party intrusion.[443] As human (in)capacities, modern privacy law should embrace more than it has common human intellectual and behavioral limitations vis-à-vis new technology and the effect of personal data processing on the collective.[444] To this end, this chapter suggests a shift of privacy regulation to a more output- and downstream-based control, perceivably in the form of a fair processing standard which can be leveraged to better balance risks and opportunities of personal data processing for the individual and for society.[445]

In addition to these building blocks, we summarized in Chapter 2 an existing standard previously used to assess how effectively countries and systems have implemented privacy and data protection laws.[446] It has been observed that effec-

440 Supra Chapter 2 A. II. Human (in)capacities.

441 Supra Chapter 2 A. II. 3. Individual and collective privacy.

442 Supra Chapter 1 The privacy landscape in the U.S. and in the EU.

443 Supra Chapter 2 A. I. Technical capacities.

444 Supra Chapter 2 A. II. Human (in)capacities.

445 Supra Chapter 2 B. Output and downstream regulation and Chapter 2 A. II. 3. Individual and collective privacy.

446 Supra Chapter 2 C. Effective implementation of privacy regulation.

tive privacy protection is often characterized by whether organizations commonly discuss privacy on the level of top management, whether they task high-status employees to liaise on privacy matters inside and outside the organization, and whether privacy is a common decision-making category within organizations.[447] Conversely, a system ideally encourages organizations to task their privacy professionals with a broad mandate, sets incentives for organizations to disclose compliance shortcomings so that they can be improved, and generally and meaningfully enforces privacy compliance.[448]

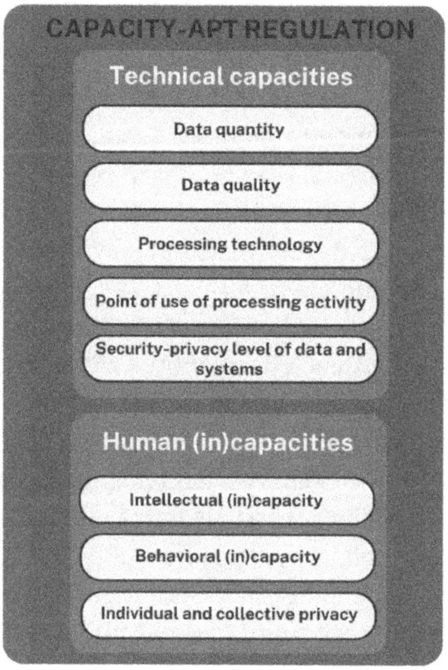

Figure 3: Capacity-apt regulation

447 Bamberger and Mulligan (n 287) 241–242; similarly in Solove, 'The Myth of the Privacy Paradox' (n 155) 49–50; Dempsey and others (n 129), 2, 8.

448 Bamberger and Mulligan (n 287) 242–243; Dempsey and others (n 129), 2, 11; Schwartz and Pfeifer (n 19), 177.

Chapter 3
Assessing the COPRA bill

Building on the building blocks for a modern privacy law and including the categorization of modern privacy risks in Chapter 2, this chapter discusses the second hypothesis of this study, namely the question whether and how effectively COPRA mitigates against modern privacy challenges of individuals and of society.[449] We examine how COPRA addresses technical capacities and human (in)capacities to understand whether the bill is a capacity-apt proposal which would strengthen the *status quo* of U.S. federal privacy law.

COPRA is a bill for a federal consumer privacy law which was first introduced to the 116th Congress of the U.S. on December 3, 2019, and, a second time, to the 117th Congress of the U.S. on April 11, 2021.[450] COPRA is a concise bill of only 22 provisions with a comprehensive approach to broadly regulate data processing.[451] The bill is not legally binding until it is passed by the legislature. By summer 2024, the bill has been read twice and referred to the *Senate Committee for Commerce, Science, and Transportation* where its status remains pending.[452] COPRA's uncertain fate is shared by other recent proposals for a federal comprehensive privacy law such as the *American Data Privacy and Protection Act*, H.R. 8152, and the *American Privacy Rights Act of 2024*.[453] Despite the passing of comprehensive privacy laws in several U.S. states, no comprehensive bill has yet been enacted on a federal level, the primary reasons of a private right of action and of the preemption of state law we will discuss further down below.[454]

We begin our analysis with a conceptual anchoring of the COPRA bill as articulated in the COPRA preparatory report and the text of the bill itself (sub Chapter 3 A. Consumer privacy rights: A conceptual change in U.S. privacy law?). A better understanding about whether COPRA is a continuation of the traditionally market-centered U.S. privacy law or whether COPRA diverts U.S. privacy law towards

---

449 See supra Chapter 2 A. Categorization of modern privacy risks – a call for capacity-apt regulation.

450 U.S. Congress, 'Consumer Online Privacy Rights Act' [2019] 116th Congress, Senate 2968; U.S. Congress, 'Consumer Online Privacy Rights Act' [2021] 117th Congress, Senate 3195.

451 Sub Chapter 3 C. I. Material scope of application.

452 U.S. Congress, 'U.S. Congress, Consumer Online Privacy Rights Act' (n 448).

453 U.S. Congress, 'American Data Privacy and Protection Act' 117th Congress, House of Representatives 8152; Committee on Energy and Commerce (n 93).

454 Supra Chapter 1 A. Concept and status of U.S. privacy law; sub Chapter 3 B. COPRA and the preemption of existing privacy law; Chapter 3 E. II. 1. Private right of action; cf. Scholz, 'Private rights of action in privacy law' (n 160) 1642; Dempsey and others (n 129), 4.

https://doi.org/10.1515/9783112215715-004

an EU-inspired fundamental rights approach will provide a helpful basis for interpreting COPRA's data processing provisions later on in this chapter.[455] We then position COPRA within the broader U.S. legal framework by examining to which extent the bill co-exists with or preempts established U.S. federal and state privacy law (sub Chapter 3 B. COPRA and the preemption of existing privacy law). At the core of Chapter 3, we undertake a detailed analysis of COPRA's processing rules with a focus on individual and collective privacy (sub Chapter 3 D. Regulating data processing activities).[456] Finally, we look at the new privacy compliance obligations COPRA sets for processing entities in the U.S., and how the bill strives to strengthen privacy oversight and enforcement both by the authorities and by the individual consumer (sub Chapter 3 E. COPRA compliance, oversight, and enforcement).

A. Consumer privacy rights: A conceptual change in U.S. privacy law?

Whereas Europe understands data protection as a constitutionally granted fundamental right on which individual data protection rights are founded, the U.S. has traditionally justified privacy regulation in federal and state privacy laws as statutory corrections to observed market failures without a constitutional basis.[457] According to the preparatory COPRA report, the traditional U.S. approach has led to a vacuum in consumer control.[458] Highlighting the mounting importance of U.S. online-retail and mobile applications for U.S. consumers and the U.S. economy, the report points to a growing worry and concern among U.S. consumers about the use and protection of their personal data: U.S. consumers want to know whether *"their data is protected, how it is used, and to whom it is sold"*. Given the current lack of comprehensive privacy protection for U.S. consumers outside of regulated industries, the report deplores that *"consumers do not have clear rights to protect their data"* and urges the legislator to grant consumers *"the specific data rights they need in the digital economy"*, in particular a *"general right to access one's data"* and a *"right to have data deleted or corrected"*.[459]

Prima facie, this strong reception of individual consumer rights, and in particular of an individual data right to access, correct, and delete personal data, could

455 Supra Chapter 1 The privacy landscape in the U.S. and in the EU.
456 Supra Chapter 2 A. II. 3. Individual and collective privacy.
457 Schwartz and Pfeifer (n 19), 119, 122–127; see generally supra Chapter 1 The privacy landscape in the U.S. and in the EU.
458 Cantwell (n 54) 3, 8.
459 Ibid 3.

indicate a change of course in U.S. privacy law *post* COPRA: Does the bill want to establish inalienable privacy rights for the individual consumer crafted after or, at least, closely informed by the European data protection law?[460] Although the COPRA report does not admit it openly, the following findings confirm the European influence on the COPRA report and bill: First, on her personal website, Senator *Cantwell*, the leading author and sponsor of the COPRA report and bill, explicitly mentions the passing of the GDPR in the year 2016 and calls for the U.S. to follow the EU's example of data protection regulation.[461] This indicates the Senator is familiar with European data protection law, that she thinks positively about aspects of EU data protection regulation, and, finally, that she is motivated to implement privacy regulation in the U.S. alike or similar to the GDPR. Secondly, the COPRA report urges to implement some of the same data protection rights which can be found in EU law, namely the right to access and data rectification in Art. 8 para. 2 sentence 2 EU CFR and the right to access, rectification and erasure of personal data in Art. 15 para. 1, 16 and 17 para. 1 GDPR. Given that the cited provisions in the EU CFR and the GDPR existed long before the drafting of the COPRA report and bill, they were available as examples for their corresponding provisions in Sec. 102 (a), 103, and 104 COPRA.[462] Thirdly, the terminology used in Sec. 102 (a), 103, and 104 COPRA is highly similar to the articles in the EU CFR and the GDPR. The term *right to access* in Sec. 102 (a) COPRA is almost identical to *right of access* used in Art. 8 para. 2 sentence 2 CFR and to the English version of Art. 15 para. 1 GDPR. The terms *right to delete* and *right to correct* appear to be a consciously chosen simplification and translation into plain English of the terms *erasure* and *rectification* in Art. 17 para. 1 and Art. 16 GDPR. The more formal terms in the English version of the GDPR can be explained as an attempt to harmonize the English with the French terminology in the GDPR of *rectification* and *effacement*.[463]

Yet it would be missing the full picture to only focus on selected language in the COPRA report and bill and on the reference to EU data protection law on the COPRA author's personal website. A re-use of the label of individual data rights and the copying of selected data rights from EU data protection law by itself does not suffice to bridge the dogmatic gap which exists between U.S. privacy law and EU

---

460 Schwartz and Pfeifer (n 19), 122–127.

461 Maria Cantwell, 'Shopping online?: It's time lawmakes join Cantwell's efforts to protect your privacy' (2019) <https://www.cantwell.senate.gov/news/news-about-maria/editorial-shopping-online-its-time-lawmakers-join-cantwells-efforts-to-protect-your-privacy> accessed 25 January 2021.

462 Sub Chapter 3 D. II. 1. Data control rights.

463 The French version of the GDPR can be found at European Parliament and Council, 'Réglement général sur la protection des données' 2016 <https://eur-lex.europa.eu/legal-content/FR/TXT/HTML/?uri=CELEX:32016R0679> accessed 3 November 2023.

data protection law. Given the EU data protection's constitutional foundation with *a-priori* data protection rights which are independent from statutory law, an equivalent in U.S. privacy law would require individual privacy rights inalienable by statutory law, and thus arguably an amendment to the U.S. Constitution.[464] However, COPRA does not propose individual privacy rights as *a-priori* or *non-consequential* consumer rights. Instead, COPRA data rights remain conceptually linked and consequential to market situations.

Already the title of the CORPA bill itself gives an indication of this conceptual foundation: The bill is called the Consumer *Online* Privacy Rights Act – its primary goal is the regulation of a market situation, *i.e.* the consumer-business relationship in the digital or internet-based economy in which consumer privacy rights predominantly serve as a response-tool to market failures. Moreover, in the COPRA preparatory report, the starting point of the argument for individual privacy rights is the market: Under the title of *"privacy concerns in the digital economy"*, the report discusses numerous examples of market failure that justify individual privacy rights, *e.g.* data breaches, unwanted collection of personal data by companies, online profiling and targeting, data-driven discrimination, and internet-connected devices.[465] In each of these cases, stronger privacy protection and reinforced individual privacy rights are a consequence of undesired market phenomena and privacy rights are a (consequential) regulatory decision to counter-balance market shortcomings.[466] Notably, only once does the COPRA report offer an alternative narrative to the market failure rhetoric to promote privacy: In the section about online profiling and targeting, the report positively highlights the business value and growing potential of online advertisement to then argue that an increase in privacy transparency – the consumer knowing that she is being targeted and that she is watching tailored advertisement – will ultimately increase consumers' trust in companies thus resulting in higher website traffic and advertisement revenue.[467] Irrespective of whether this reasoning is convincing, such pro-market justification for stronger privacy protection remains an argument built on the functioning of the market rather than on an EU-like constitutional rights approach.[468]

Last but not least, the bill provides for an update to existing U.S. federal privacy law in the form of statutory law and does not follow EU data protection's funda-

464 Cf. Stefan Ernst, 'Art. 1' in Boris Paal and Daniel Pauly (eds), *DSGVO, BDSG* (C.H. Beck 2021) para. 4–7; cf. Schwartz and Pfeifer (n 19), 132–134; Solove and Schwartz (n 60) 1436; see generally supra Chapter 1 B. Concept and status of EU data protection law.

465 Cantwell (n 54) 3.

466 Cf. Schwartz and Pfeifer (n 19), 132, 155–156; Solove and Schwartz (n 60) 1436.

467 Cantwell (n 54) 6–7.

468 Cf. Schwartz and Pfeifer (n 19), 117–119.

mental rights approach.[469] Neither the COPRA report nor the bill suggests any amendment to the U.S. Constitution. COPRA's preemption clause in Sec. 302 (c) COPRA is a case in point: With a detailed discussion of the preemption clause to follow, we can already say that Sec. 302 (c) COPRA does not shield COPRA data rights from being limited or altered by existing statutory law, by a new legislative initiative on the federal level, or by the U.S. Constitution.[470]

In sum, despite new consumer data rights in COPRA and a noticeable influence of EU data protection law on the COPRA report and some provisions of the bill, the conceptual anchoring of U.S. federal privacy law *post* COPRA remains market-based and founded in statutory law; COPRA does not adopt the EU's fundamental rights approach.[471]

B. COPRA and the preemption of existing privacy law

As a federal act of legislation, COPRA risks conflicting with existing federal privacy law such as the *Health Insurance Portability and Accountability Act*, Public Law No. 104–191,[472] or the *Children's Online Privacy Protection Act*, 15 U. S.C. §§ 6501–6506,[473] with existing state privacy law such as the *California Online Privacy Protection Act*, California Business and Professional Code §§ 22575–22579, and with common law or statutory causes of action for civil relief.[474] For instance, the examples listed above overlap in their material scope of application regulating data or information which can be used to identify a specific individual, see the definition of health information according to § 160.103 Health Insurance Portability and Accountability Act, of personal information according to § 312.2 Children's Online Privacy Protection Act, and of personally identifiable information according to § 22577(a) California Online Privacy Protection Act. As a consequence, consumers may struggle to identify and argue the correct legal basis for their claim. Whereas a consumer may demand access and correction to her personally identifiable information pursuant to § 22575(b)(2) California Online Privacy Protection Act only if and to the extent a website operator's privacy policy stipulates such rights, Sec. 102 (a) and 104 COPRA guarantee the consumer the same rights.[475]

---

469 Supra Chapter 1 B. Concept and status of EU data protection law.

470 See sub Chapter 3 B. COPRA and the preemption of existing privacy law.

471 Cf. Schwartz and Pfeifer (n 19), 122–127; Streinz (n 12) 15–16.

472 Solove and Schwartz (n 60) 683–684.

473 Ibid 1157–1159.

474 Cf. Dempsey and others (n 129), 4 pointing to the fact that the question about preemption of state privacy law has been at the center of the debate about passing a federal privacy law.

This triggers the question of preemption: Can a Californian consumer invoke the favorable COPRA provisions instead of the more restrictive provision in the California Online Privacy Protection Act? More broadly speaking, what is the relationship between COPRA and existing federal or state U.S. privacy law, does COPRA preempt or supersede existing privacy law?

COPRA answers the question of preemption in Sec. 302 (c) COPRA. The bill will only preempt or supersede existing federal, state, or common law if and to the extent such law *directly conflicts* with COPRA provisions. However, the bill does not contain a definition of what constitutes a direct conflict. A direct conflict is likely to be found in cases and to the extent consumers can invoke a right with identical consequences in law (*Rechtsfolge*). In the example above, a consumer's right to access her personal data follows from both Sec. 102 (a) COPRA and, provided a privacy policy exists, from § 22575(b)(2) California Online Privacy Protection Act. In Sec. 302(c) sentence 2 COPRA, the bill further clarifies that no direct conflict is present when existing law *"affords a greater level of protection to individuals protected under this Act"*. It follows *e contrario* that COPRA will preempt conflicting federal, state, or common law in cases of direct conflict only if and to the extent the threshold of privacy protection granted therein is *lower* than the threshold granted by COPRA. In the example above, Sec. 102 (a) and 104 COPRA preempt § 22575(b)(2) California Online Privacy Protection Act because the COPRA provisions guarantee a right to access and correct covered data without any further condition and are thus more favorable to the consumer than is Californian State privacy law.

Conceptually speaking, COPRA will thus establish, within its scope of application, a *minimum standard of privacy protection* in U.S. federal, state, and common law.[476] The political reason for a minimum standard rather than imposing the strict preemption of conflicting privacy laws is that it will likely help secure the support for the passing of COPRA of U.S. states and state representatives from progressive privacy cultures and state privacy laws. A case in point is California and its *California Consumer Privacy Act of 2018*, California Civil Code § 1798.100–178.199.[477] Otherwise, state representatives such as from California might be inclined to

475 Sub Chapter 3 D. II. 1. Data control rights.

476 For a general overview supra Chapter 1 A. Concept and status of U.S. privacy law.

477 Cf. Gregory Voss, 'Cross-Border Data Flows, the GDPR, and Data Governance' 2020 Washington International Law Journal 485, 498–499; Dempsey and others (n 129), 4; on the role of California and its progressive privacy culture and law cf. Louisa Specht-Riemenschneider, 'Data access rights – A comparative perspective' in Bundesministerium der Justiz und für Verbraucherschutz and Max-Planck-Institut für Innovation und Wettbewerb (eds), *Data Access, Consumer Interests and Public Welfare* (Nomos 2021) 411–412.

oppose a federal privacy bill which effectively lowers the standard of protection provided by their own state privacy law.

In Chapter 4, the minimum privacy standard established in the U.S. by COPRA will be of relevance when we examine whether the U.S. offers an adequate level of data protection according to Art. 45 para. 1 and 2 GDPR, the threshold for a legitimate transfer of EU personal data to the U.S.[478] We will assess whether the protection granted under the U.S. law and system *post* COPRA is essentially equivalent to the level of protection provided by EU data protection law.[479]

C. Scope of application

Some of the updates COPRA brings to U.S. consumer privacy law can already be discerned from the bill's scope of application. In the below, we examine with occasional reference to existing U.S. federal and state privacy law COPRA's material (sub I. Material scope of application), personal (sub II. Personal scope of application), and territorial scope of application (sub III. Territorial scope of application).

I. Material scope of application

COPRA applies across industries and sectors (and for online and offline activities)[480], it is comprehensive in its material scope of application. This is different from the historically targeted regulation of specific industries and sectors in U.S. federal privacy law.[481]

The comprehensive approach of the bill can be derived from the fact that COPRA's material scope of application does not contain a limitation to specific entities, industries, sectors, risk-situations, or types of processing activities. Unlike, for instance, the *Health Insurance Portability and Accountability Act*, Public Law No. 104–191, which according to 45 C.F.R. § 160.102 applies only to *"health plans, health care clearinghouses, and health care providers"* and not to whoever processes an individual's health information,[482] COPRA's material scope of application is broader and binds whichever entity or person processes covered data pursuant to

---

478 Cf. Daniel Pauly, 'Art. 45' in Boris Paal and Daniel Pauly (eds), *DSGVO, BDSG* (C.H. Beck 2021) para. 1; Hladjk, 'Art. 45' (n 49) para. 3.

479 Sub Chapter 4 U.S. adequacy *post* COPRA.

480 Online and offline processing is in scope of COPRA sub Chapter 3 C. I. 1. Processing activities.

481 Solove and Schwartz (n 60) 1033; supra Chapter 1 A. Concept and status of U.S. privacy law.

482 Ibid 683–684.

Sec. 2 (9) (A) (ii) COPRA and that falls into the scope of the *FTC Act*, 15 U. S. C. § 41–58, the federal law which establishes the FTC, its authority, and ways of working.[483] COPRA's comprehensive approach can also be identified in Sec. 110 (f) and (g) COPRA: For topics such as data and IT-security, entities which comply with the listed federal privacy laws including the *Fair Credit Reporting Act*, 15 U. S. C. 1681 et seq.,[484] and the *Health Insurance Portability and Accountability Act*, Public Law No. 104–191,[485] are deemed in compliance with the corresponding provisions in COPRA. In other words, although COPRA does apply to these entities (and hence across industries and sectors), they can demonstrate compliance with COPRA by meeting the IT- and data-security requirements set out in their respective sectoral privacy regulation.

As an exception to the rule, there is a carve-out from COPRA's material scope of application for companies which are not subject to the FTC Act. In other words, COPRA does not govern the processing of covered data by entities excluded from the FTC Act pursuant to § 45 (a) (2) FTC Act which extends to various types of financial institutions, airlines, and telecommunications carriers.[486] Importantly, the carve-out is not to be mistaken for a deliberate decision by COPRA to preserve the traditional sectoral approach in U.S. federal privacy law.[487] Rather, it appears the bitter pill which had to be swallowed to give the bill teeth: Exempting certain entities from COPRA's scope of application is the necessary consequence of tasking the FTC with the enforcement of the bill. The FTC has historically been the single most relevant federal agency investigating and enforcing privacy violations in the U.S.[488] Tasking the FTC to enforce COPRA meant that COPRA's material scope of application had to be crafted after the scope of application of the FTC Act and including its exemptions. The FTC's role and resources for the enforcement of COPRA will be discussed below.[489]

1. Processing activities

COPRA regulates data processing activities which it broadly defines in Sec. 2 (16) COPRA as *"any operation or set of operations performed on covered data [...]"*.[490]

483 Supra Chapter 1 A. Concept and status of U.S. privacy law.
484 Cf. Solove and Schwartz (n 60) 974–975.
485 Cf. ibid 683–684.
486 Cf. ibid 1106.
487 Supra Chapter Chapter 1 A. Concept and status of U.S. privacy law.
488 Cf. Hoofnagle (n 80) 98–100; Solove and Schwartz (n 60) 1106–1107.
489 Sub Chapter 3 E. II. 2. FTC and state authorities.
490 The objective of broadly capturing processing activities is highlighted in the COPRA report at Cantwell (n 54) 3.

COPRA focuses on electronic forms of data processing as illustrated by the bill's title Consumer *Online* Privacy Rights Act and the bill's tailored provisions on modern data-focused technology such as in Sec. 2 (2) and Sec. 108 (b) COPRA about algorithmic decision-making. Still, COPRA's scope of application is not limited to electronic processing of covered data. This follows from the broad definition in Sec. 2 (16) COPRA which includes as processing activity any *"collection, analysis, organization, structuring, retaining, using, or otherwise handling of covered data"*; given the comprehensive category of *otherwise handling* of covered data, COPRA hence equally governs physical or manual processing activities like sorting through printed lists of covered data.

The bill furthermore singles out and delineates from general processing activities the transfer of covered data to a third party in exchange for a consideration or for a commercial purpose. COPRA subjects the transfer of covered data for a commercial purpose to tailored regulation which does not apply to processing activities generally: According to Sec. 105 (b) and Sec. 2 (26) COPRA, consumers have a right to opt out of commercially motivated transfers of their covered data.[491] Thereby, the bill establishes a control mechanism not at the initial point and time of the first data disclosure but later on in the processing chain (downstream) and giving weight to how the covered data is used (output).[492] It is worth noting that for the fine-tuning within the material scope of application COPRA applies point of use regulation at the moment of the transfer of covered data for a commercial purpose and from one processing entity to another.[493] This is because the bill associates a structural risk with commercially motivated transfers of covered data. As the COPRA report explains, transfers of personal data for a commercial purpose have largely gone unregulated in the U.S.[494] For companies which capitalize on consumer profiling and targeted advertisement, this *laissez-faire* in data commercialization has brought large benefits.[495] As a common practice, they have traded with personal data without the individual's approval and often even without their knowing about it. This practice has provoked a lack of transparency about the processing of personal data, a loss of consumer control about their personal data, and sometimes digital discrimination based on personal data.[496] By applying point of

---

491 For the technical implementation COPRA suggests sub Chapter 3 D. II. 2. Privacy information management system.

492 Supra Chapter 2 B. Output and downstream regulation.

493 Supra Chapter 2 A. I. 4. Point of use of the processing activity.

494 Cantwell (n 54) 6; Hoofnagle, 'Privacy Self-Regulation: A Decade of Disappointment' (n 77) 382.

495 Cantwell (n 54) 6; Bygrave (n 59) 9.

496 Cantwell (n 54) 3, 8; Bygrave (n 59) 9; Hoofnagle, 'Privacy Self-Regulation: A Decade of Disappointment' (n 77) 382.

use regulation, COPRA is able to address privacy risks caused by data commercialization with more targeted privacy regulation, for instance, the bill proposes a new technical solution for consumers to register their opt-out against transfers in so-called *privacy information management system* which will be examined in detail below.[497]

COPRA's extensive material scope of application will likely subject the vast majority of imaginable processing activities to the bill's regulation. This may prompt critics of overregulation similar to the ones which have been voiced against the GDPR, *e.g.* that COPRA's broad scope of application burdens small- and mid-sized entities with compliance cost.[498] To this point, COPRA offers a response which builds on three risk-based elements: First, the default regulatory threshold for covered data processing is lower in COPRA than it is in other existing privacy regulation and including in EU data protection regulation. Under COPRA, entities are generally free to engage in (basic) processing activities of non-sensitive covered data without having to organize and document consent or other legally required processing justifications as known from the GDPR.[499]

Secondly, the bill leverages the risk category of data quantity to exempt from its scope of application altogether low-risk processing entities as defined in the small-entities exemption rule in Sec. 2 (9) (C) and Sec. 2 (23) COPRA; the exemption for individuals and small processing entities will be discussed in detail below together with additional COPRA provisions which build on data quantity regulation.[500]

Thirdly, COPRA substantially facilitates the work of the media by way of a legal privilege for the processing of *publicly available information* according to Sec. 105 (c) (4) and Sec. 2 (18) COPRA and of *newsworthy information of legitimate public concern to the public* according to Sec. 110 (e) COPRA. For the former, no consumer consent is necessary where the individual has consciously disclosed sensitive covered data to the public (Sec. 2 (18) COPRA);[501] the latter exempts newsworthy information from the provisions in Title I of COPRA altogether. In essence, for media-relevant information this means an opt-in consent is not required for sensitive covered data, consumers cannot opt out of the processing of their data and they have no right to request the deletion of their data. The legal privilege can be explained by the strong protection of free speech, the free flow of information, and

---

497 Sub Chapter 3 D. II. 2. Privacy information management system.

498 Cf. Institut der deutschen Wirtschaft (n 22) 12.

499 Supra Chapter 1 B. Concept and status of Eu data protection law.

500 See sub Chapter 3 C. II. 2. Quantitative assessment of covered entities; Chapter 3 E. I. 3. Certification obligations.

501 The definition of covered data and sensitive covered data will be discussed sub Chapter 3 C. I. 2. (Sensitive) covered data.

the work of the media as provided for by the First Amendment of the U.S. Constitution.[502]

It is important to point out that privacy protection under COPRA in the realm of free speech and of a free press is, however, not reduced to ashes: The effect of the language *newsworthy information of legitimate public concern* is that journalists and media houses will have to conduct a balancing test weighing individual privacy concerns against the public interest.[503] By consequence, although the (constitutional) baseline remains the unrestricted flow of information which journalists are free to use, in exceptional circumstances limitations to personal data use are imperative, *e.g.* when paramount individual privacy interests are at stake. Also, the carve-out for newsworthy information in Sec. 110 (e) COPRA does not fully exempt journalists and media houses from the regulatory scrutiny of COPRA: Despite their activities being privileged under Title I of COPRA, they remain subject to the bill's general oversight and compliance rules as set out in Title II, also with regard to their journalistic processing activities.[504]

In all, COPRA's material scope of application broadly captures the processing of covered data irrespective of specific industries or sectors. The bill thereby updates existing U.S. privacy law with a comprehensive federal privacy regulation with only a few exemptions for companies outside the scope of the FTC Act and for small entities as defined in Sec. 2 (9) (C) and Sec. 2 (23) COPRA.

2. (Sensitive) covered data

In contrast to traditional U.S. privacy law, COPRA broadly captures covered data irrespective of specific industries, sectors, or protected consumer groups.[505] In Sec. 2 (8) (A) COPRA, the bill defines as covered data any *"information that identifies, or is linked or reasonably linkable to an individual or a consumer device including derived data"*. Thereby, the bill breaks with traditional definitions of regulated data which typically mirror the U.S. sectoral focus of their respective act or regula-

---

502 Schwartz and Pfeifer (n 19), 134; European Commission, 'Commission Implementing Decision on the adequacy of the protection provided by the EU-U.S. Privacy Shield' C(2016)4176, Annex II III. 2. Journalistic Exceptions; European Commission, 'Commission Implementing Decision on the adequate level of protection of personal data under the EU-US Data Privacy Framework' (n 39) Annex I III. Supplemental Principles 2. Journalistic Exceptions.

503 Amy Gajda, 'Privacy, Press, and the Right to Be Forgotten in the United States' [2018] Washington Law Review 201, 257–259.

504 COPRA's provisions about oversight and compliance are examined sub Chapter 3 E. I. Processing entities' compliance.

505 Supra Chapter 1 A. Concept and status of U.S. privacy law.

tion: Consider, for example, the *Fair Credit Reporting Act* which only governs *"the communication of any information [...] bearing on a consumers creditworthiness, credit standing, credit capacity, character, general reputation, personal characteristics, or mode of living"*, see 15 U. S.C. 1681a,[506] and the *Health Insurance Portability and Accountability Act* which is restricted to *"protected health information"* that is *"created or received by a health care provider, health plan, public health authority, employer, life insurer, school or university, or health care clearinghouse; and relates to the past, present, or future physical or mental health or condition of an individual; the provision of health care to an individual; or the past, present, or future payment for the provision of health care to an individual"*, see 45 C.F.R. § 160.103.[507] Contrary to these narrow definitions of regulated information in existing U.S. consumer privacy law, COPRA expands its material scope of application to generally cover all personal data.

From regular covered data in Sec. 2 (8) (A) COPRA, the bill distinguishes so-called sensitive covered data as laid out in Sec. 2 (20) COPRA the processing of which triggers a higher regulatory threshold: Whereas the processing of regular covered data is generally permitted without a legal basis or the consumers' consent, the legitimate processing of sensitive covered data requires the consumers' prior affirmative express consent (opt-in) pursuant to Sec. 105 (c) (1) and (2) COPRA.[508] The delineation of sensitive covered data from general covered data is the result of an abstract evaluation of the risk the consumer faces when personal data is being processed. In existing U.S. privacy law and in European data protection law, such risk evaluation of personal data is commonly based solely on data quality or the content of the information: Data which is *"reasonably and objectively thought to be intrusive, offensive, or otherwise invade[s] personal privacy"*[509] when used illegitimately is considered sensitive data because of the harm the consumer frequently suffers when compared to the disclosure of non-sensitive personal data.[510] For instance, Art. 9 para. 1 GDPR protects as special categories of personal data information whose quality or content is thought to be particularly sensitive and formative for the data subject and her identity.[511] Remarkably, COPRA's approach to defining sensitive covered data goes beyond data quality

506 Cf. Solove and Schwartz (n 60) 974–975.

507 Cf. ibid 683–684.

508 For a detailed discussion about input versus output-based control supra Chapter 2 B. Output and downstream regulation.

509 Cf. Cate (n 30) 369; Ohm (n 182) 104–105.

510 Cf. Paul Ohm, 'Changing the Rules: General Principles for Data Use and Analysis' in Julia Lane and others (eds), Privacy, big data, and the public good (Cambridge University Press 2014) 104–105.

511 Frenzel, 'Art. 9' (n 183) para. 6.

and equally leverages the modern privacy risk categories of point of use regulation and of the use of a particular processing technology.[512]

The familiar criterion of data quality is applied to define sensitive covered data, for example, in Sec. 2 (20) (A) through (D), (H), (I), and (L) COPRA: The bill designates as sensitive covered data information whose data quality is generally viewed as intrusive when used illegitimately, for instance a consumer's social security and passport number, her health data, and any information revealing the consumer's sexual orientation. In comparison, point of use regulation is the explanation why sensitive covered data in COPRA comprises geolocation information according to Sec. 2 (20) (E) COPRA, specific covered data stored on a consumer's device according to Sec. 2 (20) (K) COPRA, and the tracking of covered data across third party websites and services as set out in Sec. 2 (20) (J) COPRA. The structural risks associated with the use of a specific modern processing technology such as big data technology are the reason why Sec. 2 (11) COPRA marks out so-called *derived data* and Sec. 2 (27) COPRA regulates *"other forms of persistent or probabilistic identifiers"*. In the below, we briefly examine each of the above examples of point of use- and of processing technology-based regulation; however, we do not attempt to suggest solutions to their shortcomings which are still apparent.

Sec. 2 (20) (E) COPRA regulates geolocation data as sensitive covered data in an effort to face a moving target. Recent studies have revealed the accuracy and effectiveness of geolocation information; in general, as little as four spatio-temporal data points suffice to identify about 95 % of individuals.[513] With the likely trend of growing technical capacities, fewer data points will be necessary to identify an individual in the future.[514] Hence, COPRA's targeted point of use regulation is a well-reasoned effort to create clarity about the regulation and strict scrutiny for geolocation data.[515]

Secondly, in Sec. 2 (20) (J) COPRA, the bill categorizes as sensitive covered data any information which is derived from tracking consumers over time and across third party websites and online services. Such third-party tracking is common practice in the U.S. and elsewhere; already in the year 2011, all of the top 100 most-visited websites in the U.S. used third-party cookies to track users.[516]

---

512 Supra Chapter 2 A. I. 3. Processing technology and 4. Point of use of the processing activity.

513 Montjoye and others (n 231); Bilogrevic (n 231) 216–220; see already supra Chapter 2 A. I. 3. Processing technology.

514 Cf. Bilogrevic (n 231) 216–220; Ohm (n 182) 105.

515 With the same suggestion to regulate geolocation data Ohm (n 182) 104–105.

516 Chris Hoofnagle and others, 'Behavioral Advertising: The Offer You Can't Refuse' 2012 Harvard Law & Policy Review 273, 280.

COPRA now acknowledges the structural risk related to third-party tracking which had previously been unregulated in the U.S.[517] COPRA's point of use regulation strives to increase transparency and control of third-party tracking by empowering consumers to decide whether their covered data can be tracked and by establishing accountability for processing entities to organize consumer's opt-in consent.

Thirdly, point of use regulation also is the reason for a strengthened protection of content on consumers' devices. According to Sec. 2 (20) (K) COPRA, specific data stored on a consumer device including calendar information, phone and text logs, photos and videos is regulated as sensitive covered data irrespective of the actual data quality or content it contains. This is because of *where* the data is stored or processed and because of the structural privacy risk commonly associated with the storage or processing location, *i.e.* the consumer's internet-connected devices. Above, we have discussed the structural risk that comes with the new *scale and degree of integration* of modern consumer devices into all aspects of everyday life and their oftentimes insufficient level of data and privacy security.[518] As a counter-measure to this structural risk, COPRA applies point of use regulation with effect similar to a *zone of privacy* around consumer devices as proposed by *Veil* and *Cohen.*[519]

Finally, COPRA applies processing technology-based regulation when it targets the methodology and characteristic elements of big data, machine-learning, and artificial intelligence technology. To this end, Sec. 2 (11) COPRA regulates so-called *derived data* which includes information obtained by statistical methods such as probabilities and deductions which are commonly used in the above named technologies: "[...] *covered data that is created by the derivation of information, data, assumptions, or conclusions from facts, evidence, or another source of information or data about an individual, household, or device used by an individual or household*". Similarly, Sec. 2 (27) COPRA captures statistical calculations commonly used in modern processing technology and which may allow identifying individuals even without traditional covered or personal data: COPRA's definition of covered data now explicitly comprises *"other forms of persistent or probabilistic identifiers that can be used to identify a particular individual, a household, or a*

517 Cf. Cantwell (n 54) 6.

518 Jeremy Siegel, 'When the Internet of Things Flounders: Looking into GDPR-Esque Security Standards for IoT Devices in the United States from the Consumers' Perspective' 2020(1) Journal of High Technology Law 189, 200–202; Peppet (n 105), 133–140; supra Chapter 2 A. I. 5. Security-privacy level of data and systems.

519 Veil (n 15), 695; Cohen (n 261) 143; Ohm (n 182) 105; generally supra Chapter 2 A. I. 4. Point of use of the processing activity.

device".[520] Embracing the fast evolution of modern data processing technology, in Sec. 2 (20) (N) COPRA the bill empowers the FTC to amend the definition of sensitive covered data if necessary.[521]

To summarize, COPRA updates existing U.S. privacy law by establishing a broad definition of covered data which spans across sectoral personal data and protected consumer groups. The bill distinguishes between general and sensitive covered data for which it sets a higher regulatory processing threshold. Starting from a general definition of sensitive covered data which is based on the classic criterion of data quality, COPRA embraces modern privacy risks by additionally designating as sensitive covered data information which is sensitive because of the point of use of the processing activity or because of the use of a particular processing technology.

II. Personal scope of application

In its personal scope of application, COPRA extends privacy protection broadly to any consumer whose covered data is being processed irrespective of a specific marketplace situation or whether the consumer belongs to particular group of vulnerable individuals. This is different from the classic approach in U.S. privacy law where the personal scope of application of a particular privacy act mirrors the regulated sector or consumer group.[522] For instance, the *Children's Online Privacy Protection Act*, 15 U. S.C. §§ 6501–6506, only protects children under the age of 13 years against websites gathering their data, see § 312.2.[523]

COPRA's approach now resembles EU data protection law where all data subjects are protected according to Art. 4 para 1 in connection with Art. 1 para. 1 and Art. 2 para. 1 GDPR. However, COPRA does not follow the EU's one-size-fits-all approach of equally regulating all data controllers, irrespective of their size and of the personal data they process.[524] Instead, the bill applies data quantity-based regulation to distinguish between low-, moderate-, and high-risk processing entities and

520 There are indications that modern processing technology in the near future no longer depends and is increasingly able to circumvent the use of covered data or personal data to identify an individual, cf. Gasser (n 11) 200; Ohm (n 182) 105; Barocas and Nissenbaum (n 216) 55–56; Solove, 'Privacy Self-Management and the Consent Dilemma' (n 78) 1889–1890; generally supra Chapter 2 A. I. 3. Processing technology.

521 This answers to the call that regulation must remain flexible and contain tools to keep up with the fast evolution in modern processing technology, cf. Ohm (n 182) 104–105.

522 For the traditional approach, see supra Chapter 1 A. Concept and status of U.S. privacy law.

523 Cf. Solove and Schwartz (n 60) 1157–1159.

524 Cf. Albrecht and Jotzo (n 151) 64; von Lewinski, 'Art. 2' (n 63) para. 5.

persons.[525] As we will examine in the below, by treating each of these categories of processing entities differently, COPRA has more flexibility to adjust regulation to specific processing entities then has the GDPR.[526]

1. Protection of the consumer

By its title *Consumer* Online Privacy Rights Act and several of its provisions such as Sec. 2 (8) (A) and Sec. 2 (16) COPRA, the bill protects the U.S. consumer irrespective of any marketplace situation or of her qualification as a vulnerable consumer as protected under *e.g.* the *Children's Online Privacy Protection Act*, 15 U. S.C. §§ 6501–6506.[527] As the exception to the rule, in Sec. 2 (8) (B) (ii) COPRA, the bill excludes from its personal scope of application employees, *i.e.* consumers or individuals who act in the context of an employment relationship.[528]

Unlike German or EU legal terminology might suggest (*Verbraucher* as defined in § 13 German Civil Code), COPRA's personal scope of application is not restricted to a business-to-consumer interaction, for instance as typically found in a purchasing situation; instead, the bill protects the individual or natural person generally. COPRA alike existing U.S. federal privacy law uses the term *consumer* interchangeably with the terms individual or person.[529] This can be seen in Sec. 2 (14) COPRA which defines the individual as any "*natural person residing in the U.S.*". Also, in the definition of covered data in Sec. 2 (8) (A) COPRA, the bill references to data which allows to identify "*an individual or a consumer device*". Similarly, Sec. 105 (b) (2) (B) (ii) COPRA uses both terms interchangeably when it calls for "*clear and conspicuous opt-out notices and consumer friendly mechanisms to allow an individual to opt out of transfers of covered data*". More broadly in U.S. federal privacy law, the interchangeable use of the terminology can be found in the 1988 *Video Privacy Protection Act*, 18 U.S. Code § 2710, which defines in § 2710 (a) (1) the term *consumer* and already in § 2710 (a) (3) uses the term *person* instead of consumer in its definition of personal identifiable information: "*information which identifies a person as having requested or obtained specific video materials or service materials from a video tape service provider*".

525 Supra Chapter 2 A. I. 1. Data quantity.

526 Sub Chapter 3 C. II. 2. Quantitative assessment of covered entities and Chapter 3 E. I. 3. Certification obligations.

527 Cf. Solove and Schwartz (n 60) 1157–1159.

528 For clarity, employment-related data processing is in the scope and subject to COPRA's point of use regulation, sub Chapter 3 D. I. 2. a. Point of use regulation.

529 Cf. the use of terminology in Hoofnagle, 'Privacy Self-Regulation: A Decade of Disappointment' (n 77) 397–398; Solove and Schwartz (n 60) 1031–1037.

A likely explanation of the terminology in COPRA and in U.S. privacy law is the origins of privacy law in the U.S.: Historically, U.S. privacy law has addressed shortcomings in the marketplace, a situation in which the individual who faces a counterpart, typically a business, is commonly referred to as the *consumer*.[530]

Hence, in comparison to existing U.S. federal privacy law, COPRA protects the individual broadly irrespective of a marketplace situation or any qualification as a vulnerable consumer group.

2. Quantitative assessment of covered entities

COPRA applies data quantity-based regulation to distinguish between different sizes of entities and the quantity of data they process and offers tailored regulation based on the associated risk levels.[531] There are different rules for three categories of processing entities: According to Sec. 2 (9) (C) and Sec. 2 (23) COPRA, small businesses are exempted from COPRA's scope of application altogether, the majority of the bill's processing provisions applies to (general) covered entities as described in Sec. 2 (9) (A) and (C) together with Sec. 101 COPRA; finally, additional rules apply to large data companies above the threshold set in Sec. 2 (15) COPRA in comparison to general covered entities. How does COPRA measure the size and the data quantity of a processing entity? Generally speaking, the bill stipulates for an integrated assessment over a given period of time of the company's volume of sales, of the percentage of revenue the company attributes to data commercialization, and of the quantity and quality of covered data the processing entity processes.

According to Sec. 2 (23) together with Sec. 2 (9) (C) COPRA, small businesses are exempted from COPRA's scope of application when they meet the cumulative criteria of an annual average gross revenue of less than 25 million USD in 3 consecutive years, whereby only less than 50 % of their revenue may be attributed to the commercial trading of covered data, and in any year the processing of covered data does not exceed 100,000 individuals, households, or devices. Effectively, Sec. 2 (23) together with Sec. 2 (9) (C) COPRA excludes from COPRA's scope of application any small scale processing of covered data including person-to-person or household communication. This is a very valid effort of COPRA to spare low-risk processing of covered data from potentially burdensome privacy regulation in daily life and per-

530 Supra Chapter 1 A. Concept and status of U.S. privacy law.
531 Supra Chapter 2 A. I. 1. Data quantity.

sonal settings such as in small mom-and-pop stores or intra-community communication.[532]

Instead, the bill's privacy regulation focuses on covered data processing above this *de minimis* threshold. Notably, COPRA designates a medium processing risk to general processing entities which process the data quantity of at least 100,000 but less than 5 million individuals, devices, or households annually. According to Sec. 2 (20) COPRA, the threshold covers both the processing of general covered data and of its subcategory of sensitive covered data. Importantly, however, *e contrario* Sec. 2 (15) COPRA it follows that a medium processing risk is justified only to the extent a processing entity does not process sensitive covered data of 100,000 or more individuals, households, or devices.

If a processing entity has processed in any given year sensitive covered data of 100,000 or more individuals, devices, or households, it qualifies as a high-risk large data holder according to Sec. 2 (15) COPRA and must comply with additional COPRA provisions which we will discuss further below.[533] The threshold for the processing of general covered data to qualify as a large data holder is met when a processing entity process general covered data of 5 million or more individuals, devices, or households. Here, the filter of sensitive covered data within the framework of data quantity regulation works as a catalyst and quality control: The bill associates an elevated structural risk with the processing of sensitive covered data and compared to the processing of regular covered data; hence, processing entities which process a high quantity of sensitive covered data qualify as high-risk large data holders earlier than other processing entities which process general covered data.[534]

In sum, COPRA applies data quantity-based privacy regulation and data regulation on a sliding scale as visualized in figure 4 below when it treats processing entities and persons differently according to the risk associated with their respective processing activities. Thereby, the bill spares low-risk processing activities, entities, and persons from potentially burdensome implementation and compliance costs while putting extra scrutiny on companies whose data practices have frequently been shown to be prone to elevated privacy risks.[535]

532 Similarly, Solove and Schwartz, 'ALI Data Privacy: Overview and Black Letter Text' (n 95) 1265, who call to exclude low-risk personal data processing such as person-to-person communication from the scope of application of their model privacy law cf. Chapter 1 § 1 (b) (2); cf. Institut der deutschen Wirtschaft (n 18) 12.

533 Sub Chapter 3 E. I. 3. Certification obligations.

534 Supra Chapter 3 C. I. 2. (Sensitive) covered data.

535 Cf. Solove, 'Privacy Self-Management and the Consent Dilemma' (n 78) 1881, 1889–1890; Scholz, 'Private rights of action in privacy law' (n 160) 1678–1683.

Figure 4: Data quantity-based privacy regulation

III. Territorial scope of application

COPRA's privacy regulation reaches beyond U.S. boarders. The bill's privacy provisions apply to covered processing entities irrespective of whether they are registered or operate from within or from outside of U.S. territory as long as they process a U.S. consumer's covered data. This can be derived from Sec. 2 (14) together with Sec. 2 (8) and Sec. 101 (a) COPRA which set out that data of *"any natural person residing in the U.S."* is protected, irrespective of the legal or operational seat of the processing entity whereby covered. Notably, the use of the terms *residing* in Sec. 2 (14) COPRA and *resident* in Sec. 301 (b) (1) COPRA and Sec. 301 (b) (1) (C) COPRA indicates that a mere passing-through or short-term visit to the U.S. would not suffice to qualify for COPRA privacy protection or for a processing entity to be subject to COPRA upon the processing of a visitor's personal data; instead, a prolonged stay and the administrative status of residency is the required trigger for COPRA's applicability.

COPRA's transborder territorial scope of application resembles the GDPR's market-centered approach (*Marktortprinzip*): In Art. 3 (2) GDPR, the EU privacy regulation subjects to its rule data controllers without an EU establishment when they offer goods or services to data subjects in Europe or monitor behavior of people in the EU.[536] Given that today the processing of covered data can technically be executed from anywhere in the world provided there is internet connectivity, COPRA's broad extraterritorial applicability appears necessary to effectively protect U.S. consumers' privacy expectations. In fact, recent history demonstrates how covered data of U.S. consumers was misused by foreign processing entities without any physical or legal presence in the U.S.: *Musical.ly*, a corporation registered in

536 Kai von Lewinski, 'Art. 3' in Martin Eßer, Philipp Kramer and Kai von Lewinski (eds), *DSGVO/BDSG* (Carl Heymanns Verlag 2023) para. 11–20; Hennemann, 'Wettbewerb der Datenschutzrechtsordnungen' (n 19) 879–882; Streinz (n 12) 34–35.

the Cayman Islands with a principal place of business in Shanghai, China, which later merged into the social-media provider *TikTok* has been found to illegitimately process personal data of children in the U.S.[537]

D. Regulating data processing activities

The core of the update to existing U.S. privacy law are COPRA's provisions regulating the processing of covered data. To examine the second hypothesis of this study whether COPRA is a capacity-apt privacy regulation which effectively addresses the modern privacy risks illustrated in Chapter 2, we will discuss in the below which building blocks for a modern privacy law the bill introduces to U.S. privacy law and whether and how some of the bill's new concepts and means embrace the technical capacities of modern data-focused technology and the human (in)capacities commonly found when consumers use and interact with modern technology.[538]

This chapter primarily looks at COPRA's Title I – Data Privacy Rights, Sec. 101–110 COPRA. In Sec. 102–105 COPRA, the bill introduces data rights of the individual consumer so they can better control how their covered data is processed. In Sec. 101, 106–110 COPRA, the bill establishes guardrails to covered data processing which bind processing entities irrespective of an individual consumer's taking action, hence they fall into the category of collective privacy as defined in Chapter 2.[539] We will structure our analysis of the COPRA processing provisions by starting with the latter set of rules which govern collective privacy (sub Chapter 3 C. I. Data rights of the collective) before we examine COPRA's data rights of the individual consumer (sub Chapter 3 C. II. Data rights of the individual consumer).

---

537 Federal Trade Commission, 'USA v Musical.ly, complaint for civil penalties' (2019) 4 <https://www.ftc.gov/system/files/documents/cases/musical.ly_complaint_ecf_2-27-19.pdf> accessed 15 July 2022.

538 Supra Chapter 2 Building blocks for a modern privacy law.

539 Supra Chapter 2 A. II. 3. Individual and collective privacy.

I. Data rights of the collective

Privacy is an essential supra-individual value and privacy regulation can work as an important tool for the greater good of the collective.[540] We discussed arguments and examples of the collective dimension of privacy regulation above in Chapter 2 A. II. 3. Individual and collective privacy. For instance, while privacy regulation has traditionally focused on preventing processing entities from engaging in harmful processing activities, it can equally influence how covered data is used for advancements in medicine and to foster innovation generally.[541]

Compared to existing U.S. consumer privacy law, privacy as a supra-individual value and the appreciation of how it contributes to the greater good of society seems to be a relatively new notion.[542] Only on a state level and not in statutory law, and, as far as can be seen, not on a federal level has U.S. privacy law conspicuously addressed covered data processing from an angle of collective privacy.[543] Inspired by the European data protection regulation and its *Principles related to the processing of personal data* in Art. 5 GDPR, the *California Consumer Privacy Act of 2018*, California Civil Code § 1798.100–178.199, first introduced on a state level generally binding processing guardrails which regulate processing activities irrespective of an individual consumer's taking action.[544] In § 1798.100 (a) (1) California Consumer Privacy Act, the law stipulates for businesses to inform consumers about the purpose for which personal identifiable information is collected and used and to respect the limitations of the disclosed processing purpose; the preceding EU example clearly is the purpose limitation principle in Art. 5 para. 1 lit. b GDPR.[545] According to § 1798.100 (a) (3) California Consumer Privacy Act, businesses must furthermore inform about and adhere to time limitations when storing personal identifiable information, an obligation crafted after the EU principle of storage limitation in Art. 5 para. 1 lit. e GDPR.[546] Finally, pursuant to § 1798.100 (c) California Consumer Privacy Act, businesses may only collect, use, retain, or share personal

540 Cohen (n 261) 148f.; Solove, 'The Myth of the Privacy Paradox' (n 155) 34; Solove, 'Privacy Self-Management and the Consent Dilemma' (n 78) 1881; Gasser (n 11) 198; Hoffmann-Riem (n 3) 111–112.

541 Cf. Determann, 'Healthy Data Protection' (n 16) 262–265, 277.

542 Cf. Determann (n 8) 128.

543 The *Fair Information Practices Principles* in their form of the *Privacy Act of 1974* only bind the state and not processing entities cf. Streinz (n 12) 909; Glocker points out that the principle of purpose limitation and of data minimization is anchored in the Californian Constitution, Glocker (n 91) 166–171.

544 Voss, 'Cross-Border Data Flows, the GDPR, and Data Governance' (n 477) 498–499; Glocker (n 91) 230–232.

545 Cf. Frenzel, 'Art. 5' (n 183) para. 23–25.

546 Cf. ibid para. 14–18.

identifiable information to the extent it is reasonably necessary and proportionate to achieve the disclosed processing purpose.[547] Despite some difference in wording, the objective of the provision appears to be crafted after the EU principle of data minimization in Art. 5 para. 1 lit. c GDPR.[548]

Strikingly, COPRA takes collective privacy regulation a step further than even the progressive *Californian Consumer Privacy Act*. In addition to the above cited generally applicable processing principles which reappear in COPRA, albeit not in identical wording,[549] the bill closely embraces the concept of collective privacy in an unprecedented way: First and foremost, Sec. 101 COPRA stipulates a generally applicable fair processing standard focused on the processing output and according to which processing entities and persons must adhere to good data practices which benefit the collective (sub Chapter 3 D. I. 1. COPRA's fair processing standard). Furthermore, Sec. 108 (a) and (b) COPRA apply point of use regulation and processing technology-based regulation as described supra in Chapter 2 to set generally applicable guardrails for processing entities irrespective of an individual consumer's privacy preference or choice (sub Chapter 3 D. I. 2. Point of use regulation and regulation of data quality and sub Chapter 3 D. I. 3. Regulating specific processing technology). Finally, the collective dimension of privacy is the main driver for the COPRA provisions related to preventing processing entities from contractually abridging consumers' privacy rights in Sec. 109 COPRA, to establish adequate security-privacy levels of data and systems according to Sec. 107 (a) and (b) COPRA, and to tackle the privacy risk caused by forged content on the internet as regulated in Sec. 205 COPRA (sub Chapter 3 D. I. 5. Purpose limitation, data minimization, limitations on waivers of privacy rights; Chapter 3 D. I. 6. Data security; Chapter 3 D. I. 7. Digital content forgery).

1. COPRA's fair processing standard

Under the title of *duty of loyalty*, Sec. 101 COPRA establishes a fair data processing standard for processing entities which reads

> *(a) In General: A covered entity shall not*
>
> *(1) engage in a deceptive data practice or a harmful data practice; or*
> *(2) process or transfer covered data in a manner that violates any provision of this Act.*

547 Glocker (n 91) 169–171.

548 Cf. Roßnagel (n 18) para. 118–121.

549 Sub Chapter 3 D. I. 5. Purpose limitation, data minimization, limitations on waivers of privacy rights.

(b) Definitions

(1) Deceptive data practice: The term "deceptive data practice" means an act or practice involving the processing or transfer of covered data in a manner that constitutes a deceptive act or practice in violation of section 5(a)(1) of the Federal Trade Commission Act (15 U. S. C. 45(a)(1)).
(2) Harmful data practice: The term "harmful data practice" means the processing or transfer of covered data in a manner that causes or is likely to cause any of the following:

(A) Financial, physical, or reputational injury to an individual.
(B) Physical or other offensive intrusion upon the solitude or seclusion of an individual or the individual's private affairs or concerns, where such intrusion would be offensive to a reasonable person.
(C) Other substantial injury to an individual.

In scope with the bill's scope of application, the fair processing standard in Sec. 101 COPRA binds processing entities generally and for all of their processing activities in the form of a catch-all provision (*Generalklausel*), it applies across industries and sectors and protects consumers irrespective of their personal privacy preferences or choices.[550] It follows that the overall objective of Sec. 101 COPRA is to ensure a commonly applicable standard of covered data use which can generally be regarded as fair for the individual and the collective.[551]

Sec. 101 COPRA defines what constitutes fair data processing by combining both open and adaptive language and a link to legal privacy standards that are well-established in U.S. privacy statute and case law. On the one hand, Sec. 101 (a) (1) 2nd alternative COPRA in combination with Sec. 101 (b) (2) (A) and (C) COPRA prohibit any harmful data practice "*likely to cause* [...] *financial, physical, or reputational injury*" or any "*other substantial injury to an individual*" and Sec. 101 (a) (2) COPRA bans any processing or processing result which violates a COPRA provision. On the other hand, Sec. 101 (a) (1) 1st alternative COPRA together with Sec. 101 (b) (1) COPRA link to the FTC standard in § 45(a)(1) FTC Act which bars any "*deceptive act or practice*" and Sec. 101 (a) (1) 2nd alternative COPRA in connection with Sec. 101 (b) (2) (B) COPRA incorporate into COPRA established U.S. privacy case law which we will examine in more detail in the below.[552]

This hybrid approach of combining a broad COPRA definition of a harmful data practice or violation of the bill together with the reference to established priv-

550 Supra Chapter 3 C. Scope of application.
551 Supportive of the idea of a fair processing standard for instance Veil (n 15), 695; von Lewinski, 'Einführung' (n 17) para. 13; Solove, 'Privacy Self-Management and the Consent Dilemma' (n 78) 1901–1902; Solove, 'The Myth of the Privacy Paradox' (n 155) 50; supra Chapter 2 A. II. 3. Individual and collective privacy.
552 Solove and Schwartz (n 60) 67–68, 1105, 1270; Solove and Hartzog (n 385), 628–638.

acy thresholds can prove advantageous in at least two ways: First, the open and adaptive language in Sec. 101 (a) (1) 2nd alternative, (b) (2) (A) and (C) CORPA enables the bill to evolve over time, to qualify illegitimate processing or transfer activities according to context and situations, and to integrate privacy expectations of individuals, groups of individuals and of society. What constitutes fair data processing can be constantly refined and rebalanced considering the technical and human (in)capacities which influence the output. This capacity of COPRA to adapt to evolving change is a key factor to be able to strike the right risk balance in covered data use between protection and enablement.[553] By contrast, EU data protection regulation's rigid input-control appears less receptive of data processing context, situations, and evolving privacy expectations.[554]

Secondly, the reference in Sec. 101 (a) (1) 1st alternative, (b) (1) COPRA and Sec. 101 (a) (1) 2nd alternative COPRA, (b) (2) (B) COPRA to well-established U.S. privacy thresholds provides legal certainty and guidance in the framework of an otherwise new and untested privacy law for companies to plan and implement privacy-compliant business behavior, for the FTC to operate and enforce on a clear mandate, and for the judiciary to leverage existing case law and to arrive at coherent new decisions. In Sec. 101 (a) (1) 1st alternative, (b) (1) COPRA, the bill links to Sec. 5(a)(1) FTC Act, 15 U. S. C. 45(a)(1), which reads: "*unfair or deceptive acts or practices in or affecting commerce* [...] *are hereby declared unlawful.*" Since the FTC was first tasked to enforce consumer privacy in 1995, the definition has developed into a set of rule-like categories of illegitimate business practices which processing entities must avoid when engaging in data processing activities.[555] For instance, the FTC has held as deceptive acts or practices when companies did not adhere to their privacy promises, both explicitly stated in their privacy policy or implied, *e.g.* when they disregarded consumers' registered privacy settings and preferences, or how companies obtained personal data.[556] Notably, COPRA only references to *deceptive* acts or practices in Sec. 5(a)(1) FTC Act, 15 U. S. C. 45(a)(1), not to the FTC provision's mentioning of an *unfair* act or practice. The reason is to preserve the autonomous interpretation of COPRA's own fair processing definition as set out in Sec. 101 (a) (1) and (2) COPRA which is not identical to the FTC standard of an unfair act or practice, for instance, because it encloses the COPRA definition of a harmful data act in Sec. 101 (a) (1) 2nd alternative, (b) (2) (A) and (C) CORPA as well as existing U.S. privacy case law in torts in Sec. 101 (a) (1) 2nd alternative, (b) (2) (B) COPRA.

553 Cf. Hennemann, 'Wettbewerb der Datenschutzrechtsordnungen' (n 19) 868; von Lewinski, 'Einführung' (n 17) para. 34–36; Schaub (n 265) 345–362.

554 Cf. Frenzel, 'Frenzel, Art. 9' (n 181) para. 6; cf. Gasser (n 11) 197; Hoeren (n 172), 10.

555 Solove and Schwartz (n 60) 1105.

556 Solove and Hartzog (n 387), 628–638; Solove and Schwartz (n 60) 1270.

In Sec. 101 (a) (1) 2nd alternative, (b) (2) (B) COPRA, the bill stipulates as a harmful data practice a *"physical or other offensive intrusion upon the solitude or seclusion of the individual or the individual's private affairs or concerns, where such intrusion would be offensive to a reasonable person"*. With minor linguistic adaptions, this definition is crafted after the privacy tort standard as set out in Restatement (Second) of Torts § 652B. Its origins date back to as early as 1960 when *William Prosser*, a U.S. legal scholar, laid out four privacy torts of which the above-said *intrusion upon seclusion* tort is the first.[557] The intrusion upon seclusion tort focuses on *how* information is obtained, *i.e.* whether the collection of the information was facilitated by an intrusive behavior.[558] Until today, the so-called *Prosser privacy torts* are governing U.S. tort law and heavily influence how U.S. legal scholars and practitioners think about and practice privacy law.[559]

Finally, it is worth noting that COPRA's fair processing standard applies output-based regulation in its assessment of processing activities.[560] In contrast to input regulation alike in Art. 6 para. 1 and Art. 9 para. 1 and 2 GDPR, Sec. 101 (a) (1) and (2) COPRA focuses on the processing result or output, for instance in Sec. 101 (a) (2) COPRA which asks whether the outcome of a processing activity "[…] *violates any provision of this Act*". But it is not only an undesired processing result which may render a processing activity or processing output unfair in the sense of Sec. 101 COPRA. COPRA's fair processing standard applies an output-based control broadly when it also scrutinizes whether the processing activity as such is objectionable: Both the term data *practice* in Sec. 101 (a) (1), (b) (1) COPRA and the expression *"process*[ing] *or transfer of covered data in a manner that* […]" in Sec. 101 (a) (2), (b) (2) COPRA give evidence to the fact that the COPRA fair processing standard encompasses a control about *how* covered data is processed, not only *to which effect*. In line with our arguments in the above, COPRA's choice for output-based regulation is laudable because output-based regulation in privacy is generally better suited to mitigate against the technical capacities of modern data-focused technology and to embrace common human (in)capacities such as ignorance or passivity about data processing.[561]

To summarize, the fair processing standard in Sec. 101 (a) (1) and (2) COPRA broadly binds processing entities to process covered data in compliance with the

557 Cf. Solove and Schwartz (n 60) 67–68.

558 Ibid 135.

559 Cf. ibid 68–69; cf. European Commission, 'Commission Decision on the adequacy of the protection provided by the safe harbour principles and related frequently asked questions issued by the US Department of Commerce' C(2000)2441, Annex IV A. Damages for Breaches of Privacy.

560 Supra Chapter 2 B. Output and downstream regulation.

561 Supra Chapter 2 B. Output and downstream regulation.

bill and without harm to the individual or the collective. To this end, COPRA applies broad output-based control by combining a new definition of a harmful data practice and references to established and well-respected thresholds in U.S. privacy law. The bill thereby provides flexibility to adjust to evolving context while providing legal certainty and continuity in privacy law to the benefit of the U.S. judiciary and processing entities.

2. Point of use regulation and regulation of data quality

An update to existing U.S. consumer privacy law and, as far as can be seen, to privacy law globally is COPRA's paternalistic – albeit limited in scope to a finite number of clearly identified risk situations – point of use regulation in Sec. 108 (a) COPRA which protects individuals and the collective by way of a strict processing ban against discriminatory processing activities and processing results.

Alike Sec. 101 (a) COPRA, Sec. 108 (a) COPRA targets processing entities and owners of technical capacities and does not depend on the action of the individual consumer.[562] Focusing on the processing entities and owners of technical capacities rather than on the individual consumer is a consequence of COPRA's acknowledging that human (in)capacities frequently cloud or render impossible good decision-making by individuals when they are exposed to covered data processing. As discussed in Chapter 2 A. II. 1. Intellectual (in)capacity, an individual consumer's consent often appears but a fiction in situations in which the consumer is confronted with a take-it-or-leave-it situation or in which high-stake goods or services are contingent upon the disclosure and consent to process the consumers' covered data.[563] Consumers' cognitive limitations lead to and reinforce common human behavioral (in)capacity vis-à-vis modern data-focused technology when consumers show passivity, ignorance, and disinterest instead of acting on their data rights when they are entitled to do so.[564]

Despite the fact that privacy regulation which gravitates around the individual consumer can provide only imperfect protection, the alternative of setting privacy regulation to solely focus on processing entities or to run on government-defined processing preferences and rules without regard to individual privacy preference and choice would mean contradicting fundamental beliefs and constitutional

562 Owners of technical capacities are defined supra Chapter 2 A. II. Human (in)capacities.

563 Kramer, 'Art. 6' (n 104) para. 25; Hoffmann-Riem (n 3) 166; Veil (n 15), 686, 688–689; Solove, 'Privacy Self-Management and the Consent Dilemma' (n 50) 1881; Zuiderveen Borgesius and others (n 30); Cate (n 30) 364–365; Maisch (n 238) 298.

564 Specht (n 298) 422; European Commission (n 29) 2; Voigt (n 28) 93; Ebner, 'Information Overload 2.0?' (n 28) 365–366; generally supra Chapter 2 A. II. 2. Behavioral (in)capacity.

rights of autonomy and self-determination of the individual both in the U.S. and the EU: In U.S. consumer privacy law, the individual is seen as innately sovereign to decide how her personal data is being processed; in the EU model, in particular Art. 8 para. 2 EU CFR clearly shows that the data subject's consent to the processing of her data is enshrined in EU data protection law.[565] Thus, a purely paternalistic privacy regulation with government-defined processing rules which ignore individual consumers' privacy preferences and choices is no feasible alternative either.

This is why COPRA choses a processing baseline which values individual consumers' privacy preferences, *e.g.* consumers can demand the deletion of their covered data pursuant to Sec. 103 COPRA and opt-out of unwanted transfers according to Sec. 105 (b) (1) COPRA, to which the bill applies, as an exception to the rule, the paternalistic processing ban in Sec. 108 (a) COPRA which disregards individual privacy choices. The exception is clearly circumscribed and limited in scope to high-risk processing situations by a combination of point of use regulation, data quality regulation, and output-based regulation.[566] In a few narrowly defined high-risk point of use situations (to be discussed in detail sub Chapter 3 D. I. 2. a. Point of use regulation), Sec. 108 (a) COPRA bans the processing of a set of specific covered data or data quality (to be examined sub Chapter 3 D. I. 2. b. Regulated data quality) when the processing activity or the processing result (*i.e.* output-based regulation) proves discriminatory for the individual consumer or the collective.

Remarkably, in the realm of the Sec. 108 (a) COPRA processing ban not even the individual's express consent or a balancing test with other conflicting interests may justify the processing of covered data. COPRA thereby goes beyond Art. 6 para. 1 and Art. 9 para. 1 GDPR which generally prohibit the processing of personal data and special categories of personal data but nonetheless leave room for alternative processing justifications when the consumer's consent is not present, for instance, the processing of personal data may be permissible to pursue a legitimate interest of the data controller according to Art. 6 para. 1 lit. f GDPR and the processing of special categories of personal data may be justified according to Art. 9 para. 2 lit. h GDPR when it serves preventive or occupational medicine.[567] To this point, it is worth noting that outside of EU data protection law, the *EU Digital Services Act* has recently introduced an obligation similar to the one in Sec. 108 (a) COPRA applicable to the providers of online platforms as defined in Art. 3 lit. i EU

565 Schwartz and Pfeifer (n 19), 132, 155–156; Leonie Wittershagen, *The Transfer of Personal Data from the European Union to the United Kingdom post-Brexit* (De Gruyter 2023) 11–12; Paal and Pauly (n 317) para. 16; supra Chapter 1 The privacy landscape in the U.S. and the EU.

566 The categories are presented supra Chapter 2 A. I. 2. Data quality, 4. Point of use of the processing activity, and Chapter 2 B. Output and downstream regulation.

567 Kramer, 'Art. 6' (n 104) para. 64–89; Greve, 'Art. 9' (n 199) para. 31–33.

Data Services Act: According to Art. 26 para. 3 Digital Services Act and Recital 69 sentence 3 Digital Services Act, providers of online platforms are now banned from using Art. 9 para. 1 GDPR special categories of personal data for targeted advertisement based on profiling.[568]

Like EU data protection law, existing U.S. consumer privacy law including the progressive *California Consumer Privacy Act* of 2018, California Civil Code § 1798.100–178.199, equally lacks a processing ban similar to Sec. 108 (a) COPRA. The closest resemblance bears § 1798.125 California Consumer Privacy Act according to which "*business shall not discriminate against a consumer because the consumer exercised any of the consumer's rights under this title*". Although the provision is output-oriented by prohibiting discriminatory processing results, it does not go as far as to prohibit the processing of specific data quality and in specific point of use situations as such. Hence, the processing ban in Sec. 108 (a) COPRA is broader and more nuanced than § 1798.125 California Consumer Privacy Act.

In all, COPRA's output-based processing ban in Sec. 108 (a) COPRA is new compared to existing U.S. privacy law and to the GDPR. It opts for paternalistic privacy protection in a limited scope to protect the individual and the collective against discriminatory processing practices and results.

a. Point of use regulation

The point of use situations in which the output-based processing ban applies are exhaustively listed in Sec. 108 (a) (1) (A) COPRA: The bill deems as high-risk processing situations commercially motivated processing activities which are linked to housing, employment, credit, and education.[569] With regard to employment situations and given that COPRA's material scope of application excludes the processing of employee data within an employer employee relationship according to Sec. 2 (8) (B) (ii), (12) COPRA, Sec. 108 (a) COPRA applies to all other employment-related processing activities outside of this relationship such as a job search or an application.

In line with the considerations in Chapter 2 about point of use regulation, COPRA singles out these situations because it associates with them structural privacy risks which are commonly not found in ordinary processing situations. In short, decisions related to housing, employment, credit, and education are often high-stake for consumers because a large sum of money, a long-term commitment, or a potentially life-impacting opportunity is at stake, and, by consequence, an

---

568 Simon Gerdemann and Gerald Spindler, 'Das Gesetz über digitale Dienste (Digital Services Act) (Teil 2)' 2023 GRUR 115, 119.

569 Generally on the concept supra Chapter 2 A. I. 4. Point of use of the processing activity.

unfavorable decision is likely to have a considerable impact on their life. Moreover, these situations are frequently characterized by a power and information imbalance between the consumer and the other party.[570] In the U.S. and following some notorious business malpractice, the point of use situations of housing, employment, credit, and education have been the subject of vivid discussion both in academia and in public media which has led, in some instances, to targeted regulation which pre-dates COPRA.[571]

How does the point of use regulation in Sec. 108 (a) COPRA compare to the protection provided for data subjects under the GDPR? The latter addresses the structural privacy risk of information and power imbalance not by point of use regulation but within the category of free consent, hence, actor-focused in the relation between data controller and data subject. According to Art. 4 para. 11, 6 para. 1 lit. a, 9 para. 2 lit. a together with Recital 43 sentence 1 and Recital 42 sentence 5 GDPR, consent is no valid legal ground for a processing activity *"in a specific case where there is a clear imbalance between the data subject and the controller, in particular where the controller is a public authority and it is therefore unlikely that consent was freely given in all the circumstances of that specific situation"*. The GDPR expressly calls out personal data processing by public authorities in which the data subject is subordinated to the authority of the government (*Über-/Unterordnungsverhältnis*), a situation in which she lacks the freedom to decide about how and which subject matter to contract about because the contract principles of freedom of contract (*Vertragsfreiheit*) and private autonomy (*Privatautonomie*) do not apply.[572] Here, the historic roots of EU data protection law show when the GDPR focuses on protecting the data subject against personal data processing by the government.[573] Similar situations of subordination can be argued in an educational setting where a school or university acts as a body of public law, or in an employment relationship in which the employee must fear negative consequences if she opposes her employer's request to process her personal data.[574]

We can see from the above how the protection provided by the GDPR's free consent-filter and Sec. 108 (a) COPRA overlap in the processing situations of educa-

---

570 Cf. Ebner, *Weniger ist Mehr?* (n 29) 190–191.

571 Katyal (n 52), 56; Cantwell (n 54) 8; for example, the Equal Credit Opportunity Act (15 U. S.C. 1691 et seq.); the Fair Credit Reporting Act (15 U. S.C. 1681 et seq.); and the Fair Housing Act (42 U. S.C. 3601 et seq.).

572 Martin Eßer, 'Art. 4' in Martin Eßer, Philipp Kramer and Kai von Lewinski (eds), *DSGVO/BDSG* (Carl Heymanns Verlag 2023) para. 102.

573 Supra Introduction; Detterbeck (n 13) para. 504; Veil (n 15), 686, 689.

574 Stefan Ernst, 'Art. 4' in Boris Paal and Daniel Pauly (eds), *DSGVO, BDSG* (C.H. Beck 2021) para. 71; Eßer, 'Art. 4' (n 571) para. 102.

tion and employment (to the extent covered by Sec. 108 (a)). By contrast, in a business-to-consumer processing situation which is shaped by the principles of freedom of contract and private autonomy such as in the high-risk situations of housing and credit, the GDPR's free consent-filter would likely fail. Consequently, COPRA's Sec. 108 (a) COPRA seems more apt than the GDPR to address structural privacy risks in business-to-consumer processing situations. Taking into account that the majority of data processing today occurs in the private realm and government-controlled processing is marginal, COPRA provides broader and more effective protection for consumers in the point of use situations regulated by Sec. 108 (a) COPRA.[575]

b. Regulated data quality

Sec. 108 (a) (1) COPRA lists as regulated data quality *"an individual's or class of individuals actual or perceived race, color, ethnicity, religion, national origin, sex, gender, gender identity, sexual orientation, familial status, biometric information, lawful source of income, or disability"*. All of the listed covered data individually and conjointly represent human qualities which are particularly sensitive because they define the individual's identity (although many of them are listed also as sensitive covered data in Sec. 2 (20) COPRA, they are not identical); any one or several of these qualities can easily be misused to discriminate against consumers.[576] The enumerated data quality partly overlaps with and exceeds the list of special categories of personal data in Art. 9 para. 1 GDPR. Whereas Sec. 108 (a) (1) COPRA covers national origin, gender, gender identity, familial status, and lawful source of income which are not named in Art. 9 para. 1 GDPR, unlike COPRA the EU provision additionally lists trade union membership and political opinions.[577] Both provisions aim at preventing discriminatory data processing by subjecting designated data quality to a higher regulatory threshold than regular covered data.[578]

Interestingly, Sec. 108 (a) (1) COPRA and Art. 9 para. 1 GDPR use a different technical regulatory approach to prevent discrimination. Whereas Art. 9 para. 1 GDPR follows a strict input-based regulatory approach by directly prohibiting the processing of the special categories of personal data unless a legal justification as set out in Art. 9 para. 2 lit. a-j GDPR is present, Sec. 108 (a) (1), (a) (1) (B) COPRA prohibits the processing of any *"covered data on the basis"* of the regulated data quality and *"in a manner that unlawfully segregates, discriminates against, or otherwise*

575 Cf. Cantwell (n 54) 9.

576 Cf. ibid 8; Ohm (n 182) 104–105; Katyal (n 52), 56, 71–73; Cate (n 30) 369.

577 Greve, 'Art. 9' (n 199) para. 1; Frenzel, 'Art. 9' (n 183) para. 6–9.

578 Greve, 'Art. 9' (n 199) para. 2; Frenzel, 'Art. 9' (n 183) para. 6.

makes unavailable to the individual [...] *the goods, services, facilities, privileges, advantages, or accommodations of any place of public accommodation*".

Thereby, Sec. 108 (a) (1), (a) (1) (B) COPRA, first, applies output-based regulation prohibiting the processing if either the processing *manner* or the processing *result* are discriminatory to the consumer or a group of consumers. We have examined the advantages of output-based regulation in comparison to input-based regulation above.[579] Secondly, the effect of Sec. 108 (a) (1) COPRA's regulating *any* covered data when processed "*on the basis of*" the listed data quality causes a substantial widening of the provision's scope of application and, as a result, of its processing ban. Contrary to the approach in Art. 9 para. 1 GDPR of prohibiting the processing of special categories of personal data, it is not only the listed data quality itself which must not be processed in a discriminatory manner or leading to a discriminatory result but any general covered data may fall under Sec. 108 (a) COPRA's processing ban if the combined elements of data quality, point of use, and output regulation are met.[580] Imagine a processing activity in which the discriminatory-prone data quality listed in Sec. 108 (a) (1) COPRA is not used directly but only indirectly because it informs, motivates, or influences a particular processing activity. For instance, the provision's processing ban may prohibit the use of an algorithm which was trained on data quality enumerated in Sec. 108 (a) (1) COPRA such as that all of the covered data is from people of Muslim faith but which later on does not require the actual input of such discriminatory-prone data to produce an output; still, the trained algorithm continues to operate *on the basis* of the data quality regulated by Sec. 108 (a) (1) COPRA.[581] Another example is consumer profiling for which general covered data is collected and subsequently processed *on the basis* of any of the regulated data quality with the effect that a particular consumer is not shown a job offer that is visible to other consumers.[582]

Sec. 108 (a) (1) COPRA's regulatory approach, hence, gives more importance than does Art. 9 para. 1 GDPR's direct prohibition to processing context and the fast evolution of technical capacities.[583] There are good reasons for COPRA's approach: Instead of using a finite list of data quality as set out in Art. 9 para. 1 GDPR, proces-

579 The concept of input and output-based regulation and the advantages of an output-based approach are explained supra Chapter 2 B. Output and downstream regulation; Gasser (n 11) 198; Hoeren (n 172), 10.

580 Cf. Frenzel, 'Art. 9' (n 183) para. 6–9.

581 Cf. Hoffmann-Riem (n 3) 64–65; cf. Katyal (n 52), 58.

582 Cf. Katyal (n 52), 56 on how *Meta* has been shown to profile consumers to show or hide advertisement on housing, credit, and employment.

583 Cf. a critique of the limited effect of Art. 9 para. 1 GDPR which is largely ignorant to context and only incompletely lists special categories of personal data Frenzel, 'Art. 9' (n 183) para. 7.

sing today may instead take recourse to less regulated data with the same effect of a discriminatory processing activity or a discriminatory processing result, *e.g.* when an area code is used instead of a consumer's perceived race or religion or when non-personal data is combined to identify and discriminate against consumers.[584] The trend of increasingly capable processing technology and a growing availability of data quantity likely accelerates this phenomenon that the use of highly regulated covered data can be substituted by using less or non-regulated data to arrive at the same results.[585]

To conclude, Sec. 108 (a) (1) COPRA leverages point of use, data quality, and output-based regulation to protect consumers in a paternalistic manner without the consumers' possibility to consent to the regulated processing of their covered data. As an exception to the generally processing friendly rules in COPRA, the provision is strictly limited in scope to high-risk processing situation and binds the technology owner and processing entity instead of the consumer. The provision thereby protects consumers in its scope of application in a more effective way than does existing anti-discrimination provisions in privacy law and including in Art. 9 para. 1 GDPR in EU data protection law.

3. Regulating specific processing technology

For algorithmic decision-making, artificial intelligence, and machine learning technology as defined in Sec. 2 (2) COPRA, the bill enhances its regulation in Sec. 108 (a) (1) COPRA with additional safeguards in Sec. 108 (b) (1) COPRA which are targeted at some of the processing technology's specific privacy risks. Notably, COPRA's technology-targeted provisions in Sec. 108 (b) (1) COPRA are limited in scope alike Sec. 108 (a) (1) COPRA to the processing of covered data in high-risk processing situations related to housing, employment, credit, and education.[586] This demonstrates the bill's technology-targeted regulation in Sec. 108 (b) (1) COPRA first and foremost serves the purpose of strengthening the consumer's protection against discrimination as set out in Sec. 108 (a) (1) COPRA when artificial intelligence technology is used to process her covered data.[587]

Building on the categories of modern privacy risks in Chapter 2, technology owners and consumers frequently face privacy challenges specific to artificial intelligence, machine learning, and algorithmic decision-making technology which

---

584 Cf. Cantwell (n 54) 8; Peppet (n 183), 117–124; generally supra Chapter 2 A. I. 2. Data quality.

585 Cf. Ohm (n 182) 105; Barocas and Nissenbaum (n 216) 55–56; supra Chapter 2 A. I. 3. Processing technology.

586 Supra Chapter 3 D. I. 2. a. Point of use regulation.

587 Cf. Katyal (n 52), 58; Cantwell (n 54) 8.

do not occur with other processing technology. For instance, a common misconception would be to think of artificial intelligence, machine learning, and algorithmic decision-making technology as bias-free mathematical operations. If algorithmic decision-making technology is but math, one could conclude, the technology as such is neutral and trustworthy, and only subsequently do privacy challenges arise when the technology is deployed.[588] In reality, the technology's privacy shortcomings commonly stem from insufficient data quality and built-in defects early on in the development of the technology at the input stage (which data quality is fed into the technology?), at the training stage (is data accurately labeled or categorized?), or at the programming stage (have the algorithm models been cleansed of given biases?).[589] Later on when the technology is deployed, and since built-in defects are rarely transparent to the outside user, it is often difficult to identify and mitigate existing misfunctions of the technology.[590]

Moreover, individual corrective action of affected consumers, *e.g.* a consumer demanding the correction of inaccurate covered data according to Sec. 104 (1) COPRA, is typically without lasting effect on the functioning of artificial intelligence, machine learning, and algorithmic decision-making technology since the technology is built on and path-dependent on a foundation of data which is largely immune against individual or small-scale corrections.[591] To say it differently, individual privacy actions, even if aggregated over time, do not amount to the scale and effect needed to meaningfully influence how artificial intelligence, machine learning, and algorithmic decision-making technology is developed and works in practice.[592]

As means to address these technology-specific privacy challenges, COPRA choses the tool of impact assessments as set out in Sec. 108 (b) (1) (A) COPRA. According to 108 (b) (1) and (2) COPRA, impact assessments must be conducted on an annual basis for which technology owners may rely on external auditors and experts to conduct the assessment. Although impact assessments are no new idea, consider for example data protection impact assessments as required in EU data protection law by Art. 35 para. 1 sentence 1 GDPR, COPRA's approach is notable because the bill explicitly demands, and thereby elevates to a legal standard, the examination of how the algorithmic decision-making process was developed, which design- and training-data was used, and how the process and data was tested

588 Katyal (n 52), 58; Hoffmann-Riem (n 3) 62–63.
589 Cf. Katyal (n 52), 68; Ohm (n 182) 107; Hoffmann-Riem (n 3) 62–63.
590 Hoffmann-Riem (n 3) 62–63.
591 Cf. Solove, 'Privacy Self-Management and the Consent Dilemma' (n 78) 1881, 1886–1888; Lev-Aretz and Strandburg (n 16), 295; Solove, 'The Limitations of Privacy Rights' (n 226) 10–17.
592 Solove, 'The Limitations of Privacy Rights' (n 226) 17.

for accuracy, fairness, bias, and discrimination. By requiring technology owners to ensure an assessment and quality control during the input-, training-, and programming stage of the development work, Sec. 108 (b) (1) (A) COPRA cuts through to the root cause of insufficient data quality and human (in)capacity.[593] The objective is to strengthen collective privacy by compensating what individual data rights are unable to achieve for their lack of scale and effect.[594]

By contrast, Art. 35 para. 3 lit. a and para. 7 lit. a GDPR, which stipulate data protection impact assessments for automated decision-making, do not spell out an explicit standard to test for data quality in design- and training-data and during the development work of the technology. Similarly, guiding material by EU data protection authorities about how to conduct impact assessments still lack a clear recommendation to focus on data quality and software development work.[595] Also, there is no obligation for technology owners to conduct risk assessments on a recurring and annual basis; pursuant to Art. 35 para. 11 GDPR, a review of a conducted assessment is mandatory only when there is a change of risk in the processing activity.[596]

Finally, as a critique of Sec. 108 (b) (1) COPRA, the bill's regulation of specific processing technology should arguably apply more broadly than in the defined high-risk processing situations of housing, employment, credit, and education. Taking into account how artificial intelligence, machine learning, and algorithmic decision-making technology is increasingly used in practice, the structural privacy risks linked to the specific processing technology do not seem less pertinent in other processing situations.[597] The bill's technology-specific regulation should thus be considered a mere first step in a necessary development to broadly regulate structural privacy risks linked to specific processing technology.[598]

To summarize, Sec. 108 (b) (1) COPRA obliges technology owners of artificial intelligence, machine learning, and algorithmic decision-making technology to conduct and document recurring and detailed impact assessments when they plan to deploy the technology in high-risk processing situations. In particular, technology owners must evaluate whether and how the technology was developed to avoid

---

593 Supra Chapter 2 B. I. 2. Data quality; cf. Katyal (n 52), 56, 67–77; European Data Protection Supervisor (n 21) 10; Hoffmann-Riem (n 3) 64–65; German Data Ethics Commission (n 6) 8 (4th bullet point); Hoeren (n 172), 10.

594 Sub Chapter 3 D. II. 1. Data control rights; Stollhoff, 'Art. 16' (n 198) para. 20–21; Solove, 'The Limitations of Privacy Rights' (n 226) 17.

595 Commission Nationale de l'Informatique et des Libertés (n 209).

596 Raum (n 208) para. 66.

597 Cf. Katyal (n 52), 56.

598 Cf. President of the United States, 'Executive Order on the Safe, Secure, and Trustworthy Development and Use of Artificial Intelligence' (n 242); European Parliament (n 244); supra Chapter 2 B. I. 3. Processing technology.

discriminatory outputs, and whether high-quality data was used in the development process. Thereby, Sec. 108 (b) (1) COPRA offers an effective solution to address the technology-specific privacy challenges of data quality, human (in)capacities and collective privacy.

4. Transparency and information obligations

COPRA stipulates in Sec. 102 (b) COPRA transparency and information obligations for processing entities to inform consumers about relevant processing aspects of their covered data. To counter-act human intellectual (in)capacity when consumers grapple to understand how their covered data is being processed, Sec. 102 (b) COPRA aims at increasing transparency and information generally and for all of consumers and irrespective of the marketplace situation they act in.[599] Although, systemically speaking, the bill places these obligations as a data right of the individual consumer in Title I Data Privacy Rights,[600] the provision binds processing entities and does not require an individual consumer's taking action. In the terminology of this study, COPRA's transparency and information obligations hence belong to the category of collective privacy.[601]

Similar broadly applicable transparency and information obligations without industry focus were first introduced to U.S. privacy law by § 1798.100 (b) California Consumer Privacy Act.[602] In terms of content, COPRA and the *California Consumer Privacy Act* overlap in what must be communicated to the consumer, *i.e.* the contact of the processing entity, the categories of collected covered data, the processing purpose, the storage time of the collected data, an explanation of the consumer's data control rights.[603] COPRA additionally requires the disclosure of information about data transfers and the processing entity's data security program according to Sec. 102 (b) (3) and (6) COPRA.[604] A comparison to information obligations under EU data protection law follows further below.[605]

---

599 Acquisti and Grossklags (n 226) 364, 371, 374; Ebner, *Weniger ist Mehr?* (n 29) 45–48; Specht (n 298) 167–168; Sandfuchs (n 298) pp. 218–221; Cate (n 30) 360–361; Solove, 'Privacy Self-Management and the Consent Dilemma' (n 78) 1880, 1881–1882, 1886; Solove, 'The Myth of the Privacy Paradox' (n 155) 43–44; Voigt (n 28) 90–91; Veil (n 15), 687–689; Thaler and Sunstein (n 188) 31–60; Lev-Aretz and Strandburg (n 16), 287; supra Chapter 2 A. II. 1. Intellectual (in)capacity.

600 Sub Chapter 3 D. II. Data rights of the individual consumer.

601 Supra Chapter 2 A. II. 3. Individual and collective privacy.

602 Cf. Glocker (n 91) 150–154.

603 Cf. ibid 155–157.

604 Sub Chapter 3 D. I. 6. Data security.

605 Sub Chapter 4 B. I. 5. Transparency and information rights.

In contrast to § 1798.100 (b) California Consumer Privacy Act, Sec. 102 (b) COPRA stipulates a strict form requirement which arguably results in less effective protection for the consumer. Whereas according to *California Consumer Privacy Act*, processing entities are free choose in which form they inform consumers – consider in particular *ex contrario* § 1798.130 (a) (5) California Consumer Privacy Act according to which processing entities may publish a privacy policy but can also directly inform the consumer via other means such as via email –, the effect of Sec. 102 (b) COPRA is that processing entities are limited to the use of privacy policies as a tool to inform consumers. As a consequence of the bill's restricted focus on the use of privacy policies, which are routinely provided on processing entities' websites, COPRA lacks concrete instructions about the moment or time when the processing entity must inform consumers about relevant processing activities. This is unlike § 1798.100 (a) California Consumer Privacy Act which binds processing entities to inform the consumer "*at or before the point of* [data] *collection*". COPRA, on the other hand, expects the consumer to actively consult a company's privacy policy to obtain information. Hence, under COPRA, the onus to receive relevant processing information effectively shifts from the processing entity to the consumer.[606]

Arguably, COPRA's default rule to utilize privacy policies as a means to inform consumers is softened in situations in which processing entities must obtain a consumer's affirmative express consent. This is the case, first, in Sec. 102 (d) COPRA before any material change in a processing entity's processing activity or privacy policy materializes, and, secondly, in Sec. 105 (c) (2) COPRA according to which processing entities must obtain consumers' opt-in consent before they process or transfer of sensitive covered data.[607] Although both provisions do not *expressis verbis* stipulate an obligation to directly inform the consumer, a teleological interpretation suggests that processing entities must comprehensively inform the consumer *prior* to asking for consent and so that the consumer understands what she is asked to approve. It follows that a request to consent must be sent to the consumer accompanied by sufficient information about the expected processing activity and so that the consumer has a basis for her decision-making.[608]

By contrast, for processing entities, no such obligation to directly inform consumers follows from Sec. 105 (b) (2) COPRA which establishes the bill's privacy information management system. Although Sec. 105 (b) (2) (B) (ii) COPRA calls for "*clear and conspicuous opt-out notices*" to be sent to consumers as part of the regis-

---

606 Cf. Solove, 'The Limitations of Privacy Rights' (n 226) 10–17; Solove, 'The Myth of the Privacy Paradox' (n 155) 5.

607 Supra Chapter 3 C. I. 2. (Sensitive) covered data.

608 Cf. supra Chapter 2 A. II. 1. Intellectual (in)capacity.

ter, it follows from the provision's purpose and addressee that the provision binds the register's administrator and not processing entities.[609]

In all, COPRA prompts processing entities to rely on privacy policies to inform consumers about relevant processing activities. Conversely, consumers are expected to consult the website and privacy policy of processing entities to learn about how their covered data is being processed. Only exceptionally are processing entities required to *directly* inform consumers before they ask for consumers' opt-in consent. As a consequence, COPRA's transparency and information obligations appear less detailed and, ultimately, less favorable for consumers than similar provisions in the *California Consumer Privacy Act*.

5. Purpose limitation, data minimization, limitations on waivers of privacy rights

Sec. 106 and 109 COPRA are additional examples of how COPRA protects collective privacy. Instead of addressing the individual consumer, the provisions bind processing entities by establishing generally applicable data processing rules, irrespective of whether an individual consumer has acted upon a data right.[610]

Under the title of *Right to Data Minimization*, Sec. 106 COPRA sets out both, a principle of purpose limitation and a principle of data minimization. According to Sec. 106 (1) COPRA, the purpose of a processing activity must be spelled out in the processing entity's privacy policy, the processing entity must have obtained the consumer's affirmative express consent according to Sec. 106 (2) COPRA, or the processing must serve one of the purposes exhaustively listed in Sec. 106 (3) together with Sec. 110 (d) COPRA, *i.e.* to deliver an order or service, to recall a product, to maintain IT systems and services, to detect or prevent IT incidents or other malicious activities, to save an individual from death or a serious physical harm, to comply with the law, or to conduct scientific, historical, or statistical work.[611]

Purpose limitation as a privacy concept is not new and has been around since the 1973 *Fair Information Practices Principles*.[612] In EU data protection law, it is enshrined in Art. 5 of the 1981 *Convention for the Protection of Individuals with Regard to Automatic Processing of Personal Data* and in Art. 5 para. 1 lit. b GDPR

609 Supra Chapter 3 D. II. 2. Privacy information management system.

610 Supra Chapter 2 A. II. 3. Individual and collective privacy.

611 A comparison with EU data protection law follows sub Chapter 4 B. I. 1. Data processing principles.

612 U.S. Department of Health, Education and Welfare (n 68); supra Chapter 1 A. Concept and status of U.S. privacy law.

which goes back to Art. 6 of the 1995 *EU Data Protection Directive*.[613] In the U.S., FTC privacy enforcement actions have repeatedly sanctioned broken *"privacy promises"* when processing entities processed covered data for purposes different from the ones stated in their privacy policies.[614] Yet until COPRA, no generally applicable principle of purpose limitation had been codified in U.S. federal privacy law. It was the *California Consumer Privacy Act* which first introduced in § 1798.100 (c) the principle of purpose limitation to U.S. state privacy law.[615] Sec. 106 COPRA now elevates the purpose limitation principle from state privacy law to a federal standard.

Closely connected to the principle of purpose limitation, Sec. 106 COPRA also stipulates that processing entities may only process covered data to the extent the processing is *"reasonably necessary, proportionate, and limited"* to the processing purpose. Together with Sec. 107 (b) (3) COPRA, which requires processing entities to delete or render permanently unusable covered data which is no longer necessary for the purpose it was collected, Sec. 106 COPRA holds processing entities to minimize data use.

As a consequence of the broad application of COPRA's purpose limitation and data minimization principle, Sec. 106 COPRA is mostly ignorant of the functioning and characteristics of specific modern data-focused technology. In Chapter 2 B. I. 3. Processing technology, we examined why and how purpose limitation and data minimization likely conflict with technology like big data, *e.g.* because the technology depends on and leverages the existence of large quantities of high-quality data, often without regard to the original purpose of collection.[616] Effectively, enforcing COPRA's data minimization and purpose limitation without embracing modern technology's potential to do good could make us forego important advancements in science and technology.[617] Instead, a modern privacy law is better advised to leverage a more nuanced approach, for instance by strengthening output-based regulation and data quality-control.[618]

Furthermore, Sec. 109 (1) and (2) COPRA restricts a processing entity's ability to condition the provision of goods or services to the consumers' waiving their COPRA

---

613 Cf. Kramer, 'Art. 5' (n 269) para. 5; Frenzel, 'Art. 5' (n 178) para. 5; supra Chapter 1 B. Concept and status of EU data protection law.

614 Hoofnagle, *Federal trade commission privacy law and policy* (n 79) 156–158; Glocker, (n 91) 166; Solove and Hartzog (n 385), 628–638; Solove and Schwartz (n 60) 1034.

615 Cf. Glocker (n 91) 230–232; Kramer, 'Art. 5' (n 269) para. 5; Frenzel, 'Art. 5' (n 178) para. 5; Voss, 'Cross-Border Data Flows, the GDPR, and Data Governance' (n 477) 498.

616 Hoffmann-Riem (n 3) 175; Streinz (n 12) 945–946.

617 Cf. Determann, 'Healthy Data Protection' (n 16) 262–265, 277; Determann (n 8) 141.

618 Similarly Hoffmann-Riem (n 3) 176; supra Chapter 2 A. I. 3. Processing technology.

privacy rights in whole or in part. The provision addresses the phenomenon that consumers frequently lack the intellectual or behavioral capacity to negotiate privacy-friendly transactions, *e.g.* because the consumer waives her data rights to gain access to the desired goods or services.[619] To mitigate, Sec. 109 (1) COPRA stipulates that processing entities must without exception adhere to the bill's collective privacy provisions in Sec. 101 (a) COPRA (fair processing), Sec. 105 (a) COPRA (data portability), and Sec. 106–109 COPRA (data minimization and purpose limitation, data security, the technology-neutral and technology-targeted discrimination protection, and the waiver limitation itself).[620] According to Sec. 109 (2) (A), (B), and (C) COPRA, the data rights of the individual consumer in Sec. 102–105 COPRA may only be waived if the consumer grants affirmative express consent within an already established business-to-consumer relationship initiated by the consumer, and where the processing is *strictly necessary* and *required* to provide the goods or services requested by the consumer.

To summarize, Sec. 106 and 109 COPRA establish generally applicable processing principles which require processing entities to respect collective privacy. COPRA limits how processing entities can nudge consumers into waiving their data privacy rights, and COPRA establishes the processing principles of purpose limitation and data minimization.

6. Data security

Given the scale and integration of modern data-focused technology and covered data use into daily life, adequate security-privacy levels of data and systems are paramount to safeguard privacy.[621] By way of example, we highlighted in the above how internet-connected consumer devices are particularly prone to security failures and vulnerable to malicious attacks because of their commonly insufficient security.[622]

Despite the obvious need for robust security, until today, U.S. privacy law has lacked a clear mandate for technology owners to ensure adequate data- and IT-se-

---

619 Cf. Solove, 'The Myth of the Privacy Paradox' (n 155) 5; Solove, 'Privacy Self-Management and the Consent Dilemma' (n 78) 1881, 1886–1888; Zuiderveen Borgesius and others (n 30), 354, 360 et seq.; Veil (n 15), 686, 688–689.

620 Supra Chapter 2 A. II. 3. Individual and collective privacy.

621 Cf. Cantwell (n 54) 9; Solove, 'The Myth of the Privacy Paradox' (n 155) 37; Hoffmann-Riem (n 3) 68–70, 276–277; Kessel (n 274) 23–24.

622 Supra Chapter 2 A. I. 5. Security-privacy level of data and systems; Scott Peppet, 'Regulating the Internet of Things: First Steps Toward Managing Discrimination, Privacy, Security & Consent' 2014 (93) Texas Law Review 85, 133–140; cf. Cantwell (n 54) 4.

curity for consumer devices.[623] As a consequence of U.S. privacy law's patchwork character of sector-specific regulation, there is no federal privacy law which generally stipulates adequate data security.[624] Also, it is unclear whether and which U.S. authority would look into IT-security issues at all; exceptionally, the FTC has enforced flawed IT-security in a few occasions as either a deviation from a processing entity's explicit security promises in its privacy policy or when the security failure met the threshold of an unfair or deceptive (privacy) practice.[625] Short from IT-security laws, some U.S. states have introduced so-called data-breach notification obligations which require processing entities to notify authorities when data breaches occur; yet the scope of many of these data-breach notification laws is narrow, *e.g.* personal data is defined as only the consumer's name and social security, driver's license, bank account, or credit card number, which leaves the majority of security shortcomings unregulated.[626]

COPRA now closes this gap by broadly stipulating reasonable data security in Sec. 107 (a) COPRA irrespective of a specific industry sector or the covered data at stake. Outside of regulated sectors, security-privacy levels of data and systems are thereby elevated from a discretionary decision of processing entities to a mandatory privacy standard. As recommended in Chapter 2, the bill follows a risk-based approach when it mandates context-apt security-privacy levels instead of incorporating fixed audit- and security standards.[627] According to Sec. 107 (a) sentence 2 COPRA, when adopting data security, processing entities must consider "*the volume and nature of the covered data at issue*" which links to the risk categories of data quantity and data quality. Moreover, Sec. 107 (b) (1) COPRA require processing entities to evaluate the respective data security risks associated with particular processing technology and human (in)capacities "*reasonably foreseeable risks to, and vulnerabilities* [...] *including* [...] *human vulnerabilities*" and to take preventive and corrective mitigation steps against identified risks pursuant to Sec. 107 (b) (2) COPRA.

In sum, Sec. 107 (a) and (b) CORPA update existing U.S. federal privacy law with context-adaptive security-privacy levels. In the mid- and long-term, the broadly applicable new legal obligation should catalyze the development of new effective, scalable, and accountable security-privacy measures.[628]

---

623 Ibid 136.

624 Supra Chapter 1 A. Concept and status of U.S. privacy law; Solove and Schwartz (n 60) 1033; Peppet (n 623), 136.

625 Cf. Solove and Schwartz (n 60) 1270; Solove and Hartzog (n 385), 628–638; Hoofnagle, *Federal trade commission privacy law and policy* (n 79) 163.

626 Peppet (n 623), 136; Solove and Schwartz (n 60) 1236–1239.

627 Supra Chapter 2 A. I. 5. Security-privacy level of data and systems.

628 Cf. Gasser (n 11) 207–208.

7. Digital content forgery

In Sec. 205 COPRA, the bill addresses the relatively new phenomenon of digital content forgery, *i.e.* fabricated digital content which appears authentic. Much discussed are, for instance, so-called *deep fakes*, video, and imagery material synthesized from existing content which show a synthetic person act and talk as if it was a real human-being.[629] There is evidence that deep fakes have been used, for example, in the context of the 2016 U.S. presidential election in an attempt to influence voters.[630]

Sec. 205 COPRA identifies fake digital content as a privacy risk because of how covered data can be (mis-)used to create synthetic content.[631] This is in line with COPRA's broader objective to protect the consumer and society against undesired processing consequences by regulating how covered data is used and to which effect, rather than restricting the initial disclosure and use of personal data in the style of EU data protection law.[632] To protect collective privacy, COPRA suggests technology-targeted regulation aimed at digital content forgeries. The bill does not yet offer specific remedies. Instead, it tasks outside expertise with developing such regulation: The *National Institute of Standards and Technology*, an expert agency on security-related issues in the U.S., shall lead a formal investigation into the source, use, application, the most pressing harms, and the targeted audience of digital content forgery; later on, the institute shall suggest how to detect and confront digital content forgery.

In the European Union, a similar effort to address the risks associated with fabricated online content has recently been passed into law. In November 2022, the *Digital Services Act* took effect which requires providers of intermediary services such as online and social media platforms to take action against illegal content and disinformation on their platform. According to Art. 16 Digital Services Act, services providers are expected to set up so-called notice and action mechanisms whereby consumers can notify them about allegedly illegal content which they must take down.[633]

---

629 Eric Craypo, 'Deep Fakes' (2019) <https://vision.berkeley.edu/posts/deep-fakes> accessed 22 April 2022; Bobby Chesney and Danielle Citron, 'Deep Fakes: A looming challenge for Privacy, Democracy, and National Security' 2019 California Law Review 1753, 1758–1760.

630 Craypo (n 628).

631 Chesney and Citron (n 628), 1771–1786.

632 Supra Chapter 2 A. II. 3. Individual and collective privacy.

633 European Parliament and Council 'European Parliament and Council, 'Regulation (EU) 2022/2065 on a Single Market for Digital Services and amending Directive 2000/31/EC' (n 145) 277/1.

In all, COPRA identifies in Sec. 205 COPRA the new privacy risk of digital content forgery. The bill outlines first steps how root causes of digital content forgery can be identified and how technology-targeted regulation can be conceived.

II. Data rights of the individual consumer

Complementing COPRA's collective privacy provisions, the bill stipulates in Title I Data Privacy Rights, Sec. 102–105 COPRA, a set of privacy rules aimed at broadly empowering the individual consumer to defend her privacy interests.[634] Whereas the bill's collective privacy provisions such as its fair processing standard in Sec. 101 COPRA address processing entities and not the consumer, COPRA's individual data rights focus on the individual consumer in an effort to remedy the fact that existing U.S. consumer privacy law *"does not provide the consumer the specific data rights they need in the digital economy"*.[635] As described in Chapter 1, U.S. privacy protection has traditionally been a patchwork of state and federal laws primarily focused on regulating deficiencies in specific marketplace situations.[636] The effect of such regulation has been inconsistent consumer rights at best and, many times, blank spots of unregulated marketplace situations in which, in the absence of a privacy law, the consumer has no control about her personal data at all.[637] Against this background, the objective of COPRA's data rights of the individual is to establish a minimum standard level of privacy rights for consumers across different U.S. states and irrespective of marketplace situations.[638]

Interestingly, Title I COPRA – Data Privacy Rights uses the term data *rights* which resembles EU data protection law terminology, consider, for example, the title of Chapter 3 of the GDPR *Rights of the data subject.* The use of EU terminology might lead readers to assume the U.S. legislator wanted to adopt from EU data protection law the fundamental rights model characterized by a constitutionally granted individual right to privacy as the foundation for individual data protection rights.[639] However, as argued above, this assumption would be too far-fetched. Despite similar terminology, COPRA preserves important conceptual and regulatory differences which are characteristic for U.S. consumer privacy law.

634 Supra Chapter 2 A. II. 3. Individual and collective privacy.
635 Cantwell (n 54) 3.
636 Supra Chapter 1 A. Concept and status of U.S. privacy law.
637 Cf. Solove and Schwartz (n 60) 1033; Cate (n 30) 369–370.
638 For a detailed discussion about COPRA's preemptive effect supra Chapter 3 B. COPRA and preemption of existing U.S. privacy law.
639 Schwartz and Pfeifer (n 19), 122–127; supra Chapter 1 B. Concept and status of EU privacy law.

First and foremost, U.S. consumer privacy law including COPRA do not grant constitutional(-ly anchored) privacy rights, COPRA's conceptual anchor point remains the imperfect data marketplace with privacy law offering the necessary corrective tools for the consumer to confront processing entities.[640]

In the below, we will first look at COPRA's data rights of the individual consumer (sub Chapter 3 D. II. 1. Data control rights), after which we will discuss how COPRA establishes a technical solution to facilitate individual consumers' privacy choices (sub Chapter 3 D. II. 2. Privacy information management system).

1. Data control rights

As a central quest of COPRA, Sec. 102–105 COPRA introduce on a federal level broadly applicable data control rights for the individual consumer.[641] COPRA stipulates the right to demand access or the deletion of covered data (Sec. 102 (a) COPRA and 103 COPRA), to have inaccurate covered data corrected (Sec. 104 COPRA), to request that covered data be transported to a third party, the right to decide about the processing of sensitive covered data and the right to object against transfers of covered data to any third party (Sec. 105 (a), (b), and (c) COPRA). In the below, we will trace the COPRA individual data control rights back to their likely origin, compare them with the *status quo* in U.S. consumer privacy law, and link them to the technical and human (in)capacities and building blocks for a modern privacy law illustrated in Chapter 2.[642] Not in this chapter but later on in this study, we will compare how the COPRA data control rights compare to the EU data protection law and the Rights of the data subject as set out in Art. 12–23 GDPR.[643]

All of the COPRA data control rights appear closely crafted after existing U.S. state consumer privacy rights, more precisely, they resemble rights as first introduced to U.S. privacy law by the *California Consumer Privacy Act of 2018*, California Civil Code § 1798.100–178.199. Politically speaking, COPRA's legacy in the currently most progressive of U.S. state privacy laws is sensible to help secure the support of Californian voters and representatives in passing COPRA as a U.S. federal bill.[644] Otherwise, introducing a federal privacy bill that ignores or lowers the Californian privacy threshold would leave Californian voters without the incentive to support the bill.[645]

640 Supra Chapter 3 A. Consumer privacy rights: A conceptual change in U.S. privacy law?
641 Cantwell (n 54) 3.
642 Supra Chapter 2 Building blocks for a modern privacy law.
643 Sub Chapter 4 B. I. 3. Data rights of the data subject.
644 On the role of California and its influence on U.S. privacy law Specht-Riemenschneider, 'Data access rights – A comparative perspective' (n 475) 411–412; Glocker (n 91) 230–232.
645 Cf. Voss, 'Cross-Border Data Flows, the GDPR, and Data Governance' (n 477) 498–499.

First, the consumer's data control right according to Sec. 102 (a) COPRA to access and retain a copy of her covered data collected by a processing entity and to inquire about data transfers to third parties resembles the access and transparency rights in § 1798.100 (a) and (d) and § 1798.110 California Consumer Privacy Act. The latter is slightly more extensive than the COPRA provision because it additionally grants consumers the right to inquire about the source from which their data has been collected.[646] The right to inquire about covered data in COPRA and the California Consumer Privacy Act aims at counterbalancing common human intellectual (in)capacity, consumers should have the right and means to learn about the data quality and quantity of their covered data as processed by processing entities.[647]

Secondly, COPRA establishes in Sec. 103 COPRA a general data control right to request the deletion of collected covered data. The COPRA deletion right matches § 1798.105 (a) California Consumer Privacy Act.[648] Both the COPRA and the California Consumer Privacy Act right to have covered data deleted entail an obligation for the processing entity pursuant to Sec. 103 (2) 1st alternative COPRA and § 1798.105 (c) California Consumer Privacy Act to inform any service provider to which the entity has transferred covered data about the consumer's deletion request so that the service provider can equally delete the transferred data. *Glocker* explains how in the U.S. the right to have covered data deleted is the exception to the rule of free speech in the *marketplace of ideas*, and how the California Consumer Privacy Act consequently does not extend to third parties whose data sharing would often be considered free speech.[649] By contrast, Sec. 103 (2) 2nd alternative COPRA does extend the processing entity's obligation to inform third parties following a data transfer about the consumer's request to have covered data deleted, a regulatory choice which effectively means stronger privacy protection for the consumer.

Thirdly, Sec. 104 COPRA grants the consumer a right to have inaccurate covered data corrected. The COPRA provision again follows the example of the data control right first introduced to U.S. privacy law by the California Consumer Privacy Act in § 1798.106 (a).[650] Both the data control rights to have covered data corrected or deleted in COPRA and the California Consumer Privacy Act grant consumers the means to address and improve inferior data quality with processing entities.[651] Yet the scope of the provisions is limited to the individual consumer's covered data, an

646 Cf. Glocker (n 91) 116–125.

647 Cf. ibid 116; critical Lev-Aretz and Strandburg (n 16), 295; supra Chapter 2 A. II. 1. Intellectual (in)capacity.

648 Cf. Glocker (n 91) 134–139.

649 Ibid.

650 Cf. ibid 145–147.

651 Supra Chapter 2 A. I. 2. Data quality.

individual is not entitled to have an entire data set reviewed and corrected beyond her covered data even if she contends the dataset as a whole suffers from biases to her disadvantage.[652] This is why the data control rights to correct and delete individual pieces of covered data will likely remain without much effect on the overall structural risk of inferior data quality as described in Chapter 2.[653]

Fourthly, COPRA grants a general right to data portability in Sec. 105 (a) COPRA whereby the consumer can request for her covered data to be exported in a form which can be understood by a human-being and, if desired, (re-)used by a third party. A similar provision can be found in § 1798.100 (d) California Consumer Privacy Act which stipulates the processing entities' obligation to render available, upon request, collected covered data in a portable and readily usable format.[654] The portability right addresses the consumers' frequent impasse that they find themselves locked in with their covered data stored on a particular platform or with a particular processing entity and unable to move their collected covered data to a more attractive new platform or processing entity – a situation which drastically reduces competition in the digital marketplace.[655] The idea is that by mandating collected covered data to be portable and interoperable, the consumer can counteract modern data risks such as data quality, data quantity, and the usage of restricting data processing technology which lay at the root of the lock-in phenomenon.[656] However, the data control right's limitations are both technical and human, *e.g.* moving data from one processing entities to another is frequently impaired by incompatible data formats or software solutions, the sheer quantity and dispersity of data lets it seem doubtful that even the aggregated effect of consumers' action could amount to meaningfully influence the structural privacy risk of inferior data quality.[657]

Fifthly, the consumer's right in Sec. 105 (b) (1) COPRA to object against the onward transfer of her covered data finds its predecessor in § 1798.120 (a) California Consumer Privacy Act.[658] The data control right addresses the modern privacy risk of data quantity as well as human intellectual (in)capacity.[659] Often, consumers are unaware of data commercialization and how processing entities trade their cov-

---

652 Cf. Katyal (n 52), 56, 71–73.

653 Cf. Solove, 'The Limitations of Privacy Rights' (n 226) 17.

654 Cf. Glocker (n 91) 133.

655 Cf. Lev-Aretz and Strandburg (n 16), 273–274.

656 Supra Chapter 2 A. I. 1. Data quantity, 2. Data quality, and 3. Processing technology.

657 Cf. Solove, 'The Limitations of Privacy Rights' (n 226) 10–17; Solove, 'The Myth of the Privacy Paradox' (n 155) 5; cf. Batura and Peeters (n 186) 5.

658 Glocker (n 91) 81–86.

659 Supra Chapter 2 A. I. 1. Data quantity; supra Chapter 2 A. II. 1. Intellectual (in)capacity.

ered data to amass large quantities of data and to make a profit.[660] Besides, the complexity of data trading and sharing deteriorates transparency and accountability to the detriment of consumers; regularly, consumers struggle to understand which processing entity can access their covered data or bears the ultimate responsibility in case a privacy violation occurs.[661] Against this background, it appears that it is the implementation of COPRA's right to object in the form of its privacy information management system set out in Sec. 105 (b) (1) (B), (b) (2) COPRA which has the best chance of impacting data commercialization and data trading in the U.S.[662]

In sum, COPRA's data rights of the individual consumer are an improvement to the *status quo* of U.S. federal privacy law because they broadly empower the consumer irrespective of industry-specific privacy regulation to take privacy-friendly action. COPRA mostly retakes the privacy standard as first introduced to U.S. state privacy law by the *California Consumer Privacy Act of 2018* and establishes it on a federal level. All of COPRA's data rights of the individual consumer require the trigger of the individual consumer's taking action and exercising her data control rights vis-à-vis a processing entity. Without the activation of this trigger, the individual data control rights have no effect. The dependency on individual consumer action is the reason why the bill's individual control rights, even if seen in the aggregate, will likely fall short of effectively addressing the modern privacy risks described in Chapter 2, in particular technical capacities such as data quality, data quantity, and processing technology which are structural privacy risks in nature.[663] To counter-act these structural risks, it is instead necessary to have privacy regulation at scale and independent from the individual consumers' privacy decisions, a regulatory angle COPRA addresses by way of its data rights of the collective.[664]

In COPRA, Sec. 105 (b) (1) COPRA is a regulatory downstream provision according to which the consumer may oppose to the transferring of her covered data to a third party. The right to opt out applies throughout the processing chain and may be invoked by the consumer at any moment after the initial data disclosure and whenever the processing entity wishes to share or transfer covered data with another processing entity.[665] The right to opt out of data transfers has been a

660 Cf. Cantwell (n 54) 3, 8; supra Chapter 2 A. I. 1. Data quantity.

661 Cf. Solove, 'The Myth of the Privacy Paradox' (n 155) 43–44; Solove, 'The Limitations of Privacy Rights' (n 226) 10–17; supra Chapter 2 A. II. Intellectual (in)capacity.

662 Supra Chapter 3 D. II. 2. Privacy information management system.

663 Cf. Lev-Aretz and Strandburg (n 16), 295; Solove, 'Privacy Self-Management and the Consent Dilemma' (n 78) 1881, 1886–1888.

664 Supra Chapter 3 D. I. Data rights of the collective.

665 Supra Chapter 3 D. I. 4. Transparency and information obligations.

well-established element of U.S. federal privacy law where it counter-balances the generally permitted processing of personal data absent of a specific processing limitation.[666] For example, § 6802 (b) of the *Gramm-Leach-Bliley Act*, Public Law No. 106–102, 15 U. S.C. §§ 6801 to 6809, entitles individuals to opt out of the transfer of personal data from regulated financial institutions to third parties. According to § 1681b subsection (e) of the *Fair Credit Reporting Act*, 15 U. S.C. § 1681 et seq., consumers may choose to have their name and address excluded from consumer reporting (opt out). To this point, it is worth noting how COPRA takes into account the practical difficulty for consumers to opt out downstream vis-à-vis the multitude of individual processing entities which are commonly involved in data sharing and transfer.[667] COPRA proposes a technical mechanism to ensure the opt-out right in Sec. 105 (b) (1) COPRA can be effectuated downstream on a large scale. Further down below, we will discuss the proposed privacy information management system set forth in Sec. 105 (b) (1) (B) in connection with Sec. 105 (b) (2) COPRA.[668]

Another provision with downstream effect is Sec. 105 (c) (1) and (2) COPRA which stipulates an opt-in requirement for the processing of sensitive covered data.[669] Whereas Sec. 105 (c) (2) COPRA explicitly addresses the downstream situation of onward transfers of sensitive covered data from one processing entity to another which require the consumer's prior affirmative express consent, the language in Sec. 105 (c) (1) COPRA is broader and also encompasses upstream control when the consumer must be asked for opt-in consent already at the first disclosure of sensitive covered data and irrespective of a transfer situation. That Sec. 105 (c) (1) COPRA has downstream effect becomes clear where sensitive covered data is processed beyond the initial processing entity, subsequent processing entities must equally obtain the consumer's prior affirmative express consent to legitimately process her sensitive covered data.

Similar to Sec. 105 (c) (1) COPRA, other processing rules in COPRA apply both upstream and downstream. Alike the general data processing principles in Art. 5 para. 1 lit. a-f GDPR which shape data processing upstream and downstream, the bill's mirroring principles of data minimization and purpose limitation in Sec. 106 COPRA apply throughout the processing chain.[670] The same is true for COPRA's fair processing standard in Sec. 101 COPRA, as well as its provisions in Sec. 108 (a) and

---

666 Schwartz and Pfeifer (n 19), 120.

667 Cantwell (n 54) 5; Solove, 'Privacy Self-Management and the Consent Dilemma' (n 78) 1881, 1886–1888.

668 In more detail sub Chapter 3 D. II. 2. Privacy information management system.

669 Supra Chapter 3 C. I. 2. (Sensitive) covered data.

670 Supra Chapter 3 D. I. 5. Purpose limitation, data minimization, limitation on waivers of privacy rights.

(b) COPRA which have downstream effect when they govern how covered data can be used later on in the processing chain and subsequent to the first disclosure of the data.[671]

Finally, Sec. 102 (d) COPRA is a conspicuous example of downstream regulation because at any moment after the initial data disclosure and when covered data is processed downstream, the processing entity must provide direct notification to the consumer prior to materially changing their processing practices or privacy policy.[672] In particular, the provision aims at mitigating against human intellectual and behavioral limitations including passivity and inaction by confronting consumers with privacy choices when their initial expectation about how covered data is being processed no longer holds true.[673]

In all, this chapter argues that downstream privacy regulation is a necessary and effective approach to protect the individual consumer and the collective in today's data reality.[674] Although COPRA leverages some downstream regulation, it does not use the full potential downstream regulation offers. The critique is that although substantial processing provisions targeting technical capacities would be needed, COPRA remains close to traditional U.S. federal privacy regulation focusing instead in its downstream provisions on human (in)capacities and putting the onus on the consumer to take action. Sec. 105 (b) (1) COPRA, a consumer's right to oppose onward transfers of her covered data, is a case in point. By contrast, in the recommended direction of regulating technical capacities downstream aim COPRA's point of use and technology-targeted rules in Sec. 108 (a) and (b) COPRA, albeit (too) limited in scope, and COPRA's fair processing standard in Sec. 101 COPRA whose broad scope applies downstream but which lacks technology-specific language.[675]

2. Privacy information management system

The technical capacities of today's data processing make it difficult for consumers to engage with processing entities efficiently and effectively, *e.g.* when consumers

671 Supra Chapter 3 D. I. 1. COPRA's fair processing standard and Chapter 3 D. I. 2. Point of use regulation and regulation of data quality and Chapter 3 D. I. 3. Regulating specific processing technology.

672 Supra Chapter 3 D. I. 4. Transparency and information obligations.

673 Cf. Specht (n 298) 422; Voigt (n 28) 93–95; Ebner, 'Information Overload 2.0?' (n 28) 365–366.

674 Supra Chapter 2 A. 3. Individual and collective privacy.

675 Supra Chapter 3 D. I. 1. COPRA's fair processing standard and Chapter 3 D. I. 2. Point of use regulation and regulation of data quality and Chapter 3 D. I. 3. Regulating specific processing technology.

want to act upon their data rights.[676] Essentially, too many processing entities are involved in the processing of the individual consumer's personal data so that the individual could meaningfully interact with processing entities one by one.[677]

For the right to object against onward transfers of covered data in Sec. 105 (b) (1) COPRA, the bill acknowledges this practical difficulty and establishes a technical mechanism to enable consumers to opt out with little effort and with a large-scale effect. In Sec. 105 (b) (1) (B) in connection with Sec. 105 (b) (2) COPRA, the bill introduces a centrally organized register for consumers to permanently record their wish to opt out of onward transfers of their covered data. The idea is a one-stop solution which according to Sec. 105 (b) (2) (B) (i) COPRA minimizes the number of opt-outs the consumer must make vis-à-vis processing entities. Since the COPRA register allows consumers to manage their privacy preferences centrally, the technical solution is called a privacy information management system.[678] Conversely, processing entities are required pursuant to Sec. 105 (b) (1) (B) COPRA to integrate into their workflow the consumers' processing decision as registered in the privacy information management system and to honor their opt-out. To this end, processing entities and their website, product, or service must first inquire with the central register about the consumer's privacy preference before covered data can be forwarded to another processing entity.

COPRA's privacy information management system is a centralized, technology- and processing entity-agnostic system. This facilitates the register's management and maintenance and makes compliance with the register better policeable than a combination of decentralized privacy information management systems. The technology- and processing entity-agnostic setup ensures the system is compatible with whatever processing technology processing entities use; it leaves little room for product-based or company-based workarounds, *e.g.* a product configuration by which the consumer's consent to data transfers and commercialization is mandatory to access the processing entities' goods or services.[679] By contrast, decentralized and voluntary privacy information management systems, where they existed, have mostly proven ineffective because processing entities were free to choose to

676 Cf. Cantwell (n 54) 5; Solove, 'The Myth of the Privacy Paradox' (n 155) 30.

677 Solove, 'Privacy Self-Management and the Consent Dilemma' (n 78) 1881, 1886–1888; Lev-Aretz and Strandburg (n 16), 295; Specht-Riemenschneider (n 171) 422.

678 A similar definition of privacy information management systems can be found at European Data Protection Supervisor, 'Personal Information Management System' (2021) <https://edps.europa.eu/data-protection/our-work/subjects/personal-information-management-system_en> accessed 8 September 2023.

679 By contrast cf. Zuiderveen Borgesius and others (n 30), 354, 360 et seq; Hoofnagle, 'Privacy Self-Regulation: A Decade of Disappointment' (n 77) 382; Solove, 'Privacy Self-Management and the Consent Dilemma' (n 78) 1881.

engage with them or to ignore them; the voluntary solutions lacked the market penetration the mandatory COPRA system will have.[680] Based on the information in the central register, processing entities can easily be held accountable when their processing practice runs contrary to a consumer's registered opt-out.

COPRA does not specify whether consumers only have the choice to generally opt out of all onward transfers or whether they are allowed to register their opt-out in more detail, for instance that they wish to solely opt out of data transfers to specific processing entities or concerning a particular data quality of their covered data.[681] Technically, a more nuanced registration of a consumer's opt-out would, of course, be possible.

Also, the register stipulates for clear and conspicuous notices to be sent to the consumer according to Sec. 105 (b) (2) (B) (ii) COPRA and a consumer-friendly way to check and alter one's opt-out decision for the future. However, the text of the provision does not specify who shall be responsible for sending such notices. Given the nature and functioning of the privacy information management system as a centrally managed system which runs independently from particular processing entities, an interpretation of Sec. 105 (b) (2) (B) COPRA suggests for the addressee of the provision and responsible entity of the privacy information management system to send out the notices, *i.e.* the system provider or administrator rather than individual processing entities.

As a consequence, the notices according to Sec. 105 (b) (2) (B) (ii) COPRA are not governed by Sec. 102 (b) COPRA which addresses processing entities and not the provider or administrator of the privacy information management system. In particular, this means the content of the notices according to Sec. 105 (b) (2) (B) (ii) COPRA may differ from the one stipulated in Sec. 102 (b) COPRA.[682]

COPRA's privacy information management system furthermore embraces human (in)capacities such as passivity and inaction towards data management. The central register prompts the consumer to record her privacy decision with little effort while the stakes of her decision are immediately discernible because her opt-out is valid for all pertinent processing activities. This should motivate consumers to voice their privacy preference and act upon their individual data right to oppose data transfers more than the cumbersome alternative *pre* COPRA of engaging with processing entities one by one.[683] In the U.S., similar government-ini-

680 Cf. Blankertz and Specht-Riemenschneider (n 351) 29.

681 Cf. supra Chapter 2 A. I. 2. Data quality.

682 For a detailed discussion of COPRA's transparency and information obligations supra Chapter 3 D. I. 4. Transparency and information obligations.

683 Cf. Solove, 'Privacy Self-Management and the Consent Dilemma' (n 78) 1881, 1886–1888; Lev-Aretz and Strandburg (n 16), 295; Specht-Riemenschneider (n 171) 422.

tiated central registers have been met with high consumer interest and acceptance, for instance the *Telemarketing Do-not-call Registry* currently counts about 221 million registered telephone numbers.[684]

The idea of technical solutions for data and privacy management is not new. As early as since the 1970s, technical means to better protect privacy have been discussed: First, as ancillary measures to data processing in the form of so-called privacy enhancing technology, *e.g.* data management and encryption tools, and, more recently, as an integrated component of a product's or a solution's processing operations – *privacy by design* describes the idea that the consumers' privacy choices and regulatory requirements are built into the product itself.[685] The technical mechanism of COPRA's central privacy information management system in Sec. 105 (b) (2) COPRA builds on the successful model of the *Telemarketing Do-not-call Registry* which was introduced by the FTC in 2003 to protect consumers from unwanted marketing calls.[686] Telemarketers are required to preemptively check whether the targeted consumer has opted-out of marketing calls and registered her preference in the Do-not-call Registry. In case the consumer's telephone number appears in the register, telemarketers are not allowed to contact the consumer, otherwise they risked being fined.[687] In the European Union, an example of the use of privacy information management systems can be found in Art. 26 para. 1 and 2 of the German *Telecommunication and Digital Services Data Privacy Act* and which we discussed in Chapter 2.[688]

Likely, privacy information management systems will further evolve with new technology, *e.g.* they could take the form of privacy bots which cater processing information to the level of understanding and interest of individual consumers and they could identify and execute on their respective privacy preferences.[689] Moreover, it is easily conceivable already with existing technology that privacy information management systems can be further fine-tuned to address modern privacy risks in a more nuanced manner, imagine when individual systems are configured

---

684 Federal Trade Commission, 'The Do Not Call Registry' (2013) <https://www.ftc.gov/news-events/topics/do-not-call-registry> accessed 15 May 2022.

685 Gasser (n 11) 203–204; Hoffmann-Riem (n 3) 143–144; Hacker (n 143) 559–561.

686 Cf. Hoofnagle, 'Privacy Self-Regulation: A Decade of Disappointment' (n 77) 379; Federal Trade Commission (n 683); Glocker (n 91) 81–82.

687 The FTC reports that it has collected, until today, a total of USD 178 million in civil penalties and USD 112 million in disgorgements, Federal Trade Commission, 'Enforcement Do-not-call-Registry' (2018) <https://www.ftc.gov/news-events/topics/do-not-call-registry/enforcement> accessed 14 November 2023.

688 Cf. Glocker (n 91) 97–98; supra Chapter 2 A. II. 2. Behavioral (in)capacity.

689 Cf. Ebner, *Weniger ist Mehr?* (n 29) 129–130.

to offer and execute different degrees of privacy protection in different point of use situations, for instance a stronger privacy protection when a consumer's private home or private sphere is concerned,[690] or according to particular intellectual (in) capacities, for instance a higher threshold could be required for the transferring of personal data of children.[691] To conclude, the advantage of COPRA's technical solution of a central privacy information management system over the traditional one-by-one consumer decision vis-à-vis each processing entity is that it is effective, scalable, and holds processing entities accountable.[692]

III. Interim summary

In regulating covered data processing, COPRA leverages many of the building blocks for a modern privacy law illustrated in Chapter 2.[693] The bill strengthens collective privacy by requiring processing entities to adhere to a fair processing standard set out in Sec. 101 COPRA.[694] The provision is output-based and scrutinizes whether the processing activity and its result are in line with the bill's provisions and broader U.S. privacy law and case-law. Collective privacy also is the reason for COPRA's point of use and data quality regulation in Sec. 108 (a) COPRA. In a defined number of high-risk processing situations and for specific data quality the bill mandates a strict processing ban if the output of the processing activity is discriminatory. This paternalistic decision to regulate covered data processing irrespective of the individual consumer's choice and action gives testimony to how COPRA embraces modern structural privacy risks in specific point of use situations in which the consumer appears as particularly vulnerable.[695]

In Sec. 108 (b) COPRA and Sec. 205 COPRA, the bill's focus is on privacy risks which are associated with a particular processing technology. Whereas Sec. 108 (b) COPRA stipulates additional obligations for processing entities which rely on algorithmic decision-making technology as the foundational building blocks of

690 Cf. Veil (n 15), 695; Cohen (n 261) 143.

691 Cf. German Data Ethics Commission (n 6) 12; Art. 29 Working Party, 'Stellungnahme zum Schutz der personenbezogenen Daten von Kindern' [2009] WP 160, 3; Albrecht and Jotzo (n 124) 80; in the same direction of stricter protection for children § 1798.135 (c) (5) Californian Consumer Privacy Act stipulates an opt-in instead of an opt-out requirement for consumers under the age of 16 years old regarding the sale or sharing of their personal information.

692 Cf. Gasser (n 11) 207–208; Hoffmann-Riem (n 3) 143–144, 196–198.

693 Supra Chapter 2 Building blocks for a modern privacy law.

694 Supra Chapter 3 D. I. 1. COPRA's fair processing standard.

695 Supra Chapter 3 D. I. 2. Point of use regulation and regulation of data quality.

artificial intelligence and big data technology, Sec. 205 COPRA identifies structural privacy risks with the modern data phenomenon of digital content forgery.[696]

Additional general processing obligations for all processing entities and irrespective of an individual consumer's taking action are set out in Sec. 102 (b) COPRA (transparency and information obligations), Sec. 106 COPRA (purpose limitation and data minimization), Sec. 109 (1) and (2) COPRA (limitation on waivers of privacy rights), and Sec. 107 (a) and (b) COPRA (adequate data security).[697]

Furthermore, COPRA introduces to U.S. federal privacy law broadly applicable data rights of the individual consumer which acknowledge and attempt to mitigate against some of the human (in)capacities consumers commonly struggle with when interacting with modern data-focused technology. This is a *novum* compared to U.S. privacy law *pre* COPRA which has gravitated around specific marketplace situations in which consumers had only limited control rights, if at all.[698] In Sec. 102–105 COPRA, the bill now grants consumer control rights to access, correct, delete, and transfer their covered data irrespective of specific marketplace situations.[699] Pursuant to Sec. 105 (c) (1) and (2) COPRA, consumers must be asked for their affirmative express consent (opt-in) before any of their sensitive covered data is being processed.[700] At any moment downstream, consumers may opt-out of unwanted data transfers according to Sec. 105 (b) (1) COPRA.[701] COPRA acknowledges common human intellectual and behavioral shortcomings such as passivity and the incapacity to deal with the multitude of processing entities typically involved in data processing when it establishes in Sec. 105 (b) (1) (B) in connection with Sec. 105 (b) (2) COPRA a technical one-stop solution in which consumers can register their privacy choices. This so-called privacy information management system should enable consumers to control more effectively than *pre* COPRA how their covered data can be processed.[702]

Although COPRA's processing provisions should thus result in an overall strengthening of U.S. federal consumer privacy law, aspects of COPRA are still worth criticizing. For example, we have argued in Chapter 2 how downstream privacy regulation is an effective approach to protect the individual consumer and the

---

696 Supra Chapter 3 D. I. 3. Regulating specific processing technology and Chapter 3 D. I. 7. Digital content forgery.

697 Supra Chapter 3 I. 4–6 Transparency and information obligations; Purpose limitation, data minimization, limitation on waivers of privacy rights; Data security.

698 Supra Chapter 1 A. Concept and status of U.S. privacy law.

699 Supra Chapter 3 D. II. Data rights of the individual consumer.

700 Supra Chapter 3 C. I. 2. (Sensitive) covered data.

701 Supra Chapter 3 D. II. Data rights of the individual consumer.

702 Supra Chapter 3 D. II. 2. Privacy information management system.

collective in today's data reality and how such downstream regulation should ideally focus on technical capacities.[703] Although COPRA leverages some downstream regulation, *e.g.* in Sec. 105 (b) (1) COPRA, it is far from utilizing its full potential. Path-dependent on traditional privacy regulation, COPRA's downstream regulation still too much depends on the individual consumer's taking action instead of tasking the owners of technical capacities in the form of substantive processing provisions. The point of use, data quality, and processing technology targeted regulation in Sec. 108 (a) and (b) COPRA is a step into the right direction of recommended privacy regulation; however, its scope of application is narrow with no effect on processing activities outside of its control. Finally, the catch-all fair processing standard in Sec. 101 COPRA tasks processing entities and applies downstream, yet it lacks technical capacity-apt language, so whether and how technical capacities are regulated will largely depend on how the standard will be implemented and interpreted.[704]

E. COPRA compliance, oversight, and enforcement

This chapter looks beyond COPRA's processing rules and examines how the bill strives to strengthen privacy compliance, oversight, and enforcement in the U.S. To assess whether the COPRA updates can set the foundation for a more effective privacy system compared to *pre* COPRA, we apply the benchmark described in Chapter 2 including *Bamberger/Mulligan's* standard to assess how effectively privacy regulation has been implemented.[705]

To this end, we will first examine how COPRA mandates processing entities to organize and maintain their corporate privacy compliance practice (sub Chapter 3 E. I. Processing entities' compliance) to then discuss how COPRA strengthens privacy oversight and enforcement outside of organizations by authorities and the individual consumer (sub Chapter 3 E. II. Oversight and enforcement).

---

703 Supra Chapter 2 A. 3. Individual and collective privacy; Chapter 2 A. I. Technical capacities.
704 Supra Chapter 3 D. I. 1. COPRA's fair processing standard and Chapter 3 D. I. 2. Point of use regulation and regulation of data quality; Chapter 3 D. I. 3. Regulating specific processing technology.
705 Supra Chapter 2 A. I. Technical capacities, II. Human (in)capacities, and Chapter 2 C. Effective implementation of privacy regulation.

I. Processing entities' compliance

COPRA introduces various new privacy compliance obligations for processing entities. Whereas some apply to all covered processing entities, others only apply to so-called large data holders. The bill defines large data holders in Sec. 2 (15) COPRA as processing entities which either process sensitive covered data of more than 100,000 persons, devices, or households or general covered data of more than 5 million persons, devices, or households per calendar year.[706] This risk-based approach of regulating processing entities based on their size and the data quantity they process has been described in Chapter 2 as privacy regulation on a sliding scale.[707] This study has argued that such data quantity-based privacy regulation on a sliding scale is convincing.[708] On average, large data holders pose a structural privacy risk which general covered processing entities do not.[709] By addressing processing entities which have accumulated large quantities of covered data and by subjecting them to heightened scrutiny, COPRA takes concrete steps to better mitigate against the modern privacy risk of data quantity.[710] In the below, we will highlight which compliance obligations are mandatory for all covered entities and which only apply to large data holders.

1. Privacy and data security officers

For all processing entities covered by COPRA and irrespective of their size or the data quantity they process, the bill stipulates in Sec. 202 (a) (1) and (2) COPRA the requirement to designate at least one privacy and one data security officer. Until today, the nomination of a privacy and a data security officer has not been a binding standard in existing U.S. federal and state privacy law. Among the many sector-specific federal privacy laws, a few already contain similar obligations while others do not: For example, the *Gramm-Leach-Bliley Act*, 15 U. S.C. § 6801–6809, § 6821–6827, together with the FTC's *Standards for Safeguarding Customer Information* require companies to designate a qualified individual to implement and supervise a company's information security program.[711] Also, the *Health Insurance Port-*

---

706 For a more detailed discussion of large data holders supra Chapter 3 C. II. 2. Quantitative assessment of covered entities.

707 Supra Chapter 2 A. I. 1. Data quantity.

708 Cantwell (n 54) 5; cf. the critique of the GDPR's one-size-fits-all approach which burdens small entities with high implementation costs Institut der deutschen Wirtschaft (n 22) 12.

709 Cf. Solove, 'Privacy Self-Management and the Consent Dilemma' (n 78) 1881; Bygrave (n 59) 9–11; German Data Ethics Commission (n 6) 8.

710 Supra Chapter 2 A. I. 1. Data quantity.

711 Cf. Solove and Schwartz (n 60) 1034–1035.

ability and Accountability Act, Public Law No. 104–191, requires companies according to Sec. 164.530(a)(1) to designate a privacy official.[712] By contrast, the most progressive privacy law on a state level, California's *Consumer Privacy Act* of 2018, does not require companies to designate a privacy and data security professional.[713] COPRA now establishes a federal privacy compliance standard that processing entities must nominate a privacy and a data security officer irrespective of the industry they operate in. The COPRA obligation to appoint a data security officer to work hand in hand with the privacy officer is particularly noteworthy, it answers to this study's call to better acknowledge security-privacy levels of data and systems.[714] As a consequence, processing entities will have to allocate technical expertise, authority, and resources to better mitigate against security privacy risks.[715] The new role and function within processing entities which comes with additional resources should also help to further elevate data security to a decision-making category within organizations when products and services are being developed and deployed.[716]

To ensure privacy and data security officers' authority within their organizations, COPRA delineates in broad strokes their mandate and the compliance tasks they are expected to fulfill. According to Sec. 202 (b) (1) COPRA, privacy and data security officers are responsible to implement and supervise a written privacy and data security program to safeguard covered data *"throughout the life cycle of development and operational practice of the covered entity's products and services"*, *e.g.* they must implement safeguards around their organization's data processing, help shape privacy robust product and service development, and conduct privacy training for staff.[717] Besides, Sec. 202 (b) (2) COPRA tasks the privacy and data security officer to annually conduct privacy and data security risk assessments, and to ensure good data hygiene and quality.[718] With regard to *Bamberger/Mulligan's* recommendation to appoint high-status employees as data privacy officers, COPRA again takes a risk-based approach and generally leaves it to the covered entity to decide about the seniority of the employees they recruit as privacy and data security officer.[719] However, for large data holders, the bill explicitly stipulates privacy

712 Cf. ibid 683–684.
713 Glocker (n 91) 180.
714 Supra Chapter 2 A. I. 5. Security-privacy level of data and systems.
715 With similar recommendations Determann, 'Healthy Data Protection' (n 16) 270–271, 273; Floridi (n 143) 235–236, 243; Maisch (n 238) 107–118, 340; Hacker (n 143) 559–561.
716 Cf. Hoffmann-Riem (n 3) 62–63; Bamberger and Mulligan (n 287) 241–242.
717 Cf. Solove and Schwartz (n 60) 1034.
718 Supra Chapter 2 A. I. 2. Data quality.
719 Bamberger and Mulligan (n 287) 241–242.

accountability obligations for high status employees which we will discuss below.[720]

To summarize, the above shows how COPRA follows *Bamberger/Mulligan's* recommendation that companies nominate privacy officials, that they broadly mandate them to interpret and implement processing rules, and that processing entities elevate privacy to a decision-making category.[721] In particular, COPRA stipulates privacy professionals' responsibility to ensure adequate security-privacy levels of data and systems and data quality. Together, the update will substantially strengthen corporate privacy responsibility and privacy on the ground in the U.S. *post* COPRA.

2. Whistleblower protection

All covered entities under COPRA must introduce measures to protect whistleblowers when they disclose confidential information related to perceived privacy shortcomings from inside processing entities. To this end, Sec. 204 (a) (1) and (2) COPRA prohibits the discrimination of employees who take lawful actions to disclose information or testify to federal government, a state attorney general, or to a company official about any act or omission which they reasonably believe is a privacy violation. In case of a discrimination, Sec. 204 (b) COPRA entitles whistleblowers to seek judicial redress with the possibility to obtain their reinstatement with the same seniority status, a substantial salary compensation, as well as other consequential damages. Finally, Sec. 204 (c) and (d) COPRA bans the use of waivers or pre-dispute arbitration agreements which limit whistleblowers' protection.

In line with *Bamberger/Mulligan's* elements of a strong privacy system, the general objective of the bill's provisions on whistleblower protection is to foster a culture of transparency and information disclosure in which privacy shortcomings and breaches can surface from inside organizations to the responsible privacy officer in the organization or to the outside.[722] History has shown how important developments in U.S. privacy law and EU data protection law have been triggered by the activity of whistleblowers such as *Snowden*.[723] In the European Union, it is directive (EU) 2019/1937 *on the protection of persons who report breaches of Union law* which aims at better protecting whistleblowers. Until 17 December 2023, EU Member States will have to conclude the final step of trans-

---

720 Sub Chapter 3 E. I. 3. Certification obligations.

721 Bamberger and Mulligan (n 287) 242–243.

722 Cf. ibid; Dempsey and others (n 129), 2, 11.

723 Supra Chapter 1 A. Concept and status of U.S. privacy law; Chapter 1 B. Concept and status of EU data protection law.

posing the directive into national law with binding obligations also for companies with 50 to 249 employees.[724]

3. Certification obligations

For large data holders only, COPRA stipulates additional privacy accountability obligations which do not apply to general covered entities.[725] Under the title *Executive responsibility* Sec. 201 COPRA requires the chief executive officer of a large data holder to annually certify to the FTC together with the company's privacy and data security officer about the company's privacy compliance program, measures, and about how the company ensures effective reporting. The obligation to certify sets the ground for a personal liability of the top-management of large data holders.[726] As a consequence, any false certification about a company's privacy compliance is potentially sanctionable directly against the top-management. And so is any inaction of the top-management following the reporting of privacy shortcomings within processing entities: For instance, the internal reporting about a privacy breach puts the management on notice with the consequence that any inaction thereafter by the management may appear as negligence. Following *Bamberger/Mulligan's* recommendations, Sec. 201 COPRA effectively establishes privacy responsibility for high-status employees which, in turn, pushes the topics of data privacy and data security on the company's board agenda. These additional accountability rules for large data holders are without precedent *pre* COPRA and, hence, mean a strengthening of the existing U.S. privacy law and system.

II. Oversight and enforcement

Beyond processing entities' internal privacy compliance programs and measures, meaningful oversight and enforcement from outside of processing entities play an essential role in strong privacy systems.[727] *Pre* COPRA, oversight and enforcement of U.S. consumer privacy law have been criticized as weak. During decades of industry self-regulation, processing entities have been allowed to set their own processing rules and have mainly been held accountable to whether they break their

724 European Parliament and Council, 'Directive 2019/1937 of the European Parliament and the of the Council on the protection of persons who report breaches of Union law' OJL 30/517.
725 Supra Chapter 3 C. II. 2. Quantitative assessment of covered entities.
726 Cf. Bamberger and Mulligan (n 287) 241–242.
727 Cf. ibid 242–243.

privacy policy promises.[728] Most of the privacy oversight and enforcement actions have been handled by the FTC.[729] With limited resources and enforcement powers, the FTC has, on average, brought 10 enforcement actions per year, most of them settled without becoming case law.[730]

Looking forward, this chapter examines which form of oversight and enforcement would foster a stronger privacy system in the U.S. and whether COPRA stipulates for such updates. As we will see in the below, there are multiple examples in U.S. law in and beyond the privacy realm which indicate that a combination of oversight and enforcement by private individuals (sub Chapter 3 E. II. 1. Private right of action) and by government agencies and state authorities (sub Chapter 3 E. II. 2. FTC and state authorities) could be advantageous in comparison to the *pre* COPRA system which primarily relied on the FTC's taking action.[731] In any event, both oversight and enforcement by private individuals and by state authorities should ideally provide for effective remedies in line with COPRA's double goal of protecting individual and collective privacy to adequately redress harmed individuals and to deter processing entities from acting against the law.[732]

1. Private right of action

Private oversight and enforcement by way of a private right of action means that the individual consumer is entitled to directly seek redress for a contested privacy violation by suing a processing entity at court.[733] Whether U.S. federal consumer privacy law should contain such a private right of action has been the topic of intense debate and is one of the main reasons why until today no federal privacy law has been passed.[734] The hope and for others the fear about a federal private right of action is that it would trigger a great number of private enforcement

728 Supra Chapter 1 A. Concept and status of U.S. privacy law.

729 Kühnl (n 311) 248–253; supra Chapter 1 A. Concept and status of U.S. privacy law.

730 Cf. Solove and Schwartz (n 60) 1106–1107; Voss, 'Obstacles to transatlantic harmonization of data privacy law in context' (n 36) 424; Hoofnagle, *Federal trade commission privacy law and policy* (n 79) 117–118, 159; Hoofnagle, 'Privacy Self-Regulation: A Decade of Disappointment' (n 77) 382; Solove and Hartzog (n 385).

731 Scholz, 'Private rights of action in privacy law' (n 160) 8–9, 57–58; Dempsey and others (n 129), 26; Zachary Clopton, 'Redundant Public-Private Enforcement' 2016 69 Vanderbilt Law Review 285, 295–299; Hoffmann-Riem (n 3) 207–208.

732 Dempsey and others (n 129), 3, 21–23; supra Chapter 2 A II. 3. Individual and collective privacy.

733 Cf. Scholz, 'Private rights of action in privacy law' (n 160) 1645.

734 Dempsey and others (n 129), 4; Scholz, 'Private rights of action in privacy law' (n 160) 1645; the other topic of debate has been about the preemption of state privacy laws by COPRA supra Chapter 3 B. COPRA and the preemption of existing privacy law.

actions and litigation.[735] Increased litigation would likely produce more pertinent privacy case law than a system that only relies on enforcement by state authorities; more case law, in turn, could help further shape and develop U.S. federal privacy law and its implementation.[736] Also, the increase in litigation may have a deterrent effect on processing entities to avoid violating privacy processing and compliance rules.[737]

For the individual consumer, private oversight and enforcement in privacy matters has the advantage that it can often happen much earlier and be more efficient and effective than enforcement by state authorities. Since most personal data processing relevant to the consumer happens in the relationship between the consumer and the processing entity, the consumer typically becomes aware of privacy wrongs much earlier than a state authority which sits outside of this relationship, *e.g.* when a processing entity does not answer to a consumer's request to access her personal data.[738] Instead of logging a complaint, waiting for, and depending on a state authority to react, a private right of action allows the consumer to take action herself.[739] Considering FTC's currently scarce privacy enforcement practice of about 10 enforcement actions per year, such direct access to courts would likely strengthen consumer's privacy protection.[740]

While a private right of action is not new in U.S. law generally and in U.S. privacy law in particular, a COPRA update would set a federally binding standard in a currently divided landscape of private oversight and enforcement in U.S. consumer privacy law. On a state level, some jurisdictions do not recognize a private right of action at all, others have established or propose a private right of action, albeit often limited in scope to specific privacy violations only. For example, the private right of action as set out in § 1798.150 *California Consumer Privacy Act* is restricted to cases of insufficient security-privacy levels of data and systems when non-encrypted or non-redacted data is stolen or leaked.[741] Similarly, the States of Pennsylvania, Florida, Kentucky, Maine, Mississippi, and Wisconsin restrict private enforcement to specific privacy violations only; by contrast, among the jurisdictions which broadly recognize a private right of action are the States of New

735 Danielle Keats Citron and Daniel Solove, 'Privacy Harms' 2022 Boston University Law Review 793, 815, 821; Dempsey and others (n 129), 3.

736 Cf. Hoofnagle, 'Privacy Self-Regulation: A Decade of Disappointment' (n 77) 382; Solove and Schwartz (n 60) 1033–1034; 1089.

737 Cf. Scholz, 'Private rights of action in privacy law' (n 160) 1647.

738 Ibid 1688.

739 Ibid 1645.

740 Cf. Clopton (n 730), 296.

741 Keats Citron and Solove (n 734), 810–811, 813.

Jersey, Alaska, Georgia, Massachusetts, North Carolina, Rhode Island, Washington, New York.[742] A private right of action in privacy law exists also on a federal level, for example in the *Telephone Consumer Protection Act* 47 U. S.C. § 277(c)(5), in the *Video Privacy Protection Act* 18 U. S.C. § 2710(c), and in the *Fair Credit Reporting Act* 15 U. S.C. §§ 1681n, 1681o.[743] Beyond privacy law, private enforcement has been an important element of oversight and enforcement in environmental law, for instance, the *Clean Water Act* has allowed citizens to bring a claim according to 33 U. S.C. § 1365 against any other person, the U.S., or any governmental agency that is allegedly in conflict with the act, in antitrust law which stipulates for a private right of action in 15 U. S.C. § 15 *Antitrust Act*, and in securities law which recognizes private enforcement in 15 U. S.C. § 78r and § 78t *Securities Exchange Law* to sanction misleading statements and insider trading.[744]

Where it exists in U.S. law, private oversight and enforcement in privacy matters has regularly been met with two common obstacles: First, individuals who contend a violation of their privacy rights have often struggled to demonstrate standing as a necessary precondition for bringing a claim.[745] Standing is typically defined as an injury in fact which must be concrete and particularized.[746] The problem with privacy infringements is that they often remain intangible injuries, that consumers do not succeed in proving the emotional distress inflicted by a privacy violation, and that the compounded future risk of a privacy violation mostly is difficult to assess, *e.g.* what is the likelihood that leaked personal data will be misappropriated by third parties and what could be the damage?[747] The second common obstacle has been the widespread usage of arbitration clauses in consumer contracts by which the consumer waives her right to go to court.[748] For consumers, consenting to arbitration and waiving their right to a court proceeding has often been a choice of take-it-or-leave-it if they wished to obtain a particular good or service.[749]

COPRA now introduces to U.S. federal privacy law a broad and strong private right of action which seemingly overcomes the above-listed constraints. According to Sec. 301 (c) (1) COPRA, any alleged violation of the bill is actionable for the individual consumer; COPRA's private right of action is not limited in scope to a particu-

742 IAPP (n 65).

743 Keats Citron and Solove (n 734), 810–811, 813.

744 Clopton (n 730), 295–299; Dempsey and others (n 129), 3, 23.

745 Wischmeyer (n 87) 71–72; Glocker (n 91) 205–206.

746 Keats Citron and Solove (n 734), 800–801; Glocker (n 91) 205–206.

747 Keats Citron and Solove (n 734), 796–797, 816–817.

748 Scholz, 'Private rights of action in privacy law' (n 160) 1653, 1667.

749 Ibid.

lar privacy infringement. Besides, any contested violation of COPRA *per definitionem "constitutes a concrete and particularized injury in fact"* according to Sec. 301 (c) (3) COPRA which removes the consumer's need to demonstrate standing. Sec. 301 (d) (1), (2) and (3) COPRA bans the use of pre-dispute arbitration agreements and any waiver of the consumer's right to participate in a joint, class, or collective enforcement action.

Moreover, COPRA's private right of action is linked to effective remedies which are aligned with the bill's dual policy goal of individual and collective privacy.[750] Pursuant to Sec. 301 (c) (2) (A), (C), (D) COPRA, wronged consumers are entitled to claim monetary compensation between $ 100 and $ 1000 per violation per day as well as the reimbursement of attorney fees and litigation cost. Additionally, courts may find for equitable, declaratory, or other appropriate relief to rectify the suffered harm which includes specific performance, *e.g.* ordering a processing entity to comply with a consumer's request according to Sec. 102 (a) COPRA to access her covered data. As a remedy of deterrence and to foster collective privacy, Sec. 301 (c) (B) COPRA explicitly allows courts to impose punitive damages on processing entities, *i.e.* penalties which exceed the consumer's suffered damage and which are intended to punish the processing entity and to deter others from engaging in similar behavior.[751]

In all, COPRA's private right of action applies more broadly and provides for more severe remedies than what has previously existed in U. S. federal privacy law and including the private right of action in § 1798.150 California Consumer Privacy Act. COPRA thereby follows *Bamberger/Mulligan's* recommendation to set a framework of meaningful privacy oversight and enforcement.[752]

2. FTC and state authorities

Besides oversight and enforcement by private individuals, in Sec. 301 (a) and (b) COPRA, the bill tasks the FTC and other state authorities to ensure privacy compliance with COPRA. Compared to individual consumer's taking action, oversight and enforcement by the FTC and other state authorities is advantageous in at least three ways: First, it allows for monitoring and oversight of data processing activities on a large scale in a way that is not feasible for the individual consumer. Oversight and enforcement authorities may request access to large quantities of business information or even a constant flow of information from processing entities

750 Cf. Dempsey and others (n 129), 3, 21–23.
751 Cf. Scholz, 'Private rights of action in privacy law' (n 160) 1657.
752 Bamberger and Mulligan (n 225) 242–243.

to the supervisor.[753] The *Securities Exchange Committee*, for instance, receives millions of reports from securities firms every day which it scrutinizes for anomalies.[754] Similarly, in privacy matters several FTC settlement agreements already today require large technology companies to have their privacy and data security compliance monitored on a continuous basis by third-party examiners.[755] Given the technical capacities of modern data processing such as data quantity, data quality, and the use of particular processing technology, large-scale monitoring and oversight by the FTC and other state authorities seem better suited than punctual discovery of information in private enforcement to stay on top of pertinent industry developments, changes in market behavior, and technological innovation.[756]

Secondly, to cope with the technical capacities of modern data processing, the FTC and state authorities may leverage a high number of specialized technical staff for its monitoring and enforcement activities to whom individual consumers have no broad access.[757] To do so effectively, the FTC's current resources will likely have to be re-balanced towards a more technically trained workforce: Whereas most of the large federal agencies in the U.S. already employ primarily technical staff such as engineers, IT specialists, and accountants, 97 % of the FTC's current workforce have a legal and only 3 % a technical background.[758]

Last but not least, oversight and enforcement by the FTC and state authorities can focus on collective privacy more than private enforcement commonly does.[759] For example, where a privacy harm is dispersed among many consumers and is too small a cause of action to yield a successful or impactful result in a private litigation, enforcement by the FTC and state authorities can better account for compounded future risks of privacy shortcomings or for aggregated harm.[760] Moreover, the FTC and state authorities can systematically probe and enforce technical capacities such as data quality, the use of particular processing technology, and security-privacy levels of data and systems which cause structural privacy risks beyond the individual consumer.[761]

---

753 Cf. Dempsey and others (n 129), 5–6.

754 Dempsey and others (n 129), 9.

755 This applies to some of the largest U.S. technology companies in the United States, cf. Dempsey and others (n 129), 5–6.

756 Supra Chapter 2 A. I. Technical capacities; Dempsey and others (n 129), 9.

757 Cf. Dempsey and others (n 129), 5–7.

758 Cf. Dempsey and others (n 129), 5–6 who explain that the high ratio of legal staff is due to the FTC's historic focus on investigations rather than monitoring.

759 Dempsey and others (n 129), 3 and 14; supra Chapter 3 D. II. Data rights of the individual consumer.

760 Dempsey and others (n 129), 5–6; Keats Citron and Solove (n 734), 814.

761 Supra Chapter 2 A. I. Technical capacities.

To enable effective public oversight and enforcement, COPRA significantly strengthens the resources of the FTC. Sec. 301 (a) (1) (A) COPRA sets out that a new bureau for consumer privacy shall be set up which must match the existing FTC bureau for consumer protection and competition in terms of structure, size, and organization. Today, the FTC's consumer protection bureau employs a total of 493 full times employees of which only 63 full time employees work on consumer privacy matters as part of the division of privacy and identity protection.[762] The COPRA update effectively means that the FTC staffing for consumer privacy will rise to a total of 493 full time employees, in other words a staff increase of more than 780 % compared to the status quo *pre* COPRA. Additional resources for the FTC may likely come from the so-called *Data privacy and security relief fund* in which money payments resulting from civil penalties or enforcement actions are collected. According to Sec. 301 (a) (4) (A) and (C) COPRA, the FTC is tasked to set up the fund and provide monetary relief to victims of privacy violations, for technological research which benefits the enforcement of COPRA, or to educate consumers and businesses about privacy. Such use of the fund money may help ease some of the common human intellectual (in)capacities highlighted in Chapter 2 which frequently catalyze privacy risks including poor decision-making and inaction by consumers regarding the processing of their personal data.[763] Overall, COPRA sets out a framework for the FTC to engage in privacy education, research, and policy-making more actively than *pre* COPRA.[764]

Moreover, the FTC's mandate to monitor and enforce consumer privacy will be broadened. Where § 18 (a) (1) (B) FTC Act previously limited FTC privacy enforcement to cases of deceptive practice which met the threshold of "[...] *to the consumer's detriment*" or of unfair practice "*likely to cause substantial injury to consumers*", Sec. 301 (a) (2) COPRA now establishes that any violation of the bill is actionably by the FTC.[765] *Post* COPRA, the FTC is granted independent litigation authority according to Sec. 301 (a) (2) and (3) (A) and (C) COPRA to commence enforcement proceedings against any violation of COPRA. Further below in this study, we will discuss the enforcement means the FTC can rely on and which sanctions it has available.[766]

---

762 Federal Trade Commission, 'Congressional Budget Justification Fiscal Year 2022' (2022) 141 <https://www.ftc.gov/system/files/documents/reports/fy-2022-congressional-budget-justification/fy22cbj.pdf> accessed 12 February 2023.

763 Supra Chapter 2 A. II. Human (in)capacities; Acquisti and Grossklags (n 226) 368, 371; Specht (n 298) 167–168; Cate (n 30) 360–361.

764 On the importance of privacy education and the role the oversight and enforcement authorities can play Sandfuchs (n 298) 108; Schrems (n 307) 204–206; European Data Protection Supervisor (n 21) 5.

765 Cf. Keats Citron and Solove (n 734), 814, 816.

766 Sub Chapter 4 B. II. 1. Public oversight and enforcement.

Finally, in addition to FTC oversight and enforcement, Sec. 301 (b) (1) COPRA empowers state attorney generals and state consumer protection officers to bring civil claims when they believe their state residents' interests have been affected. According to Sec. 301 (b) (1) (A) to (D) COPRA, state attorney generals and consumer protection officers may obtain the enjoinment of any act or practice violating COPRA, civil penalties, and damages or other compensation for the harmed individuals.

We conclude from the above that COPRA's update significantly strengthens the FTC's resources and mandate to oversee and enforce compliance with the bill compared to the status *pre* COPRA. With additional help from state attorney generals and consumer protection officers, the FTC will be in a better position to safeguard collective privacy, in particular by leveraging its capability to monitor on a large scale, to deploy technically trained staff to investigate technical capacities of modern data processing, and by systemically probing and enforcing structural privacy such as data quality, the use of particular processing technology, and security-privacy levels of data and systems. *Post* COPRA and in line with *Bamberger/Mulligan's* recommendation for a robust privacy system, the FTC will hence be better able than before the update to meaningfully monitor and enforce consumer privacy in the U.S.[767]

F. Interim summary

Measured against the benchmark set out in Chapter 2, COPRA can be considered a meaningful update to existing U.S. federal privacy law. The concise bill of 22 provisions leverages many of the building blocks illustrated above and offers new concepts and means which mitigate against technical capacities and human (in)capacities linked to modern data processing.[768]

First, COPRA updates the marketplace-centered approach of U.S. federal privacy law with its comprehensive privacy regulation which applies across industries and sectors.[769] It thereby sets a minimum standard of privacy protection across U.S. states. Other privacy laws on a federal or state level remain in effect to the extent they provide for more rigorous privacy protection compared to COPRA.[770] The consequence is that COPRA does not solve today's challenge of processing entities in the U.S. to navigate a fragmented and complex U.S. privacy land-

767 Bamberger and Mulligan (n 225) 242–243.

768 Supra Chapter 2 Building blocks for a modern privacy law.

769 Supra Chapter 3 C. I. Material scope of application.

770 Supra Chapter 3 B. COPRA and the preemption of existing privacy law.

scape.[771] However, the new minimum standard in U.S. privacy law will likely make it easier for processing entities to streamline their efforts towards privacy compliance across jurisdictions by demonstrating compliance with COPRA.

COPRA's baseline of generally permitted processing of covered data remains close to the U.S. traditional regulatory approach of unrestricted data processing in the absence of any opposing rule.[772] Instead, COPRA generally focuses on output-based regulation such as in Sec. 101, and 108 (a) and (b) COPRA where privacy regulation is triggered when the processing activity produces an undesired result or is *per se* considered objectionable, *e.g.* because it builds on discriminatory data quality as in Sec. 108 (a) (1) COPRA.[773] In today's data reality where *inter alia* the generation and use of high-quality data should be an aspired goal of privacy regulation, such output-based regulation has been shown to be advantageous for the data economy and innovation compared to input regulation known from EU data protection law.[774]

To strengthen individual consumer's privacy, COPRA's processing baseline is subsequently modified when processing entities must obtain the consumer's affirmative express consent (opt-in) prior to any processing of sensitive covered data according to Sec. 105 (c) (1) and (2) COPRA.[775] The bill embraces common human (in)capacities in its provisions about individual privacy, *e.g.* its privacy information management system where consumers can centrally register their opt-out against unwanted data transfers in Sec. 105 (b) (1) (B) and Sec. 105 (b) (2) COPRA, and the data control rights in Sec. 102–105 COPRA.[776]

An important focus of COPRA is collective privacy and how owners of technical capacities and processing entities can be tasked to ensure effective privacy protection for the individual and society.[777] To this end, the bill leverages output- and downstream-based regulation and provisions which focus on the point of use of the

771 Cf. Business Roundtable, 'CEO letter to members of the U.S. Senate and House of Representatives' (2019) <https://s3.amazonaws.com/brt.org/BRT-CEOLetteronPrivacy-2.pdf> accessed 6 June 2020.

772 Supra Chapter 1 A. Concept and status of U.S. privacy law.

773 Supra Chapter 2 B. Output and downstream regulation; Chapter 3 D. I. 1. COPRA's fair processing standard; Chapter 3 D. I. 2. Point of use regulation and regulation of data quality; Chapter 3 D. I. 3. Regulating specific processing technology.

774 Gal and Aviv (n 19), 363–364; supra Chapter 2 B. Output and downstream regulation.

775 Supra Chapter 3 C. I. 2. (Sensitive) covered data.

776 Supra Chapter 3 D. II. Data rights of the individual consumer; Chapter 2 A. II. Human (in)capacities; Chapter 3 D. II. 1. Data control rights; Chapter 3 D. II. 2. Privacy information management system.

777 Supra Chapter 2 A. II. 3. Individual and collective privacy; Chapter 3 D. I. Data rights of the collective.

processing activity, on specific data quality and the use of particular processing technology such as in Sec. 101, 108 (a) and (b), 205 COPRA.[778]

With the same objective, COPRA furthermore tightens processing entities' compliance obligations. For instance, processing entities will have to designate privacy and data security officers, maintain reasonable security practices, and conduct annual risk assessments about how they use covered data and particular processing technology.[779] Remarkably, COPRA considers structural privacy risks linked to the quantity of covered data that is being processed when it applies a risk-based approach based on data quantity regulation. As set out in Sec. 2 (9) (C), Sec. 2 (23), Sec. 2 (15) COPRA, the bill exempts small businesses which process little covered data and puts additional scrutiny on so-called large data holders which process large quantities of covered data or a substantial amount of sensitive covered data.[780] Such large data holders are subject to additional compliance and accountability obligations, *e.g.* their top-management must annually certify in person about the their companies' compliance efforts (which may trigger a personal liability for top-management in matters of privacy).[781]

Finally, COPRA introduces a hybrid approach of oversight and enforcement by the FTC, state authorities, and the private consumer. The bill substantially strengthens the FTC by bolstering its resources and broadening its mandate which will help the FTC to remain, *post* COPRA, the most important state actor to monitor and enforce compliance with U.S. federal privacy law.[782] Importantly, COPRA additionally provides for a broad and strong private right of action for individual consumers to bring privacy matters to court themselves. The consequence will likely be an increase in enforcement and litigation action in privacy matters, a development this study argues will ultimately render U.S. consumer privacy law more robust.[783]

By way of concluding this study's analysis of COPRA, we want to highlight that the above core points hold true also for the recent *American Privacy Rights Act*. The author and sponsor of COPRA *Senator Cantwell* released the draft text of the American Privacy Rights Act as a bi-partisan proposal in April 2024 together with the Republican Chair of the House Energy & Commerce Committee *Representative*

---

778 Supra Chapter 2 B. Output and downstream regulation; Chapter 3 D. I. 1. COPRA's fair processing standard; Chapter 3 D. I. 2. Point of use regulation and regulation of data quality; Chapter 3 D. I. 3. Regulating specific processing technology; Chapter 3 D. 7. Digital content forgery.

779 Supra Chapter 3 E. I. 1. Privacy and data security officers; Chapter 3 D. I. 6. Data security; Chapter 3 D. I. 3. Regulating specific processing technology.

780 Supra Chapter 3 C. II. 2. Quantitative assessment of covered entities.

781 Supra Chapter 3 E. I. 3. Certification obligations.

782 Supra Chapter 3 E. II. 2. FTC and state authorities.

783 Supra Chapter 3 E. II. 1. Private right of action.

Cathy McMorris Rodgers.[784] The American Privacy Rights Act closely resembles COPRA, often to the point of identical concepts, structure and content: It would broadly apply across industries and sectors (Sec. 2 (10) (A)), establish the same consumer data control rights as COPRA (Sec. 5 (a)), and require processing entities to obtain the consumer's prior affirmative express consent (opt-in) to process any sensitive covered data (Sec. 11 (b)). It would establish a centralized privacy information management system where consumers can register their privacy preferences (Sec. 6 (b)) and, in an effort to promote collective privacy, prohibit processing when the output or effect is harmful or discriminating (Sec. 7 (a) and (b), Sec. 12 (b), Sec. 13 (a)). Alike COPRA, the American Privacy Rights Act sets out comprehensive privacy compliance obligations for covered entities including annual certification obligations for the top-management of large data holders (Sec. 10 (a) (2) (B)). The American Privacy Rights Act equally proposes to strengthen the FTC's oversight and enforcement resources and authority (Sec. 17 (a) and (b)) while recognizing in Sec. 19 (a) a private right of action for consumers to bring civil claims against covered entities for alleged violations of the law. Last but not least, pursuant to Sec. 20 (a) the American Privacy Rights Act preempts all state privacy law except for some listed exceptions. In this point of preemption of state law, the American Privacy Rights Act is more ambitious than Sec. 302(c) sentence 2 COPRA according to which only less onerous state privacy law would be preempted.[785] The desired effect of a full preemption of state privacy law according to Sec. 20 (a) (1) (A) American Privacy Rights Act is to *"establish a uniform national data privacy and data security standard in the United States to prevent administrative costs and burdens placed on interstate commerce"*. The above shows that the American Privacy Rights Act alike COPRA can be considered a meaningful update to existing U.S. federal privacy law when measured against the benchmark set out in Chapter 2 of this study.

784 Committee on Energy and Commerce (n 93).

785 Supra Chapter 3 B. COPRA and the preemption of existing privacy law.

Chapter 4
U.S. adequacy *post* COPRA

Given the paramount importance of personal data exchange between the EU and the U.S. for economy and society, Chapter 4 of this study examines the legal state of exporting personal data protected by the GDPR from the EU to the U.S. *post* COPRA and compared to the situation *pre* COPRA.[786] In particular, this chapter asks whether the U.S. *post* COPRA would qualify as a third country which broadly offers an adequate level of data protection according to Art. 45 para. 1 and 2 GDPR. Could the privacy concepts and means introduced by COPRA – when viewed in the aggregate – be considered a strong enough update to existing U.S. privacy law for the European Commission to recognize according to Art. 45 para. 3 sentence 1 GDPR that the U.S. and U.S. privacy law *post* COPRA ensure an adequate level of data protection?

The question arises because Art. 44 sentence 1 GDPR bans the transfer of personal data from the EU to third countries unless the export fulfills the requirements of one of the transfer mechanisms provided for in Chapter V, see Art. 44–50 GDPR.[787] Accordingly, personal data may only be transferred to the U.S. if, first, an adequacy decision exists by the European Commission and by which the U.S. is granted adequacy status according to Art. 45 para. 1 sentence 1 and para. 3 sentence 1 GDPR, secondly, if the controller or processor provide for appropriate safeguards according to Art. 46 para. 1 and 2 GDPR and which ensure enforceable data subject rights and effective legal remedies, or, thirdly, in the exceptional case of a derogation according to Art. 49 para. 1 sentence 1 and 2 GDPR.[788] Since a transfer

786 Consider the quantity of data exchanged between the EU and the U.S. which exceeds any other data flow supra Introduction and A. Scope, thesis, and structure of the study; Eurostat (n 38); WIPO (n 37) 33; cf. Schwartz and Pfeifer (n 19), 117–118; Hoffmann-Riem (n 3) 289–290; Hamilton and Quinlan (n 39) 25; Schwartz, 'Global Data Privacy: The EU Way' (n 61) 799; European Commission, 'Commission Implementing Decision on the adequate level of protection of personal data under the EU-US Data Privacy Framework' (n 39) Annex III Letter of the International Trade Administration within the U.S. Department of Commerce p. 2.
787 Cf. Art. 44 sentence 2 GDPR; Recital 101 sentence 3 GDPR; *C-311/18 – Schrems II* (n 52) para. 92; Julian Wagner, 'The transfer of personal data to third countries under the GDPR: when does a recipient country provide an adequate level of protection?' 2018 8(4) International Data Privacy Law 318, 319; Moritz Hennemann, 'Wettbewerb der Datenschutzrechtsordnungen' 2020(4) RabelsZ 864, 883; Schwartz, 'Global Data Privacy: The EU Way' (n 61) 784–785; Streinz (n 12) 36.
788 *C-311/18 – Schrems II* (n 52) para. 91–93; Julian Wagner, 'The transfer of personal data to third countries under the GDPR: when does a recipient country provide an adequate level of protection?' 2018 8(4) International Data Privacy Law 318, 320.

https://doi.org/10.1515/9783112215715-005

based on an adequacy decision is treated like a transfer between EU Member States without additional requirements according to Art. 45 para. 1 sentence 2 GDPR and Recital 103 sentence 2 GDPR, adequacy for many businesses is the most convenient transfer mechanism.[789]

However, until today no adequacy decision exists which recognizes that the U.S. privacy law and system *per se* and without a tailor-made protection framework for EU personal data provide for an adequate level of data protection.[790] The U.S. has never formally requested the EU Commission to broadly examine the level of data protection in the U.S., reportedly, because politicians have doubted whether the traditional sectoral privacy approach, the lack of general data rights for individuals, and the reliance on industry self-regulation with limited prospects for individuals to seek redress for privacy violations would leave the Commission much room for a positive decision.[791] Instead, the U.S. government and the EU Commission have repeatedly attempted to implement more narrow adequacy decisions tailored only to the transfer and the processing of personal data of EU data subjects to and in the U.S. whereby they adjust in this narrow scope of application the level of protection in the U.S. to the EU standard.[792]

These attempts have failed to bring a lasting solution to cross-Atlantic personal data transfer though: First, the Commission's decision (EC) 2000/520 based on the *Safe Harbor* principles was invalidated by the CJEU in C-362/14 Schrems/Data Protection Commissioner ("*Schrems-I*").[793] After the *Safe Harbor* principles were updated in the form of the *EU-U.S. Privacy Shield* and approved by the Commission in the decision (EC) 2016/1250, the CJEU subsequently voided the Commission's deci-

---

789 Cf. European Commission, 'Commission Implementing Decision on the adequate level of protection of personal data under the EU-US Data Privacy Framework' (n 39) para. 2 sentence 2, para. 8 sentence 1; cf. Hennemann (n 49), 883–884; Pauly (n 49) para. 1; Hladjk, 'Art. 45' (n 49) para. 3.

790 European Commission, 'Adequacy Decisions' (2024) <https://commission.europa.eu/law/law-topic/data-protection/international-dimension-data-protection/adequacy-decisions_en> accessed 27 June 2024.

791 Murphy (n 88), 250; Schwartz, 'Global Data Privacy: The EU Way' (n 61) 794; cf. Voss, 'Obstacles to transatlantic harmonization of data privacy law in context' (n 36) 431–445; supra Chapter 1 A. Concept and status of U.S. privacy law.

792 European Commission, 'Commission Implementing Decision on the adequate level of protection of personal data under the EU-US Data Privacy Framework' (n 39); European Commission, 'Commission Implementing Decision on the adequacy of the protection provided by the EU-U.S. Privacy Shield' (n 500); European Commission, 'Commission Decision on the adequacy of the protection provided by the safe harbour principles and related frequently asked questions issued by the US Department of Commerce' (n 558).

793 European Commission, 'Commission Decision on the adequacy of the protection provided by the safe harbour principles and related frequently asked questions issued by the US Department of Commerce' (n 558); *C-362/14 – Schrems I* (n 110); Pauly, 'Art. 45' (n 476) para. 12–16.

sion in C-311/18 Facebook Ireland/Schrems ("*Schrems-II*").[794] The latest attempt is the 2023 *US-EU Data Privacy Framework,* recognized by the Commission in its decision (EU) 2023/1795, and which still has to prove that it can survive legal challenges.[795]

It is noteworthy that rather than assessing the *Safe Harbor* and the *EU-U.S. Privacy Shield* principles in their entirety, the Court's critique in *Schrems-I* and *Schrems-II* primarily revolved around U.S. intelligence activities and their effect on EU data subjects.[796] In particular, the CJEU criticized a lack of limitations to derogations and interferences with data protection rights in U.S. national security law which allowed U.S. authorities the bulk collection and processing of personal data of EU data subjects, insufficient control and oversight of such surveillance practices, and inadequate remedies for EU data subjects to protect them against abusive data processing activities.[797]

The Court's focus in *Schrems-I* and *Schrems-II* on U.S. intelligence activities and their impact on the protection of personal data in the U.S. raises the following challenge for this study and the examination of the data protection level provided by COPRA: The likely remedy to the CJEU critique lies in a demarcation and limitation of U.S. intelligence activities; such activities, however, and their scope and limitation are typically not spelled out in data protection or data privacy law itself, rather they are subject to a country's separate body of law regarding national defense and security. A case in point is the broad exemption for national security, defense, and public security in the EU data protection law in Recital 16 and Art. 23 para. 1 lit. a–c GDPR.[798] Similarly, COPRA does not itself contain express checks and balances vis-à-vis U.S. intelligence activities. Sec. 302 (a) (1) and (2) COPRA clarifies that the bill does not limit the authority of any executive agency or provision of federal law unless expressly stated otherwise.[799] As a consequence, COPRA by itself does not

794 European Commission, 'Commission Implementing Decision on the adequacy of the protection provided by the EU-U.S. Privacy Shield' (n 500); *C-311/18 – Schrems II* (n 52); Pauly, 'Art. 45' (n 476) para. 24c.

795 European Commission, 'Commission Implementing Decision on the adequate level of protection of personal data under the EU-US Data Privacy Framework' (n 39); NOYB, 'European Commission gives EU-US data transfers third round at CJEU' (2023) <https://noyb.eu/en/european-commission-gives-eu-us-data-transfers-third-round-cjeu> accessed 25 February 2025.

796 Cf. Murphy (n 88), 257–258, 262; see also the EU Commission's summary in European Commission, 'Commission Implementing Decision on the adequate level of protection of personal data under the EU-US Data Privacy Framework' (n 39) para. 5 sentences 2 and 3.

797 *C-362/14 – Schrems I* (n 110) para. 81–95; *C-311/18 – Schrems II* (n 52) para. 174–184.

798 The CJEU's take to not allow similar exceptions for national security in U.S. privacy law has been criticized as *hypocritical* by Streinz (n 12) 9–10.

799 Also supra Chapter 3 B. COPRA and the preemption of existing privacy law.

suffice to mitigate the shortcomings pointed out by the CJEU in *Schrems-I* and *Schrems-II*. Instead, we have to look at recent developments in U.S. law outside of COPRA which address U.S. intelligence activities: First, in October 2022 U.S. *President Biden* issued *Executive Order no. 14086 on Enhancing Safeguards For U.S. Signals Intelligence Activities* ("EO") whose very purpose is to address the breaking points enounced in *Schrems-I* and *Schrems-II*.[800] In particular, the EO aims at implementing limitations on, and control and oversight of U.S. surveillance activities, and establishes a review body for individuals who seek redress for privacy violations.[801] Secondly, the EU Commission and the U.S. government have jointly worked towards an updated transfer and processing framework for EU personal data which is called the *EU-U.S. Data Privacy Framework*.[802] On July 10, 2023, the Commission published its *Implementation decision C(2023) 4745 final on the adequate level of protection of personal data under the EU-U.S. Data Privacy Framework*.[803] In large parts of its adequacy decision, the EU Commission discusses how the framework, the EO, and additional material together mitigate against the risk of excessive surveillance activities and insufficient protection for EU data subjects.[804]

Given the scope of this study which focuses on COPRA and the update it brings to U.S. privacy law, it will be for a separate discussion to examine whether the EU-U.S. Data Privacy Framework and recent developments in U.S. law ensure adequate protection for EU data subjects against U.S. intelligence activities. In the below, we will thus restrict our assessment to the COPRA provisions and whether, apart from the above illustrated discussion about U.S. intelligence activities and their impact on EU data subjects, they adequately protect personal data of EU data subjects which is transferred to the U.S. To this end, we will briefly summarize the EU adequacy threshold (sub Chapter 4 A. The adequacy threshold), the benchmark

---

800 President of the United States, 'Executive Order on Enhancing Safeguards For United States Signals Intelligence Activities' (2022) <https://www.whitehouse.gov/briefing-room/presidential-actions/2022/10/07/executive-order-on-enhancing-safeguards-for-united-states-signals-intelligence-activities/> accessed 14 October 2022.

801 Ibid Sec. 2 a) to c) Signals Intelligence Activities and Sec. 2 d) Data Protection Review Court.

802 European Commission, 'Commission Implementing Decision on the adequate level of protection of personal data under the EU-US Data Privacy Framework' (n 39) Annex I.

803 Ibid; President of the United States (n 796).

804 European Commission, 'Commission Implementing Decision on the adequate level of protection of personal data under the EU-US Data Privacy Framework' (n 39) 88–100; Annex III Letter of the International Trade Administration within the U.S. Department of Commerce p. 10 U.S. Government Access to Personal Data; Annex VI Letter of the U.S. Department of Justice; Annex VII Letter of the Office of the Director of National Intelligence Office if General Counsel.

against which we will then assess the level of data protection provided by COPRA, to finally conclude about whether the EU Commission should recognize the U.S. *post* COPRA as a country that ensures an adequate level of data protection (sub Chapter 4 B. Data protection level in the U.S. *post* COPRA).

A. The adequacy threshold

The transfer mechanism of adequacy is set out in Art. 45 para. 1, 2, and 3 GDPR, however, the article lacks a definition of what adequacy actually is.[805] A comprehensive definition of the term and concept is missing also in CJEU case law, in its rulings the court has instead marked out shortcomings which speak against an adequate level of data protection.[806] Another approximation is the list of non-exhaustive criteria in Art. 45 para. 2 lit. a-c GDPR the EU Commission must consider when assessing the level of data protection in a third country.[807] Among these criteria, in particular Art. 45 para. 2 lit. a and b GDPR stick out which highlight that an adequate level of data protection largely depends on a country's legal privacy framework, the existence of supervisory authorities and the country's enforcement practice – we will detail these elements sub Chapter 4 A. I. Legal framework applicable to personal data processing in the EU and sub Chapter 4 A. II. Supervisory authority and enforcement in the EU.[808]

Recital 104 sentence 3 GDPR further clarifies the third country must guarantee a level of data protection *"essentially equivalent"* to the protection in the EU. The language is taken directly from the *Schrems-I* ruling in which the CJEU held that a third country must provide for an actual level of protection of fundamental rights and freedoms essentially equivalent to the one guaranteed in the EU.[809] Yet whether and to which extent this requires third countries to closely retake EU data protection law has been the topic of intense debate. Whereas a very strict interpretation demands a third country to adopt the majority of GDPR core concepts and means almost *verbatim*, a more flexible interpretation argues that a third country's data protection law and system may differ from the GDPR and the

---

805 Cf. Wagner (n 785), 319.

806 Cf. Hennemann, 'Wettbewerb der Datenschutzrechtsordnungen' (n 19) 889; *C-362/14 – Schrems I* (n 110); *C-311/18 – Schrems II* (n 52); supra Chapter 4 U.S. adequacy *post* COPRA.

807 Hennemann, 'Wettbewerb der Datenschutzrechtsordnungen' (n 19) 885–886; Pauly, 'Art. 45' (n 476) para. 4; Hladjk, 'Art. 45' (n 476) para. 7–11; Wittershagen (n 564) 59 f.

808 Art. 29 Data Protection Working Party, 'Adequacy Referential' (2017) Working Paper 254 rev01, 5–6; Pauly, 'Art. 45' (n 476) para. 4.

809 *C-362/14 – Schrems I* (n 110) para. 73, 74.

EU system as long as it offers a comparably strong protection for EU data subjects.[810] For this study, taking a position in this debate is important because it determines the benchmark against which we assess the U.S. data protection level *post* COPRA.

On one end of the spectrum, the *European Data Protection Board* ("EDPB") advocates for a strict interpretation of the adequacy threshold; it has endorsed, adopted, and updated in *Working Paper 254* the adequacy guidelines spelled out in *Working Paper 12* of the *Article 29 Data Protection Working Party*, the EDPB's predecessor until May 2018.[811] Accordingly, a third country's law is expected to contain the "*basic content and procedural/enforcement data protection principles and mechanisms*" and "*should reflect, and be consistent with the concepts*" present in EU data protection law.[812] Countries should adopt the GDPR concept of input-control, the processing principles of purpose limitation, proportionality, data retention, security and confidentiality, transparency, they must provide for data subject rights of access, rectification, erasure, and objection to personal data processing, and restrictions on onwards transfers.[813] Moreover, their law should expressly discuss special categories of personal data and automated decision-making and profiling as set out in Art. 9, 10, and 22 GDPR.[814] To pointedly summarize, the EDPB essentially expects third countries to retake almost the complete set of core concepts and means of the GDPR to a level of detail that even specific data rights have to be copied.[815]

This narrow interpretation of the adequacy threshold by the EDPB in Working Paper 254 has been rightfully criticized by *Hennemann* and others as too restrictive. Art. 45 para. 1, 2, and 3 GDPR does not call for a literal copying of EU data protection law and rather sets the framework for a legal comparison between different laws and systems and their functionality and context.[816] The interpretation suggested by the EDPB seems too restrictive also when compared to CJEU case law and the practice of the EU Commission: *Schrems-I* and *Schrems-II* were clear about an essentially equivalent level of data protection not requiring an identical retake of the

---

810 Cf. Art. 29 Data Protection Working Party, 'Adequacy Referential' (n 804); Hennemann, 'Wettbewerb der Datenschutzrechtsordnungen' (n 19) 890–891.

811 Wittershagen (n 564) 66–68; Hennemann, 'Wettbewerb der Datenschutzrechtsordnungen' (n 19) 888..

812 Art. 29 Data Protection Working Party, 'Adequacy Referential' (n 804) 5.

813 Ibid 5–6.

814 Ibid 6–7.

815 Cf. Hennemann, 'Wettbewerb der Datenschutzrechtsordnungen' (n 19) 888.

816 Cf. ibid 890–891; Koch, Magnus and Winkler von Mohrenfels (n 54) § 13 para. 11–14; Kischel (n 53) § 3 para. 179–197; Wittershagen (n 564) 68.

GDPR.[817] Instead, the EU Commission shall evaluate according to Art. 45 para. 3 GDPR a third country's *"system as a whole"* and whether it *"delivers the required level of protection"*.[818] The Commission may *"recognise a diverse range of privacy systems, representing different legal traditions"*.[819] An instructive example of the Commission's recent practice is the adequacy decision about Japan and its legislative framework and system.[820] Because Japan and the EU's enforcement concepts and practice in data protection matters differ greatly, the Commission looked at the functionality and the effect of the Japanese enforcement practice. In particular, the Commission focused on the issuance of non-binding recommendations in response to privacy violations pursuant to Art. 42 para. 1 *Japanese Act on the Protection of Personal Information.*[821] *Prima facie*, the harmed individual's recourse to a non-binding recommendation without legal effect appears to be too weak a remedy to meet the EU standard of data protection which according to Art. 47 para. 1 and 2 EU Charter of Fundamental Rights grants individuals a right to *"effective remedy before a tribunal"*.[822] Nevertheless, in its adequacy decision about Japan, the EU Commission relied on a functional analysis and on the effect of the Japanese remedy-system as a whole when it explicitly acknowledged the line of escalation in the Japanese enforcement practice according to which a data controller's failure to comply with a non-binding recommendation regarding the processing of personal data of EU subjects warrants the issuance of a binding order which, if ignored, constitutes a criminal offense.[823]

---

817 *C-362/14 – Schrems I* (n 110) para. 73, 74; CJEU, 'C-311/18 – Schrems II' (n 52) para. 94; European Commission, 'Communication from the Commission to the European Parliament and the Council: Exchanging and Protecting Personal Data in a Globalised World' COM(2007)7 final, 6; European Commission, 'Commission Implementing Decision on the adequate protection of personal data by the United Kingdom' C(2021)4800 final, 2.

818 European Commission, 'Commission Implementing Decision on the adequate protection of personal data by the United Kingdom' (n 816) 2; European Commission, 'Commission Implementing Decision on the adequate level of protection of personal data under the EU-US Data Privacy Framework' (n 39) para. 3 sentence 2, para. 4 sentence 1–4.

819 European Commission, 'Communication from the Commission to the European Parliament and the Council' (n 816) 7.

820 European Commission, 'Commission Implementing Decision on the adequate protection of personal data by Japan under the Act on the Protection of Personal Information' C(2019)304, para. 4; Hennemann, 'Wettbewerb der Datenschutzrechtsordnungen' (n 19) 890.

821 Wang (n 33), 679–683; European Commission, 'Commission Implementing Decision on the adequate protection of personal data by Japan under the Act on the Protection of Personal Information' (n 816) para. 101–102; Schwartz, 'Global Data Privacy: The EU Way' (n 61) 788–790.

822 Wang (n 33), 674–678; *C-311/18 – Schrems II* (n 52) para. 186–187.

823 European Commission, 'Commission Implementing Decision on the adequate protection of personal data by Japan under the Act on the Protection of Personal Information' (n 816) para. 101–102.

In sum, the EU adequacy standard according to Art. 45 para. 1, 2, and 3 GDPR and as interpreted by the CJEU in *Schrems-I* and *Schrems-II* does not require a "*point-to-point replication of Union rules*";[824] even when a third country's law and system differ from the EU law and system, they may still qualify as providing for an essentially equivalent data protection level to the one established in the European Union.[825]

I. Legal framework applicable to personal data processing in the EU

According to Art. 45 para. 1, 2, and 3 and Recital 104 sentence 3 GDPR, the level of data protection in a third country must be essentially equivalent to the level of data protection in the EU. In the European Union, data protection is guaranteed by a combination of legislative acts and of CJEU case law, most of all in EU primary law Art. 7 (Respect for private and family life), Art. 8 (Protection of personal data), and Art. 47 (Right to an effective remedy and to a fair trial) of the *Charter of Fundamental Rights of the European Union* ("ECFR"), Art. 16 (Right to data protection) of the *Treaty on the Functioning of the European Union* ("TFEU"), in EU secondary law the GDPR, and in the *Schrems-I* and *Schrems-II* rulings.[826] Additional protection is granted to EU citizens by Art. 8 para. 1 (Right to respect for private and family life) of the *European Convention on Human Rights* because all of the EU Member States, however not the European Union itself, have ratified the convention.[827]

In the following, we will focus on a selection of provisions the European Commission and the CJEU have highlighted as indispensable for the level of data protection in the EU, in particular as discussed in the recent adequacy decisions of the Commission about the UK, Japan, the EU-U.S. Privacy Shield, and the EU-U.S. Data

---

824 European Commission, 'Commission Implementing Decision on the adequate protection of personal data by the United Kingdom' (n 813) para. 4; European Commission, 'Commission Implementing Decision on the adequate level of protection of personal data under the EU-US Data Privacy Framework' (n 39) para. 3 sentence 2, para. 4 sentence 1–4.

825 *C-362/14 – Schrems I* (n 110) para. 73, 74; *C-311/18 – Schrems II* (n 52) para. 94; European Commission, 'Commission Implementing Decision on the adequate protection of personal data by the United Kingdom' (n 813) para. 3–4; European Commission, 'Commission Implementing Decision on the adequate protection of personal data by Japan under the Act on the Protection of Personal Information' (n 816) para. 3.

826 European Commission, 'Commission Implementing Decision on the adequate level of protection of personal data under the EU-US Data Privacy Framework' (n 39) para. 3 sentence 2; Commission Implementing Decision on the adequate protection of personal data by the United Kingdom (n 606) 2; *C-362/14 – Schrems I* (n 110); *C-311/18 – Schrems II* (n 52); Wittershagen (n 564) 9–10.

827 Wittershagen (n 564) 19–21; *C-311/18 – Schrems II* (n 52) para. 97–99.

Privacy Framework.[828] First and foremost, the processing principles in Art. 5 para. 1 GDPR of lawfulness, fairness, and transparency (lit. a), purpose limitation (lit. b), data minimization (lit. c), accuracy of personal data (lit. d), storage limitation (lit. e), and integrity and confidentiality of personal information (lit. f) and in Art. 5 para. 2 GDPR of accountability form the framework applicable to the processing of personal data of EU data subjects.[829] The importance of the principles is highlighted also by the fact that any violation is directly sanctionable against processing entities according to Art. 83 para. 5 lit. a GDPR and may entail administrative fines of up to 20'000 EUR or up to 4 % of a company's total annual turnover.[830]

The principle of lawfulness, fairness, and transparency in Art. 5 para. 1 lit. a GDPR stipulates *if* and *how* personal data of EU data subjects can be processed.[831] Any processing must be fair which, drawing on Art. 8 para. 2 sentence 1 ECFR, presupposes that EU data subjects whose personal data is being processed have consented to the processing or that another legitimate basis permits the processing.[832] Contrary to the EDPB's interpretation in Working Paper 254, the principle does not

828 European Commission, 'Commission Implementing Decision on the adequate protection of personal data by the United Kingdom' (n 813); European Commission, 'Commission Implementing Decision on the adequate protection of personal data by Japan under the Act on the Protection of Personal Information' (n 816); European Commission, 'Commission Implementing Decision on the adequacy of the protection provided by the EU-U.S. Privacy Shield' (n 500); *C-311/18 – Schrems II* (n 52); *C-362/14 – Schrems I* (n 110); European Commission, 'Commission Implementing Decision on the adequate level of protection of personal data under the EU-US Data Privacy Framework' (n 39).

829 European Commission, 'Commission Implementing Decision on the adequate protection of personal data by the United Kingdom' (n 813) para. 24–46, 83–84; European Commission, 'Commission Implementing Decision on the adequate protection of personal data by Japan under the Act on the Protection of Personal Information' (n 816) para. 39–56, 60–64; European Commission, 'Commission Implementing Decision on the adequacy of the protection provided by the EU-U.S. Privacy Shield' (n 500) para. 19–23, 28; European Commission, 'Commission Implementing Decision on the adequate level of protection of personal data under the EU-US Data Privacy Framework' (n 39) para. 13–28; Julian Wagner, 'The transfer of personal data to third countries under the GDPR: when does a recipient country provide an adequate level of protection?' 2018 8(4) International Data Privacy Law 318, 331; Frenzel, 'Art. 5' (n 178) para. 11; Kramer, 'Art. 5' (n 269) para. 1–2, 5, 9.

830 Cf. Eike Frenzel, 'Art. 83' in Boris Paal and Daniel Pauly (eds), *DSGVO, BDSG* (C.H. Beck 2021) para. 23–24.

831 European Commission, 'Commission Implementing Decision on the adequate level of protection of personal data under the EU-US Data Privacy Framework' (n 39) para. 13; European Commission, 'Commission Implementing Decision on the adequate protection of personal data by the United Kingdom' C(2021)4800 final, para. 24–26; European Commission, 'Commission Implementing Decision on the adequate protection of personal data by Japan under the Act on the Protection of Personal Information' (n 816) para. 44–51; Wagner (n 8), 329; Wittershagen (n 564) 32–33.

832 Frenzel, 'Art. 5' (n 178) para. 14–18; Wittershagen (n 564) 11–12.

limit a third country's regulatory approach to the GDPR's input-control regime whereby according to Art. 6 para. 1 GDPR personal data processing is prohibited unless explicitly justified.[833] Instead, the EU Commission has repeatedly held that fair processing can be achieved in a regime which uses a mixed approach of opt-out for non-sensitive personal data and an input-control or opt-in for sensitive personal data.[834] In fact, acknowledging different levels of data protection for general personal data and sensitive personal data, a concept the GDPR refers to as *special categories of personal data* as set out in Art. 9 para. 1 and Art. 10 GDPR, has frequently been recognized as another essential element of EU data protection,[835] and an opt-in requirement in a third country's data protection law for the processing of sensitive personal data arguably is a manifestation of this element.

Secondly, the GDPR principle of purpose limitation in Art. 5 para. 1 lit. b GDPR is paramount to data protection in the European Union.[836] Linking back to Art. 8 para. 2 sentence 1 ECFR, the principle establishes that any data processing must be restricted to a *"specific, explicit, and legitimate purpose"*. Thereby, EU data protection law renders illicit any unlimited and uncontrolled processing of personal data.[837] It follows that data controllers and processors must specify data

---

833 Cf. Art. 29 Data Protection Working Party, 'Adequacy Referential' (n 804) 5; Hennemann, 'Wettbewerb der Datenschutzrechtsordnungen' (n 19) 887–888; for a discussion of input- and output-control supra Chapter 2 B. Output and downstream regulation.

834 European Commission, 'Commission Implementing Decision on the adequate protection of personal data by Japan under the Act on the Protection of Personal Information' (n 816) para. 45, 65–69, Annex I (1) special care-required data; European Commission, 'Commission Implementing Decision on the adequacy of the protection provided by the EU-U.S. Privacy Shield' (n 500) para. 22, Annex II 2. Choice c.

835 Cf. European Commission, 'Commission Implementing Decision on the adequate level of protection of personal data under the EU-US Data Privacy Framework' (n 39) para. 16–19; Commission Implementing Decision on the adequate protection of personal data by the United Kingdom (n 606) para. 27–42; European Commission, 'Commission Implementing Decision on the adequate protection of personal data by Japan under the Act on the Protection of Personal Information' (n 816) para. 65–69; European Commission, 'Commission Implementing Decision on the adequacy of the protection provided by the EU-U.S. Privacy Shield' (n 500) para. 22, Annex II 2. Choice c.

836 Wagner (n 785), 329; Kramer, 'Art. 5' (n 269) para. 22; Frenzel, 'Art. 5' (n 178) para. 23–25; Wittershagen (n 564) 33–35; cf. European Commission, 'Commission Implementing Decision on the adequate protection of personal data by the United Kingdom' (n 813) para. 43–44; European Commission, 'Commission Implementing Decision on the adequate protection of personal data by Japan under the Act on the Protection of Personal Information' (n 816) para. 39–43, 52–54; European Commission, 'Commission Implementing Decision on the adequacy of the protection provided by the EU-U.S. Privacy Shield' (n 500) para. 21–22; European Commission, 'Commission Implementing Decision on the adequate level of protection of personal data under the EU-US Data Privacy Framework' (n 39) para. 13.

837 Cf. *C-311/18 – Schrems II* (n 52) para. 173–176; Kramer (n 51) para. 22–33.

retention times and store data only as long as it serves the defined processing purpose.[838]

Another fundamental cornerstone of data protection in the EU are, thirdly, the rights of the data subject as set out in Chapter 3 Art. 12 through 23 GDPR. In particular, these rights empower EU data subjects to obtain from the data controller access to their personal data according to Art. 15 para. 1 GDPR, and to rectify or erase personal data according to Art. 16 and 17 para. 1 GDPR.[839] Building on the Art. 5 para. 1 lit. a GDPR principle of fairness and transparency, the EU data subjects rights also comprise extensive information rights which require the data controller to share with the data subject pertinent information related to the intended processing and as set out in Art. 13 para. 1 to 3 and 14 para. 1 to 4 GDPR.[840]

Furthermore, appropriate security-privacy levels which safeguard the processing of personal data of EU data subjects pursuant to Art. 5 para. 1 lit. f GDPR are an essential component of the data protection level granted in the EU.[841] Whereas

---

838 Cf. European Commission, 'Commission Implementing Decision on the adequate level of protection of personal data under the EU-US Data Privacy Framework' (n 39) para. 22 sentence 1; Commission Implementing Decision on the adequate protection of personal data by the United Kingdom (n 606) para. 46; European Commission, 'Commission Implementing Decision on the adequate protection of personal data by Japan under the Act on the Protection of Personal Information' (n 816) para. 55–56.

839 European Commission, 'Commission Implementing Decision on the adequate level of protection of personal data under the EU-US Data Privacy Framework' (n 39) para. 29; European Commission, 'Commission Implementing Decision on the adequate protection of personal data by the United Kingdom' (n 813) para. 52–54; European Commission, 'Commission Implementing Decision on the adequate protection of personal data by Japan under the Act on the Protection of Personal Information' (n 816) para. 81–94; European Commission, 'Commission Implementing Decision on the adequacy of the protection provided by the EU-U.S. Privacy Shield' (n 500) para. 25; Wittershagen (n 564) 45–48.

840 Paal and Hennemann, 'Art. 13' (n 219) para. 4; Martin Eßer, 'Art. 13' in Martin Eßer, Philipp Kramer and Kai von Lewinski (eds), *DSGVO/BDSG* (Carl Heymanns Verlag 2023) para. 5; European Commission, 'Commission Implementing Decision on the adequate level of protection of personal data under the EU-US Data Privacy Framework' (n 39) para. 25; European Commission, 'Commission Implementing Decision on the adequate protection of personal data by the United Kingdom' (n 813) para. 49–50; European Commission, 'Commission Implementing Decision on the adequate protection of personal data by Japan under the Act on the Protection of Personal Information' (n 816) para. 60–64; European Commission, 'Commission Implementing Decision on the adequacy of the protection provided by the EU-U.S. Privacy Shield' (n 500) para. 20, Annex II Principles 1 Notice.

841 Kramer, 'Art. 5' (n 269) para. 55–56; cf. European Commission, 'Commission Implementing Decision on the adequate level of protection of personal data under the EU-US Data Privacy Framework' (n 39) para. 23; Commission Implementing Decision on the adequate protection of personal data by the United Kingdom (n 606) para. 47–48; Commission Implementing Decision on the adequate protection of personal data by Japan under the Act on the Protection of Personal Information (n 609) para. 57–59; Commission Implementation Decision on the adequacy of the protection provided by the EU-U.S. Privacy Shield (n 322) para. 24.

Art. 24 para. 1 GDPR spells out the data controller's obligation to implement appropriate technical and organizational measures to protect the processing of personal data, Art. 32 para. 1 and 2 GDPR and Recital 83 GDPR more broadly set forth a general obligation for meaningful IT-security according to which data controllers and processors are held to assess the risk-level associated with a particular processing activity and to apply appropriate technical and organizational measures to hedge against them. In particular, they must take into account "*the state of the art, the costs of implementation and the nature, scope, context, and purposes of* [the] *processing*".[842]

Fifthly, to avoid the circumvention of the level of data protection granted in the EU, EU data protection law strictly limits onward transfers, *i.e.* the transfer of personal data of EU data subjects from the EU to third countries.[843] To this end, Art. 44 sentence 1 GDPR prohibits any onward transfer of personal data outside of the designated transfer-mechanisms laid out in Chapter V, see Art. 45–49 GDPR. Conversely, the transfer mechanisms ensure within their respective scope and limitation that transferred personal data is processed in a third country according to the same or essentially equivalent standards as within the EU.[844]

Finally, a characteristic of EU data protection law is set forth in Art. 23 para. 2 GDPR and Art. 52 para. 1 sentence 1 and 2 ECFR according to which any derogations from and limitations to the protection of personal data must be provided for by law and must be themselves defined and finite in scope and application.[845] The legal

842 Cf. Kramer and Meints (n 293) para. 1–2.

843 European Commission, 'Commission Implementing Decision on the adequate level of protection of personal data under the EU-US Data Privacy Framework' (n 39) para. 37; European Commission, 'Commission Implementing Decision on the adequate protection of personal data by the United Kingdom' (n 813) para. 74–82; European Commission, 'Commission Implementing Decision on the adequate protection of personal data by Japan under the Act on the Protection of Personal Information' (n 816) para. 47, 75–80; European Commission, 'Commission Implementing Decision on the adequacy of the protection provided by the EU-U.S. Privacy Shield' (n 500) para. 28.

844 *C-311/18 – Schrems II* (n 52) para. 96; Jörg Hladjk, 'Art. 46' in Martin Eßer, Philipp Kramer and Kai von Lewinski (eds), *DSGVO/BDSG* (Carl Heymanns Verlag 2023) para. 4–7; Daniel Pauly, 'Art. 46' in Boris Paal and Daniel Pauly (eds), *DSGVO, BDSG* (C.H. Beck 2021) para. 7–8.

845 *C-362/14 – Schrems I* (n 110) para. 92; *C-311/18 – Schrems II* (n 52) para. 176; European Commission, 'Commission Implementing Decision on the adequate protection of personal data by the United Kingdom' (n 813) para. 55–67; European Commission, 'Commission Implementing Decision on the adequate protection of personal data by Japan under the Act on the Protection of Personal Information' (n 816) para. 113 and Annex 2 Collection and use of personal information by Japanese public authorities for criminal law enforcement and national security purposes; European Commission, 'Commission Implementing Decision on the adequacy of the protection provided by the EU-U.S. Privacy Shield' (n 500) para. 68–76; European Commission, 'Commission Implementing Decision on the adequate level of protection of personal data under the EU-US Data Privacy Framework' (n 39) para. 4 sentence 4; para. 88 and 89; Wittershagen (n 564) 12–13; 48–49.

basis for an interference must hence stipulate for any derogation or limitation to remain within the limits of what is necessary and proportionate while expressly imposing minimum safeguards to protect EU data subjects against abuse.[846] As a case in point, a derogation or limitation from fundamental privacy rights as protected by Art. 7 and Art. 8 ECFR may be necessary because of opposing public interests such as national security or criminal justice.[847] Yet whatever the conflicting interest which justifies an interference with EU data subjects' fundamental rights, in *Schrems-II* the CJEU held with an explicit reference to Art. 52 para. 1 sentence 1 ECFR that the "*essence of those rights and freedoms*" must remain respected.[848]

II. Supervisory authority and enforcement in the EU

Data protection in the European Union is furthermore characterized by the work of independent supervisory authorities whose task it is to monitor and enforce compliance with data protection rules and to advise and assist EU data subjects in exercising their rights.[849] According to Art. 45 para. 2 lit. b GDPR, the EU Commission will assess whether a third country manages to ensure comparable privacy oversight and enforcement.[850]

Art. 8 para. 3 ECFR and Art. 16 para. 2 sentence 2 TFEU are at the foundation of Chapter 6 Art. 51–59 GDPR which spell out in detail the EU's oversight and enforcement mechanism.[851] According to Art. 51 para. 1 GDPR and Art. 52 para. 1 and 4 GDPR, each EU Member State must maintain at least one independent and sufficiently staffed supervisory authority. Independence means a supervisory authority must be

846 *C-311/18 – Schrems II* (n 52) para. 176; Wittershagen (n 564) 13–15; Art. 29 Data Protection Working Party, 'Adequacy Referential' (n 804) 9.
847 *C-311/18 – Schrems II* (n 52) para. 172; cf. European Commission, 'Commission Implementing Decision on the adequate protection of personal data by the United Kingdom' (n 813) para. 51.
848 *C-311/18 – Schrems II* (n 52) para. 174; Wittershagen (n 564) 13–15.
849 Art. 29 Data Protection Working Party, 'Adequacy Referential' (n 804) 6–8; cf. Schwartz, 'Global Data Privacy: The EU Way' (n 61) 808–811; Wittershagen (n 564) 49–51.
850 European Commission, 'Commission Implementing Decision on the adequate protection of personal data by the United Kingdom' (n 813) para. 85–103; European Commission, 'Commission Implementing Decision on the adequate protection of personal data by Japan under the Act on the Protection of Personal Information' (n 816) para. 95–102; European Commission, 'Commission Implementing Decision on the adequacy of the protection provided by the EU-U.S. Privacy Shield' (n 500) para. 30–37; European Commission, 'Commission Implementing Decision on the adequate level of protection of personal data under the EU-US Data Privacy Framework' (n 39) para. 47, 58.
851 Kai von Lewinski, 'Art. 51' in Martin Eßer, Philipp Kramer and Kai von Lewinski (eds), *DSGVO/BDSG* (Carl Heymanns Verlag 2023) para. 1, 10–13.

autonomous from a country's executive power and must have the authority to issue binding decisions.[852] Today, an array of independent supervisory authorities exists both on an EU and on a national level with Germany leading the race and counting 18 data protection authorities for its 16 Länder.[853] Arguably, this institutionalization of data protection has strongly contributed to the level of data protection in the EU.[854]

Furthermore, Art. 47 sentence 1 in connection with Art. 7 and 8 ECFR entitle EU data subjects to seek effective judicial review in data protection matters. Accordingly, Art. 45 para. 2 lit. a in connection with para. 3 sentence 1 and Recital 104 sentence 4 GDPR require the Commission to examine a third country's enforcement system as to whether there exist *"effective and enforceable data subject rights and effective administrative and judicial redress for the data subjects whose personal data are being transferred"*.[855] In light of Art. 47 sentence 2 ECFR, judicial redress refers to the right of an EU data subject to bring a legal action before an independent and impartial court of law.[856] Effective redress in the sense of Art. 47 sentence 1 ECFR and Art. 45 para. 2 lit. a GDPR comprises the individual's right to claim monetary damages for harm suffered due to privacy violations.[857]

---

852 Cf. *C-311/18 – Schrems II* (n 52) para. 195–196; Art. 29 Data Protection Working Party, 'Adequacy Referential' (n 804) 6–8; Wittershagen (n 564) 49–51.

853 Bundesbeauftragter für den Datenschutz und die Informationsfreiheit, 'Germany data protection authorities' (2022) <https://www.bfdi.bund.de/DE/Service/Anschriften/Laender/Laender-node.html> accessed 9 September 2022; European Data Protection Board, 'Member State data protection authorities' (2022) <https://edpb.europa.eu/about-edpb/about-edpb/members_en> accessed 31 October 2022.

854 Cf. Schwartz, 'Global Data Privacy: The EU Way' (n 61) 808–811; Thomas Streinz, 'The Evolution of European Data Law' in Paul P Craig and Gráinne de Búrca (eds), *The evolution of EU law* (Oxford University Press 2021) 920–922.

855 *C-311/18 – Schrems II* (n 52) para. 188; European Commission, 'Commission Implementing Decision on the adequate level of protection of personal data under the EU-US Data Privacy Framework' (n 39) para. 65.

856 *C-311/18 – Schrems II* (n 52) para. 194; *C-362/14 – Schrems I* (n 110) para. 95; European Commission, 'Commission Implementing Decision on the adequate level of protection of personal data under the EU-US Data Privacy Framework' (n 39) para. 89 sentences 3 and 4.

857 Art. 29 Data Protection Working Party, 'Adequacy Referential' (n 804) 8; cf. European Commission, 'Commission Implementing Decision on the adequate protection of personal data by the United Kingdom' (n 813) para. 104–111; European Commission, 'Commission Implementing Decision on the adequate protection of personal data by Japan under the Act on the Protection of Personal Information' (n 816) para. 103–112, 137–150; European Commission, 'Commission Implementing Decision on the adequacy of the protection provided by the EU-U.S. Privacy Shield' (n 500) para. 38–63, Annex 1 and 2; European Commission, 'Commission Decision on the adequacy of the protection provided by the safe harbour principles and related frequently asked questions issued by the US Department of Commerce' (n 558) Art. 1 para. 1 b; Annex IV Damages for Breaches of Privacy, Legal Authorizations and Mergers and Takeovers in U.S. Law; European Commission, 'Commission Implementing Deci-

B. Data protection level in the U.S. post COPRA

Already a first look at COPRA and at the update it brings to existing U.S. privacy law reveals that the bill improves the decision-making basis for the EU Commission's adequacy assessment according to Art. 45 para. 3 sentence 1 GDPR.[858] This is because *pre* COPRA it was difficult to broadly assess the level of privacy protection in the U.S. due to the fragmentation of the law caused by its traditional sectoral approach, different layers of U.S. privacy law on a federal and state level, and white spaces left in between existing privacy laws which, in the words of the COPRA authors, essentially left U.S. consumers without *"the specific data rights they need in the digital economy"*.[859] By contrast, COPRA now adopts an omnibus approach to the regulation of covered data according to Sec. 2 (9) (A) (ii) and Sec. 302 (a), (b), and (c) COPRA and will therefore, for the first time in U.S. consumer privacy law history, broadly regulate on a federal level the processing of covered data irrespective of sectors and industries.[860] Within its scope of application, the bill will establish according to Sec. 302 (c) COPRA a minimum level of federal data privacy protection in the U.S. only to be surpassed by more rigorous federal or State privacy protection.[861] For the adequacy assessment according to Art. 45 para. 1 sentence 1 and para. 2 (a) and (b) GDPR this means if the COPRA provisions meet the EU adequacy threshold, the U.S., within the scope of the COPRA, would provide for protection of personal data transferred from the EU to the U.S. essentially equivalent to the one in the EU.

On the other hand, any transfer of personal data to the U.S. outside of the scope of application of COPRA would not benefit from such finding and would have to be assessed separately. With regard to COPRA's scope of application, two aspects stand out which limit the protection of EU personal data transferred from the EU to the U.S. First, it follows from Sec. 2 (14) together with Sec. 2 (8) (A) COPRA that the bill protects covered data from U.S. residents.[862] Consequently, information which meets the criteria of covered data in Sec. 2 (8) (A) COPRA but does not stem from U.S. residents is outside the bill's personal scope of application. This means personal data of EU data subjects when transferred to the U.S. does not automatically fall

---

sion on the adequate level of protection of personal data under the EU-US Data Privacy Framework' (n 39) para. 65.

858 Cf. Murphy (n 88), 250; supra Chapter 4 U.S. adequacy *post* COPRA.

859 Cantwell (n 54) 3; Solove and Schwartz (n 60) 1033; Solove and Schwartz, 'ALI Data Privacy: Overview and Black Letter Text' (n 95) 1254, 1284; supra Chapter 1 A. Concept and status of U.S. privacy law.

860 Supra Chapter 3 C. I. Material scope of application.

861 Supra Chapter 3 B. COPRA and the preemption of existing privacy law.

862 Supra Chapter 3 C. II. 1. Protection of the consumer.

under the protection of COPRA. Instead, a link would have to be made that EU personal data is deemed covered data as set out in Sec. 2 (8) (A) COPRA or that it enjoys the same protection as covered data of U.S. residents according to Sec. 2 (14) COPRA. Arguably, this could be implemented in a form similar to the EU-U.S. Data Privacy Framework, a set of rules which applies in addition to COPRA for EU personal data which is transferred to the U.S.[863]

Secondly, according to Sec. 2 (9) (A) (i) COPRA the bill's scope of application carves out processing entities which are not subject to the FTC Act.[864] As a consequence, EU personal data, even if deemed covered data according to Sec. 2 (8) (A) COPRA, is not protected by COPRA if it is transferred to an entity in the U.S. which is not governed by the FTC Act, for instance to financial institutions, airlines, or telecommunications carriers.[865] Due to the close link between COPRA's scope of application and the FTC's supervisory and enforcement power, an approach similar to the EU-U.S. Data Privacy Framework does not seem feasible by which protection is extended to EU data if send to processing entities that are not governed by COPRA.[866] Rather, the material scope of application of COPRA constitutes the limit of the EU Commission's adequacy assessment, and, consequently, any transfer to an entity not covered by COPRA would not benefit from a COPRA adequacy finding and would have to be assessed separately.

With COPRA as the object of this study, we will focus in the below on transfers within the scope of the bill and will disregard transfers to entities not covered by COPRA. To understand the level of protection COPRA provides for personal data sent from the EU to the U.S., we will examine both the legal framework applicable to personal data processing in the U.S. *post* COPRA (sub Chapter 4 B. I. Legal framework applicable to personal data processing in the U.S. *post* COPRA), and the supervisory authority and enforcement practice in the U.S. *post* COPRA (sub Chapter 4 B. II. Supervisory authority and enforcement in the U.S. *post* COPRA).

---

863 European Commission, 'Commission Implementing Decision on the adequate level of protection of personal data under the EU-US Data Privacy Framework' (n 39) Annex I.

864 Supra Chapter 3 C. I. Material scope of application.

865 Cf. Solove and Schwartz (n 60) 1106.

866 For a detailed discussion about the link between COPRA's scope of application and the FTC supervisory and enforcement competence supra Chapter 3 C. I. Material scope of application.

I. Legal framework applicable to personal data processing in the U.S. *post* COPRA

According to Art. 45 para. 3 sentence 1 and Art. 45 para. 2 lit. a GDPR, we first look at the legal framework *post* COPRA applicable to the processing of personal data which is exported from the EU to the U.S. and in the scope of COPRA. The benchmark we apply is whether COPRA provides for general processing principles alike in Art. 5 para. 1 and 2 GDPR (sub Chapter 4 B. I. 1. Data processing principles), special safeguards for the processing of special categories of personal data as set out in Art. 9 para. 1 GDPR (sub Chapter 4 B. I. 2. Special categories of personal data), data subject rights similar to the rights in Chapter 3 Art. 12 through 23 GDPR (sub Chapter 4 B. I. 3. Data rights of the data subject), whether the bill sets limitations to derogations from data rights similar to the stipulation in Art. 52 para. 1 sentence 1 and 2 ECFR (sub Chapter 4 B. I. 4. Limitations to derogations), how COPRA's transparency and information rights compare to Art. 13 para. 1–3 and Art. 14 para. 1–4 GDPR (sub Chapter 4 B. I. 5. Transparency and information rights), which obligations the bill sets for processing entities to maintain adequate security-privacy levels similar to Art. 24 para. 1 GDPR and Art. 32 para. 1 and 2 GDPR (sub Chapter 4 B. I. 6. Data security), and, finally, whether COPRA sufficiently restricts onward transfers as set out in the GDPR in Art. 44 sentence 1 (sub Chapter 4 B. I. 7. Rules on onward transfers of personal data).[867]

1. Data processing principles

Personal data transferred to the U.S. should be processed with essentially the same effect as set out by the EU data processing principles in Art. 5 para. 1 and 2 GDPR.[868] COPRA discusses the Art. 5 para. 1 lit. a GDPR principles of a lawfulness and fairness in different provisions. With regard to the lawfulness of the data collection and pro-

867 For a detailed presentation of the EU adequacy threshold and regarding the legal framework applicable to personal data processing supra Chapter 4 A. I. Legal framework applicable to personal data processing in the EU.

868 European Commission, 'Commission Implementing Decision on the adequate protection of personal data by the United Kingdom' (n 813) para. 24–46, 83–84; European Commission, 'Commission Implementing Decision on the adequate protection of personal data by Japan under the Act on the Protection of Personal Information' (n 816) para. 39–56, 60–64; European Commission, 'Commission Implementing Decision on the adequacy of the protection provided by the EU-U.S. Privacy Shield' (n 500) para. 19–23, 28; European Commission, 'Commission Implementing Decision on the adequate level of protection of personal data under the EU-US Data Privacy Framework' (n 39) para. 13–28; Wagner (n 586), 331; Frenzel, 'Art. 5' (n 178) para. 11; Kramer, 'Art. 5' (n 269) para. 1–2, 5, 9.

cessing, COPRA follows a mixed regime of input- and output-based control with additional safeguards in high-risk processing situations.[869] The EU Commission has not opposed against such a mixed control regime where the effect is a comparably strong protection for EU data subjects.[870] Sec. 105 (c) (1) together with Sec. 2 (20) COPRA stipulate for input-control for the processing of sensitive covered data for which processing entities must obtain a consumer's prior affirmative express consent.[871] For general covered data, COPRA follows the traditional U.S. opt-out approach.[872] The extensive definition of sensitive covered data in Sec. 20 (20) (A) to (N) COPRA together with the opt-in requirement in Sec. 105 (c) (1) COPRA effectively means a substantial carve-out to the classic U.S. output-control baseline and a strong shift closer to the GDPR's input-based control regime.[873] Besides, for general covered data a comparably strong protection to the EU standard is achieved by ancillary measures: According to Sec. 108 (a) (1) (A) COPRA, the bill sets very strict processing restrictions for covered data in the high-risk point of use situations of housing, employment, credit, education.[874] Additionally, Sec. 105 (b) and 105 (b) (2) (B) COPRA guarantee consumers an efficient and effective right to object against the transfer of covered data to third parties by providing for a privacy information management system where consumers can centrally register their opt-out decisions.[875]

Art. 5 para. 1 lit. a GDPR's requirement of fairness is explicitly written into COPRA's Sec. 101 (a) (1) and (2).[876] The COPRA fair processing standard arguably

---

869 Supra Chapter 4 A. I. Legal framework applicable to personal data in the EU; supra Chapter 2 B. Output and downstream regulation.

870 Cf. European Commission, 'Commission Implementing Decision on the adequate level of protection of personal data under the EU-US Data Privacy Framework' (n 39) para. 15, 27, Annex I II. Principles 2. Choice; Commission Implementing Decision on the adequate protection of personal data by Japan under the Act on the Protection of Personal Information (n 635) para. 45, 65–69, Annex I (1) special care-required data; Commission Implementation Decision on the adequacy of the protection provided by the EU-U.S. Privacy Shield (n 337) para. 22, Annex II 2. Choice c; cf. Solove and Schwartz (n 60) 1544.

871 Supra Chapter 3 C. I. 2. (Sensitive) covered data.

872 Schwartz and Pfeifer (n 19), 120; supra Chapter 1 A. Concept and status of U.S. privacy law; supra Chapter 2 B. Output and downstream regulation.

873 Supra Chapter 3 C. I. 2. (Sensitive) covered data; sub Chapter 4 B. I. 2. Special categories of personal data.

874 Supra Chapter 3 D. I. 2. Point of use regulation and regulation of data quality.

875 Supra Chapter 3 D. II. 2. Privacy information management system.

876 European Commission, 'Commission Implementing Decision on the adequate level of protection of personal data under the EU-US Data Privacy Framework' (n 39) para. 13; European Commission (n 831), para. 24–26; Commission Implementing Decision on the adequate protection of personal data by Japan under the Act on the Protection of Personal Information (n 655) para. 44–51; Wagner (n 8), 329; Wittershagen (n 564) 32–33.

exceeds the scope and effect of the GDPR principle. This is because the provision works as an effective output-control provision and is sufficiently detailed yet flexible in its protection of individual and collective privacy. CORPA's fair processing standard achieves this balance by integrating in Sec. 101 (a) (1) and (2) COPRA established privacy case law in U.S. tort law and relevant privacy decisions by the FTC while leaving sufficient room for interpretation of what could constitute fair processing in the future.[877]

The principles of purpose, storage limitation, and data minimization as set out in Art. 5 para. 1 lit. b, c, and e GDPR form part of the different sections in Sec. 106 (1) to (3) COPRA and in Sec. 107 (b) (3) COPRA, the bill's central provision about data security.[878] Under the title of data minimization, Sec. 106 (1) to (3) COPRA restricts the processing of covered data to what is reasonably necessary, proportionate, and limited to the legitimate processing purpose. According to Sec. 106 (1) and (2) COPRA, the processing purpose must either be spelled out in a company's privacy policy or the company must have obtained from the consumer affirmative express consent to the processing. Alternatively, the processing purpose must be listed in the exhaustive list of allowed processing purposes in Sec. 106 (3) together with Sec. 110 (d) COPRA. Finally, Sec. 107 (b) (3) COPRA explicitly stipulates that covered data must no longer be stored once the processing purpose has been fulfilled or no longer justifies the processing.[879]

The principle of data accuracy in Art. 5 para. 1 lit. d GDPR is manifested in COPRA in several provisions.[880] Sec. 104 (1) COPRA entitles the individual to correct incorrect or incomplete information in covered data with the subsequent obligation for processing entities according to Sec. 104 (2) COPRA to instruct any service provider or third party to equally correct received data.[881] COPRA additionally reg-

877 Supra Chapter 3 D. I. 1. COPRA's fair processing standard.

878 Wagner (n 785), 329; Kramer, 'Art. 5' (n 269) para. 22; Frenzel, 'Art. 5' (n 178) para. 23–25; Wittershagen (n 564) 33–35; cf. European Commission, 'Commission Implementing Decision on the adequate protection of personal data by the United Kingdom' (n 813) para. 43–44; European Commission, 'Commission Implementing Decision on the adequate protection of personal data by Japan under the Act on the Protection of Personal Information' (n 816) para. 39–43, 52–54; European Commission, 'Commission Implementing Decision on the adequacy of the protection provided by the EU-U.S. Privacy Shield' (n 500) para. 21–22; European Commission, 'Commission Implementing Decision on the adequate level of protection of personal data under the EU-US Data Privacy Framework' (n 39) para. 13.

879 Supra Chapter 3 D. I. 5. Purpose limitation, data minimization, limitations on waivers of privacy rights.

880 European Commission, 'Commission Implementing Decision on the adequate level of protection of personal data under the EU-US Data Privacy Framework' (n 39) para. 20–21.

881 Supra Chapter 3 D. II. 1. Data control rights.

ulates data accuracy in its technology-neutral point of use regulation in Sec. 108 (a) (1) COPRA, in its technology-targeted regulation in Sec. 108 (b) (1) COPRA, and in its fair processing standard in Sec. 101 (a) (1) and (2) COPRA; in all of these provisions, inaccurate, incomplete, and biased covered data is scrutinized to avoid discriminatory or unfair processing outputs.[882]

Finally, COPRA addresses the essence of what Art. 5 para. 2 GDPR stipulates as a data controllers' accountability to document and prove compliance with the GDPR's processing provisions.[883] Compared to the U.S. consumer privacy law and system *pre* COPRA, among COPRA's most fundamental updates are the heightened compliance and accountability requirements for processing entities which, in several aspects, exceed EU accountability standards. Under COPRA, all processing entities must appoint privacy and data security officers as set out in Sec. 201 (a) (2) COPRA whose responsibility according to Sec. 202 (b) COPRA comprises the implementation and supervision of privacy and data security programs.[884] Exceeding the EU standard, COPRA sets strict accountability obligations for large data holders whose top-management must annually certify to the FTC according to Sec. 201 (a) and Sec. 2 para. 15 COPRA about their organizations' privacy compliance.[885] Furthermore, COPRA explicitly recognizes the importance of whistleblowers as a means to enforce accountability because they can help surface from within organizations privacy compliance violations. To this end, Sec. 204 (a) COPRA protects employees against repressive measures by their employers when they chose to disclose confidential information related to alleged privacy compliance violations.[886]

A comparison between COPRA and the principle of transparency and consumers' information rights as set out in Art. 5 para. 1 lit. a and Art. 13 para. 1–3 and Art. 14 para. 1–4 GDPR follows further below (sub Chapter 4 B. I. 5. Transparency and information rights); and so does a comparison between COPRA and the processing principle of data integrity and confidentiality as set out in Art. 5 para. 1 lit. f GDPR (sub Chapter 4 B. I. 6. Data security). For the above discussed processing principles as set out in Art. 5 para. 1 lit. a-e and para. 2 GDPR, we conclude that COPRA sets forth essentially the same and sometimes even a more rigorous protection for EU data subjects than the protection present in the EU.

---

882 Supra Chapter 3 D. I. 2. b. Regulated data quality; Chapter 3 D. I. 3. Regulating specific processing technology; Chapter 3 D. I. 1. COPRA's fair processing standard.

883 Kramer, 'Art. 5' (n 269) para. 61, 64; Article 29 Data Protection Working Party (n 441), 7–8; supra Chapter 4 A. I. Legal framework applicable to personal data processing in the EU.

884 Supra Chapter 3 E. I. 1. Privacy and data security officers.

885 Supra Chapter 3 E. I. 3. Certification obligations.

886 Supra Chapter 3 E. I. 2. Whistleblower protection.

2. Special categories of personal data

To meet the EU adequacy standard, COPRA must provide for specific safeguards for the processing of special categories of data as set out in Art. 9 para. 1.[887] The bill distinguishes between general covered data and sensitive covered data which it defines extensively in Sec. 2 (20) (A) to (N) COPRA: Covered data qualifies as sensitive data not only because of its data quality or content but also when the point of use situation in which the data was collected or processed poses an elevated risk of privacy violation; for instance, sensitive covered data under COPRA comprises geolocation information pursuant to Sec. 2 (20) (E) COPRA, religious beliefs and trade union membership as set out in Sec. 2 (20) (H) COPRA, covered data which is tracked across services and platforms according to Sec. 2 (20) (J) COPRA, and selected information which is stored on an individual's device according to Sec. 2 (20) (K) COPRA.[888] Overall, COPRA's definition of sensitive covered data covers all of the aspects EU data protection law protects as special categories of personal data in Art. 9 para. 1. As a consequence, such personal data when transferred from the EU to the U.S. will be treated in the U.S. as sensitive covered data.[889]

For the processing and the transfer of sensitive covered data, COPRA sets a higher threshold than for the processing of general covered data: According to Sec. 105 (c) (1) and (2) COPRA, processing entities are required to obtain the consumers' affirmative consent or opt-in ahead of any processing or transfer of sensitive covered data.[890] The effect of the opt-in requirement for sensitive covered data is an input-control regime which closely resembles the one in EU data protection law as spelled out in Art. 6 para. 1 and Art. 9 para. 1 and 2 GDPR.[891]

Derogations from this input-control for the processing and transferring of sensitive covered data are of an exceptional nature, they are provided for by law and are exhaustively defined in Sec. 105 (c) (4) COPRA and in Sec. 110 (d) (1) (A) to (H) COPRA. A detailed discussion including regarding their respective limitations follows further below (sub Chapter 4 B. I. 4. Limitations to derogations). In light of the above, we conclude that COPRA provides for safeguards for the processing of specific categories of personal data compared to EU data protection law.

887 European Commission, 'Commission Implementing Decision on the adequate level of protection of personal data under the EU-US Data Privacy Framework' (n 39) para. 16–19; Art. 29 Data Protection Working Party, 'Adequacy Referential' (n 804) 6–7.

888 Supra Chapter 3 C. I. 2. (Sensitive) covered data.

889 Provided EU personal data is deemed covered data according to Sec. 2 (8) (A) COPRA or enjoys equal protection to covered data of U.S. residents as set out in Sec. 2 (14) COPRA, supra Chapter 4 B. Data protection level in the U.S. *post* COPRA.

890 Supra Chapter 3 B. I. 2. (Sensitive) covered data.

891 Supra Chapter 1 B. Concept and status of EU data protection law; Chapter 2 B. Output and downstream regulation.

3. Data rights of the data subject

When personal data is transferred to third countries, EU data subjects should have data rights to control their personal data vis-à-vis the processing entities.[892] COPRA introduces broadly applicable data control rights to U.S. privacy law in Sec. 102–105 COPRA. According to Sec. 102 (a) and (b) (2) COPRA, data subjects may demand access to their covered data without justification. The COPRA right to access covers the essential elements laid out in Art. 15 para. 1, para. 2, and para. 3 sentence 1 GDPR, in particular, processing entities must provide consumers with a copy or accurate representation of their covered data in a human-readable format according to Sec. 102 (a) (1) COPRA. Besides, Sec. 102 (b) (2) COPRA stipulates that as part of their privacy policies processing entities must inform about the categories of processed data and the processing purpose, and Sec. 102 (a) (2) COPRA requires processing entities to disclose any third parties which have received covered data as well as the purpose of the transfer.[893] Data subjects are thus in a position to demand access to personal data also from third parties and down the processing chain.

According to Sec. 103 and Sec. 104 COPRA, data subjects may request processing entities to delete their covered data and to correct inaccurate covered data.[894] COPRA furthermore requires processing entities to follow up with third parties which have received the consumer's covered data so that they as well delete or correct covered data pursuant to Art. 103 (2) and Sec. 104 (2) COPRA. The level of protection provided by these COPRA data control rights corresponds to the EU data subject rights in Art. 16, Art. 17 para. 1, and Art. 19 GDPR.

Furthermore, according to Sec. 105 (c) (1) and (2) COPRA data subjects are entitled to object against the processing and transferring of their sensitive covered data comparable to the right in Art. 21 para. 1 GDPR.[895] They may also object against transfers of their general covered data to third parties pursuant to Sec. 105

---

892 Cf. European Commission, 'Commission Implementing Decision on the adequate protection of personal data by the United Kingdom' (n 813) para. 52–54; European Commission, 'Commission Implementing Decision on the adequate protection of personal data by Japan under the Act on the Protection of Personal Information' (n 816) para. 81–94; European Commission, 'Commission Implementing Decision on the adequacy of the protection provided by the EU-U.S. Privacy Shield' (n 500) para. 25; European Commission, 'Commission Implementing Decision on the adequate level of protection of personal data under the EU-US Data Privacy Framework' (n 39) para. 29–32; Wittershagen (n 564) 45–48.

893 This matches the Access Principle in European Commission, 'Commission Implementing Decision on the adequate level of protection of personal data under the EU-US Data Privacy Framework' (n 39) Annex I III. 8. lit. a i-iii Access.

894 Ibid.

895 Supra Chapter 4 B. I. 2. Special categories of personal data.

(b) (1) (A) COPRA.[896] Data subjects may do so generally against all transfers and by leveraging the efficient and effective technical solution of a privacy information management system set out in Sec. 105 (b) (2) (B) and Sec. 105 (b) (2) COPRA, or against individual transfers as planned and disclosed by the processing entity in their privacy policies according to Sec. 102 (b) (3) COPRA.[897] Yet as a consequence of COPRA's processing baseline, whereby general covered data can be processed without a legal justification, the bill's right to object does not extend to the processing of general covered data.[898] Also, the bill does not contain a provision equivalent to Art. 18 para. 1 GDPR to restrict the processing of personal data.[899] COPRA instead compensates with the more targeted protection of a processing ban in the high-risk processing situations described in Sec. 108 (a) (1) COPRA.[900] Besides, data subjects are protected because they may object according to Sec. 102 (d) COPRA against any material changes in the processing practice and privacy policies of processing entities.[901] Together, these measures provide for comparably strong protection as set out in Art. 18 para. 1 and Art. 21 para. 1 GDPR because data processing is or can be sufficiently restricted at the choice of data subjects or by law, in particular in high-risk processing situations.

A right to portability of personal data similar to Art. 20 para. 1 GDPR can be found in Sec. 105 (a) COPRA. Whereas the GDPR provision speaks of the data controller's obligation to share the data in a "*commonly used format and machine-readable format*", potentially risking the export of data which is actually incompatible with the system or solution of the data receiver, Sec. 105 (a) (2) COPRA more adequately stipulates for portable data to be "*interoperable*". In essence, the COPRA and the GDPR provision pursue the same objective of ameliorated data portability.[902]

896 Supra Chapter 3 D. II. 1. Data control rights.

897 Supra Chapter 3 D. II. 2. Privacy information-management system.

898 Cf. the mixed approach of output-based control for general covered data with input-control for sensitive covered data has been approved before in European Commission, 'Commission Implementing Decision on the adequate protection of personal data by Japan under the Act on the Protection of Personal Information' (n 816) para. 45, 65–69, Annex I (1) special care-required data; European Commission, 'Commission Implementing Decision on the adequacy of the protection provided by the EU-U.S. Privacy Shield' (n 500) para. 22, Annex II 2. Choice c.

899 Cf. Susanne Stollhoff, 'Art. 18' in Martin Eßer, Philipp Kramer and Kai von Lewinski (eds), *DSGVO/BDSG* (Carl Heymanns Verlag 2023) para. 2, 5 who points out the character of Art. 18 para. 1 GDPR as an interim measure often leading to data correction or deletion and whose importance in EU data protection law is therefore limited.

900 Supra Chapter 3 D. I. 2. Point of use regulation and regulation of data quality.

901 Supra Chapter 3 D. I. 4. Transparency and information obligations.

902 In line with the recommendation of data standardization and compatibility supra Chapter 2 A. I. 2. Data quality.

Finally, EU data protection law according to Art. 22 para. 1 GDPR shields data subjects from being subjected to automated decision-making and profiling without human oversight and control.[903] Although COPRA lacks an identical provision, it provides for similar effective protection in at least two ways: First, its technology-targeted regulation in Sec. 108 (b) COPRA subjects algorithmic-decision making and profiling to heightened scrutiny in the form of impact assessments which go beyond the scope of the EU standard in Art. 35 para. 1 and para. 7 lit. a to lit. d GDPR, in particular the COPRA processing impact assessment directly aims at mitigating against the root cause of poor data quality.[904] Secondly, COPRA specifically regulates processing situations in which processing entities most likely use algorithmic decision-making and profiling technology, namely in data-based decisions about housing, employment, credit, and education.[905] In these high-risk processing situations, the bill stipulates an absolute processing ban if the processing itself or its output manifests a discriminatory result.[906] Together, COPRA's technology-targeted and its technology-neutral regulation in Sec. 108 (a) and (b) COPRA protect against discriminatory processing activities and results, the objective EU data protection law pursues in Art. 22 para. 1 GDPR regarding automated decision-making and profiling.[907]

In light of the above-discussed data rights, we conclude the level of data protection in the U.S. *post* COPRA is essentially equivalent to the EU standard because COPRA's provisions provide EU data subjects with a comparably strong protection.

4. Limitations to derogations

Any restrictions to and derogations from COPRA's privacy protection and data control rights must be provided for by law and must be themselves limited in scope and application.[908] In COPRA, Sec. 110 (a), (c), and (d) are the central provisions

---

903 Cf. Mario Martini, 'Art. 22' in Boris Paal and Daniel Pauly (eds), *DSGVO, BDSG* (C.H. Beck 2021) para. 8.

904 Supra Chapter 3 D. I. 3. Regulating specific processing technology.

905 Cf. European Commission, 'Commission Implementing Decision on the adequate level of protection of personal data under the EU-US Data Privacy Framework' (n 39) para. 35 sentence 1–3.

906 Supra Chapter 3 D. I. 2. Point of use regulation and regulation of data quality.

907 Cf. Katyal (n 52), 56, 71–73; European Data Protection Supervisor (n 21) 10; supra Chapter 2 A. I. 2. Data quality.

908 Supra Chapter 4 A. I. Legal framework applicable to personal data processing in the EU; *C-362/14 – Schrems I* (n 110) para. 92; *C-311/18 – Schrems II* (n 52) para. 176; European Commission, 'Commission Implementing Decision on the adequate protection of personal data by the United Kingdom' (n 813) para. 55–67; European Commission, 'Commission Implementing Decision on the adequate protection of personal data by Japan under the Act on the Protection of Personal

which spell out restrictions and derogations to the bill's data control rights of the individual in Sec. 102–105 COPRA.[909] First, Sec. 110 (a) (1) (A) and Sec. 110 (c) (1) COPRA excuse the processing entity if the requestor's identity cannot be verified despite mandatory inquiries as set out in Sec. 110 (a) (2) COPRA or in case the processing entity finds meeting the request is *"demonstrably impossible"*. To this regard, Sec. 110 (a) (3) COPRA clarifies that a large number of requests will not amount to an impossibility for the processing entity, that processing entities have an obligation to minimize any burden and inconvenience for consumers when verifying their identity, and that the exercising of any data right shall be free of charge for the consumer according to Sec. 110 (b) COPRA.[910] Building on the legal dogma of *impossibilium nulla est obligatio*, the limitation in Sec. 110 (a) (1) (A) COPRA thus appears sufficiently restricted to cases in which processing entities are factually unable to act upon a consumer's request.

Secondly, Sec. 110 (a) (1) (B) and (c) (6) COPRA which by reference integrates Sec. 110 (d) (1) (A) COPRA allow a derogation if necessary to complete a transaction or fulfill a contract. The exception corresponds with the processing justification in EU data protection law of performing contractual obligations according to Art. 6 para. 1 lit. b GDPR.[911] Similarly, legal obligations or overriding interests of the processing entity such as the performance of internal audits, system maintenance, or the detection and protection against security incidents may justify the continuous processing of covered data according to Sec. 110 (c) (2) and Sec. 110 (c) (6) together with Sec. 110 (d) (1) (B), (C), (D), (E), (G) COPRA. Moreover, such *"legitimate* [interest to pursue] *internal testing"* is a valid derogation from COPRA's processing ban in high-risk processing situations in Sec. 108 (a) (2) COPRA.[912] EU data protection law equally recognizes data controllers' legal obligations and overriding legitimate interests as processing justifications according to Art. 6 para. 1 lit. c and lit. f and Art. 9 para. 2 lit. b GDPR.[913]

Information' (n 816) para. 113 and Annex 2 Collection and use of personal information by Japanese public authorities for criminal law enforcement and national security purposes; European Commission, 'Commission Implementing Decision on the adequacy of the protection provided by the EU-U.S. Privacy Shield' (n 500) para. 68–76; European Commission, 'Commission Implementing Decision on the adequate level of protection of personal data under the EU-US Data Privacy Framework' (n 39) para. 31; Wittershagen (n 393) 12–13.

909 Supra Chapter 3 D. II. 1. Data control rights.

910 Similarly in Art. 12 para. 2, 5 and 6 GDPR cf. Martin Eßer, 'Art. 12' in Martin Eßer, Philipp Kramer and Kai von Lewinski (eds), *DSGVO/BDSG* (Carl Heymanns Verlag 2023) para. 18, 34.

911 Kramer, 'Art. 6' (n 104) para. 28–56.

912 Supra Chapter 3 C. I. 2. Point of use regulation and regulation of data quality.

913 Kramer, 'Art. 6' (n 104) para. 64–89.

Thirdly, COPRA provides for a derogation to data control rights according to Sec. 110 (c) (6) together with Sec. 110 (d) (1) (F) COPRA if the processing can spare an individual from suffering serious harm. The derogation closely resembles the processing justification of protecting vital interests of the data subject or another natural person as set forth in EU data protection law in Art. 6 para. 1 lit. d and Art. 9 para. 2 lit. c GDPR.[914]

Fourthly, Sec. 110 (c) (3), (4), (5) 2nd alternative COPRA allow for derogations regarding publicly available information, the publication of newsworthy information, and the exercise of free speech, all of which enjoy strong protection under the First Amendment of the U.S. Constitution.[915] The same objective serve the tailored exceptions in Sec. 105 (c) (4) CORPA regarding the processing and transferring of sensitive covered data and the media privilege in Sec. 110 (e) COPRA. All of the derogations are sufficiently limited in scope and application because the definition and the necessary balancing test for publicly available information in Sec. 2 (18) (A) and (B) and for newsworthy information of legitimate public concern in Sec. 110 (c) (4) COPRA effectively factor in the data subject's privacy interests.[916] Besides, similar privileges which guarantee public access to information exist in EU data protection law, consider, for instance, the derogations in Art. 85 para. 2 and Recital 153 sentence 3 GDPR regarding personal data in news archives and press libraries, and Art. 9 para. 2 lit. e GDPR which permits the processing of personal data to the extent the data subject has manifestly chosen to publicize the information.[917]

Fifthly, Sec. 110 (c) (6) together with Sec. 110 (d) (H) COPRA privileges the processing of covered data for the purpose of scientific, historical, or statistical research in the public interest, a derogation which EU data protection law equally recognizes in Art. 89 para. 2 and 3, Art. 5 para. 1 lit. e, Art. 21 para. 6, Art. 17 para. 3 lit. d, Art. 14 para. 5 lit. b, Art. 9 para. 2 lit. j GDPR.[918]

---

914 Greve, 'Art. 9' (n 199) para. 23 and 31; ibid 56–58.

915 Cf. Schwartz and Pfeifer (n 19), 134–135; cf. European Commission, 'Commission Implementing Decision on the adequacy of the protection provided by the EU-U.S. Privacy Shield' (n 500) Annex II III. 2. Journalistic Exceptions.

916 Cf. Gajda (n 323), 257–259; a detailed discussion about what constitutes publicly available information, newsworthy information of legitimate public concern, and the balancing test they require supra Chapter 3 C. I. 1. Processing activities.

917 Kai von Lewinski, 'Art. 85' in Martin Eßer, Philipp Kramer and Kai von Lewinski (eds), *DSGVO/BDSG* (Carl Heymanns Verlag 2023) para. 16–19; Greve, 'Art. 9' (n 199) para. 26.

918 Cf. Holger Greve, 'Art. 89' in Martin Eßer, Philipp Kramer and Kai von Lewinski (eds), *DSGVO/BDSG* (Carl Heymanns Verlag 2023) para. 12–13; cf. European Commission, 'Commission Implementing Decision on the adequate protection of personal data by the United Kingdom' (n 813) para. 71.

Finally, Sec. 110 (d) (1) COPRA explicitly limits any restriction in its subsections to what is *reasonably necessary, proportionate, and limited* to the purpose of the restriction. The bill hereby retakes the EU data protection terminology whose legal concept implies a careful balancing of the interest to process personal data against the data subject's interest to preserve her privacy and her right to keep the essence of her protection untouched.[919] Whether the U.S. interpretation of this terminology will live up to EU expectations is for the EU Commission to monitor over time; according to Art. 45 para. 4 and 5 sentence 1 GDPR, a valid adequacy decision may be revoked should the U.S. fall short of the EU standard.[920]

Conversely, it is important to point out that the EU-like terminology in Sec. 110 (d) (1) COPRA does not apply to Sec. 110 (c) (1) to (5) COPRA because it precedes the balancing test (*systemic interpretation*). Still, the restrictions in 110 (c) (1) to (5) COPRA appear sufficiently limited in scope and application nevertheless: First, Sec. 110 (c) (2) COPRA independently establishes a strict purpose limitation "[...] *is not processed or transferred for any purpose other than such specific activities*". Secondly, impossibility in Sec. 110 (c) (1) COPRA only goes as far as objectively demonstrable and within the limits set by Sec. 110 (a) (3), (b), (c) (1) COPRA.[921] Thirdly, the limitations of the free-speech restrictions in Sec. 110 (c) (3), (4), (5) COPRA are linked to the limitation-setting balancing test against the data subject's interests mentioned above.[922] Finally, the restrictions to COPRA data rights of the individual consumer and motivated by legal and other legitimate interests of the processing entity in Sec. 110 (c) (2) COPRA largely overlap with the derogations in Sec. 110 (d) (1) (B), (C), (D), and (E) COPRA to which the necessary, proportionate, and purpose-bound limitation in Sec. 110 (d) (1) COPRA applies directly.

In sum, COPRA's restrictions and derogations to data control rights and the protection of EU data subjects come with clear limitations in scope and application. In particular, the bill introduces to U.S. federal privacy law the test known from EU data protection law that any restriction in the subsections of Sec. 110 (d) (1) COPRA must be necessary, proportionate, and limited to the purpose of the restriction.

---

919 *C-311/18 – Schrems II* (n 52) para. 176; Wittershagen (n 564) 13–15; Art. 29 Data Protection Working Party, 'Adequacy Referential' (n 804) 9; supra Chapter 4 A. I. Legal framework applicable to personal data processing in the EU.

920 Cf. European Commission, 'Commission Implementing Decision on the adequate level of protection of personal data under the EU-US Data Privacy Framework' (n 39) para. 208–209.

921 See a more detailed explanation of the limitations in Sec. 110 (a) (3), (b), (c) (1) COPRA at the beginning of this chapter.

922 For a detailed discussion of publicly available information, newsworthy information of legitimate public concern, and the balancing test they require supra Chapter 3 C. I. 1. Processing activities; cf. Gajda (n 323), 257–259.

This is why in regard of the above, COPRA offers a level of data protection essentially equivalent to the standard in the European Union.

5. Transparency and information rights

Data subjects are entitled to receive detailed information about how their personal data is being processed also after their data is transferred from the EU to the U.S.[923] EU data protection law stipulates for these information rights in its transparency principle in Art. 5 para. 1 lit. a GDPR and in Art. 13 para. 1 to 3 and 14 para. 1 to 4 GDPR.[924]

COPRA contains a similar right to transparency in Sec. 102 (b) COPRA which stipulates the information the processing entity must provide to the data subject. According to Sec. 102 (b) (1), (2), (3) COPRA, the processing entity must disclose its identity, the contact details of their privacy and security officers, the categories of covered data it processes, the processing purpose, and whether it transfers data to service providers and third parties including information about their identity. In this regard, COPRA requires the same information to be shared than do Art. 13 para. 1 lit. a, b, d and Art. 14 para. 1 lit. a, b, d, and e GDPR.[925] According to Sec. 102 (b) (4), (5), and (6) COPRA, processing entities must furthermore provide information about how long covered data is being stored, which data control rights data subjects have available and how they can exercise their rights, as well as a description of the processing entity's data minimization and data security policies. There is an overlap with the required information as set out in Art. 13 para. 2 lit. a and Art. 14 para. 2 lit. a GDPR regarding the storage time, and in Art. 13 para. 2 lit. b, d and Art. 14 para. 2 lit. c, e GDPR regarding data subject rights and how data subjects may lodge a complaint.[926] COPRA notably goes beyond the EU standard when it demands the explanation of a data controller's minimization and data security pol-

923 Cf. European Commission, 'Commission Implementing Decision on the adequate level of protection of personal data under the EU-US Data Privacy Framework' (n 39) para. 25; European Commission, 'Commission Implementing Decision on the adequate protection of personal data by the United Kingdom' (n 813) para. 49–50; European Commission, 'Commission Implementing Decision on the adequate protection of personal data by Japan under the Act on the Protection of Personal Information' (n 816) para. 60–64; European Commission, 'Commission Implementing Decision on the adequacy of the protection provided by the EU-U.S. Privacy Shield' (n 500) para. 20, Annex II Principles 1 Notice.

924 Cf. Eßer, 'Art. 13' (n 836) para. 5; Paal and Hennemann, 'Art. 13' (n 173) para. 4; Ebner, *Weniger ist Mehr?* (n 29) 171–183, 255–266.

925 Ebner, *Weniger ist Mehr?* (n 29) 172–173, 177, 256, 257–258.

926 Ibid 193–194, 197, 260–262.

icy.[927] By contrast, COPRA does not retake language closely linked to proprietary concepts and means in the GDPR, such as the obligation to inform about EU transfer mechanisms to transfer personal data of European data subjects to third countries according to Art. 13 para. 1 lit. f and Art. 14 para. 1 lit. f GDPR,[928] and language linked to the EU's input-based control regime and processing justifications in Art. 13 para. 1 lit. d, para. 2 lit. c, e and Art. 14 para. 2 lit. b, and d GDPR.[929] This is a consequence of COPRA's primarily output-based control regime though; as argued above, an identical retake of GDPR language and provisions is not required to meet the adequacy standard.[930] When viewed in the aggregated, the content of the COPRA transparency and information obligations in Sec. 102 (b) (1) to (7) COPRA closely match the EU standard.

Similar to EU data protection law, processing entities must provide the above-illustrated information to the data subject in an easily accessible and understandable way.[931] Whereas Art. 12 para. 1 sentence 1, Recital 58 sentence 1 and Recital 39 sentence 3 GDPR detail that information must be communicated in a *"concise, transparent, intelligible and easily accessible form"* and in *"clear and plain language"*,[932] Sec. 102 (b) COPRA demands the disclosure in a *"conspicuous and readily accessible manner"* and, according to Sec. 102 (c) COPRA, in all languages the processing entity provides its goods or services.

Unlike in EU data protection law, in COPRA the use of privacy policies is the default means to inform consumers according to Sec. 102 (b) (2) COPRA: *"A covered entity shall make publicly and persistently available* [...] *a privacy policy that provides a detailed and accurate representation of the entity's processing and data transfer activities."* Only exceptionally does COPRA demand direct notifications to data subjects when processing entities must obtain an individual's affirmative express consent according to Sec. 102 (d) COPRA prior to any material changes in their privacy policy or practice, or according to Sec. 105 (c) (1) and (2) COPRA prior to processing or transferring of any sensitive covered data.[933] A similar direct

927 Supra Chapter 3 D. I. 5. Purpose limitation, data minimization, limits on waivers of privacy rights.

928 Cf. Eßer, 'Art. 13' (n 836) para. 31–32.

929 Cf. ibid para. 28, 42, 44; Paal and Hennemann, 'Art. 13' (n 219) Art. 14 para. 27, 29.

930 Commission Implementing Decision on the adequate protection of personal data by the United Kingdom (n 652) para. 4; European Commission, 'Commission Implementing Decision on the adequate level of protection of personal data under the EU-US Data Privacy Framework' (n 39) para. 3 sentence 2, para. 4 sentence 1–4.

931 Ebner, *Weniger ist Mehr?* (n 29) 78.

932 Eßer, 'Art. 12' (n 907) para. 4–10.

933 Supra Chapter 3 C. I. 2. (Sensitive) covered data; Chapter 3 D. I. 4. Transparency and information obligations.

notice is required pursuant to Sec. 105 (b) (2) (B) (ii) COPRA regarding consumer's right to object against transfers.[934] In comparison, EU data protection law appears more open and leaves it to the discretion of data controllers according to Art. 12 para. 1 sentence 2 GDPR to decide in which (written) form to inform the data subject.[935] Still, although EU data protection law does not set the use of privacy policies as the default means to inform data subjects, Recital 58 sentence 2 GDPR clarifies that EU data protection law does recognize information on a website and by way of a privacy policy as a legitimate form of informing data subjects.[936] It follows that, in this regard and despite COPRA's mandating of the broad use of privacy policies, the bill does not substantially deviate from the EU standard.

As a consequence of COPRA's focus on the use of privacy policies, the bill mostly lacks guidance about the point in time when the data subjects must receive processing information. Whereas Art. 13 para. 1, 2, 3 and Art. 14 para. 3 GDPR clearly stipulate when the data subject must be informed, *e.g.* at the time when personal data is first obtained,[937] the logic in COPRA is that processing entities shall keep privacy policies *"persistently available"* according to Sec. 102 (b) (2) COPRA and that it is the data subject's onus to consult the processing entity's website and privacy policy to obtain processing information. Exceptionally, data subjects receive direct notices according to Sec. 105 (c) (1), (2), and Sec. 102 (d) COPRA prior to the processing of sensitive covered data or prior to the processing entity's substantially changing its privacy policy or processing activity.[938] By contrast, when general covered data is processed under COPRA, there will often be no direct communication between the processing entity and the data subject because processing entities are not required to engage with the data subject prior to the processing of general covered data.[939] Sec. 105 (b) (2) (B) (ii) COPRA which stipulates the consumer's right to object against transfers of her general covered data is no exception, the provision binds the service provider of COPRA's privacy information management system rather than the processing entity and is vague about when the information and notice needs to be provided to the consumer.[940] With COPRA's focus on the use of privacy policies and its lack of guidance about when consumers must

---

934 Supra Chapter 3 D. II. 2. Privacy information management system.

935 Eßer, 'Art. 12' (n 907) para. 13.

936 Ibid para. 13, 16.

937 Cf. Martin Eßer, 'Art. 14' in Martin Eßer, Philipp Kramer and Kai von Lewinski (eds), *DSGVO/BDSG* (Carl Heymanns Verlag 2023) para. 33, 34, 36–39; Paal and Hennemann, 'Art. 13' (n 219) Art. 13 para. 12, 33.

938 Supra Chapter 3 C. I. 2. (Sensitive) covered data; Chapter 3 D. I. 4. Transparency and information obligations; Chapter 3 D. II. 2. Privacy information management system.

939 Supra Chapter 3 C. I. 2. (Sensitive) covered data.

940 Supra Chapter 3 D. II. 2. Privacy information management system.

obtain necessary processing information, it is easy to imagine a situation in which the data subject could be left unaware of her general covered data being processed, and, as a consequence of her intellectual incapacity, could fail to consult a processing entity's privacy policy to learn about relevant processing information.[941]

Does this mean COPRA provides for a lower level of transparency and information rights compared to the EU standard? Instead of insisting on a retake of EU data protection law, we examine in a functional analysis of the above-cited COPRA provisions whether the bill effectively ensures that data subjects receive information about important processing activities.[942] First, COPRA stipulates for direct information to data subjects in particularly risk-prone processing situations before sensitive covered data is processed according to Sec. 105 (c) (1), (2) COPRA, before any processing activity materially changes according to Sec. 102 (d) COPRA, and in connection with the data subject's right to object to transfers according to Sec. 105 (b) (2) (B) (ii) COPRA.[943] In other cases, the default reference to privacy policies and without a direct notice to data subjects is the consequence of COPRA's primarily output-based processing control.[944] The adequacy of such output-based control regime has repeatedly been confirmed by the EU Commission in previous EU-U.S. adequacy decisions.[945] Hence, in light of the above, COPRA's transparency and information rights in the aggregate provide for an adequate level of protection for EU data subjects.

---

941 Supra Chapter 2 A. II. 1. Intellectual (in)capacity.

942 Cf. Hennemann, 'Wettbewerb der Datenschutzrechtsordnungen' (n 19) 890–891; Koch, Magnus and Winkler von Mohrenfels (n 53) § 13 para. 11–14; Kischel (n 53) § 3 para. 179–197; Wittershagen (n 564) 68.

943 Supra Chapter 4 B. I. 2. Special categories of personal data; Chapter 3 C. I. 2. (Sensitive) covered data; Chapter 2 B. Output and downstream regulation.

944 Ibid.

945 Cf. European Commission, 'Commission Implementing Decision on the adequate level of protection of personal data under the EU-US Data Privacy Framework' (n 39) para. 25–27, Annex I II. Principles 1. b. Notice and 2. Choice; European Commission, 'Commission Implementing Decision on the adequacy of the protection provided by the EU-U.S. Privacy Shield' (n 500) para. 20, Annex II II. Principles 1. b. Notice 2. a. Choice; European Commission, 'Commission Decision on the adequacy of the protection provided by the safe harbour principles and related frequently asked questions issued by the US Department of Commerce' (n 558) Annex I Notice and Choice; the UK adopted the GDPR transparency and information obligations *verbatim* cf. European Commission, 'Commission Implementing Decision on the adequate protection of personal data by the United Kingdom' (n 813) para. 49–50.

6. Data security

The U.S. *post* COPRA must provide for adequate data security for personal data of EU data subjects.[946] According to Art. 5 para. 1 lit. f GDPR, Art. 24 para. 1 GDPR, and Art. 32 para. 1 and 2 GDPR, EU data protection law in particular requires controllers and processors to adapt technical and organizational measures which consider *inter alia* the state of the art, the cost of implementation and the nature, scope, context, and purpose of the processing.[947] In the U.S. *post* COPRA, Sec. 107 (a) together with Sec. 107 (b) (2) COPRA stipulate processing entities' obligation to maintain "*reasonable data security practices*" including "*administrative, technical, or physical safeguards*" which shall be "*appropriate to the volume and nature of the covered data*". Additionally, Sec. 107 (b) (1) COPRA clarifies that such practices must take into account "*any reasonably foreseeable risks*". Together, COPRA thereby links the required security-privacy level of data and systems to the modern processing risks described in this study as technical capacities and human (in)capacities.[948] Sec. 107 (a) and (b) (1) and (2) COPRA demonstrate how the bill closely follows the EU model of mandating context-apt security-privacy levels which factor in the risk level of relevant processing activities.[949] In comparison to U.S. privacy law *pre* COPRA, the bill mitigates against the lack of general guidance about whether and which data security is necessary, and whose responsibility it is to implement appropriate corrective and preventive measures.[950] *Post* COPRA, the level of data security for personal data of EU data subjects thus appears essentially equivalent to the standard in EU data protection law.

---

946 Cf. European Commission, 'Commission Implementing Decision on the adequate level of protection of personal data under the EU-US Data Privacy Framework' (n 39) para. 23; Commission Implementing Decision on the adequate protection of personal data by the United Kingdom (n 606) para. 47–48; Commission Implementing Decision on the adequate protection of personal data by Japan under the Act on the Protection of Personal Information (n 609) para. 57–59; Commission Implementation Decision on the adequacy of the protection provided by the EU-U.S. Privacy Shield (n 322) para. 24.

947 Supra Chapter 4 A. I. Legal framework applicable to the processing of personal data in the EU; Kramer, 'Art. 5' (n 269) para. 55–56; Kramer and Meints (n 293) para. 1–2.

948 Supra Chapter 2 A. I. Technical capacities and II. Human (in)capacities.

949 For a more detailed discussion supra Chapter 3 D. I. 6. Data security.

950 Supra Chapter 3 D. I. 6. Data security; Peppet (n 183), 136; Hoofnagle, *Federal trade commission privacy law and policy* (n 79) 163; Solove and Schwartz (n 60) 1270; Solove and Hartzog (n 385), 628–638.

7. Rules on onward transfers of personal data

COPRA must provide for limitations on onward transfers so that the protection of personal data sent from the EU to the U.S. cannot be undermined by further transfers.[951] Based on a review of previous adequacy findings by the EU Commission, this requires in particular that data subjects are informed about any transfer and have a choice to approve or object against the transfer, that the transfer is limited to specified processing purposes, that it occurs on the basis of a contract between the processing entity and the third party (or comparable arrangements within a corporate group), and that by such contract the third party commits to provide for adequate protection for the personal data it receives.[952]

COPRA establishes generally applicable rules which govern the transfer of covered data from a processing entity to a service provider or third party, irrespective of whether the data recipient is located in the U.S. or elsewhere. Without reference to their place of operation or registration, COPRA defines third parties in Sec. 2 (24) (A) (1) and (2) COPRA as any entity which *"processes or transfers third party data and which is not a service provider"*, and in Sec. 2 (25) COPRA third party data as *"covered data transferred by a processing entity to a third party"*. A service provider, on the other hand, processes data *"in the course of performing a service or function on behalf of, and at the direction of* [...] *another covered entity"* as set out in Sec. 2 (21) (A) COPRA.[953] Consequently, EU personal data in the U.S. is safeguarded by the bill's transfer rules including in situations of onward transfers in which personal data of EU data subjects is transferred from the U.S. to recipients outside of the U.S.[954]

---

951 European Commission, 'Commission Implementing Decision on the adequate level of protection of personal data under the EU-US Data Privacy Framework' (n 39) para. 37; supra Chapter 4 A. I. Legal framework applicable to personal data processing in the EU.

952 Ibid para. 37–43; European Commission, 'Commission Decision on the adequacy of the protection provided by the safe harbour principles and related frequently asked questions issued by the US Department of Commerce' (n 558) Annex I p. 2; European Commission, 'Commission Implementing Decision on the adequacy of the protection provided by the EU-U.S. Privacy Shield' (n 500) para. 27–29; European Commission, 'Commission Implementing Decision on the adequate protection of personal data by Japan under the Act on the Protection of Personal Information' (n 816) para. 75–80; the UK adopted the GDPR transfer regime Art. 44–49 GDPR without changes Commission Implementing Decision on the adequate protection of personal data by the United Kingdom (n 632) para. 74–82.

953 Supra Chapter 3 C. I. Material scope of application.

954 Provided personal data of EU data subjects is deemed covered data according to Sec. 2 (8) (A) COPRA or enjoys the same protection as U.S. residents' data according to Sec. 2 (14) COPRA; supra Chapter 4 B. Data protection level in the U.S. *post* COPRA.

First, COPRA ensures data subjects receive information about their right to object against any transfer of their covered data to third parties according to Sec. 105 (b) (1) (A) and (2) (B) (ii) COPRA.[955] Prior to any transfer of sensitive covered data, data subjects must be informed and expressly consent to the transfer according to Sec. 105 (c) (2) COPRA.[956] Sec. 102 (b) (3) (A) and (B) COPRA stipulates that transfer information must include the category of service providers and the identify of third parties to which covered data is transferred as well as the transfer purpose.[957] Secondly, COPRA's principle of purpose limitation in Sec. 106 (1), (2), (3) COPRA ensures any onward transfer only takes place within the limits of specified processing purposes.[958] Furthermore, Sec. 203 (a), (b), and (c) COPRA delineate accountability obligations for processing entities, third parties, and service providers which transfer and receive covered data. In particular, Sec. 203 (a) (1) and (4) (A) COPRA binds service providers to only process covered data within the limits of the processing entity's instructions, and to assist processing entities in fulfilling any consumer requests. Importantly, Sec. 203 (a) (5) COPRA clarifies that service providers have to be compliant with COPRA as "[they] *have the same responsibilities and obligations as a covered entity with respect to such data under all other provisions of this Act.*" With regard to third parties, according to Sec. 203 (b) (1) and (2) COPRA, they "*shall not process data for a purpose that is inconsistent with the expectations of a reasonable individual*", and they are subject to the "*same responsibilities and obligations* [under COPRA] *as a covered entity*". Finally, Sec. 203 (c) (1) (A) and (B) COPRA stipulate that processing entities are responsible to select service providers and third parties with diligence and that they must conduct "*reasonable oversight* [...] *to ensure compliance with the applicable requirements of* [COPRA]"; effectively, the due diligence obligation sets the basis for processing entities' liability if they fail to monitor and react to any incompliance of the data receivers in connection with the data transfer.

The above shows how COPRA closely resembles EU data protection law in that onward transfers must remain limited to specified purposes, that data subjects must be informed about the transfers, and that data subjects have a choice about the transfer of their covered data. Yet under EU data protection law, the link between the data controller and data processor or third party in a third country

955 Supra Chapter 3 D. II. 2. Privacy information management system; Sec. 105 (b) COPRA binds the provider of COPRA's privacy information management system and not the processing entities; the provision is not clear about the point in time when the data subject must receive the information, supra Chapter 4 B. I. 5. Transparency and information rights.

956 Supra Chapter 3 C. I. 2. (Sensitive) covered data.

957 Supra Chapter 4 B. I. 5. Transparency and information rights.

958 Supra Chapter 4 B. I. 1. Data processing principles.

that transfer or receive personal data arguably is closer than in COPRA because of the EU requirement for a written contract or a comparable arrangement within a corporate group as the framework for the data transfer and any further processing as set out in Art. 28 para. 3 sentence 1 and Art. 46 para. 2 lit. b–c GDPR.[959] Under COPRA, by contrast, no contractual basis is required for the transferring of covered data from the processing entity to the service provider or third party. Instead, as seen above, the bill's approach builds on the general applicability of COPRA so that processing entities, service providers, and third parties are directly subjected to its regulation for the processing of covered data according to Sec. 2 (8) and (16) COPRA,[960] and on the accountability obligations in Sec. 203 (a), (b), (c) COPRA by which the bill extends the obligation to comply with COPRA also to service providers and third parties outside of the U.S.

Does the lack of a contractual arrangement for a data transfer under COPRA mean that EU data subjects are less protected in the U.S. and compared to the EU standard? The legal effect of Sec. 203 (a) (5) and (b) (2) COPRA is that service providers and third parties outside of the U.S. must fully comply with COPRA so that the same level of protection for covered data exists in and outside of the U.S. Hence, to the extent COPRA provides for adequate protection of EU personal data in the U.S., personal data which is transferred from the U.S. onwards to a third party outside of the U.S. enjoys the same protection as in the U.S. The desired consequence of COPRA's transfer provisions is the same as the EU transfer mechanism's goal in Art. 46 para. 2 lit. b-c GDPR to raise, within a given framework, the level of protection in a third country to the EU standard.[961] A difference between COPRA and EU data protection law is that EU-like contractual arrangements can arguably accompany personal data transfers in a more complete and nuanced manner than the COPRA provisions do. For instance, following the *Schrems-II* decision, parties may be legally required to contractually agree on additional safeguards as a reaction to the actual level of data protection within the receiving country, *e.g.* encrypting personal data to shield it against the risk of government access in the U.S.[962] Also, neither the accountability obligations in Sec. 203 (a), (b), (c) COPRA nor elsewhere in COPRA does the bill provide for obligations of the service provider or third party to notify the processing entity in case of a personal data breach or a government

959 European Commission, 'Commission Implementing Decision on the adequate level of protection of personal data under the EU-US Data Privacy Framework' (n 39) para. 38; cf. Wittershagen (n 564) 188f.; cf. the specific reference to "contractual rules" in the section on restrictions on onward transfers in Art. 29 Data Protection Working Party, 'Adequacy Referential' (n 804) 6.

960 Supra Chapter 3 C. I. 1. Processing activities and 2. (Sensitive) covered data.

961 Pauly, 'Art. 46' (n 840) para. 9–11.

962 Ibid para. 12a.

request to access personal data, an obligation that the EU standard contractual clauses spell out in Clause 8.5 lit. c and Clause 14 lit. e (Module II).[963]

This is why COPRA should bolster its privacy protection regarding transfers of EU personal data with the supplemental requirement for processing entities to conclude written contracts with the receiving service provider or third party or similar arrangements for data exchanges within corporate groups comparable to EU data protection law. This could be implemented in the form of binding processing rules which govern the transferring and processing of EU personal data in addition to COPRA and with language similar to Art. 10 lit. a, b, and c EU-U.S. Data Privacy Framework.[964] Regarding the other transfer safeguards in COPRA of information, choice, and purpose limitation, the U.S. *post* COPRA provides for comparably strong rules on onward transfers of personal data than does EU data protection law.

II. Supervisory authority and enforcement in the U.S. *post* COPRA

Post COPRA, the U.S. must count the existence of at least one independent supervisory authority which effectively oversees and enforces compliance with U.S. consumer privacy law (sub Chapter 4 B. II. 1. Public oversight and enforcement).[965] Moreover, EU data subjects must have access to administrative and judicial review in privacy matters, they must be able to challenge alleged privacy shortcomings before an independent and impartial court of law (sub Chapter 4 B. II. 2. Private oversight and enforcement).[966]

1. Public oversight and enforcement

According to Sec. 301 (a) (2) and (3) (A) and (C), (b) (1) COPRA, compliance with COPRA is monitored and enforced by the FTC, by state attorney generals, and by state consumer protection officers.[967]

---

963 European Commission, 'Annex to the Commission Implementing Decision on standard contractual clauses for the transfer of personal data to third countries pursuant to Regulation (EU) 2016/679 of the European Parliament and of the Council' C(2021)3972 final; cf. European Commission, 'Commission Implementing Decision on the adequate level of protection of personal data under the EU-US Data Privacy Framework' (n 39) para. 42.

964 European Commission, 'Commission Implementing Decision on the adequate level of protection of personal data under the EU-US Data Privacy Framework' (n 39) Annex I Art. 10 lit. a, b, c.

965 Cf. supra Chapter 4 A. II. Supervisory authority and enforcement in the EU.

966 Ibid.

967 Supra Chapter 3 E. III. 2. FTC and state authorities.

To determine whether the FTC is an independent and impartial supervisory authority, we look at its organization and functioning. The Commission is composed of five commissioners who are appointed by the U.S. President and confirmed by the U.S. Senate. To minimize the risk of partisanship, no more than three commissioners may belong to the same political party.[968] Commissioners are appointed for a seven-year term and may only be removed for cause, *i.e.* inefficiency, neglect of duty, or malfeasance.[969] The office of commissioner is a full-time position, commissioners must abstain from any other remunerated activity; any violation of this compliance obligation constitutes a criminal offence which is sanctionable pursuant to 18 U. S.C. § 203 (a) and § 216 (a).[970] Finally, internal rules require commissioners and FTC employees to abstain from situations of perceived conflict of interest, *inter alia* by prohibiting the disclosure of information without the Commission's approval and by mandating "*cooling off*" periods after leaving office and before representing clients before the Commission.[971] All of this shows the FTC is an impartial and independent supervisory authority.[972]

COPRA furthermore addresses the question whether the FTC's resources and mandate suffice to effectively monitor and enforce privacy compliance.[973] To this end, Sec. 301 (a) (1) (A) COPRA substantially increases the FTC's staff and resources compared to the status *pre* COPRA.[974] Sec. 301 (a) (2) COPRA broadens the FTC's mandate, any violation of COPRA now triggers the agency's taking action.[975] According to Sec. 301 (a) (3) (C) COPRA, the FTC may bring administrative and judicial proceedings at its discretion, for instance to obtain cease and desist orders or a federal court order which prohibits a challenged processing activ-

968 Federal Trade Commission, 'Commissioners and Staff' (2022) <https://www.ftc.gov/about-ftc/commissioners-staff> accessed 12 February 2023; Hoofnagle, *Federal trade commission privacy law and policy* (n 79) 83.

969 Hoofnagle, *Federal trade commission privacy law and policy* (n 79) 83, 86; Kühnl (n 311) 249.

970 Cf. Hoofnagle, *Federal trade commission privacy law and policy* (n 79) 89.

971 Ibid 83, 89.

972 Confirmed also by European Commission, 'Commission Implementing Decision on the adequate level of protection of personal data under the EU-US Data Privacy Framework' (n 39) para. 60; Kühnl (n 311) 249.

973 Cf. Federal Trade Commission, 'Division of Privacy and Identity Protection' (2023) <https://www.ftc.gov/about-ftc/bureaus-offices/bureau-consumer-protection/our-divisions/division-privacy-and-identity> accessed 13 September 2023; Scholz, 'Private rights of action in privacy law' (n 160) 10, 13; Hoofnagle, 'Privacy Self-Regulation: A Decade of Disappointment' (n 77) 382.

974 Supra Chapter 3 E. II. 2. FTC and state authorities.

975 Ibid.

ity.[976] Regarding the protection of EU data subjects, it is worth noting that the FTC's mandate is not limited to protecting U.S. consumers and may extent to foreign consumers including EU data subjects.[977] When monitoring and enforcing COPRA, the FTC may leverage its full authority under the FTC Act according to Sec. 301 (a) (3) (A) COPRA.[978] For instance, it may investigate businesses and individuals according to § 46 (a) FTC Act, demand the disclosure of information pursuant to § 46 (b) FTC Act, and examine witnesses and subpoena their attendance according to § 49 FTC Act.[979] An additional angle for FTC oversight and enforcement finally is the accountability obligation for large data holders in Sec. 201 (a) COPRA according to which their CEO, privacy and data security officer must annually certify to the FTC about their organization's compliance with COPRA.[980]

Already since *pre* COPRA, penalties for privacy violations secured by the FTC have been severe and likely with a deterring effect on potential infringers.[981] According to § 45(m) (1) (A) and (B) FTC Act, any failure to comply with an FTC administrative order may lead to civil penalties up to 50,120 USD per violation or day in the case of a continuing violation. Such violation-based calculation has repeatedly resulted in very high penalties for processing entities whose privacy shortcomings affected a large number of consumers.[982] *Facebook*, for example, was fined 5 billion USD for its role in the *Cambridge Analytica* scandal.[983] *Twitter* had to pay 150 million USD after it failed to comply with a pre-existing FTC order which, among other issues, enforced compliance with the purpose limitation principle in the EU-U.S. Privacy Shield.[984]

---

976 Cf. Hoofnagle, *Federal trade commission privacy law and policy* (n 79) 98–100; European Commission, 'Commission Implementing Decision on the adequate level of protection of personal data under the EU-US Data Privacy Framework' (n 39) Annex I III. 11. Dispute Resolution and Enforcement lit. f FTC Action.

977 European Commission, 'Commission Implementing Decision on the adequate level of protection of personal data under the EU-US Data Privacy Framework' (n 39) Annex IV Letter Federal Trade Commission lit. b U.S. Legal Protections Benefitting EU Consumers.

978 Federal Trade Commission, 'A brief overview of the Federal Trade Commission's Investigative, law enforcement, and rulemaking authority' (2021) <https://www.ftc.gov/about-ftc/mission/enforcement-authority> accessed 12 February 2023; Hoofnagle, *Federal trade commission privacy law and policy* (n 79) 98–100.

979 Cf. Kühnl (n 311) 250–253; Hoofnagle, *Federal trade commission privacy law and policy* (n 79) 98–100.

980 Supra Chapter 3 E. II. 3. Certification obligations.

981 Cf. European Commission, 'Commission Implementing Decision on the adequate level of protection of personal data under the EU-US Data Privacy Framework' (n 39) para. 62–63.

982 Cf. ibid Annex IV Letter Federal Trade Commission III. Seeking and Monitoring Orders.

983 Federal Trade Commission (n 9).

984 Federal Trade Commission, 'FTC charges Twitter with Deceptively Using Account Security Data to Sell Targeted Ads?' (2022) <https://www.ftc.gov/news-events/news/press-releases/2022/05/ftc-charges-twitter-deceptively-using-account-security-data-sell-targeted-ads> accessed 4 August 2023.

Post COPRA, such penalties are to be deposited in the data privacy and security relief fund where they can be used according to Sec. 301 (a) (4) (A) and (B) (i), and (C) COPRA to redress harmed individuals or for general educational purposes.[985] For the above reasons, we conclude that the FTC possesses sufficient investigative and enforcement power, it may issue effective sanctions to oversee and enforce compliance with COPRA.

On the other hand, COPRA oversight and enforcement by state attorney generals and state consumer protection officers will not protect EU data subjects.[986] According to Sec. 301 (b) (1) CORPA, state attorney generals and state consumer protection officers only take action when a COPRA violation affects their state residents' interest; EU data subjects, however, are not residents of any U.S. state.

In sum, with the FTC as the principal supervisory and enforcement agency for COPRA and including for EU personal data which is transferred to the U.S., the U.S. law and system *post* COPRA fulfil the EU requirement of an independent, impartial, and effective supervisory authority.

2. Private oversight and enforcement

Post COPRA, EU data subjects must have effective and enforceable data subject rights and access to administrative and judicial review to challenge any contested mishandling of their personal data after the transfer to the U.S.[987] In particular, data subjects must be entitled to bring a legal action before an independent and impartial court of law where they have the right to claim redress including in the form of a monetary compensation.[988]

---

985 Supra Chapter 3 E. II. 2. FTC and state authorities.

986 Ibid.

987 *C-311/18 – Schrems II* (n 52) para. 188; European Commission, 'Commission Implementing Decision on the adequate level of protection of personal data under the EU-US Data Privacy Framework' (n 39) para. 65–66.

988 *C-311/18 – Schrems II* (n 52) para. 194; *C-362/14 – Schrems I* (n 110) para. 95; Art. 29 Data Protection Working Party, 'Adequacy Referential' (n 804) 8; cf. European Commission, 'Commission Implementing Decision on the adequate protection of personal data by the United Kingdom' (n 813) para. 104–111; European Commission, 'Commission Implementing Decision on the adequate protection of personal data by Japan under the Act on the Protection of Personal Information' (n 816) para. 103–112, 137–150; European Commission, 'Commission Implementing Decision on the adequacy of the protection provided by the EU-U.S. Privacy Shield' (n 500) para. 38–63, Annex 1 and 2; European Commission, 'Commission Decision on the adequacy of the protection provided by the safe harbour principles and related frequently asked questions issued by the US Department of Commerce' (n 558) Art. 1 para. 1 b; Annex IV Damages for Breaches of Privacy, Legal Authorizations and Mergers and Takeovers in U.S. Law.

In Sec. 301 (c) (1) COPRA, the bill introduces a private right of action which entitles data subjects to seek review and redress at U.S. courts for any contended privacy violation in the scope of COPRA.[989] The bill's private right of action also extents to the bill's data control rights in Sec. 102–105 COPRA according to which the data subject may claim access, deletion, correction, and portability of her covered data as well as decide about whether her sensitive covered data can be processed and transferred.[990] Importantly, the bill removes common blocking points which existed in privacy litigation *pre* COPRA, namely the difficulty to prove standing for a suffered privacy harm and the vast usage of pre-dispute arbitration clauses by which the individual renounced her right to a court proceeding.[991] First, Sec. 301 (c) (3) COPRA stipulates that every violation of a COPRA provision is deemed an injury in fact which establishes the consumer's standing in court, and, secondly, Sec. 301 (d) COPRA broadly bans the use of contract clauses which foreclose the individual's access to a court of law.[992]

Besides challenging privacy violations at U.S. courts, data subjects may lodge a complaint with the FTC to trigger an FTC investigation and enforcement measure.[993] By contrast, a review by state attorney generals and state consumer protection officers according to Sec. 301 (b) (1) COPRA is not available to EU data subjects given that they are not U.S. residents.[994] It follows that, under COPRA, EU data subjects have enforceable data subject rights. COPRA furthermore ensures data subjects can be effectively compensated. According to Sec. 301 (c) (2) (A) COPRA, data subjects may bring a civil action for money damages and courts may award consumers between 100 USD and 1000 USD per violation per day or the actual damages suffered. Moreover, in FTC enforcement actions, the Commission may collect damage payments from infringers which it may subsequently distribute to harmed individuals pursuant to Sec. 301 (a) (4) (A) and (B) (i) COPRA.[995]

To summarize, *post* COPRA, EU data subjects are entitled to challenge privacy violations before U.S. courts which can issue binding decisions including for monetary compensation. COPRA ensures EU data subjects have effective and enforceable data subject rights in the U.S. to demand and enforce access, correction, or erasure

989 Supra Chapter 3 E. II. 1. Private right of action.

990 Supra Chapter 3 D. II. 1. Data control rights.

991 Cf. Wischmeyer (n 88) 71–72; Glocker (n 91) 205–206.

992 Supra Chapter 3 E. II. 1. Private right of action.

993 Supra Chapter 4 B. II. 1. Public oversight and enforcement; European Commission, 'Commission Implementing Decision on the adequate level of protection of personal data under the EU-US Data Privacy Framework' (n 39) Annex IV Letter Federal Trade Commission lit. b U.S. Legal Protections Benefitting EU Consumers.

994 Supra Chapter 3 E. II. 2. FTC and state authorities.

995 Ibid.

of their personal data. In this regard, the protection for EU data subjects *post* COPRA is essentially equivalent to the one provided for by EU data protection law.

C. Interim summary

Provided COPRA is signed into law, the European Commission should recognize according to Art. 45 para. 3 sentence 1 and 3 GDPR that an adequate level of protection for personal data exists in the U.S. within the scope of application of COPRA and subject to the improvements suggested in Chapter 4.[996]

Instead of recognizing the whole of the U.S., the restriction to COPRA's scope of application is necessary because Sec. 2 (9) (A) (i) COPRA links the bill's protection to the scope of application of the FTC Act which excludes from the FTC's jurisdiction specific processing entities including financial institutions, airlines, and telecommunication carriers.[997] Consequently, personal data which is transferred from the EU to these processing entities in the U.S. is not subject to COPRA and does not enjoy the bill's protection. Outside of the scope of application of COPRA and disregarding the recent issuing of the *EU-U.S. Data Privacy Framework*, the U.S. currently does not provide a level of data protection essentially equivalent to the one in the EU, for instance, because of the lack of generally applicable data rights in U.S. privacy law for data subjects to control their data.[998]

A second limitation in COPRA's scope of application is caused by the definition of covered data in Sec. 2 (8) (A) together with Sec. 2 (14) COPRA according to which covered data must derive from U.S. residents.[999] Personal data of EU data subjects, however, is generally unable to meet this requirement because EU data subjects by and large do not have U.S. resident status. The consequence is that personal data of EU data subjects sent from the EU to the U.S. does not automatically fall into COPRA's scope of application and does not by itself enjoy the bill's protection. To address this issue, the U.S. government and the EU Commission should thus expressly deem personal data covered data in the sense of Art. 2 (8) (A) COPRA or clarify that EU personal data enjoys the same protection under COPRA as U.S. residents' data as set out in Sec. 2 (14) COPRA.[1000]

---

996 Supra Chapter 4 A. The adequacy threshold.

997 Supra Chapter 3 C. I. Material scope of application.

998 European Commission, 'Commission Implementing Decision on the adequate level of protection of personal data under the EU-US Data Privacy Framework' (n 39); Cantwell (n 54) 3; supra Chapter 1 A. Concept and status of U.S. privacy law.

999 Supra Chapter 3 C. II. 1. Protection of the consumer.

1000 Supra Chapter 4 B. Data protection level in the U.S. *post* COPRA.

Personal data which is transferred from the EU to the U.S. within the scope of COPRA enjoys a level of protection essentially equivalent to the one guaranteed in the EU. COPRA introduces data rights for data subjects to access, correct, delete, and transfer their personal data.[1001] It establishes generally applicable data processing principles which closely bind processing entities in how they can process personal data.[1002] The bill distinguishes between general and special categories of personal data for which a higher processing threshold applies, albeit using the different COPRA terminology of sensitive and (general) covered data.[1003] Alike the GDPR, COPRA sets guardrails how personal data may be processed when processing entities use algorithmic decision-making and profiling.[1004] The bill furthermore provides for transparency and information rights for data subjects which match the required content set out by EU data protection law.[1005] *Post* COPRA, processing entities are responsible to establish and maintain reasonable data security practices which are adequate to the processing context.[1006]

Where the bill allows for derogations from COPRA's data control rights and the bill's protection of personal data, the exceptions are spelled out by law and are limited in scope.[1007] Other possible derogations from the bill's accorded level of data protection in the U.S. which are caused by public interest and including U.S. intelligence activities are not dealt with by COPRA and are, hence, not discussed in this study.[1008]

A deviation from the level of data protection in the EU arguably are COPRA's rules about the onward transfer of covered data to service providers and third parties outside of the U.S. Whereas the GDPR according to Art. 46 para. 2 lit. b-c GDPR routinely requires, as the basis for the transfer, the signing of a contract or of a similar written arrangement, COPRA does not set an obligation for parties to enter into a written agreement. Instead, the bill aims at safeguarding the transfer and further processing by directly regulating the processing entities, service providers, and third parties, and by detailed accountability obligations for these parties.[1009] In light of the importance of a contractual basis for onward transfers in EU data protection law, this study recommends for the U.S. government and the EU Commis-

1001 Supra Chapter 4 B. I. 3. Data rights of the data subject.
1002 Supra Chapter 4 B. I. 1. Data processing principles.
1003 Supra Chapter 4 B. I. 2. Special categories of personal data.
1004 Supra Chapter 4 B. I. 3. Data rights of the data subject; supra Chapter 3 D. I. 2. Point of use regulation and regulation of data quality.
1005 Supra Chapter 4 B. I. 5. Transparency and information rights.
1006 Supra Chapter 4 B. I. 6. Data security.
1007 Supra Chapter 4 B. I. 4. Limitations to derogations.
1008 Supra Chapter 4 U.S. adequacy *post* COPRA.
1009 Supra Chapter 4 B. I. 7. Rules on onward transfers of personal data.

sion to agree on additional rules which apply to EU personal data in the U.S. and which require the signing of a written transfer agreement similar to the ones in EU data protection law prior to any onward transfer of EU personal data from the U.S. to a service provider or third party outside of the U.S.[1010]

The effective application of COPRA and the protection the bill stipulates for EU personal data is ensured by FTC oversight and enforcement. The FTC is an independent and impartial supervisory authority with the capacity to issue effective sanctions. Compared to the status *pre* COPRA, the bill substantially strengthens the resources and authority of the FTC in privacy matters.[1011] Beyond enforcement and oversight by the FTC, COPRA establishes a private right of action which guarantees data subjects access to U.S. courts where they may claim the enforcement of their data rights including access, correction, and erasure of their personal data, and may remedy suffered data protection harms including in the form of a monetary compensation.[1012]

Provided the above-suggested improvements regarding the definition of covered data and the requirement of a contractual basis for onward transfers are implemented, COPRA provides for comparably strong protection for data subjects and their personal data than the one guaranteed by EU data protection law. The EU Commission should thus recognize the U.S. and for transfers within the scope of application of COPRA as a country which provides for adequate data protection.

1010 Supra Chapter 4 A. I. Legal framework applicable to personal data processing in the EU.
1011 Supra Chapter 4 B. II. 1. Public oversight and enforcement.
1012 Supra Chapter 4 B. II. Private oversight and enforcement.

Summary and outlook

The analysis in Chapter 3 and Chapter 4 illustrates how U.S. consumer privacy law in the form of COPRA in many aspects converges towards EU data protection law. For example, COPRA is a comprehensive federal privacy law which applies broadly across sectors and industries,[1013] the bill introduces EU-inspired data control rights for the individual consumer,[1014] elements of collective privacy such as generally applicable data processing principles,[1015] and tightened compliance obligations for processing entities.[1016] Yet the foundation of U.S. consumer privacy law *post* COPRA remains fundamentally different from EU data protection law's constitutional basis.[1017] A continuous discussion about why, what, and how we should regulate personal data processing in the U.S. and in the EU thus seems inevitable. Rather than insisting on the U.S. and third countries' adopting European regulatory concepts and means, law- and policymakers should learn from each other and work towards a common understanding about what and how personal data should be regulated.[1018] To this end, Chapter 2 suggests building blocks for a modern privacy law which gravitate around common processing phenomena and modern privacy risks routinely found in the EU, in the U.S., and elsewhere because of the processing technology we use and how we use it. The categories of modern privacy risks presented in this study each consist of a subset of technical capacities which shape personal data processing and of common human (in)capacities of those who prepare, conduct, or are exposed to processing technology and processing activities.[1019] Looking into the future, working towards common privacy building blocks about what and how we regulate personal data processing may be useful also when we discuss international regulatory standards, *e.g.* in the context of international data transfers.[1020]

1013 Supra Chapter 3 C. I. Material scope of application.

1014 Supra Chapter 3 D. II. 1. Data control rights and Chapter 4 B. I. 3. Data rights of the data subject.

1015 Supra Chapter 4 B. I. 1. Data processing principles.

1016 Supra Chapter 3 E. I. Processing entities' compliance.

1017 Cf. Cantwell (n 459); supra Chapter 3 A. Consumer privacy rights: A conceptual change in U.S. privacy law?

1018 Gstrein and Zwitter (n 31), 5–7; cf. Hennemann, 'Wettbewerb der Datenschutzrechtsordnungen' (n 19) 888.

1019 Supra Chapter 2 B. Categorization of modern privacy risks – a call for capacity-apt regulation.

1020 Cf. Gstrein and Zwitter (n 31), 23; Chander and Schwartz (n 43), 48; with the idea to align on "*a new (digital) Bretton Woods*" Douglas W Arner, Giuliano Castellano and Eriks Selga, 'The Transnational Data Governance Problem' 2022 Berkeley Technology Law Journal 624, 692–696; Elizabeth Denham, 'A new Bretton Woods for Data' (2021), 09:00–09:47 <https://www.oii.ox.ac.uk/news-events/videos/a-new-bretton-woods-for-data/> accessed 12 June 2024.

https://doi.org/10.1515/9783112215715-006

For EU law- and policymakers, COPRA can be a source of inspiration because of how the bill proposes mitigation measures against some of today's privacy risks which differ from EU data protection law. For instance, COPRA's use of output- and downstream-based regulation such as in the form of COPRA's fair processing standard in Sec. 101 COPRA arguably is superior to the GDPR's input- and upstream-control to address technical and human (in)capacities.[1021] The fair processing standard effectively shifts the onus from the individual consumer on to processing entities to take responsibility that their processing activities and results are fair, *e.g.* that they do not discriminate against the consumer or a group of individuals.[1022] Also, such output-based control likely encourages data competition and innovation better than does the GDPR's input regulation.[1023] More competition together with measures to encourage the generation of high-quality data could increase overall data quality.[1024] Better data quality, in turn, may serve as a basis for innovation and the evolution of new technologies such as artificial intelligence and big data to better serve the individual consumer and the collective.[1025]

Another source of inspiration can be COPRA's privacy information management system, a central register for consumers to record their privacy preferences. The system's technology-agnostic character and mandatory use positions it as an efficient and effective tool for consumers to better control how their covered data is being processed.[1026] COPRA's privacy information management system is superior to alternative solutions of a decentralized and voluntary character which have been tested before but have failed to reach sufficient market penetration.[1027] Finally, COPRA strives to strengthen collective privacy. It introduces concepts and means which, at times, exceed the protection guaranteed under EU data protection law. For instance, in Sec. 108 (a) COPRA the bill introduces a generally applicable strict processing ban to use particularly sensitive covered data in high-risk processing situations and if the processing activity or the processing result is discriminatory.[1028] The strict processing ban in specific point of use situations builds on the

1021 Supra Chapter 2 B. Output and downstream regulation; Solove, 'The Myth of the Privacy Paradox' (n 155) 50; Hoffmann-Riem (n 3) 73–75; Solove, 'The Limitations of Privacy Rights' (n 187) 10–17.

1022 Supra Chapter 4 D. I. 1. COPRA's fair processing standard; cf. von Lewinski, 'Einführung' (n 17) para. 13; Solove, 'Privacy Self-Management and the Consent Dilemma' (n 78) 1901–1902.

1023 Cf. Gal and Aviv (n 19), 363–364; Lev-Aretz and Strandburg (n 16), 269–270, 308–309.

1024 Cf. Lev-Aretz and Strandburg (n 16), 269–270; supra Chapter 2 B. Output and downstream regulation; Batura and Peeters (n 186) 5; European Data Protection Supervisor (n 21) 21–22.

1025 Cf. Katyal (n 52), 56, 67–77; cf. Hoffmann-Riem (n 3) 62–63.

1026 Supra Chapter 4 D. II. 2. Privacy information management system.

1027 Cf. Blankertz and Specht-Riemenschneider (n 351) 29.

1028 Supra Chapter 3 D. I. 2. b. Regulated data quality.

idea of regulated online spaces in which the individual and the collective are protected from potentially harmful processing activities in a paternalistic manner and without regard to individual processing preferences because of the importance of these regulated spaces for all of society.[1029]

Still, COPRA is not the end of the journey to a modern privacy law. The bill can be criticized *inter alia* for stopping short of the full potential of downstream regulation, for instance because its provisions which address technical capacities such as in a particular point of use situation or the use of specific data quality in Sec. 108 (a) COPRA only apply within a very narrow scope of application.[1030] Also, a substantial part of COPRA's privacy regulation still depends on the individual consumer's taking action despite clear evidence that human capacity is limited both intellectually and behaviorally.[1031] For example, the bill's data rights of the individual consumer and the consumer's right to opt out of unwanted data transfers in Sec. 102–105 COPRA require the consumer to confront processing entities about how they process her covered data.[1032]

This study also shows how privacy regulation, concepts, and means in the U.S. and COPRA in many elements have been inspired by EU data protection law and how they are now evolving beyond some of the traditional solutions in the GDPR.[1033] At the same time, the European Union has begun to advance data regulation beyond data protection law in the form of the *Digital Services Act*, the *Digital Markets Act*, the *Data Governance Act*, the *Data Act*, and the *AI Act*.[1034] Remarkably, these new EU data regulations seem to integrate some of the building blocks for a modern privacy law presented in Chapter 2, several of which the COPRA bill proposes as an update to U.S. privacy law. For example, data quantity-based regulation such as in Sec. 2 (9) (C), Sec. 2 (23), Sec. 2 (15) COPRA, whereby small business are exempted from some of COPRA's compliance obligations and large data holders are subject to heightened scrutiny, is used in the recent *EU Digital Services Act* which

---

1029 Cf. Cohen (n 261) 143; Ohm (n 182) 105; supra Chapter 2 A. I. 4. Point of use of the processing activity.

1030 Supra Chapter 3 D. I. 2. Point of use regulation and regulation of data quality.

1031 Supra Chapter 2 A. II. 1. Intellectual (in)capacity; Chapter 2 A. II. 2. Behavioral (in)capacity.

1032 Supra Chapter 3 D. II. Data rights of the individual consumer.

1033 For a summary of the American Privacy Rights Act and how the proposal compares to COPRA supra Chapter 3. F. Interim summary; for U.S President Biden's Executive Order on the Safe, Secure, and Trustworthy Development and Use of Artificial Intelligence supra Chapter 2 A. I. 3. Processing technology.

1034 Cf. European Commission, 'A European strategy for data: Communication from the Commission to the European Parliament, the Council, A European strategy for data: Communication from the Commission to the European Parliament, the Council, the European Economic and Social Committee and the Committee of the Regions' (n 24).

treats *very large online platforms* and *very large online search engines* differently from regular providers of intermediary services, for instance in Art. 14 para. 1, 4, 5 and 6 about a company's terms and conditions.[1035] Also, Art. 26 para. 3 EU Digital Services Act leverages a combination of data quality, point of use, and processing technology-specific regulation similar to Sec. 108 (a) and (b) COPRA when it prohibits providers of online platforms to use special categories of personal data in profiling and for targeted advertisement.[1036]

The *EU AI Act* governs how artificial intelligence technology and products should be used downstream and without harmful effect, *inter alia* by establishing regulatory guardrails in Art. 10 para. 1–4, Art. 12 para. 1 and 2, Art. 13 para. 1–3, and Art. 15 para. 1 about the use of high-quality data, good data governance and meaningful transparency.[1037] Similar to the strict processing ban in Sec. 108 (a) COPRA, Chapter II Art. 5 para. 1 and 2 AI Act sets out when the use of artificial intelligence technology is banned altogether. The AI Act's prohibited practices seem to be largely motivated by the same data processing risks as illustrated in Chapter 2 of this study: Art. 5 para. 1 lit. c prohibits the use of artificial intelligence technology and products for social monitoring (*point of use of the processing activity*), Art. 5 para. 1 lit. d bans real-time remote biometric identification systems (*processing technology*), and Art. 5 para. 1 lit. a is triggered when the outcome or effect of use of artificial intelligence technology or products is harmful (*output-based regulation to protect individual and collective privacy*).

While the use of common building blocks in these new EU data regulations may foster convergence, the recent laws have given rise to further questions of interpretation and enforcement. For instance, considerable friction exists between the provisions of the GDPR and the new *EU Data Governance Act* and the *EU Data Act* which aim at facilitating data access and usage.[1038] Also, the multitude of enforcement authorities in the EU may come at the cost of a consistent and effective oversight and enforcement of the new regulations. Consider, for example, the *EU AI Act* which sets out for Member States' national data protection supervisory authorities or new market surveillance authorities to oversee and enforce provisions of the regulation (*e.g.* the monitoring of high-risk AI systems according to Art. 70 para. 1 and Art. 74 para. 8) while it creates an additional authority on the EU level (the new *AI Office* is tasked to *inter alia* monitor general-purpose AI models

1035 Cf. European Parliament and Council, 'Regulation (EU) 2022/2065 on a Single Market for Digital Services and amending Directive 2000/31/EC' (n 145) Recital 76.
1036 Gerdemann and Spindler (n 567), 119.
1037 European Parliament (n 249); supra Chapter 3 D. I. Data rights of the collective.
1038 Cf. Louisa Specht-Riemenschneider, 'Datennutz und Datenschutz: Zum Verhältnis zwischen Datenwirtschaftsrecht und DSGVO' [2023] ZEuP 639, 642–644.

according to Art. 66 and Art. 75 para. 1).[1039] This is different to COPRA or a comparable federal U.S. privacy law for which the FTC has oversight and enforcement power across U.S. states and could therefore help to ensure a consistent and effective application of the law.[1040]

To conclude, the use of common building blocks in U.S. privacy law such as in COPRA and in the new EU data regulations highlights the opportunity for law- and policymakers across the Atlantic (and the globe) to agree on a modern understanding about what and how personal data processing should be regulated. On this journey to a modern privacy law and framework, the comparative study of privacy and data protection law may offer valuable insight, inspiration, and guidance.

1039 European Parliament (n 249).

1040 Supra Chapter 4. B. II. 1. Public oversight and enforcement.

References

Acquisti Alessandro and Grossklags Jens, 'What Can Behavioral Economics Teach Us about Privacy?' in Alessandro Acquisti (ed), *Digital privacy: Theory, technologies, and practices* (Auerbach Publications 2008).

Albrecht Jan Philipp, 'Das neue EU-Datenschutzrecht – von der Richtlinie zur Verordnung' 2016(32(2)) CR 88.

Albrecht Jan Philipp and Jotzo Florian, *Das neue Datenschutzrecht der EU* (Nomos 2017).

Alt Ulrich, 'Datensicherheit, Datenschutz und Technik – ein risikoorientierter Ansatz' 2020 Der Sachverständige 169.

Apple, 'Family Privacy Disclosure for Children' (2022) <https://www.apple.com/legal/privacy/en-ww/parent-disclosure/> accessed 2 July 2022.

Aris Gkoulalas-Divanis, Bettini Claudio (ed), *Handbook of mobile data privacy* (Springer 2018).

Arner Douglas W, Castellano Giuliano and Selga Eriks, 'The Transnational Data Governance Problem' 2022 Berkeley Technology Law Journal 624.

Art. 29 Data Protection Working Party, 'Working Party on the Protection of Individuals with regard to the Processing of Personal Data' (1999) Working Paper 15.

Art. 29 Data Protection Working Party, 'Stellungnahme zum Schutz der personenbezogenen Daten von Kindern' (2009) Working Paper 160.

Art. 29 Data Protection Working Party, 'Adequacy Referential' (2017) Working Paper 254 rev01.

Auer-Reinsdorff Astrid and Conrad Isabell (eds), *Handbuch IT- und Datenschutzrecht* (C.H. Beck 2019).

Bamberger Kenneth A and Mulligan Deirdre K, *Privacy on the Ground: Driving Corporate Behavior in the United States and Europe* (MIT Press 2015).

Barocas Salon and Nissenbaum Helen, 'Big Data's End Run around Anonymity and Consent' in Julia Lane and others (eds), *Privacy, big data, and the public good* (Cambridge University Press 2014).

Batura Olga and Peeters Roel, 'EU Commission DG Internal Policies, Policy Department for Economic, Scientific, and Quality of Life Policies: European Union data challenge' (2021) <https://www.europarl.europa.eu/RegData/etudes/BRIE/2021/662939/IPOL_BRI(2021)662939_EN.pdf> accessed 3 October 2023.

Becker Maximilian, 'Ein Recht auf datenerhebungsfreie Produkte' 2017 JZ 170.

Bernes-Lee Tim, 'Proposal of an information management system' (1989) <http://info.cern.ch/Proposal.html> accessed 10 August 2023.

Bernes-Lee Tim and Fischetti Mark, *Weaving the web: The original design and ultimate destiny of the world wide web by its inventor* (Harper Collins 1999).

Bilogrevic Igor, 'Privacy in Geospatial Applications and Location-Based Social Networks' in Claudio B Aris Gkoulalas-Divanis (ed), *Handbook of mobile data privacy* (Springer 2018).

Blankertz Aline and Specht-Riemenschneider Louisa, 'What regulation for data trusts should look like' (2021) <https://www.stiftung-nv.de/sites/default/files/regulation_for_data_trusts_0.pdf> accessed 8 September 2023.

Bosche Ann and others, 'Unlocking Opportunities in the Internet of Things' (2018) <https://www.bain.com/contentassets/5aa3a678438846289af59f62e62a3456/bain_brief_unlocking_opportunities_in_the_internet_of_things.pdf> accessed 20 December 2020.

Bradford Anu, *The Brussels Effect: How the European Union rules the world* (Oxford University Press 2021).

Bundesbeauftragter für den Datenschutz und die Informationsfreiheit, 'Germany data protection authorities' (2022) <https://www.bfdi.bund.de/DE/Service/Anschriften/Laender/Laender-node.html> accessed 9 September 2022.

https://doi.org/10.1515/9783112215715-007

Bundesministerium der Justiz und für Verbraucherschutz and Max-Planck-Institut für Innovation und Wettbewerb (eds), Data Access, Consumer Interests and Public Welfare (Nomos 2021).

Burri Mira (ed), *Big data and global trade law* (Cambridge University Press 2021).

Business Roundtable, 'CEO letter to members of the U.S. Senate and House of Representatives' (2019) <https://s3.amazonaws.com/brt.org/BRT-CEOLetteronPrivacy-2.pdf> accessed 6 June 2020.

Bygrave Lee, *Data privacy law: An international perspective* (Oxford University Press 2014).

Bygrave Lee, 'The 'Strasbourg Effect' on data protection in light of the 'Brussels Effect': Logic, mechanics and prospects' 2021 40(105460) Computer Law & Security Review 1.

Cantwell Maria, 'Shopping online?: It's time lawmakes join Cantwell's efforts to protect your privacy' (2019) <https://www.cantwell.senate.gov/news/news-about-maria/editorial-shopping-online-its-time-lawmakers-join-cantwells-efforts-to-protect-your-privacy> accessed 25 January 2021.

Cantwell Maria, 'The State of Online Privacy and Data Security' (2019) <https://www.cantwell.senate.gov/imo/media/doc/The%20State%20of%20Online%20Privacy%20and%20Data%20Security.pdf> accessed 6 August 2020.

Cate Fred H, 'The Failure of Fair Information Practice Principles' in Jane Winn (ed), *Consumer Protection in the Age of the 'Information Economy'* (Ashgate 2007).

Chander Anupam and Schwartz Paul, 'Privacy and/or Trade' 2022 University Chicago Law Review forthcoming <https://papers.ssrn.com/sol3/papers.cfm?abstract_id=4038531> accessed 8 September 2023.

Chesney Bobby and Citron Danielle, 'Deep Fakes: A looming challenge for Privacy, Democracy, and National Security' 2019 California Law Review 1753.

Clopton Zachary, 'Redundant Public-Private Enforcement' 2016 69 Vanderbilt Law Review 285.

Cohen Julie, *Configuring the Networked Self* (Yale University Press 2012).

Commission Nationale de l'Informatique et des Libertés, 'Private Impact Assessment: Methodology' (2022) <https://www.cnil.fr/en/privacy-impact-assessment-pia> accessed 31 October 2023.

Committee on Energy and Commerce, 'Committee Chairs Rodgers, Cantwell Unveil Historic Draft Comprehensive Data Privacy Legislation' (2024) <https://energycommerce.house.gov/posts/committee-chairs-rodgers-cantwell-unveil-historic-draft-comprehensive-data-privacy-legislation> accessed 23 May 2024.

Council of Europe, 'Convention for the Protection of Individuals with regard to Automatic Processing of Personal Data' (1981) <https://rm.coe.int/1680078b37> accessed 24 February 2023.

Council of Europe, 'Update to Convention for the Protection of Individuals with regard to Automatic Processing of Personal Data' (2018) <https://search.coe.int/cm/Pages/result_details.aspx?ObjectId=09000016807c65bf> accessed 24 February 2023.

Craig Paul P and Búrca Grainne de (eds), *The evolution of EU law* (Oxford University Press 2021).

Craypo Eric, 'Deep Fakes' (2019) <https://vision.berkeley.edu/posts/deep-fakes> accessed 22 April 2022.

Datta Amit, Tschantz Michael C and Datta Anupam, 'Automated Experiments on Ad Privacy Settings' 2015 Proceedings on Privacy Enhancing Technologies 92.

Dempsey James and others, 'Breaking the Privacy Gridlock: A Broader Look at Remedies' (2021) SSRN Journal <https://dx.doi.org/10.2139/ssrn.3839711> accessed 30 October 2023.

Denham Elizabeth, 'A new Bretton Woods for Data' (2021) <https://www.oii.ox.ac.uk/news-events/videos/a-new-bretton-woods-for-data/> accessed 12 June 2024.

Determann Lothar, 'Healthy Data Protection' 2020(26) Michigan Telecommunications and Technology Law Review 229.

Determann Lothar, 'California Privacy Law Vectors for Data Disclosures' in Moritz Hennemann and others (eds), *Data Disclosure: Global developments and perspectives* (De Gruyter 2023).

Detterbeck Steffen, *Allgemeines Verwaltungsrecht* (C.H. Beck 2020).

Deutsche Bundesregierung, 'Datenstrategie der Bundesregierung' (2021) <https://www.bundesregierung.de/breg-de/service/publikationen/datenstrategie-der-bundesregierung-1845632> accessed 13 September 2023.

Ebner Gordian, 'Information Overload 2.0?: Datenwirtschaftsrecht IV: Die Informationspflichten gem. Art. 3 Abs. 2 Data Act-Entwurf' 2022(7) ZD 364.

Ebner Gordian, *Weniger ist Mehr*? (Nomos 2022).

Ehmann Eugen and Selmayr Martin (eds), *DSGVO* (C.H. Beck 2018).

Eßer Martin, Kramer Philipp and von Lewinski Kai (eds), *DSGVO/BDSG* (Carl Heymanns Verlag 2023).

ETSI, '4th Generation (LTE)' (2023) <https://www.etsi.org/technologies/mobile/4g?jjj=1698915313158> accessed 2 November 2023.

European Commission, 'Annex to the Commission Implementing Decision on standard contractual clauses for the transfer of personal data to third countries pursuant to Regulation (EU) 2016/679 of the European Parliament and of the Council' C(2021)3972 final.

European Commission, 'Commission Decision on the adequacy of the protection provided by the safe harbour principles and related frequently asked questions issued by the US Department of Commerce' C(2000)2441.

European Commission, 'Commission Implementing Decision on the adequate protection of personal data by Japan under the Act on the Protection of Personal Information' C(2019)304.

European Commission, 'Commission Implementing Decision on the adequacy of the protection provided by the EU-U.S. Privacy Shield' C(2016)4176.

European Commission, 'Commission Implementing Decision on the adequate protection of personal data by the United Kingdom' C(2021)4800 final.

European Commission, 'Commission Implementing Decision on the adequate level of protection of personal data under the EU-US Data Privacy Framework' C(2023)4745 final.

European Commission, 'Communication from the Commission to the European Parliament and the Council: Exchanging and Protecting Personal Data in a Globalised World' COM(2007)7 final.

European Commission, 'Data protection as a pillar of citizens' empowerment and the EU's approach to the digital transition: Two years of application of the General Data Protection Regulation' COM (2020)264 final.

European Commission, 'Report from the Commission to the European Parliament and the Council on the second annual review of the functioning of the EU-U.S. Privacy Shield' SWD(2018) 497 final.

European Commission, 'Special Eurobarometer 487a: The General Data Protection Regulation' (2019) <https://cnpd.public.lu/dam-assets/fr/actualites/international/2019/ebs487a-GDPR-sum-en.pdf> accessed 15 December 2021.

European Commission, 'A European strategy for data: Communication from the Commission to the European Parliament, the Council, A European strategy for data: Communication from the Commission to the European Parliament, the Council, the European Economic and Social Committee and the Committee of the Regions' [2020] COM(2020)66 final.

European Commission, 'Adequacy Decisions' (2024) <https://commission.europa.eu/law/law-topic/data-protection/international-dimension-data-protection/adequacy-decisions_en> accessed 27 June 2024.

European Commission, 'Proposal for a regulation – The European Health Data Space' (2022) <https://health.ec.europa.eu/publications/proposal-regulation-european-health-data-space_en> accessed 12 November 2023.

European Data Protection Board, 'Who we are' (2024) <https://edpb.europa.eu/about-edpb/about-edpb/who-we-are_en> accessed 12 June 2024.

European Data Protection Board, 'Endorsement 1/2018' (2018) <https://edpb.europa.eu/sites/default/files/files/news/endorsement_of_wp29_documents_en_0.pdf> accessed 21 October 2022.

European Data Protection Board, 'Member State data protection authorities' (2022) <https://edpb.europa.eu/about-edpb/about-edpb/members_en> accessed 31 October 2022.

European Data Protection Supervisor, 'Opinion on the European Commission's White Paper on Artificial Intelligence' (2020) <https://edps.europa.eu/data-protection/our-work/publications/opinions/edps-opinion-european-commissions-white-paper_en> accessed 26 October 2020.

European Data Protection Supervisor, 'Personal Information Management System' (2021) <https://edps.europa.eu/data-protection/our-work/subjects/personal-information-management-system_en> accessed 8 September 2023.

European Parliament, 'USB-type C to become EU's common charger by end of 2024' (2022) <https://www.europarl.europa.eu/news/en/headlines/society/20220413STO27211/usb-type-c-to-become-eu-s-common-charger-by-end-of-2024> accessed 15 January 2024.

Eurostat, 'Imports of high-tech products in 2022' (2022) <https://ec.europa.eu/eurostat/statistics-explained/index.php?title=International_trade_and_production_of_high-tech_products#Main_conclusions> accessed 20 May 2024.

Executive Office of the President, 'Big Data: Seizing Opportunities, Preserving Values' (2014) <https://obamawhitehouse.archives.gov/sites/default/files/docs/big_data_privacy_report_5.1.14_final_print.pdf> accessed 24 April 2023.

Facebook, 'Report Second Quarter Results' (2020) <https://investor.fb.com/investor-news/press-release-details/2020/Facebook-Reports-Second-Quarter-2020-Results/default.aspx> accessed 27 January 2021.

Federal Trade Commission, 'A Brief Overview of the Federal Trade Commission's Investigative, Law Enforcement, and Rulemaking Authority' (2013) <https://www.ftc.gov/about-ftc/what-we-do/enforcement-authority> accessed 6 August 2020.

Federal Trade Commission, 'The Do Not Call Registry' (2013) <https://www.ftc.gov/news-events/topics/do-not-call-registry> accessed 15 May 2022.

Federal Trade Commission, 'Enforcement Do-not-call-Registry' (2018) <https://www.ftc.gov/news-events/topics/do-not-call-registry/enforcement> accessed 14 November 2023.

Federal Trade Commission, 'USA v Musical.ly, complaint for civil penalties' (2019) <https://www.ftc.gov/system/files/documents/cases/musical.ly_complaint_ecf_2-27-19.pdf> accessed 15 July 2022.

Federal Trade Commission, 'FTC Imposes $5 Billion Penalty and Sweeping New Privacy Restrictions on Facebook' (2020) <https://www.ftc.gov/news-events/press-releases/2019/07/ftc-imposes-5-billion-penalty-sweeping-new-privacy-restrictions> accessed 14 October 2020.

Federal Trade Commission, 'A brief overview of the Federal Trade Commission's Investigative, law enforcement, and rulemaking authority' (2021) <https://www.ftc.gov/about-ftc/mission/enforcement-authority> accessed 12 February 2023.

Federal Trade Commission, 'Commissioners and Staff' (2022) <https://www.ftc.gov/about-ftc/commissioners-staff> accessed 12 February 2023.

Federal Trade Commission, 'Competition Advisory Opinions' (2022) <https://www.ftc.gov/tips-advice/competition-guidance/competition-advisory-opinions> accessed 7 March 2022.

Federal Trade Commission, 'Congressional Budget Justification Fiscal Year 2022' (2022) <https://www.ftc.gov/system/files/documents/reports/fy-2022-congressional-budget-justification/fy22cbj.pdf> accessed 12 February 2023.

Federal Trade Commission, 'FTC charges Twitter with Deceptively Using Account Security Data to Sell Targeted Ads' (2022) <https://www.ftc.gov/news-events/news/press-releases/2022/05/ftc-charges-twitter-deceptively-using-account-security-data-sell-targeted-ads> accessed 4 August 2023.

Federal Trade Commission, 'Warning about using Artificial Intelligence to Combat Online Problems' (2022) <https://www.ftc.gov/news-events/news/press-releases/2022/06/ftc-report-warns-about-using-artificial-intelligence-combat-online-problems> accessed 4 August 2023.

Federal Trade Commission, 'Division of Privacy and Identity Protection' (2023) <https://www.ftc.gov/about-ftc/bureaus-offices/bureau-consumer-protection/our-divisions/division-privacy-and-identity> accessed 13 September 2023.

Floridi Luciano, *The ethics of information* (Oxford University Press 2013).

ForgeRock, 'U.S. Consumer Data Breach Report' (2019) <https://www.forgerock.com/resources/view/92170441/industry-brief/us-7> accessed 30 September 2020.

Förster Achim, *Fair Use: Ein Systemvergleich der Schrankengeneralklausel des US-amerikanischen Copyright Act mit dem Schrankenkatalog des deutschen Urheberrechtsgesetzes* (Mohr Siebeck 2008).

Freeman Christopher and Louçã Francisco, *As time goes by: From the industrial revolutions to the information revolution* (Oxford University Press 2002).

Gajda Amy, 'Privacy, Press, and the Right to Be Forgotten in the United States' [2018] Washington Law Review 201.

Gal Michael S and Aviv Oshrit, '*The Competitive Effects of the GDPR*' 2020(3) Journal of Competition Law & Economics 349.

Gasser Urs, 'Futuring Digital Privacy' in Mira Burri (ed), *Big data and global trade law* (Cambridge University Press 2021).

Gerdemann Simon and Spindler Gerald, 'Das Gesetz über digitale Dienste (Digital Services Act) (Teil 2)' 2023 GRUR 115.

German Data Ethics Commission, 'Opinion' (2019) <https://datenethikkommission.de/wp-content/uploads/191023_DEK_Kurzfassung_en_bf.pdf> accessed 26 October 2020.

Github, 'Github company website' (2002) <https://github.com/about> accessed 3 October 2022.

Glocker Felix, *Der California Consumer Privacy Act* (Mohr Siebeck 2022).

Gola Peter (ed), *Bundesdatenschutzgesetz* (C.H. Beck 2019).

Graham-Harrison Emma and Cadwalladr Carole, 'Revealed: 50 million Facebook profiles harvested for Cambridge Analytica in major data breach' (2018) <https://www.theguardian.com/news/2018/mar/17/cambridge-analytica-facebook-influence-us-election> accessed 8 December 2020.

Gstrein Oskar Josef and Zwitter Aandrej Janko, 'Extraterritorial application of the GDPR: promoting European values or power?' (2021) 10(3) Internet Policy Review 2.

Hacker Philipp, *Datenprivatrecht* (Mohr Siebeck 2020).

Hamilton Daniel and Quinlan Joseph, 'The Transatlantic Economy 2023' (2023) https://transatlanticrelations.org/publications/transatlantic-economy-2023/ accessed 20 June 2024.

Hamm Christoph (ed), Beck'sches Rechtsanwalts-Handbuch (C.H. Beck 2022).

Heberlein Johanna, *Datenschutz im Social Web* (Nomos 2017).

Helbing Dirk, *Thinking Ahead – Essays on Big Data, Digital Revolution, and Participatory Market Society* (Springer International Publishing 2015).

Hennemann Moritz, 'Wettbewerb der Datenschutzrechtsordnungen' 2020(4) RabelsZ 864.

Hennemann Moritz, 'Datenrichtigkeit' [2020] LR 77.

Hennemann Moritz, Boshe Patricia and Meding Ricarda, 'Datenschutzrechtsordnungen in Afrika: Grundlagen, Rechtsentwicklung und Fortentwicklungspotenziale' 2021(3) ZfDR 193.

Hennemann Moritz and Ditfurth Lukas, 'Datenintermediäre und Data Governance Act' 2022(27) NJW 1905.

Hennemann Moritz, von Lewinski Kai, Wawra Daniel and Widjaja Thomas (eds), *Data Disclosure: Global developments and perspectives* (De Gruyter 2023).

Hennemann Moritz and Specht-Riemenschneider Louisa, *Data Governance Act* (Nomos 2023).

Hennemann Moritz and Steinrötter Björn, 'Data Act: Fundament des neuen EU-Datenwirtschaftsrechts?' 2022(21) NJW 1481.

Hennemann Moritz and Steinrötter Björn, 'Der Data Act: Neue Instrumente, alte Friktionen, strukturelle Weichenstellungen' 2024 NJW 1.

Hepp Andreas, 'Die Herausforderungen der Regulation und Governance von kommunikativer KI: Drei Thesen aus kommunikations- und medienwissen-schaftlicher Sicht' 2023 ZUM 553.

Hermstrüwer Yoan, *Informationelle Selbstgefährdung* (Mohr Siebeck 2015).

Hoeren Thomas, 'Thesen zum Verhältnis von Big Data und Datenqualität Erstes Raster zum Erstellen juristischer Standards' 2016(1) MMR 8.

Hoeren Thomas (ed), *Big Data und Recht* (C.H. Beck 2014).

Hoffmann-Riem Wolfgang, *Recht im Sog der digitalen Transformation* (Mohr Siebeck 2022).

Hoofnagle Chris, 'Privacy Self-Regulation: A Decade of Disappointment' in Jane Winn (ed), *Consumer Protection in the Age of the 'Information Economy'* (Ashgate 2007).

Hoofnagle Chris, *Federal trade commission privacy law and policy* (Cambridge University Press 2016).

Hoofnagle Chris, Soltani Ashkan, Good Nathaniel and Wambach Dietrich, 'Behavioral Advertising: The Offer You Can't Refuse' 2012 Harvard Law & Policy Review 273.

IAPP, 'U.S. Federal Privacy Legislation Tracker' (2023) <https://iapp.org/media/pdf/resource_center/us_federal_privacy_legislation_tracker.pdf> accessed 10 February 2023.

IAPP, 'U.S. State Privacy Legislation Tracker' (2024) <https://iapp.org/media/pdf/resource_center/State_Comp_Privacy_Law_Chart.pdf> accessed 23 May 2024.

IBM, 'What are large-language-models?' (2023) <https://www.ibm.com/topics/large-language-models> accessed 12 January 2024.

Institut der deutschen Wirtschaft, 'Wettbewerbseffekte der Europäischen Datenschutzgrundverordnung' (2020) <https://www.iwkoeln.de/fileadmin/user_upload/Studien/Report/PDF/2020/IW-Report_2020_DSGVO_und_Wettbewerb.pdf> accessed 15 December 2021.

Isaac Mike, 'Zuckerberg Plans to Integrate WhatsApp, Instagram and Facebook Messenger' *New York Times* (2019) <https://www.nytimes.com/2019/01/25/technology/facebook-instagram-whatsapp-messenger.html> accessed 10 October 2020.

Kahneman Daniel, *Thinking, fast and slow* (Penguin Books 2012).

Katyal Sonia, 'Private Accountability in the Age of Artificial Intelligence' 2019(66) UCLA Law Review 54.

Keats Citron Danielle and Solove Daniel, 'Privacy Harms' 2022 Boston University Law Review 793.

Kessel Lena, 'Vectors of data disclosure – A comparative study of the use of personal data from a legal, cultural, and information systems perspective: Cultural Influences on Personal Data Disclosure Decisions – US-American Perspectives' (2022) <https://www.jura.uni-passau.de/irdg/publikationen/research-paper-series/> accessed 15 February 2023.

Kischel Uwe, *Rechtsvergleichung* (C.H. Beck 2019).

Kloza Dariuz, 'A Behavioural Alternative To The Protection Of Privacy' in Dan J B Svantesson and Dariuz Kloza (eds), *Trans-Atlantic Data Privacy Relations As A Challenge For Democracy* (Intersentia 2017).

Koch Harald, Magnus Ulrich and Winkler von Mohrenfels Peter, *IPR und Rechtsvergleichung* (C.H. Beck 2010).

Köhler Helmut, Bornkamm Joachim and Feddersen Jörn (eds), *Gesetz gegen den unlauteren Wettbewerb* (C.H. Beck 2020).

Kühnl Christina, *Persönlichkeitsschutz 2.0* (De Gruyter 2016).

Landau Susan, 'Making Sense from Snowden: What's Significant in the NSA Surveillance Revelations' 2013 11(4) IEEE Security & Privacy 54.

Lane Julia and others (eds), *Privacy, big data, and the public good* (Cambridge University Press 2014).

Lev-Aretz Yafit and Strandburg Katherine J, 'Privacy Regulation and Innovation Policy' 2020(22) Yale Journal for Law and Technology 256.

Levmore Saul, 'The Evolutionary Force of Behavioral Economics in Law' 2021 17(2) Review of Law & Economics 465.

Von Lewinski Kai, *Die Matrix des Datenschutzes* (Mohr Siebeck 2014).

Liesching Marc, 'Fünf Jahre Netzwerkdurchsetzungsgesetz' 2023 MMR 56.

Louven Sebastian, 'Datenmacht und Zugang zu Daten' 2018 NZKart 217.

Maisch Michael Marc, *Informationelle Selbstbestimmung in Netzwerken* (Duncker & Humblot 2015).

Mannion Cara, 'Data Imperialism: The GDPR's Disastrous Impact on Africa's E-Commerce Markets' 2020 Vanderbilt Journal of Transnational Law 685.

Masing Johannes, 'Herausforderungen des Datenschutzes' 2012 NJW 2305.

Maunz Theodor and Dürig Günter (eds), *Grundgesetz* (C.H. Beck 2020).

Mayer-Schönberger Viktor and Ramge Thomas, *Reinventing capitalism in the age of big data* (John Murray 2018).

Michaels Ralf, 'The Functional Method of Comparative Law' in Mathias Reimann and Reinhard Zimmermann (eds), *The Oxford handbook of comparative law* (Oxford University Press 2019).

Michaels Ralf and Salaymeh Lena, 'Decolonial Comparative Law: A Conceptual Beginning' 2022(1) RabelsZ 166.

Montjoye Yves-Alexandre de, Hidalgo Cesar; Verleysen Michel; Blondel Vincent, 'Unique in the Crowd: The privacy bounds of human mobility' 2013 Nature 1376.

Murphy Maria Helen, 'Assessing the implications of Schrems II for EU US data flow' 2022 71 ICLQ 245.

National Center for Education Statistics, 'Tuition cost of colleges and universities' (2022) <https://nces.ed.gov/fastfacts/display.asp?id=76> accessed 24 April 2023.

National Institute of Standards and Technology, 'Privacy Framework' (2020) <https://www.nist.gov/privacy-framework> accessed 20 May 2024.

NETmundial, 'NETmundial-Multistakeholder-Document' (2014) <https://netmundial.br/wp-content/uploads/2014/04/NETmundial-Multistakeholder-Document.pdf> accessed 13 May 2022.

NOYB, 'European Commission gives EU-US data transfers third round at CJEU' (2023) <https://noyb.eu/en/european-commission-gives-eu-us-data-transfers-third-round-cjeu> accessed 25 February 2025.

OECD, 'Guidelines on the Protection of Privacy and Transborder Flows of Personal Data' [1980] <http://www.oecd.org/internet/ieconomy/oecdguidelinesontheprotectionofprivacyandtransborderflowsofpersonaldata.htm> accessed 5 August 2020.

Ohm Paul, 'Changing the Rules: General Principles for Data Use and Analysis' in Julia Lane and others (eds), *Privacy, big data, and the public good* (Cambridge University Press 2014).

Paal Boris and Hennemann Moritz, 'Big Data im Recht: Wettbewerbs- und daten(schutz)rechtliche Herausforderungen' 2017 NJW 1697.

Paal Boris and Pauly Daniel (eds), *DSGVO, BDSG* (C.H. Beck 2021).

Peppet Scott, 'Regulating the Internet of Things: First Steps Toward Managing Discrimination, Privacy, Security & Consent' 2014(93) Texas Law Review 85.

Poulsen Kevin and Mcmillan Robert, 'TikTok Tracked User Data Using Tactic Banned by Google' (2020) <https://www.wsj.com/articles/tiktok-tracked-user-data-using-tactic-banned-by-google-11597176738?mod=djemalertNEWS> accessed 12 August 2023.

President of the United States, 'Executive Order on Enhancing Safeguards For United States Signals Intelligence Activities' (2022) <https://www.whitehouse.gov/briefing-room/presidential-actions/2022/10/07/executive-order-on-enhancing-safeguards-for-united-states-signals-intelligence-activities/> accessed 14 October 2022.

President of the United States, 'Executive Order on the Safe, Secure, and Trustworthy Development and Use of Artificial Intelligence' (2023) <https://www.whitehouse.gov/briefing-room/presidential-actions/2023/10/30/executive-order-on-the-safe-secure-and-trustworthy-development-and-use-of-artificial-intelligence/> accessed 1 November 2023.

Reiling Katharina, 'Transnationale Ordnung der Digitalwirtschaft durch die Datenschutzgrundverordnung' in Christoph Krönke (ed), *Regulierung in Zeiten der Digitalwirtschaft* (Mohr Siebeck 2019).

Reimann Mathias and Zimmermann Reinhard (eds), *The Oxford handbook of comparative law* (Oxford University Press 2019).

Sandfuchs Barbara, *Privatheit wider Willen* (Mohr Siebeck 2015).

Sandfuchs Barbara and Kapsner Andreas, 'Coercing Online Privacy' 2016(12) ISJLP 185.

Sarre Frank and Pruß Michael, '§ 2 Daten, Datenbanken und Datensicherheit' in Astrid Auer-Reinsdorff and Isabell Conrad (eds), *Handbuch IT- und Datenschutzrecht* (C.H. Beck 2019).

Schaub Florian, 'Context-Adaptive Privacy Mechanisms' in Claudio B Aris Gkoulalas-Divanis (ed), *Handbook of mobile data privacy* (Springer 2018).

Scholz Lauren, 'Private rights of action in privacy law' 2022 William & Mary Law Review 1639.

Schrems Max, *Kämpf um deine Daten* (Edition a 2014).

Schrems Max, 'Open Letter on the Future of EU-US Data Transfers' (2022) <https://noyb.eu/en/open-letter-future-eu-us-data-transfers?mkt_tok=MTM4LUVaTS0wNDIAAAGEorNHTjjBStW6O3oFTK2_1LHlDiq4K83VAY5dUPTjQ9BdMwc41t0_DDUkzExb2xX9IMhhqCY1-x1t5V6M4k2WygT5ZIPWgoOaWAild53IkFDr> accessed 4 February 2023.

Schwartz Paul, 'Preemption and Privacy' 2009(118) The Yale Law Journal 902.

Schwartz Paul, 'Privacy inalienability and the regulation of spyware' 2005 Berkeley Technology Law Journal 1269.

Schwartz Paul, 'Global Data Privacy: The EU Way' 2019 New York University Law Review 771.

Schwartz Paul and Pfeifer Karl-Nikolaus, 'Transatlantic Data Privacy Law' 2017(106) Georgetown Law Journal 115.

Schweitzer Heike, 'Datenzugang in der Datenökonomie: Eckpfeiler einer neuen Informationsordnung' 2019 GRUR 569.

Seyr Sibylle, *Der effet utile in der Rechtsprechung des Europäischen Gerichtshofs* (Duncker & Humblot 2010).

Siegel Jeremy, 'When the Internet of Things Flounders: Looking into GDPR-Esque Security Standards for IoT Devices in the United States from the Consumers' Perspective' 2020(1) Journal of High Technology Law 189.

Silverstein Jason, 'Facebook data breach: Hundreds of millions of records exposed on Amazon server, according to UpGuard cybersecurity research firm' (2019) <https://www.cbsnews.com/news/millions-facebook-user-records-exposed-amazon-cloud-server/> accessed 27 January 2021.

Simitis Spiros, Hornung Gerrit and Spiecker Döhmann Indra (eds), *Datenschutzrecht* (Nomos 2019).

Solove Daniel, 'Privacy Self-Management and the Consent Dilemma' 2013(126) Harvard Law Review 1880.

Solove Daniel, 'The Limitations of Privacy Rights' 2022(30) GWU Law School Public Law Research Paper 1.

Solove Daniel, 'The Myth of the Privacy Paradox' 2021(89) The George Washington Law Review 1.

Solove Daniel and Hartzog Woodrow, 'The FTC and the New Common Law of Privacy' 2014(114) Columbia Law Review 583.

Solove Daniel and Schwartz Paul, *Information Privacy Law* (Wolters Kluwer Law & Business 2018).

Solove Daniel and Schwartz Paul, 'ALI Data Privacy: Overview and Black Letter Text' 2022 UCLA Law Review 1252.

Solti Andreas, Agarwal Sushant and Spiekermann-Hoff Sarah, 'Privacy in Location-Sensing Technologies' in Claudio Bettini Aris Gkoulalas-Divanis (ed), *Handbook of mobile data privacy* (Springer 2018).

Specht Louisa, *Diktat der Technik* (Nomos 2019).

Specht-Riemenschneider Louisa, 'Datennutz und Datenschutz: Zum Verhältnis zwischen Datenwirtschaftsrecht und DSGVO' 2023 ZEuP 638.

Specht-Riemenschneider Louisa, 'Data access rights – A comparative perspective' in Bundesministerium der Justiz und für Verbraucherschutz and Max-Planck-Institut für Innovation und Wettbewerb (eds), *Data Access, Consumer Interests and Public Welfare* (Nomos 2021).

Specht-Riemenschneider Louisa, Werry Nicola, Werry Susanne (eds), *Datenrecht in der Digitalisierung (Erich Schmidt Verlag 2020).*

Spiecker Oliver, '§ 39 Äußerungs- und Medienrecht' in Christoph Hamm (ed), *Beck'sches Rechtsanwalts-Handbuch* (C.H. Beck 2022).

Steinmüller Wilhelm, Lutterbeck Bernd, Mallmann Christoph, Harbort Uwe, Kolb Gerhard, Schneider Jochen, 'Grundfragen des Datenschutzes, Anlage 1' 1972 Drucksache VI/3826.

Strandburg Katherine J, 'Monitoring, Datafication, and Consent: Legal Approaches to Privacy in the Big Data Context' in Julia Lane and others (eds), *Privacy, big data, and the public good* (Cambridge University Press 2014).

Streinz Thomas, 'The Evolution of European Data Law' in Paul P Craig and Gráinne de Búrca (eds), *The evolution of EU law* (Oxford University Press 2021).

Susskind Jamie, *Future politics: Living together in a world transformed by tech* (Oxford University Press 2018).

Svantesson Dan Jerker B and Kloza Dariuz (eds), *Trans-Atlantic Data Privacy Relations As A Challenge For Democracy* (Intersentia 2017).

Taeger Jürgen and Gabel Detlev (eds), *DSGVO – BDSG – TTDSG: Kommentar* (Deutscher Fachverlag GmbH 2022).

Thaler Richard and Sunstein Cass, *Nudge* (Yale University Press 2009).

U.S. Bureau of Labor Statistics, 'Consumer Expenditures 2021' (2021) <https://www.bls.gov/news.release/cesan.nr0.htm> accessed 5 March 2023.

U.S. Department of Health, Education and Welfare, 'Records, Computers and the Rights of Citizens' (1973) <https://aspe.hhs.gov/reports/records-computers-rights-citizens> accessed 24 February 2023.

Veil Winfried, 'Die Datenschutz-Grundverordnung: des Kaisers neue Kleider' 2018(10) NVwZ 686–696.

Voigt Marlene, *Die datenschutzrechtliche Einwilligung: Zum Spannungsfeld von informationeller Selbstbestimmung und ökonomischer Verwertung personenbezogener Daten* (Nomos 2020).

Voss Gregory, 'Obstacles to transatlantic harmonization of data privacy law in context' 2019 University of Illinois Journal of Law, Technology & Policy 405.

Voss Gregory, 'Cross-Border Data Flows, the GDPR, and Data Governance' 2020 Washington International Law Journal 485.

Wachter Sandra, Mittelstadt Brent and Floridi Luciano, 'Why a Right to Explanation of Automated Decision-Making Does Not Exist in the General Data Protection Regulation' 2017 7(2) International Data Privacy Law 76.

Wagner Gerhard, 'Haftung von Plattformen für Rechtsverletzungen (Teil 2)' 2020 GRUR 447.

Wagner Julian, 'The transfer of personal data to third countries under the GDPR: when does a recipient country provide an adequate level of protection?' 2018 8(4) International Data Privacy Law 318.

Wang Flora, 'Cooperative Data Privacy: The Japanese Model of Data Privacy And The EU-Japan GDPR Adequacy Agreement' 2020(33) Harvard Journal of Law & Technology 661.

Wawra Daniela, 'Parameters of Personal Data Disclosure Decisions in Cross-Cultural Comparison' in Moritz Hennemann and others (eds), *Data Disclosure: Global developments and perspectives* (De Gruyter 2023).

Weichert Thilo, 'Privatheit und Datenschutz im Konflikt zwischen den USA und Europa' (2012) <https://www.datenschutzzentrum.de/uploads/vortraege/20120806-weichert-privatheit-datenschutz-konflikt-usa-europa.pdf> accessed 15 December 2022.

Westphalen Friedrich, 'Auf dem Weg zum gläsernen Bürger?' 1983 Die neue Ordnung 136.

Winn Jane (ed), *Consumer Protection in the Age of the 'Information Economy'* (Ashgate 2007).

WIPO, 'The Geography of Innovation: Local Hotspots, Global Networks' (2019) <https://www.wipo.int/edocs/pubdocs/en/wipo_pub_944_2019.pdf> accessed 15 December 2022.

Wischmeyer Thomas, *Überwachung ohne Grenzen: Zu den rechtlichen Grundlagen nachrichtendienstlicher Tätigkeiten in den USA* (Nomos 2017).

Wittershagen Leonie, *The Transfer of Personal Data from the European Union to the United Kingdom post-Brexit* (De Gruyter 2023).

World Bank, 'Individuals using the Internet' (2020) <https://data.worldbank.org/indicator/it.net.user.zs> accessed 11 August 2020.

Zuiderveen Borgesius Frederik, Kruikemeier Sanne, Boerman Sophie and Helberger Natali, 'Tracking Walls, Take-It-or-Leave-It Choices, the GDPR, and the ePrivacy Regulation' 2017(3) EDPL 353.

Zweigert Konrad and Kötz Hein, *Einführung in die Rechtsvergleichung auf dem Gebiete des Privatrechts* (Mohr Siebeck 1996).

Annex
U.S. Consumer Online Rights Act

117th CONGRESS 1st Session

S. 3195

To provide consumers with foundational data privacy rights, create strong oversight mechanisms, and establish meaningful enforcement.

IN THE SENATE OF THE UNITED STATES

November 4, 2021
Ms. Cantwell (for herself, Mr. Schatz, Ms. Klobuchar, and Mr. Markey) introduced the following bill; which was read twice and referred to the Committee on Commerce, Science, and Transportation

A BILL

To provide consumers with foundational data privacy rights, create strong oversight mechanisms, and establish meaningful enforcement.

Be it enacted by the Senate and House of Representatives of the United States of America in Congress assembled,

SECTION 1. Short title; table of contents.

(a) Short title.—This Act may be cited as the "Consumer Online Privacy Rights Act".
(b) Table of contents.—The table of contents of this Act is as follows:

SEC. 2. Definitions.

In this Act:

(1) AFFIRMATIVE EXPRES. CONSENT.—

(A) IN GENERAL.—The term "affirmative express consent" means an affirmative act by an individual that clearly communicates the individual's authorization for an act or practice, in response to a specific request that meets the requirements of subparagraph (B).

(B) REQUEST REQUIREMENTS.—The requirements of this subparagraph with respect to a request from a covered entity to an individual are the following:

(i) The request is provided to the individual in a standalone disclosure.

(ii) The request includes a description of each act or practice for which the individual's consent is sought and—

(I) clearly distinguishes between an act or practice which is necessary to fulfill a request of the individual and an act or practice which is for another purpose; and

(II) is written in easy-to-understand language and includes a prominent heading that would enable a reasonable individual to identify and understand the act or practice.
(iii) The request clearly explains the individual's applicable rights related to consent.
(C) EXPRES. CONSENT REQUIRED.—An entity shall not infer that an individual has provided affirmative express consent to an act or practice from the inaction of the individual or the individual's continued use of a service or product provided by the entity.

(2) ALGORITHMIC DECISION-MAKING.—The term "algorithmic decision-making" means a computational process, including one derived from machine learning, statistics, or other data processing or artificial intelligence techniques that makes a decision or facilitates human decision-making with respect to covered data.

(3) BIOMETRIC INFORMATION.—
(A) IN GENERAL.—The term "biometric information" means any covered data generated from the measurement or specific technological processing of an individual's biological, physical, or physiological characteristics, including—
(i) fingerprints;
(ii) voice prints;
(iii) iris or retina scans;
(iv) facial scans or templates;
(v) deoxyribonucleic acid (DNA) information; and
(vi) gait.
(B) EXCLUSIONS.—Such term does not include writing samples, written signatures, photographs, voice recordings, demographic data, or physical characteristics such as height, weight, hair color, or eye color, provided that such data is not used for the purpose of identifying an individual's unique biological, physical, or physiological characteristics.

(4) COLLECT; COLLECTION.—The terms "collect" and "collection" mean buying, renting, gathering, obtaining, receiving, accessing, or otherwise acquiring covered data by any means, including by passively or actively observing the individual's behavior.

(5) COMMON BRANDING.—The term "common branding" means a shared name, servicemark, or trademark.

(6) CONTROL.—The term "control" means, with respect to an entity—
(A) ownership of, or the power to vote, more than 50 percent of the outstanding shares of any class of voting security of the entity;

(B) control in any manner over the election of a majority of the directors of the entity (or of individuals exercising similar functions); or
(C) the power to exercise a controlling influence over the management of the entity.

(7) COMMISSION.—The term "Commission" means the Federal Trade Commission.

(8) COVERED DATA.—
(A) IN GENERAL.—The term "covered data" means information that identifies, or is linked or reasonably linkable to an individual or a consumer device, including derived data.
(B) EXCLUSIONS.—Such term does not include—
(i) de-identified data;
(ii) employee data; and
(iii) public records.

(9) COVERED ENTITY.—
(A) IN GENERAL.—The term "covered entity" means any entity or person that—
(i) is subject to the Federal Trade Commission Act (15 U. S.C. 41 et seq.); and
(ii) processes or transfers covered data.
(B) INCLUSION OF COMMONLY CONTROLLED AND COMMONLY BRANDED ENTITIES.—Such term includes any entity or person that controls, is controlled by, is under common control with, or shares common branding with a covered entity.
(C) EXCLUSION OF SMALL BUSINESS.—Such term does not include a small business.

(10) DE-IDENTIFIED DATA.—Term "de-identified data" means information that cannot reasonably be used to infer information about, or otherwise be linked to, an individual, a household, or a device used by an individual or household, provided that the entity—
(A) takes reasonable measures to ensure that the information cannot be reidentified, or associated with, an individual, a household, or a device used by an individual or household;
(B) publicly commits in a conspicuous manner—
(i) to process and transfer the information in a de-identified form; and
(ii) not to attempt to reidentify or associate the information with any individual, household, or device used by an individual or household; and
(C) contractually obligates any person or entity that receives the information from the covered entity to comply with all of the provisions of this paragraph.

(11) DERIVED DATA.—The term "derived data" means covered data that is created by the derivation of information, data, assumptions, or conclusions from facts, evidence, or another source of information or data about an individual, household, or device used by an individual or household.

(12) EMPLOYEE DATA.—The term "employee data" means—
(A) covered data that is collected by a covered entity or the covered entity's service provider about an individual in the course of the individual's employment or application for employment (including on a contract or temporary basis) provided that such data is retained or processed by the covered entity or the covered entity's service provider solely for purposes necessary for the individual's employment or application for employment;
(B) covered data that is collected by a covered entity or the covered entity's service provider that is emergency contact information for an individual who is an employee, contractor, or job applicant of the covered entity provided that such data is retained or processed by the covered entity or the covered entity's service provider solely for the purpose of having an emergency contact for such individual on file; and
(C) covered data that is collected by a covered entity or the covered entity's service provider about an individual (or a relative of an individual) who is an employee or former employee of the covered entity for the purpose of administering benefits to which such individual or relative is entitled on the basis of the individual's employment with the covered entity, provided that such data is retained or processed by the covered entity or the covered entity's service provider solely for the purpose of administering such benefits.

(13) EXECUTIVE AGENCY.—The term "Executive agency" has the meaning given such term in section 105 of title 5, United States Code.

(14) INDIVIDUAL.—The term "individual" means a natural person residing in the United States, however identified, including by any unique identifier.

(15) LARGE DATA HOLDER.—The term "large data holder" means a covered entity that, in the most recent calendar year—
(A) processed or transferred the covered data of more than 5,000,000 individuals, devices used by individuals or households, or households; or
(B) processed or transferred the sensitive covered data of more than 100,000 individuals, devices used by individuals or households, or households.

(16) PROCESS.—The term "process" means any operation or set of operations performed on covered data including collection, analysis, organization, structuring, retaining, using, or otherwise handling covered data.

(17) PROCESSING PURPOSE.—The term "processing purpose" means an adequately specific and granular reason for which a covered entity processes covered data that clearly describes the processing activity.

(18) PUBLICLY AVAILABLE INFORMATION.—
(A) IN GENERAL.—The term "publicly available information" means—
(i) information that a covered entity has a reasonable basis to believe is lawfully made available to the general public from widely distributed media; and
(ii) information that is directly and voluntarily disclosed to the general public by the individual to whom the information relates.
(B) LIMITATION.—Such term does not include—
(i) information derived from publicly available information;
(ii) biometric information; or
(iii) nonpublicly available information that has been combined with publicly available information.

(19) PUBLIC RECORDS.—The term "public records" means information that is lawfully made available from Federal, State, or local government records provided that the covered entity processes and transfers such information in accordance with any restrictions or terms of use placed on the information by the relevant government entity.

(20) SENSITIVE COVERED DATA.—The term "sensitive covered data" means the following forms of covered data:
(A) A government-issued identifier, such as a Social Security number, passport number, or driver's license number.
(B) Any information that describes or reveals the past, present, or future physical health, mental health, disability, or diagnosis of an individual.
(C) A financial account number, debit card number, credit card number, or any required security or access code, password, or credentials allowing access to any such account.
(D) Biometric information.
(E) Precise geolocation information that reveals the past or present actual physical location of an individual or device.

(F) The content or metadata of an individual's private communications or the identity of the parties to such communications unless the covered entity is an intended recipient of the communication.

(G) An email address, telephone number, or account log-in credentials.

(H) Information revealing an individual's race, ethnicity, national origin, religion, or union membership in a manner inconsistent with the individual's reasonable expectation regarding disclosure of such information.

(I) Information revealing the sexual orientation or sexual behavior of an individual in a manner inconsistent with the individual's reasonable expectation regarding disclosure of such information.

(J) Information revealing online activities over time and across third-party websites or online services.

(K) Calendar information, address book information, phone or text logs, photos, or videos maintained on an individual's device.

(L) A photograph, film, video recording, or other similar medium that shows the naked or undergarment-clad private area of an individual.

(M) Any other covered data processed or transferred for the purpose of identifying the above data types.

(N) Any other covered data that the Commission determines to be sensitive covered data through a rulemaking pursuant to section 553 of title 5, United States Code.

(21) SERVICE PROVIDER.—

(A) IN GENERAL.—The term "service provider" means a covered entity that processes or transfers covered data in the course of performing a service or function on behalf of, and at the direction of, another covered entity, but only to the extent that such processing or transferral—

(i) relates to the performance of such service or function; or

(ii) is necessary to comply with a legal obligation or to establish, exercise, or defend legal claims.

(B) EXCLUSION.—Such term does not include a covered entity that processes or transfers the covered data outside of the direct relationship between the service provider and the covered entity.

(22) SERVICE PROVIDER DATA.—The term "service provider data" means covered data that is collected by or has been transferred to a service provider by a covered entity for the purpose of allowing the service provider to perform a service or function on behalf of, and at the direction of, such covered entity.

(23) SMALL BUSINESS.—
(A) IN GENERAL.—The term "small business" means an entity that can establish that, with respect to the 3 preceding calendar years (or for the period during which the entity has been in existence if, as of such date, such period is less than 3 years) the entity does not—
(i) maintain annual average gross revenue in excess of $25,000,000;
(ii) annually process the covered data of an average of 100,000 or more individuals, households, or devices used by individuals or households; and
(iii) derive 50 percent or more of its annual revenue from transferring individuals' covered data.
(B) COMMON CONTROL; COMMON BRANDING.—For purposes of subparagraph (A), the annual average gross revenue, data processing volume, and percentage of annual revenue of an entity shall include the revenue and processing activities of any person that controls, is controlled by, is under common control with, or shares common branding with such entity.

(24) THIRD PARTY.—The term "third party"—
(A) means any person or entity that—
(i) processes or transfers third party data; and
(ii) is not a service provider with respect to such data; and
(B) does not include a person or entity that collects covered data from another entity if the two entities are related by common ownership or corporate control and share common branding.

(25) THIRD PARTY DATA.—The term "third party data" means covered data that is transferred to a third party by a covered entity.

(26) TRANSFER.—The term "transfer" means to disclose, release, share, disseminate, make available, sell, license, or otherwise communicate covered data by any means to a service provider or third party—
(A) in exchange for consideration; or
(B) for a commercial purpose.

(27) UNIQUE IDENTIFIER.—The term "unique identifier" means an identifier that is reasonably linkable to an individual, household, or device used by an individual or household, including a device identifier, an Internet Protocol address, cookies, beacons, pixel tags, mobile ad identifiers, or similar technology, customer number, unique pseudonym, or user alias, telephone numbers, or other forms of persistent or probabilistic identifiers that can be used to identify a particular individual, a household, or a device.

(28) WIDELY DISTRIBUTED MEDIA.—The term "widely distributed media" means information that is available to the general public, including information from a telephone book or online directory, a television, internet, or radio program, the news media, or an internet site that is available to the general public on an unrestricted basis, but does not include an obscene visual depiction as defined in section 1460 of title 18, United States Code.

SEC. 3. Effective date.

This Act shall take effect on the date that is 180 days after the date of enactment of this Act.

TITLE I—Data privacy rights

SEC. 101. Duty of loyalty.

(a) In general.—A covered entity shall not—
(1) engage in a deceptive data practice or a harmful data practice; or
(2) process or transfer covered data in a manner that violates any provision of this Act.

(b) Definitions.—
(1) DECEPTIVE DATA PRACTICE.—The term "deceptive data practice" means an act or practice involving the processing or transfer of covered data in a manner that constitutes a deceptive act or practice in violation of section 5(a)(1) of the Federal Trade Commission Act (15 U. S. C. 45(a)(1)).
(2) HARMFUL DATA PRACTICE.—The term "harmful data practice" means the processing or transfer of covered data in a manner that causes or is likely to cause any of the following:
(A) Financial, physical, or reputational injury to an individual.
(B) Physical or other offensive intrusion upon the solitude or seclusion of an individual or the individual's private affairs or concerns, where such intrusion would be offensive to a reasonable person.
(C) Other substantial injury to an individual.

SEC. 102. Right to access and transparency.

(a) Right to access.—A covered entity, upon the verified request of an individual, shall provide the individual, in a human-readable format that a reasonable individual can understand, with—
(1) a copy or accurate representation of the covered data of the individual processed or transferred by the covered entity; and
(2) the name of any third party to whom covered data of the individual has been transferred by the covered entity and a description of the purpose for which the entity transferred such data to such third party.

(b) Right to transparency.—A covered entity shall make publicly and persistently available, in a conspicuous and readily accessible manner, a privacy policy that provides a detailed and accurate representation of the entity's data processing and data transfer activities. Such privacy policy shall include, at a minimum—
(1) the identity and the contact information of the covered entity, including the contact information for the covered entity's representative for privacy and data security inquiries;
(2) each category of data the covered entity collects and the processing purposes for which such data is collected;
(3) whether the covered entity transfers covered data and, if so—
(A) each category of service provider and third party to which the covered entity transfers covered data and the purposes for which such data is transferred to such categories; and
(B) the identity of each third party to which the covered entity transfers covered data and the purposes for which such data is transferred to such third party, except for transfers to governmental entities pursuant to a court order or law that prohibits the covered entity from disclosing such transfer;
(4) how long covered data processed by the covered entity will be retained by the covered entity and a description of the covered entity's data minimization policies;
(5) how individuals can exercise the individual rights described in this title;
(6) a description of the covered entity's data security policies; and
(7) the effective date of the privacy policy.

(c) Languages.—A covered entity shall make the privacy policy required under this section available to the public in all of the languages in which the covered entity provides a product or service or carries out any other activities to which the privacy policy relates.

(d) Right To consent to material changes.—A covered entity shall not make a material change to its privacy policy or practices with respect to previously collected covered data that would weaken the privacy protections applicable to such data without first obtaining prior affirmative express consent from the individuals affected. The covered entity shall provide direct notification, where possible, regarding material changes to affected individuals, taking into account available technology and the nature of the relationship.

SEC. 103. Right to delete.

A covered entity, upon the verified request of an individual, shall—
(1) delete, or allow the individual to delete, any information in the covered data of the individual that is processed by the covered entity; and
(2) inform any service provider or third party to which the covered entity transferred such data of the individual's deletion request.

SEC. 104. Right to correct inaccuracies.

A covered entity, upon the verified request of an individual, shall—
(1) correct, or allow the individual to correct, inaccurate or incomplete information in the covered data of the individual that is processed by the covered entity; and
(2) inform any service provider or third party to which the covered entity transferred such data of the corrected information.

SEC. 105. Right to controls.

(a) Right to data portability.—A covered entity, upon the verified request of an individual, shall export the individual's covered data, except for derived data, without licensing restrictions—
(1) in a human-readable format that allows the individual to understand such covered data of the individual; and
(2) in a structured, interoperable, and machine-readable format that includes all covered data or other information that the covered entity collected to the extent feasible.

(b) Right To opt out of transfers.—
(1) IN GENERAL.—A covered entity—

(A) shall not transfer an individual's covered data to a third party if the individual objects to the transfer; and
(B) shall allow an individual to object to the covered entity transferring covered data of the individual to a third party through a process established under the rule issued by the Commission pursuant to paragraph (2).
(2) RULEMAKING.—
(A) IN GENERAL.—Not later than 18 months after the date of enactment of this Act, the Commission shall issue a rule under section 553 of title 5, United States Code, establishing one or more acceptable processes for covered entities to follow in allowing individuals to opt out of transfers of covered data.
(B) REQUIREMENTS.—The processes established by the Commission pursuant to this subparagraph shall—
(i) be centralized, to the extent feasible, to minimize the number of opt-out designations of a similar type that a consumer must make;
(ii) include clear and conspicuous opt-out notices and consumer friendly mechanisms to allow an individual to opt out of transfers of covered data;
(iii) allow an individual that objects to a transfer of covered data to view the status of such objection;
(iv) allow an individual that objects to a transfer of covered data to change the status of such objection;
(v) be privacy protective; and
(vi) be informed by the Commission's experience developing and implementing the National Do Not Call Registry.

(c) Sensitive data.—A covered entity—
(1) shall not process the sensitive covered data of an individual without the individual's prior, affirmative express consent;
(2) shall not transfer the sensitive covered data of an individual without the individual's prior, affirmative express consent;
(3) shall provide an individual with a consumer-friendly means to withdraw affirmative express consent to process the sensitive covered data of the individual; and
(4) is not required to obtain prior, affirmative express consent to process or transfer publicly available information.

SEC. 106. Right to data minimization.

A covered entity shall not process or transfer covered data beyond what is reasonably necessary, proportionate, and limited—

(1) to carry out the specific processing purposes and transfers described in the privacy policy made available by the covered entity as required under section 102;
(2) to carry out a specific processing purpose or transfer for which the covered entity has obtained affirmative express consent; or
(3) for a purpose specifically permitted under subsection (d) of section 110.
Covered data processing and transfers consistent with this section shall not supersede any other provision of this Act.

SEC. 107. Right to data security.

(a) In general.—A covered entity shall establish, implement, and maintain reasonable data security practices to protect the confidentiality, integrity, and accessibility of covered data. Such data security practices shall be appropriate to the volume and nature of the covered data at issue.

(b) Specific requirements.—Data security practices required under subsection (a) shall include, at a minimum, the following:
(1) ASSES. VULNERABILITIES.—Identifying and assessing any reasonably foreseeable risks to, and vulnerabilities in, each system maintained by the covered entity that processes or transfers covered data, including unauthorized access to or risks to covered data, human vulnerabilities, access rights, and use of service providers. Such activities shall include a plan to receive and respond to unsolicited reports of vulnerabilities by entities and individuals.
(2) PREVENTIVE AND CORRECTION ACTION.—Taking preventive and corrective action to mitigate any risks or vulnerabilities to covered data identified by the covered entity, which may include implementing administrative, technical, or physical safeguards or changes to data security practices or the architecture, installation, or implementation of network or operating software.
(3) INFORMATION RETENTION AND DISPOSAL.—Disposing covered data that is required to be deleted or is no longer necessary for the purpose for which the data was collected unless an individual has provided affirmative express consent to such retention. Such process shall include destroying, permanently erasing, or otherwise modifying the covered data to make such data permanently unreadable or indecipherable and unrecoverable and data hygiene practices to ensure ongoing compliance with this subsection.
(4) TRAINING.—Training all employees with access to covered data on how to safeguard covered data and protect individual privacy and updating that training as necessary.

(c) Training guidelines.—Not later than 1 year after the date of enactment of this Act, the Commission, in conjunction with the National Institute of Standards and Technology, shall publish guidance for covered entities on how to provide effective data security and privacy training as described in subsection (b)(4).

SEC. 108. Civil rights.

(a) Protections.—
(1) IN GENERAL.—A covered entity shall not process or transfer covered data on the basis of an individual's or class of individuals' actual or perceived race, color, ethnicity, religion, national origin, sex, gender, gender identity, sexual orientation, familial status, biometric information, lawful source of income, or disability—
(A) for the purpose of advertising, marketing, soliciting, offering, selling, leasing, licensing, renting, or otherwise commercially contracting for a housing, employment, credit, or education opportunity, in a manner that unlawfully discriminates against or otherwise makes the opportunity unavailable to the individual or class of individuals; or
(B) in a manner that unlawfully segregates, discriminates against, or otherwise makes unavailable to the individual or class of individuals the goods, services, facilities, privileges, advantages, or accommodations of any place of public accommodation.
(2) EXCEPTION.—Nothing in this section shall limit a covered entity from processing covered data for legitimate internal testing for the purpose of preventing unlawful discrimination or otherwise determining the extent or effectiveness of the covered entity's compliance with this Act.
(3) FTC ADVISORY OPINIONS.—A covered entity may request advice from the Commission concerning the covered entity's potential compliance with this subsection, in accordance with the Commission's rules of practice on advisory opinions.

(b) Algorithmic decision-Making impact assessment.—
(1) IMPACT ASSESSMENT.—Notwithstanding any other provision of law, a covered entity engaged in algorithmic decision-making, or in assisting others in algorithmic decision-making for the purpose of processing or transferring covered data, solely or in part to make or facilitate advertising for housing, education, employment or credit opportunities, or an eligibility determination for housing, education, employment or credit opportunities or determining access to, or restrictions on the use of, any place of public accommodation, must annually conduct an impact assessment of such algorithmic decision-making that—

(A) describes and evaluates the development of the covered entity's algorithmic decision-making processes including the design and training data used to develop the algorithmic decision-making process, how the algorithmic decision-making process was tested for accuracy, fairness, bias and discrimination; and
(B) assesses whether the algorithmic decision-making system produces discriminatory results on the basis of an individual's or class of individuals' actual or perceived race, color, ethnicity, religion, national origin, sex, gender, gender identity, sexual orientation, familial status, biometric information, lawful source of income, or disability.
(2) EXTERNAL, INDEPENDENT AUDITOR OR RESEARCHER.—A covered entity may utilize an external, independent auditor or researcher to conduct such assessments.
(3) AVAILABILITY.—The covered entity—
(A) shall make the impact assessment available to the Commission upon request; and
(B) may make the impact assessment public.
A covered entity may redact and segregate trade secrets as defined by section 1839 of title 18, United States Code, from public disclosure under this subsection.
(4) STUDY.—Not later than 3 years after the date of enactment of this Act, the Commission shall publish a report containing the results of a study, using the Commission's authority under section 6(b) of the Federal Trade Commission Act (15 U. S. C. 46(b)), examining the use of algorithms for the purposes described in this subsection. Not later than 3 years after the publication of the initial report, and as necessary thereafter, the Commission shall publish a new and updated version of such report.

SEC. 109. Prohibition on waiver of rights.

A covered entity shall not condition the provision of a service or product to an individual on the individual's agreement to waive privacy rights guaranteed by—
(1) sections 101, 105(a), and 106 through 109 of this Act; and
(2) sections 102 through 104, and 105(b) and (c) of this Act, except in the case where —
(A) there exists a direct relationship between the individual and the covered entity initiated by the individual;
(B) the provision of the service or product requested by the individual requires the processing or transferring of the specific covered data of the individual and the covered data is strictly necessary to provide the service or product; and
(C) an individual provides affirmative express consent to such specific limitations.

SEC. 110. Limitations and applicability.

(a) Verification of requests.—
(1) IN GENERAL.—A covered entity shall not permit an individual to exercise a right described in sections 102 through 105(a) if—
(A) the covered entity cannot reasonably verify that the individual making the request to exercise the right is the individual whose covered data is the subject of the request or an individual authorized to make such a request on the individual's behalf; or
(B) the covered entity reasonably believes that the request is made to interfere with a contract between the covered entity and another individual.
(2) ADDITIONAL INFORMATION.—If a covered entity cannot reasonably verify that a request to exercise a right described in sections 102 through 105(a) is made by the individual whose covered data is the subject of the request (or an individual authorized to make such a request on the individual's behalf), the covered entity shall request the provision of additional information necessary for the sole purpose of verifying the identity of the individual and shall not process or transfer such additional information for any other purpose.
(3) BURDEN MINIMIZATION.—A covered entity shall minimize the inconvenience to consumers relating to the verification or authentication of requests.

(b) Cost of access.—A covered entity shall carry out the rights described in sections 102 through 105(a) free of charge.

(c) Exceptions to sections 102 through 105(b).—A covered entity may decline to comply with an individual's request to exercise a right described in sections 102 through 105(b) if—
(1) complying with the request would be demonstrably impossible (for purposes of this paragraph, the receipt of a large number of verified requests, on its own, shall not be considered to render compliance with a request demonstrably impossible);
(2) complying with the request would prevent the covered entity from carrying out internal audits, performing accounting functions, processing refunds, or fulfilling warranty claims, provided that the covered data that is the subject of the request is not processed or transferred for any purpose other than such specific activities;
(3) the request is made to correct or delete publicly available information, and then only to the extent the data is publicly available information;
(4) complying with the request would impair the publication of newsworthy information of legitimate public concern to the public by a covered entity, or the processing or transfer of information by a covered entity for such purpose;

(5) complying with the request would impair the privacy of another individual or the rights of another to exercise free speech; or
(6) the covered entity processes or will process the data subject to the request for a specific purpose described in subsection (d) of this section, and complying with the request would prevent the covered entity from using such data for such specific purpose.

(d) Exceptions to affirmative express consent.—
(1) IN GENERAL.—A covered entity may process or transfer covered data without the individual's affirmative express consent for any of the following purposes, provided that the processing or transfer is reasonably necessary, proportionate, and limited to such purpose:
(A) To complete a transaction or fulfill an order or service specifically requested by an individual, such as billing, shipping, or accounting.
(B) To perform system maintenance, debug systems, or repair errors to ensure the functionality of a product or service provided by the covered entity.
(C) To detect or respond to a security incident, provide a secure environment, or maintain the safety of a product or service.
(D) To protect against malicious, deceptive, fraudulent, or illegal activity.
(E) To comply with a legal obligation or the establishment, exercise, or defense of legal claims.
(F) To prevent an individual from suffering harm where the covered entity believes in good faith that the individual is in danger of suffering death or serious physical injury.
(G) To effectuate a product recall pursuant to Federal or State law.
(H) To conduct scientific, historical, or statistical research in the public interest that adheres to all other applicable ethics and privacy laws and is approved, monitored, and governed by an institutional review board or a similar oversight entity that meets standards promulgated by the Commission pursuant to section 553 of title 5, United States Code.
(2) BIOMETRIC INFORMATION.—Not later than 1 year after the date of enactment of this Act, the Commission shall promulgate regulations pursuant to section 553 of title 5, United States Code, identifying privacy protective requirements for the processing of biometric information for a purpose described in subparagraph (C) or (D) of paragraph (1). Such regulations shall include—
(A) strict data processing limitations, including a prohibition on the processing of biometric information unless the covered entity has a reasonable suspicion, after a specific criminal incident involving the covered entity, that the individual may engage in criminal activity;

(B) strict data transfer limitations, including a prohibition on the transfer of biometric information to a third party other than to comply with a legal obligation or to establish, exercise, or defend a legal claim; and
(C) strict transparency obligations, including requiring disclosures in a conspicuous and readily accessible manner regarding specific data processing and transfer activities.

(e) Journalism exception.—Nothing in this title shall apply to the publication of newsworthy information of legitimate public concern to the public by a covered entity, or to the processing or transfer of information by a covered entity for that purpose.

(f) Applicability of other data privacy requirements.—A covered entity that is required to comply with title V of the Gramm-Leach-Bliley Act (15 U. S.C. 6801 et seq.), the Health Information Technology for Economic and Clinical Health Act (42 U. S.C. 17931 et seq.), part C of title XI of the Social Security Act (42 U. S.C. 1320d et seq.), the Fair Credit Reporting Act (15 U. S.C. 1681 et seq.), the Family Educational Rights and Privacy Act (20 U. S.C. 1232g; part 99 of title 34, Code of Federal Regulations), or the regulations promulgated pursuant to section 264(c) of the Health Insurance Portability and Accountability Act of 1996 (42 U. S.C. 1320d–2 note), and is in compliance with the data privacy requirements of such regulations, part, title, or Act (as applicable), shall be deemed to be in compliance with the related requirements of this title, except for section 107, with respect to data subject to the requirements of such regulations, part, title, or Act. Not later than 1 year after the date of enactment of this Act, the Commission shall issue guidance describing the implementation of this subsection.

(g) Applicability of other data security requirements.—A covered entity that is required to comply with title V of the Gramm-Leach-Bliley Act (15 U. S.C. 6801 et seq.), the Health Information Technology for Economic and Clinical Health Act (42 U. S.C. 17931 et seq.), part C of title XI of the Social Security Act (42 U. S.C. 1320d et seq.), or the regulations promulgated pursuant to section 264(c) of the Health Insurance Portability and Accountability Act of 1996 (42 U. S.C. 1320d–2 note), and is in compliance with the information security requirements of such regulations, part, title, or Act (as applicable), shall be deemed to be in compliance with the requirements of section 107 with respect to data subject to the requirements of such regulations, part, title, or Act. Not later than 1 year after the date of enactment of this Act, the Commission shall issue guidance describing the implementation of this subsection.

(h) In general.—The Commission shall have authority under section 553 of title 5, United States Code, to promulgate regulations necessary to carry out the provisions of this title.

TITLE II—Oversight and responsibility

SEC. 201. Executive responsibility.

(a) In general.—Beginning 1 year after the date of enactment of this Act, the chief executive officer of a covered entity that is a large data holder (or, if the entity does not have a chief executive officer, the highest ranking officer of the entity) and each privacy officer and data security officer of such entity shall annually certify to the Commission, in a manner specified by the Commission, that the entity maintains—
(1) adequate internal controls to comply with this Act; and
(2) reporting structures to ensure that such certifying officers are involved in, and are responsible for, decisions that impact the entity's compliance with this Act.

(b) Requirements.—A certification submitted under subsection (a) shall be based on a review of the effectiveness of a covered entity's internal controls and reporting structures that is conducted by the certifying officers no more than 90 days before the submission of the certification.

SEC. 202. Privacy and data security officers; comprehensive privacy and data security programs; risk assessments and compliance.

(a) Privacy and data security officer.—A covered entity shall designate—
(1) 1 or more qualified employees as privacy officers; and
(2) 1 or more qualified employees (in addition to any employee designated under paragraph (1)) as data security officers.

(b) Comprehensive privacy and data security programs, risk assessments, and compliance.—An employee who is designated by a covered entity as a privacy officer or a data security officer shall be responsible for, at a minimum—
(1) implementing a comprehensive written data privacy program and data security program to safeguard the privacy and security of covered data throughout the life cycle of development and operational practices of the covered entity's products or services;

(2) annually conducting privacy and data security risk assessments, data hygiene, and other quality control practices; and
(3) facilitating the covered entity's ongoing compliance with this Act.

SEC. 203. Service providers and third parties.

(a) Service providers.—A service provider—
(1) shall not process service provider data for any processing purpose other than one performed on behalf of, and at the direction of, the covered entity that transferred such data to the service provider, except that a service provider may process data to comply with a legal obligation or the establishment, exercise, or defense of legal claims;
(2) shall not transfer service provider data to a third party without the affirmative express consent, obtained by, or on behalf of, the covered entity, of the individual to whom the service provider data is linked or reasonably linkable;
(3) shall delete or de-identify service provider data after the agreed upon end of the provision of services;
(4) is exempt from the requirements of sections 102(a), 103, 104, and 105(a) with respect to service provider data, but shall, to the extent practicable—
(A) assist the covered entity from which it received the service provider data in fulfilling requests made by individuals under such sections; and
(B) shall delete, de-identify, or correct (as applicable), any service provider data that is subject to a verified request from an individual described in section 103 or 104; and
(5) is exempt from the requirements of section 106 with respect to service provider data, but shall have the same responsibilities and obligations as a covered entity with respect to such data under all other provisions of this Act.

(b) Third parties.—A third party—
(1) shall not process third party data for a purpose that is inconsistent with the expectations of a reasonable individual;
(2) may reasonably rely on representations made by the covered entity that transferred third party data regarding the expectation of a reasonable individual, provided the third party conducts reasonable due diligence on the representations of the covered entity and finds those representations to be credible; and
(3) upon receipt of any third party data, is exempt from the requirements of section 105(c) with respect to such data, but shall have the same responsibilities and obligations as a covered entity with respect to such data under all other provisions of this Act.

(c) Additional obligations on covered entities.—
(1) IN GENERAL.—A covered entity shall—
(A) exercise reasonable due diligence in selecting a service provider and conduct reasonable oversight of its service providers to ensure compliance with the applicable requirements of this section; and
(B) exercise reasonable due diligence in deciding to transfer covered data to a third party, and conduct oversight of third parties to which it transfers data to ensure compliance with the applicable requirements of this subsection.
(2) GUIDANCE.—Not later than 1 year after the date of enactment of this Act, the Commission shall issue guidance for covered entities regarding compliance with this subsection.

(d) In general.—The Commission shall have authority under section 553 of title 5, United States Code, to promulgate regulations necessary to carry out the provisions of this section.

SEC. 204. Whistleblower protections.

(a) In general.—A covered entity shall not, directly or indirectly, discharge, demote, suspend, threaten, harass, or in any other manner discriminate against a covered individual of the covered entity because—
(1) the covered individual, or anyone perceived as assisting the covered individual, takes (or the covered entity suspects that the covered individual has taken or will take) a lawful action in providing to the Federal Government or the attorney general of a State information relating to any act or omission that the covered individual reasonably believes to be a violation of this Act or any regulation promulgated under this Act;
(2) the covered individual provides information that the covered individual reasonably believes evidences such a violation to—
(A) a person with supervisory authority over the covered individual at the covered entity; or
(B) another individual working for the covered entity who the covered individual reasonably believes has the authority to investigate, discover, or terminate the violation or to take any other action to address the violation;
(3) the covered individual testifies (or the covered entity expects that the covered individual will testify) in an investigation or judicial or administrative proceeding concerning such a violation; or
(4) the covered individual assists or participates (or the covered entity expects that the covered individual will assist or participate) in such an investigation or judicial

or administrative proceeding, or the covered individual takes any other action to assist in carrying out the purposes of this Act.

(b) Enforcement.—An individual who alleges discharge or other discrimination in violation of subsection (a) may bring an action governed by the rules, procedures, statute of limitations, and legal burdens of proof in section 42121(b) of title 49, United States Code. If the individual has not received a decision within 180 days and there is no showing that such delay is due to the bad faith of the claimant, the individual may bring an action for a jury trial, governed by the burden of proof in section 42121(b) of title 49, United States Code, in the appropriate district court of the United States for the following relief:
(1) Temporary relief while the case is pending.
(2) Reinstatement with the same seniority status that the individual would have had, but for the discharge or discrimination.
(3) Three times the amount of back pay otherwise owed to the individual, with interest.
(4) Consequential and compensatory damages, and compensation for litigation costs, expert witness fees, and reasonable attorneys' fees.

(c) Waiver of rights and remedies.—The rights and remedies provided for in this section shall not be waived by any policy form or condition of employment, including by a predispute arbitration agreement.

(d) Predispute arbitration agreements.—No predispute arbitration agreement shall be valid or enforceable if the agreement requires arbitration of a dispute arising under this section.

(e) Covered Individual defined.—In this section, the term "covered individual" means an applicant, current or former employee, contractor, subcontractor, grantee, or agent of an employer.

SEC. 205. Digital content forgeries.

(a) Reports.—Not later than 1 year after the date of enactment of this Act, and annually thereafter, the Director of the National Institute of Standards and Technology shall publish a report regarding digital content forgeries.

(b) Requirements.—Each report under subsection (a) shall include the following:
(1) A definition of digital content forgeries along with accompanying explanatory materials. The definition developed pursuant to this section shall not supersede any other provision of law or be construed to limit the authority of any executive agency related to digital content forgeries.
(2) A description of the common sources in the United States of digital content forgeries and commercial sources of digital content forgery technologies.
(3) An assessment of the uses, applications, and harms of digital content forgeries.
(4) An analysis of the methods and standards available to identify digital content forgeries as well as a description of the commercial technological counter-measures that are, or could be, used to address concerns with digital content forgeries, which may include the provision of warnings to viewers of suspect content.
(5) A description of the types of digital content forgeries, including those used to commit fraud, cause harm or violate any provision of law.
(6) Any other information determined appropriate by the Director.

TITLE III—Miscellaneous

SEC. 301. Enforcement, civil penalties, and applicability.

(a) Enforcement by the Federal Trade Commission.—
(1) NEW BUREAU.—
(A) IN GENERAL.—The Commission shall establish a new Bureau within the Commission comparable in structure, size, organization, and authority to the existing Bureaus with the Commission related to consumer protection and competition.
(B) MISSION.—The mission of the Bureau established under this paragraph shall be to assist the Commission in exercising the Commission's authority under this Act and under other Federal laws addressing privacy, data security, and related issues.
(C) TIMELINE.—Such Bureau shall be established, staffed, and fully operational within 2 years of enactment of this Act.
(2) TREATMENT AS VIOLATION OF RULE.—A violation of this Act or a regulation promulgated under this Act shall be treated as a violation of a rule defining an unfair or deceptive act or practice prescribed under section 18(a)(1)(B) of the Federal Trade Commission Act (15 U. S. C. 57a(a)(1)(B)).
(3) POWERS OF COMMISSION.—
(A) IN GENERAL.—Except as provided in subparagraph (C), the Commission shall enforce this Act and the regulations promulgated under this Act in the same manner, by the same means, and with the same jurisdiction, powers, and duties as

though all applicable terms and provisions of the Federal Trade Commission Act (15 U. S.C. 41 et seq.) were incorporated into and made a part of this Act.
(B) PRIVILEGES AND IMMUNITIES.—Any person who violates this Act or a regulation promulgated under this Act shall be subject to the penalties and entitled to the privileges and immunities provided in the Federal Trade Commission Act (15 U. S.C. 41 et seq.).
(C) INDEPENDENT LITIGATION AUTHORITY.—The Commission may commence, defend, or intervene in, and supervise the litigation of any civil action under this subsection (including an action to collect a civil penalty) and any appeal of such action in its own name by any of its attorneys designated by it for such purpose. The Commission shall notify the Attorney General of any such action and may consult with the Attorney General with respect to any such action or request the Attorney General on behalf of the Commission to commence, defend, or intervene in any such action.
(4) DATA PRIVACY AND SECURITY RELIEF FUND.—
(A) ESTABLISHMENT OF RELIEF FUND.—There is established in the Treasury of the United States a separate fund to be known as the "Data Privacy and Security Relief Fund" (referred to in this paragraph as the "Relief Fund").
(B) DEPOSITS.—
(i) DEPOSITS FROM THE COMMISSION.—The Commission shall deposit into the Relief Fund the amount of any civil penalty obtained against any covered entity in any judicial or administrative action the Commission commences to enforce this Act or a regulation promulgated under this Act.
(ii) DEPOSITS FROM THE ATTORNEY GENERAL.—The Attorney General of the United States shall deposit into the Relief Fund the amount of any civil penalty obtained against any covered entity in any judicial or administrative action the Attorney General commences on behalf of the Commission to enforce this Act or a regulation promulgated under this Act.
(C) USE OF FUND AMOUNTS.—Notwithstanding section 3302 of title 31, United States Code, amounts in the Relief Fund shall be available to the Commission, without fiscal year limitation, to provide redress, payments or compensation, or other monetary relief to individuals affected by an act or practice for which civil penalties have been obtained under this Act. To the extent that individuals cannot be located or such redress, payments or compensation, or other monetary relief are otherwise not practicable, the Commission may use such funds for the purpose of consumer or business education relating to data privacy and security or for the purpose of engaging in technological research that the Commission considers necessary to enforce this Act.
(D) AMOUNTS NOT SUBJECT TO APPORTIONMENT.—Notwithstanding any other provision of law, amounts in the Relief Fund shall not be subject to apportionment

for purposes of chapter 15 of title 31, United States Code, or under any other authority.

(b) Enforcement by State attorneys general.—
(1) CIVIL ACTION.—In any case in which the attorney general of a State or a consumer protection officer of a State has reason to believe that an interest of the residents of that State has been or is adversely affected by the engagement of any covered entity in an act or practice that violates this Act or a regulation promulgated under this Act, the attorney general of the State, or a consumer protection officer of the State acting on behalf of the State, as parens patriae, may bring a civil action on behalf of the residents of the State in an appropriate district court of the United States to—
(A) enjoin that act or practice;
(B) enforce compliance with this Act or the regulation;
(C) obtain damages, civil penalties, restitution, or other compensation on behalf of the residents of the State; or
(D) obtain such other relief as the court may consider to be appropriate.
(2) NOTICE TO THE COMMISSION AND RIGHTS OF THE COMMISSION.—Except where not feasible, the State shall notify the Commission in writing prior to initiating a civil action under paragraph (1). Such notice shall include a copy of the complaint to be filed to initiate such action. If prior notice is not practicable, the State shall provide a copy of the complaint to the Commission immediately upon instituting the action. Upon receiving such notice, the Commission may intervene in such action and, upon intervening—
(A) be heard on all matters arising in such action; and
(B) file petitions for appeal of a decision in such action.
(3) PRESERVATION OF STATE POWERS.—No provision of this section shall be construed as altering, limiting, or affecting the authority of a State attorney general or a consumer protection officer of a State to—
(A) bring an action or other regulatory proceeding arising solely under the law in effect in that State; or
(B) exercise the powers conferred on the attorney general or on a consumer protection officer of a State by the laws of the State, including the ability to conduct investigations, to administer oaths or affirmations, or to compel the attendance of witnesses or the production of documentary or other evidence.
(4) VENUE; SERVICE OF PROCESS.—
(A) VENUE.—Any action brought under paragraph (1) may be brought in the district court of the United States that meets applicable requirements relating to venue under section 1391 of title 28, United States Code.

(B) SERVICE OF PROCESS.—In an action brought under paragraph (1), process may be served in any district in which the defendant—
(i) is an inhabitant; or
(ii) may be found.

(c) Enforcement by individuals.—
(1) IN GENERAL.—Any individual alleging a violation of this Act or a regulation promulgated under this Act may bring a civil action in any court of competent jurisdiction, State or Federal.
(2) RELIEF.—In a civil action brought under paragraph (1) in which the plaintiff prevails, the court may award—
(A) an amount not less than $100 and not greater than $1,000 per violation per day or actual damages, whichever is greater;
(B) punitive damages;
(C) reasonable attorney's fees and litigation costs; and
(D) any other relief, including equitable or declaratory relief, that the court determines appropriate.
(3) INJURY IN FACT.—A violation of this Act or a regulation promulgated under this Act with respect to the covered data of an individual constitutes a concrete and particularized injury in fact to that individual.

(d) Invalidity of pre-Dispute arbitration agreements and pre-Dispute joint action waivers.—
(1) IN GENERAL.—Notwithstanding any other provision of law, no pre-dispute arbitration agreement or pre-dispute joint action waiver shall be valid or enforceable with respect to a privacy or data security dispute arising under this Act.
(2) APPLICABILITY.—Any determination as to whether or how this subsection applies to any privacy or data security dispute shall be made by a court, rather than an arbitrator, without regard to whether such agreement purports to delegate such determination to an arbitrator.
(3) DEFINITIONS.—For purposes of this subsection:
(A) The term "pre-dispute arbitration agreement" means any agreement to arbitrate a dispute that has not arisen at the time of the making of the agreement.
(B) The term "pre-dispute joint-action waiver" means an agreement, whether or not part of a pre-dispute arbitration agreement, that would prohibit, or waive the right of, one of the parties to the agreement to participate in a joint, class, or collective action in a judicial, arbitral, administrative, or other forum, concerning a dispute that has not yet arisen at the time of the making of the agreement.

(C) The term "privacy or data security dispute" means any claim relating to an alleged violation of this Act, or a regulation promulgated under this Act, and between an individual and a covered entity.

SEC. 302. Relationship to Federal and State laws.

(a) Federal law preservation.—Nothing in this Act or a regulation promulgated under this Act shall be construed to limit—
(1) the authority of the Commission, or any other Executive agency, under any other provision of law; or
(2) any other provision of Federal law unless as specifically authorized by this Act.

(b) State law preservation.—Nothing in this Act shall be construed to preempt, displace, or supplant the following State laws, rules, regulations, or requirements:
(1) Consumer protection laws of general applicability such as laws regulating deceptive, unfair, or unconscionable practices.
(2) Civil rights laws.
(3) Laws that govern the privacy rights or other protections of employees, employee information, or students or student information.
(4) Laws that address notification requirements in the event of a data breach.
(5) Contract or tort law.
(6) Criminal laws governing fraud, theft, unauthorized access to information or unauthorized use of information, malicious behavior, and similar provisions, and laws of criminal procedure.
(7) Laws specifying remedies or a cause of action to individuals.
(8) Public safety or sector specific laws unrelated to privacy or security.

(c) Preemption of directly conflicting State laws.—Except as provided in subsections (b) and (d), this Act shall supersede any State law to the extent such law directly conflicts with the provisions of this Act, or a standard, rule, or regulation promulgated under this Act, and then only to the extent of such direct conflict. Any State law, rule, or regulation shall not be considered in direct conflict if it affords a greater level of protection to individuals protected under this Act.

(d) Preservation of common law or statutory causes of action for civil relief.—Nothing in this Act, nor any amendment, standard, rule, requirement, assessment, law or regulation promulgated under this Act, shall be construed to preempt, displace, or supplant any Federal or State common law rights or remedies, or any statute creating a remedy for civil relief, including any cause of action for personal injury, wrongful death, property damage, or other financial, physical, reputational, or psychological injury based in negligence, strict liability, products liability, failure to warn, an objectively offensive intrusion into the private affairs or concerns of the individual, or any other legal theory of liability under any Federal or State common law, or any State statutory law.

SEC. 303. Severability.

If any provision of this Act, or the application thereof to any person or circumstance, is held invalid, the remainder of this Act and the application of such provision to other persons not similarly situated or to other circumstances shall not be affected by the invalidation.

SEC. 304. Authorization of appropriations.

There are authorized to be appropriated to the Commission such sums as may be necessary to carry out this Act.